Coparenting

Coparenting

A CONCEPTUAL and CLINICAL EXAMINATION of FAMILY SYSTEMS

JAMES P. McHALE
KRISTIN M. LINDAHL

AMERICAN PSYCHOLOGICAL ASSOCIATION
WASHINGTON, DC

Published by
American Psychological Association
750 First Street, NE
Washington, DC 20002
www.apa.org

To order
APA Order Department
P.O. Box 92984
Washington, DC 20090-2984
Tel: (800) 374-2721; Direct: (202) 336-5510
Fax: (202) 336-5502; TDD/TTY: (202) 336-6123
Online: www.apa.org/pubs/books
E-mail: order@apa.org

In the U.K., Europe, Africa, and the Middle East, copies may be ordered from
American Psychological Association
3 Henrietta Street
Covent Garden, London
WC2E 8LU England

HQ
734
C781
2011

Typeset in Goudy by Circle Graphics, Inc., Columbia, MD

Printer: United Book Press, Baltimore, MD
Cover Designer: Berg Design, Albany, NY

The opinions and statements published are the responsibility of the authors, and such opinions and statements do not necessarily represent the policies of the American Psychological Association.

Library of Congress Cataloging-in-Publication Data

Coparenting : a conceptual and clinical examination of family systems / [edited by] James P. McHale and Kristin M. Lindahl. — 1st ed.
   p. cm.
  Includes index.
  ISBN-13: 978-1-4338-0991-0
  ISBN-10: 1-4338-0991-5
 1. Parenting, Part-time. 2. Parenting. 3. Families. I. McHale, James P. II. Lindahl, Kristin M.

  HQ755.8.C663 2011
  306.874—dc22

                          2010049941

British Library Cataloguing-in-Publication Data

A CIP record is available from the British Library.

Printed in the United States of America
First Edition

DOI: 10.1037/12328-000

To Trang, Hailey, and Christopher, who I will love forever and ever.
To Liam, who teaches his parents every day how to be the
best coparents they can be.

CONTENTS

CONTRIBUTORS

Francesca Adler-Baeder, PhD, Department of Human Development and Family Studies, Auburn University, Auburn, AL

Marcia J. Carlson, PhD, Department of Sociology, University of Wisconsin–Madison

Rebekah Levine Coley, PhD, Applied Developmental and Educational Psychology, Boston College, Chestnut Hill, MA

Tracy Donsky, JD, MSW, School for Social Work, Smith College, Northampton, MA

Rachel H. Farr, MA, Department of Psychology, University of Virginia, Charlottesville

Nicolas Favez, PhD, Department of Psychology, University of Geneva, Geneva, Switzerland

Mark E. Feinberg, PhD, Prevention Research Center for the Promotion of Human Development, Pennsylvania State University, University Park

Elisabeth Fivaz, PhD, Centre d' Etude de la Famille, University of Lausanne, Switzerland

France Frascarolo, PhD, Centre d' Etude de la Famille, University of Lausanne, Lausanne, Switzerland

James P. Gleeson, PhD, Jane Addams College of Social Work, University of Illinois at Chicago

Robin S. Högnäs, PhD, Center for Demography and Ecology, University of Wisconsin–Madison

Karina Irace, MA, Family Study Center, University of South Florida, St. Petersburg

Allison Jessee, MA, Department of Psychology, University of Illinois at Urbana–Champaign

Deborah J. Jones, PhD, Department of Psychology, University of North Carolina at Chapel Hill

Daniel J. Laxman, MA, Department of Human and Community Development, University of Illinois at Urbana–Champaign

L. Oriana Linares, PhD, Adolescent Health Center, Mount Sinai School of Medicine, New York, NY

Kristin M. Lindahl, PhD, Department of Psychology, University of Miami, Coral Gables, FL

Kerry A. Littlewood, PhD, MSW, School of Social Work, East Carolina University, Greenville, NC

Sarah C. Mangelsdorf, PhD, Weinberg College of Arts and Sciences, Northwestern University, Evanston, IL

James P. McHale, PhD, Department of Psychology and Family Study Center, University of South Florida St. Petersburg

Daniela Montalto, PhD, NYU Child Study Center, Department of Child and Adolescent Psychiatry, New York University Langone Medical Center, New York

Charlotte J. Patterson, PhD, Department of Psychology, University of Virginia, Charlottesville

Laura D. Pittman, PhD, Department of Psychology, Northern Illinois University, DeKalb

Marsha Kline Pruett, PhD, School for Social Work, Smith College, Northampton, MA

Kari-Lyn Sakuma, PhD, MPH, Prevention Research Center for the Promotion of Human Development, Pennsylvania State University, State College

Karen A. Shirer, PhD, Extension Center for Family Development, University of Minnesota, St. Paul

Anne L. Strozier, PhD, MSW, School of Social Work, University of South Florida, Tampa

ACKNOWLEDGMENTS

We'd fill an entire book simply acknowledging all those who have shaped the way we think about families and influenced our fervent belief that a coparenting framework is our best hope for creating an inclusive advocacy paradigm to improve the life chances of all children. Those whose shoulders we stand on are recognized and cited liberally throughout the volume, and this book owes to each of them and their contributions. But there are two individuals who stand out among this passionate and magnificent crowd— Salvador and Patricia Minuchin.

Over the course of a career and a life span, we can count on one hand those who have truly been game changers, individuals who influence forever the way we think about the important things in life. The Minuchins have been such a force in our generation, tirelessly championing the notion that children's life chances are improved when the individuals responsible for their care and upbringing can be helped to collaborate with one another in the child's best interests. Without once discounting or minimizing the heroic work of mothers everywhere, Salvador and Patricia nudged the field, time and time again, to broaden its lens and move toward triangular and family systems conceptualizations. As Patricia admonished developmental researchers in a landmark 1985 article,[1]

> Studies of the parent–child dyad, though valid in themselves, are properly regarded as studies of subsystems. They do not represent the child's significant reality, especially after infancy, and they do not stand in for the study of triadic parent–child systems. (p. 296)

Her provocations helped trigger the enduring transformation of a field, bridging the once distinct literatures on family theory and therapy, child development and socialization, and attachment theory and research. Now, a quarter century later, we are beginning to see the fruitful integration of these equally vital lines of theory and thought. As this volume details, this exciting synthesis is still only just beginning, and great developments lie ahead.

Salvador's vision was in many ways unparalleled. Perhaps most revolutionary and prescient among his countless contributions is his chronicling of the interplay between family dynamics and biology in families of children with psychosomatic symptoms. His recognition that recurrent patterns of problematic communication and conflict in families of children with symptoms such as asthma, diabetes, and anorexia can be tied to physiological markers of stress in children—and demonstration of how intervention-induced shifts in communication in conflict-avoiding families resulted in the alleviation of the children's physical symptoms—anticipated by decades today's major scientific interest in epigenesis and effects of social experience on brain development.

Above all, the Minuchins' work has always been culturally grounded, sensitive, and respectful. It was influenced meaningfully, Patricia once said, by the elaborate anthropological work of Beatrice and John Whiting and Leigh Minturn. The Minuchins' most recent writings—in particular *Working With Families of the Poor* (with Jorge Colapinto; Minuchin, Colapinto, & Minuchin)[2] detailing their groundbreaking work in New York with children and families in foster care settings—continue to provoke, inspire, and educate us in a way few other family scholars ever have or will. Salvador and Patricia are a national and international treasure. This book stands as one small tribute to their enduring influence and reach.

---

[1]Minuchin, P. (1985). Families and individual development: Provocations from the field of family therapy. *Child Development, 56,* 289–302. doi:10.2307/1129720

[2]Minuchin, P., Colapinto, J., & Minuchin, S. (2007). *Working with families of the poor* (2nd ed.). New York, NY: Guilford Press.

Coparenting

INTRODUCTION: WHAT IS COPARENTING?

JAMES P. McHALE AND KRISTIN M. LINDAHL

The past 15 years have seen the explosive growth of a new field of study that has come to be known as *coparenting* (McHale & Sullivan, 2008). Since the turn of the new millennium, fresh new insights and thoughtful empirical research studies explicitly guided by coparenting frameworks have made their way into the peer-reviewed literature almost every few months. But what is coparenting, and why is there a need for an entire volume taking stock of such a relatively new field of study?

Broadly speaking, coparenting is an enterprise undertaken by two or more adults who together take on the care and upbringing of children for whom they share responsibility (McHale, Lauretti, Talbot, & Pouquette, 2002). Viewed as a dynamic force in families that is related to, but also distinct from, parent–child or marital subsystems, coparenting is a framework that traces its roots most directly to Salvador Minuchin's (1974) structural family theory. In his writings, Minuchin emphasized the importance in every family of collaborative, supportive leadership provided by the family's parenting adults. Children's healthy emotional growth and development, he maintained, was best promoted in a system in which there were clear generational boundaries delineating adults, who embraced their authority and shared roles as in-charge parents, from children, who were protected by the structures that the adults created and who were permitted to be children without having to serve as caregivers for adults' emotions. In such a hierarchically organized system, even though children sometimes had to assist with adult responsibilities at an early age (e.g., helping with family work, caring for younger siblings), there was no confusion about reversal of roles. Adults were parents, and children were children, and this clarity allowed all family members (adults and children alike) to bring their psychic resources to bear on the normative developmental and relationship challenges they confronted.

As the coparenting field first took wing in earnest in the mid-1990s, its initial focus was principally on two-parent family systems and on understanding the triangular relationship system that tied together a mother, a father, and a child (McHale & Cowan, 1996). Although narrow in focus, this view that child development proceeded within the context of a multiperson relationship system was actually a watershed moment in child socialization research. For nearly 100 years, from Freud's portrayal of the mother–child relationship as the prototype for all future love relationships, through attachment theory's emphasis on the salience of children's interactions with "primary attachment figures" at century's end, children's emotional development was viewed as being shaped by dyadic, parent–child interactions and relationships—most often, mother–child relations. Indeed, as many commentators (e.g., Luepnitz, 1988; Rich, 1976; Singh, 2004) have noted, mothers have almost always been the ones held responsible for the adjustment—or maladjustment—of children (Caplan & Caplan, 1994; Kindlon & Thompson, 2000; Sax, 1997).

Things gradually began to change following an influential 1985 article in the well-respected journal *Child Development* by Patricia Minuchin directly confronting this dyadic mother–child bias. In family triads, Minuchin pointed out, each participant was simultaneously in some form of contact with each of the two others. This fundamental reality was not properly captured by dyadic conceptualizations, or even by newer conceptualizations that had begun pursuing study of "the effects of relationships on relationships"—parent–child dyads, spousal dyads, and individuals linked together through patterns of mutual influence (Hinde & Stevenson-Hinde, 1988). As Minuchin argued, it was insufficient to view triadic dynamics as an amalgam of discrete, interlocking dyads within the family. Triadic processes needed themselves to be considered as units of analysis. Reorienting the focus away from the dynamics of two-person relationship systems to the dynamics of three-person relationship systems hence demanded a reconceptualization of the emotional field in which child development proceeded.

This basic notion—that children are part of a family relationship system in which they are simultaneously cared for and socialized by multiple parenting figures—is at the core of modern coparenting theory and research. But it is not always an easy concept to grasp. Even today, most conceptualizations still err in the direction of seeing child development in the family context as a "two-plus-one" model, in which the mother's role is primary but is augmented by efforts of a second person—the child's father, the child's grandmother—who is there to provide support for the mother's child-rearing efforts and to provide the child with some positive influence him- or herself. Coparenting conceptualizations are not meant to replace or reduce the importance of maternal (or paternal) parenting influences, but rather to draw attention to the simultaneous reality that even as they are parented by individuals, children also develop and function within a triangular system in which the "rules of engagement" differ.

As McHale and Kuersten-Hogan (2004) detailed, the precise point at which the field of coparenting studies began depends on the historian. As early as the 1950s, when the family therapy movement was taking root, there were already descriptions of problems that occur when coparental partners (mothers and fathers) cannot develop reciprocal, cooperative roles. Lidz, Cornelison, Fleck, and Terry (1957) wrote about two problematic patterns seen in families of adolescent and young adult children with schizophrenia. One involved an openly antagonistic coparenting pattern in which partners undermined one another with their children and competed openly for children's affection and loyalty. The second involved overbearing parenting by one parent that was not balanced or countered, but rather was acquiesced to or otherwise enabled, by the second. In Lidz and colleagues' published cases, it was typically the father who acceded, though the dynamic could also be reversed. In both family systems, children were "caught in the middle," triangulated into problematic interadult relations.

Salvador Minuchin's seminal volume on structural family theory and therapy appeared in 1974 and presented the centrally important concepts of hierarchy and boundaries. Families, he explained, comprise a number of different subsystems, including marital, coparenting, parent–child, and sibling subsystems. In well-functioning families, adaptive emotional growth and development of children and other family members is contingent on the existence of appropriate boundaries between subsystems. When hierarchies break down, boundaries are violated, or children are triangulated into adult–adult subsystems, one or more family members signal the family's distress by exhibiting symptomatic behavior. A generation of clinical and research studies has supported many of these propositions (Andolfi, 1978; S. Minuchin, Montalvo, Guerney, Rosman, & Schumer, 1967; S. Minuchin, Rosman, & Baker, 1978; Rosenberg, 1978), and today several integrative models approach families using structural family therapy as their base (Diamond, Siqueland, & Diamond, 2003; Henggeler, Schoenwald, Borduin, Rowland, & Cunningham, 1998; Liddle, 2000; Wood, Klebba, & Miller, 2000).

Coparenting as a defined field took a further, quantum leap forward in the late 1970s and early 1980s as millions of American families began raising their children in postdivorce family systems. As concerns grew about the poor postdivorce adjustment and often severe behavior problems exhibited by children in postdivorce environments (Emery, 1982; Hetherington, Cox, & Cox, 1978; Wallerstein & Kelly, 1975), a focus soon came to be placed squarely on the continuing coparental relationship between mothers and fathers postdivorce (Ahrons, 1981). It became clear that when parents were working at cross-purposes and providing inconsistent rules and expectations for children across households, children suffered the consequences. By contrast, in families in which the adults communicated with one another about their parenting roles and their children, child development was not as severely compromised (Maccoby, Mnookin, Depner, & Peters, 1992). This evidence, in combination with the conceptual and clinical groundwork that had been laid by family systems theories and therapies, gave modern-day coparenting theory and research its conceptual and empirical base.

Although much of the focus of family systems theories was on family interiors, feminist writers such as Hare-Mustin (1978) and Luepnitz (1988) drew attention to the narrow-mindedness of looking for all answers within the family's relational field. As outlined previously, one of the more common clinical presentations in two-parent families is one in which mothers are cast as overinvolved and ineffectual and fathers as problematically underinvolved. Although much of the appeal of family therapy had been in absolving mothers of primary blame for child difficulties (by factoring fathers into the family equation), the truth was that mothers were still being viewed pathologically, without any recognition that they had been thrust by society into economically dependent, emotionally isolated, and hyper-responsible positions. Changes were needed, feminist therapists maintained, not because incompetent mothers required help but because men's assumption of their responsibilities to their children would enable mothers to move out of the "crazy-making" situation that society had foisted on them (McGoldrick, Anderson, & Walsh, 1989; Walters, Carter, Papp, & Silverstein, 1988).

Contemporary coparenting theory, although not free of the cultural assumptions and burdens of earlier theories, also provides fresh promise for understanding families in the myriad forms they take. To be sure, there are explicit assumptions that have been guiding theory and research. One is that in any coparenting system that serves the needs of children, there must be functional hierarchies and appropriate boundaries. Another is that a proper understanding of coparental alliances necessitates taking a triadic or family group level of analysis, one in which the relationship between the adults with respect to a particular child is considered. The coparenting system that evolves for different children within a family can constitute different individuals, and the nature and dynamics of the same two people's coparenting alliance may differ for different children in the family. Moreover, children themselves contribute to the particular relationship dynamic that evolves between them and their coparents.

Besides these basic core assumptions, there is one more that distinguishes the work presented in this volume from published and forthcoming work principally concerned with strengthening families through strengthening marriages. That assumption is that although coparenting is a centrally important dynamic in families headed by heterosexual married couples, coparenting is also a dynamic, potent socialization force that is characteristic of all family systems. Hence, this book complements and augments healthy marriage frameworks by taking instead the lens of healthy coparenting alliances. We are still very early in the process of learning about how coparenting systems evolve and function, and so this volume marks a moment in time—a point in the evolution of a field in which the questions still outnumber the answers. However, we have brought together for the first time diverse and broad-ranging research on coparenting from a group of contributors who have all provided leadership in this emerging field of research, studying coparenting in a wide range of family forms and systems.

Chapters in this volume address what we know about coparenting alliances in nuclear, fragile, and extended kinship systems of different ethnicities and socioeconomic circumstances, in family systems headed by gay and lesbian parents, in circumstances in which biological and foster parents must coordinate as the major coparenting figures in the child's life, and in post-divorce family systems. The volume has two interrelated goals. The first is to bring together in an integrated fashion the latest research on coparenting, covering as best as possible the full gamut of studies with diverse caretaking systems. The second is to present issues directly relevant to clinical practice, attending to both the assessment of coparenting systems and to new and promising intervention efforts.

Although all authors have approached coparenting from the same perspective—as the nature of the alliance between the two (or more) adults who together share responsibility for the child's care and upbringing—readers will note variability across chapters in how authors have operationalized the construct. Some have taken a narrower approach (e.g., Chapters 4 and 6) and others a much broader one (e.g., Chapters 2, 5, and 8). One challenge the editors faced mirrors a challenge inherent in this relatively young field of study: how to help meld sometimes disparate operationalizations of coparenting into a coherent whole. The critical questions "Who are a child's coparents?" and "What critical features define coparenting?" are not definitively decided on in this volume. This said, we believe that the stances taken by the leading researchers and clinicians currently grappling with these centrally important issues will advance conversations about the nature of coparenting and its importance for child outcomes.

The volume is presented in two parts, each reflecting the most recent evidence within the field. Part I, Theory and Empirical Research, addresses assumptions, concepts, and methods used in the study of coparenting. It provides a foundation for conceptualizing coparenting across a diverse range of families and for understanding the diverse array of individuals who can constitute a child's coparenting system. Chapters in Part I address what is known about coparenting alliances in nuclear, fragile, and extended kinship systems of different ethnicities and socioeconomic circumstances and in family systems headed by gay and lesbian parents. Part II, Applications: Assessment and Interventions to Promote Coparenting, covers clinical applications and issues relevant to mental health practice. Chapters address assessment and both preventive and intervention approaches designed to foster stronger coparenting relationships. Also included in this part are chapters concerned with specific clinical populations, addressing issues such as coordination between biological and foster parents as major coparenting figures in the child's life and between parents in postdivorce family systems.

In Part I, we present the case for studying coparenting as a family force related to, but also distinct from, marital quality and parenting behavior in understanding child adaptation, and we review the evidentiary base concerning coparenting in a range of different family systems. Chapter 1 frames the study of coparenting and the challenging theoretical and methodological issues that confront the field. Chapter 2 focuses on coparenting in two-parent nuclear families, both covering ground well familiar to researchers and practitioners versed in family systems research and presenting up-to-date data on capacities within individuals that promote optimal coparenting and studies of how coparenting shifts over the course of child development. Chapter 3 expands on and augments material reviewed in Chapter 2, addressing the unique strengths and circumstances for coparenting among various ethnic groups, including African American, Hispanic, Asian heritage, and Native American families. A cornerstone of this chapter is its emphasis on a broader conceptualization of family adopted by many ethnic groups, including the incorporation of fictive kin (i.e., nonbiologically related individuals who are considered central to the family).

Of paramount interest to many coparenting researchers are the difficulties faced by individuals who are coparenting under challenging circumstances. Chapter 4, with its focus on unmarried, low-income parents, and Chapter 5, with its focus on adolescent mothers, summarize current research in these areas, and both chapters illustrate how strong coparenting can bolster maternal as well as paternal parenting and child functioning. The role of cross-generational coparenting alliances is discussed, along with the quality of the relationship between the coparents, and some evidence is presented for how outcomes sometimes vary by ethnicity. Chapter 6 closes Part I, examining coparenting in gay and lesbian families. Gay and lesbian families are less well represented in the coparenting literature than other family types, and this chapter is among the first of its kind. Although coparenting is examined principally in terms of division of labor in this chapter, a narrower operationalization than that of other chapters, this reflects the nascency of this field of work, as relatively few studies of coparenting in same-sex families exist. Data to date have suggested that coparenting for same-sex couples is less specialized than for heterosexual parents, and parents' sentiments about "who does what" in their coparenting alliance appears more significant for same-sex couples than the actual arrangements themselves.

Part II of the volume addresses clinical applications of a coparenting approach. Ways in which children benefit when clinical practice redraws family lines to accommodate coparenting (rather than parent–child) realities are discussed. Most of the intervention work discussed in Part II shares common goals, including supporting mutual parental involvement, promoting solidarity and a strong alliance between coparents, and minimizing conflict, though the populations they target and the approaches they take in achieving these goals vary tremendously. Several innovative approaches to prevention and intervention are outlined and discussed. Among these are incorporating coparenting education into childbirth classes (Chapter 8); encouraging unmarried mothers to coparent, taking an ecoculturally valid approach (Chapter 9); using videotaped feedback to assess coparenting dynamics and affect change (Chapter 10); implementing parent education programs, parenting coordination, and mediation approaches to promote coparenting postdivorce (Chapter 11); and intervening in biological–foster parent coparenting systems within the foster care system (Chapter 12). The closing chapter in Part II, Chapter 13, discusses clinical and policy implications of coparenting in multigenerational households. The unique focus of this chapter is on children who live in a household headed by a relative other than a parent. It reviews the diversity of kinship care coparenting arrangements that are formed; the clinical issues that affect the relative caregivers, parents, and children involved; and policies that impact the quality of coparenting provided. The volume closes with a brief Afterword concerning next steps for this field of research.

In summary, this volume provides intensive treatment of the importance and implications of a coparenting approach in understanding the true caretaking context of children's lives. The book aims to provide an introduction that will be useful to researchers, practitioners, and educators. Readers will see some overlap, and also some dissonance, in the perspectives outlined in different chapters. The dissonance is intentional and welcome. It is far too premature to be divining laws, truths, and realities in this emergent field; from the diversity will come coherence. If there is any organizing premise that the contributors would endorse, we believe it would be that coparenting alliances can function as resources in all manners of family systems for virtually every child—whether that child is raised by a married heterosexual mother and father or by any and all other honorable sets of individuals who step forward to assume and share responsibility for the child's care and upbringing. With this framework guiding our efforts, we stand poised to embark on an enterprise that truly stands to serve all children and the families who care for them.

REFERENCES

Ahrons, C. R. (1981). The continuing coparental relationship between divorced spouses. *American Journal of Orthopsychiatry, 51*, 415–428. doi:10.1111/j.1939-0025.1981.tb01390.x

Andolfi, M. (1978). A structural approach to a family with an encopretic child. *Journal of Marital and Family Therapy, 4*, 25–30. doi:10.1111/j.1752-0606.1978.tb00493.x

Caplan, P. J., & Caplan, J. B. (1994). *Thinking critically about research on sex and gender*. New York, NY: HarperCollins.

Diamond, G., Siqueland, L., & Diamond, G. M. (2003). Attachment-based family therapy for depressed adolescents: Programmatic treatment development. *Clinical Child and Family Psychology Review, 6*, 107–127. doi:10.1023/A:1023782510786

Emery, R. E. (1982). Interparental conflict and the children of discord and divorce. *Psychological Bulletin, 92*, 310–330. doi:10.1037/0033-2909.92.2.310

Hare-Mustin, R. T. (1978). A feminist approach to family therapy. *Family Process, 17*, 181–194. doi:10.1111/j.1545-5300.1978.00181.x

Henggeler, S. W., Schoenwald, S. K., Borduin, C. M., Rowland, M. D., & Cunningham, P. B. (1998). *Multisystemic therapy for antisocial behavior in children and adolescents*. New York, NY: Guilford Press.

Hetherington, E. M., Cox, M., & Cox, R. (1978). The aftermath of divorce. In J. H. Stevens & M. Mathews (Eds.), *Mother-child, father-child relations* (pp. 110–155). Washington, DC: National Association for the Education of Young Children.

Hinde, R. A., & Stevenson-Hinde, J. (1988). *Relationships within families: Mutual influences*. Oxford, England: Clarendon Press.

Kindlon, D., & Thompson, M. (2000). *Raising Cain: Protecting the emotional life of boys*. New York, NY: Ballantine Books.

Liddle, H. A. (2000). *Multidimensional family therapy treatment manual*. Rockville, MD: Center for Substance Abuse Treatment.

Lidz, T., Cornelison, A. R., Fleck, S., & Terry, D. (1957). The intrafamilial environment of schizophrenic patients: II. Marital schism and marital skew. *The American Journal of Psychiatry, 114*, 241–248.

Luepnitz, D. A. (1988). *The family interpreted: Feminist theory in clinical practice*. New York, NY: Basic Books.

Maccoby, E., Mnookin, R., Depner, C., & Peters, E. (1992). *Dividing the child: Social and legal dilemmas of custody*. Cambridge, MA: Harvard University Press.

McGoldrick, M., Anderson, C. M., & Walsh, F. (1989). *Women in families: A framework for family therapy*. New York, NY: Norton.

McHale, J., & Cowan, P. (1996). Understanding how family-level dynamics affect children's development: Studies of two-parent families. *New Directions for Child and Adolescent Development, 74*.

McHale, J., & Kuersten-Hogan, R. (2004). Introduction: The dynamics of raising children together. *Journal of Adult Development, 11*, 163–164. doi:10.1023/B:JADE.0000035798.74058.ef

McHale, J., Lauretti, A., Talbot, J., & Pouquette, C. (2002). Retrospect and prospect in the psychological study of co-parenting and family group process. In J. McHale & W. Grolnick (Eds.), *Retrospect and prospect in the psychological study of families* (pp. 127–165). Hillsdale, NJ: Erlbaum.

McHale, J., & Sullivan, M. (2008). Family systems. In M. Hersen & A. Gross (Eds.), *Handbook of clinical psychology* (Vol. 2, Children and adolescents; pp. 192–226). Hoboken, NJ: Wiley.

Minuchin, P. (1985). Families and individual development: Provocations from the field of family therapy. *Child Development, 56*, 289–302. doi:10.2307/1129720

Minuchin, S. (1974). *Families and family therapy*. Cambridge, MA: Harvard University Press.

Minuchin, S., Montalvo, B., Guerney, B. G., Rosman, B. L., & Schumer, F. (1967). *Families of the slums*. New York, NY: Basic Books.

Minuchin, S., Rosman, B., & Baker, L. (1978). *Psychosomatic families: Anorexia nervosa in context*. Cambridge, MA: Harvard University Press.

Rich, A. C. (1976). *Of woman born: Motherhood as experience and institution*. New York, NY: Norton.

Rosenberg, J. B. (1978). Two is better than one: Use of behavioral techniques within a structural family therapy model. *Journal of Marital and Family Therapy, 4*, 31–40. doi:10.1111/j.1752-0606.1978.tb00494.x

Sax, P. (1997). Narrative therapy and family support: Strengthening the mother's voice in working with families with infants and toddlers. In C. Smith & D. Nylund (Eds.), *Narrative therapies with children and adolescents* (pp. 111–146). New York, NY: Guilford Press.

Singh, I. (2004). Doing their jobs: Mothering with Ritalin in a culture of mother-blame. *Social Science & Medicine, 59*, 1193–1205.

Wallerstein, J. S., & Kelly, J. B. (1975). The effects of parental divorce: Experiences of the preschool child. *Journal of the American Academy of Child and Adolescent Psychiatry, 14*, 600–616. doi:10.1016/S0002-7138(09)61460-6

Walters, M., Carter, B., Papp, P., & Silverstein, O. (1988). *The invisible web: Gender patterns in family relations*. New York, NY: Guilford Press.

Wood, B. L., Klebba, K. B., & Miller, B. D. (2000). Evolving the biobehavioral family model: The fit of attachment. *Family Process, 39*, 319–344. doi:10.1111/j.1545-5300.2000.39305.x

I

THEORY AND EMPIRICAL RESEARCH

1

COPARENTING IN DIVERSE
FAMILY SYSTEMS

JAMES P. McHALE AND KARINA IRACE

> It is unfortunate when public discourse frames as "profamily" those who
> adhere to the 1950s nuclear family as the sole standard for healthy fam-
> ilies while denouncing as "antifamily" those who hold a pluralistic view.
> Abundant research evidence shows that children can be raised well in a
> variety of family arrangements. We need to be mindful that families in
> the distant past and in cultures worldwide have had multiple, varied
> structures and that effective family processes and the quality of relation-
> ships matter most for the well-being of children.
> —F. Walsh (2006, pp. 31–32)

As Froma Walsh (2006) mused in her treatise on the growing diversity
and complexity of families in a changing world, there is certainly no dearth
of opinion about what constitutes a healthy, adaptive family. From pro-
nouncements that two-parent biological family systems are the only truly
functional family form, to observations that two-parent nuclear families are
the most fragile family form that has ever existed in the history of the planet,
pundits offer their perspectives on what it takes to create a well-adjusted,
happy child. Such conversations are pointless to children during their early
years, of course. Children see their families as a collection of individuals who
love and care for them. And children are right; in the end, their welfare in
the world will ultimately be protected and assured, to the extent maximally
possible, by the collection of individuals who step up to take responsibility for
their care and upbringing.

From this vantage point, virtually every child will be "coparented," continuously or episodically, from birth through adolescence. In a field often overwhelmed by cantankerous debates about how to define families and how to
prioritize and direct funding to help support children and families, embracing
this simple adage redirects our focus to where it should be—on valuing,

strengthening, and supporting the efforts of every family caring for children, whatever the family's composition.

The aim of this chapter is to provide an overview of the myriad of family forms in which coparenting systems develop and flourish, and the importance of these systems in the lives of children. This chapter complements and updates earlier pieces on this topic (McHale, 2009; McHale, Khazan, et al., 2002) but presents a perspective that is even more simplistic. Every child is coparented. Every family does its level best to assemble a responsible group of people to help ensure the child's survival and healthy development. Every coparenting system is as important as any other. And every coparent "counts" and matters.

DEFINING COPARENTING

Deriving a definition of coparenting is at once very simple and straightforward, and infinitely complex. Coparenting, stripped to its essence, is a shared activity undertaken by those adults responsible for the care and upbringing of children. This joint enterprise serves children best when each of the coparenting adults is capable of seeing and responding to the child as a separate person with feelings and needs different from their own and when the adults find ways to work together to cocreate a structure that adequately protects and nurtures the child. The most effective cocreated structures will be those in which there is mutual understanding, communication, and coordination between the coparenting adults about the child; trust, backing, and support of one another's efforts; and the capacity to successfully resolve the inevitable dissonance that will arise as decisions must be made about the child's best interests.

Who are a child's coparents? As the chapters throughout this book attest, attempts to offer any singular answer to this question would be misguided, if not dangerous. Claims about who a child's coparents truly are or who they should be miss the basic point that in any given family system, they are who they are. Although biological mothers are nearly always in the mix, millions of children are coparented in family systems without any knowledge of or contact with their biological mothers. The same is so for biological fathers—with the flip side of this coin being that biological fathers need not be coresident or even in regular contact with children to be considered fundamental contributors to the child's and family's coparenting system. In extended kinship systems, maternal grandmothers and sometimes grandfathers often play centrally important coparenting roles. In families headed by lesbian coparents, sperm donor fathers sometimes play a meaningful ongoing role in the child's life.

In cases in which children are removed from families and placed in foster families, meaningful connections between the foster and natal family serve the child's best interests (see Chapter 12, this volume). In other words, any child's coparents are the individuals who collaborate to socialize and nurture the child.

To those who work with families, proper understanding of who any given child's coparents "are" rests on two separate, equally important considerations. The first concerns who has ultimate decision-making authority for the child. Defining coparenting in this way places emphasis on the single one or two people who make all decisions of consequence about the child's living situation, health care, school options, and matters of legal consequence. Defined in this way, every child will not be coparented. A never-married mother, for example, will typically possess a legal right to exclude any and all individuals she decides she does not want involved in her child's life (including in many cases the child's father if the father did not sign a Recognition of Parentage when the child was born). As detailed in Chapter 13, kinship caregivers who take over for mothers when they cannot fulfill their parental roles for a time are often conceived of and portrayed in the literature as substitute caregivers or surrogate parents (Minkler & Roe, 1996) rather than as coparents. Indeed, any person or persons empowered with legal authority for the child may overrule any other individual who is contributing to the child's care and upbringing if the legally vested parent believes, rightly or wrongly, that that person is not acting in the child's best interests.

The other equally important consideration is who is really involved as family caregivers and central attachment and socialization figures in the child's life. For the child, this is the meaningful distinction. Perhaps the most lucid exposition of this perspective was Crosbie-Burnett and Lewis's (1999) distinction between the *patrifocal* system of law within the United States, which defines the family on the basis of the status of adults (i.e., legal marriage, separation, or divorce) from a *pedifocal* or child-centered family focus, in which the basic family unit includes everyone involved in the ongoing nurturance and support of a given child, regardless of actual household membership (Brooks-Gunn & Furstenberg, 1986; Stack, 1974). As Crosbie-Burnett and Lewis outlined, coparents in many African American family systems are all parental and family figures who contribute to the child's well-being and become involved in the child's support and nurturance. With the child as the focus, the center of family relations shifts away from arrangements between legally related members to arrangements that are based on the child's needs, assuring continuing responsibility for dependent children across changes in relationships among adults (cf. McHale, Lauretti, et al., 2002). It is this latter definition that supports the claim that all children will be coparented.

Family Structure and Bonding

A family would be in chaos without a definitive leadership team, clear lines of authority for decision making at critically important junctures, and an overarching and intentional protective structure that ensures consistency and continuity of care for the child across developmental time and through any changes in family membership. A family would also fall into despair and disarray without the bonds of closeness and loyalty that develop among children and adults. Children are capable of and typically form a number of different attachment relationships during their infancy and early childhood, though not an infinite number. Although each attachment serves the child's socioemotional development, the attachments are person specific and hence not interchangeable. Any time an attachment is disrupted, children suffer. Functional families recognize this and honor and value children's emotional bonds with different members of the family network.

S. Minuchin's (1974) structural family theory (S. Minuchin, Rosman, & Baker, 1978), the basis for the generation of research on coparenting detailed throughout this book, provides the most comprehensive detailing of families and their coparenting structures. In structural theory, adaptive and healthy family systems are hierarchically organized, with parenting adults clearly in charge as the system's executives. Families can comprise many different subsystems, including marital, coparenting, parent–child, and sibling subsystems. In well-functioning families, adaptive emotional growth and development of children and other family members depend on the existence of appropriate boundaries between these subsystems. However, if the family's authority structure breaks down, if family members are in too close or too distant emotional proximity, or if children are co-opted to play a role in unhealthy adult–adult relationships, then symptomatic behavior can result.

In cases in which children are co-opted, they help to maintain a false harmony in the adult–adult subsystem and thereby keep the whole family structure in order. The adults unintentionally collude in treating the child as an appendage, rather than seeing and relating to the child as a separate third person. Unfortunately, the failure of the adults to recognize and tend to the child's own needs waylays the child's healthy individuation, emotional growth, and development. In other families, problems occur not because of members being too close and enmeshed but because there is insufficient executive leadership and attentive child rearing (the main functions of the coparenting system). In situations in which there are inadequate protective structures and/or excessive emotional distance among family members, children often exit the family before they are developmentally ready; engage in dangerous risk-taking behavior; and fall prey to extrafamilial societal risks, such as drug abuse, early pregnancy, gang membership, homelessness, and victimization.

Many higher risk families manage to raise their children successfully and avert major problems such as those described previously. Those who do find ways to develop a hierarchical leadership structure along with boundaries that enable sufficient proximity, contact, and bonding among family members (Jones & Lindblad-Goldberg, 2002). Moreover, P. Minuchin, Colapinto, and Minuchin (2007) detailed how established structures, attachments, recurrent patterns, and boundaries that have meaning can often be found even in multistressed families in need of social services. They also pointed out that, unfortunately, once families come into contact with the courts, the welfare system, and protective services, family loyalty, connections, affection, and bonding get overlooked or ignored. So too do any adaptive structures the family has developed, and such structures are inevitably disrupted when children are taken for placement or members are jailed or hospitalized. As P. Minuchin et al. argued, a welcome shift in our field would be movement toward a true family-oriented approach in which clinicians and researchers would "begin to look for relevant people in the family network and accept unconventional family shape. We notice subsystems and the rules that govern family interactions, both those that lead to crises and those that indicate strength" (p. 26).

Looking Closer: Functional Family Coparenting Adaptations

Adaptive coparenting structures can be achieved in a variety of family configurations, so long as the adults who take on responsibility for the child's care and upbringing establish and honor clear coparenting boundaries. Countless families cocreate an organization with differentiated functions and expertise that keeps children monitored, protected, and safe. Operating from the family-oriented perspective articulated by P. Minuchin et al. (2007), it becomes much easier to see the adaptive and functional coparenting structures that evolve in families. Take, for example, a "single-parent family" in which a child lives with his never-married mother. Mother and son live together in the maternal grandmother's residence along with a maternal uncle, and the boy spends time with his father several days a month. Because both the boy's mother and grandmother must work to provide the income needed to make ends meet, his uncle, who has been unable to find work, provides after-school care, oversight, and life lessons to the child. When the boy's father is arrested and incarcerated for a second time, the uncle intensifies the time he spends with the child during periods when the boy would ordinarily have seen his father.

In this family, the uncle is far more than a glorified babysitter. He is vested by the family with both a trust and a responsibility to help coparent the child. He may be a good coparent, communicating with the other adults about the child's needs and worries, and perhaps even stepping in to help the child downregulate his arousal on occasions when there is bickering going on between the adults. Or he may be a poor coparent, regularly disregarding the rules of the other adults, failing to communicate with the other adults about the child's transgressions, or even contributing negatively to the child's socialization through poor role modeling. But good or bad, he is the child's coparent in a very real sense. So is the boy's father, who as before is welcomed back by the family after he is released from jail. At the same time, not every member of the boy's kin network serves a coparenting role. A different uncle, who drops by regularly for Sunday afternoon football and family get-togethers but is less well regarded by the family, may play no coparental function. Neither may the boy's paternal grandfather, who, while well loved, lives a fair distance away and sees the child only sporadically.

This family counts at least four functional coparents. Other families have more; some have fewer. There is no "ideal" or magic number of coparents. Examples of functional coparenting systems are limitless. In many three-generational families seen clinically and in research projects, grandmothers are fully functioning coparents (Wilson, 1984; see also Chapters 3, 5, and 13, this volume). Indeed, children from many ethnic backgrounds (including some lower socioeconomic Anglo families) sometimes refer to coresident grandmothers as "mom" and to their mothers as "mommy." In most cases, both women are typically quite comfortable with their monikers, and rarely do they suffer from clinically concerning patterns of enmeshment or troubling boundary violations.

Kurrien and Vo (2004) noted that in many families of Vietnamese heritage, the boundaries of coparenting systems are very flexible, and aunts and uncles have full authority to discipline children and carry out other caregiving functions on a daily basis. In many African American family systems, both blood and fictive kin play important and ongoing coparenting roles (Roy & Burton, 2007). And looking beyond the North American and Western European families most commonly studied in coparenting investigations, coparenting systems are even more diverse. For example, it is often paternal rather than maternal grandmothers who play powerful coparenting roles in Middle Eastern countries. In short, families are the ones who determine who will be involved in coparenting children.

Yet even with this inclusive view of coparenting, it would be misguided to consider every adult who interacts positively with a child as a member of the family's coparenting alliance. The visiting aunt, a beloved teacher, a growth-promoting little league or gymnastics coach, a friend's parent with whom the child sometimes shares personal information—these individuals contribute to the richness of the child's life in meaningful ways and hold a special place in the child's heart, but they are not part of the enduring, functional system that has evolved in the family to provide for the child's care and upbringing. Lines can sometimes be thin during the early stages of a child's life, when there is a uniquely important circumstance worthy of note. Specifically, a family or nonfamily caregiver who spends 8 to 10 waking hours each day with an infant or toddler de facto becomes a central attachment figure for the child. How well the caregiver coordinates with the child's parents on calming and sleep routines, toileting, and other developmental issues will have a fundamental and often lasting influence on the child's regulatory and socioemotional development. Moreover, when the caregiver is an enduring member of the family household or of the mother or father's intimate relationship system (Roy & Burton, 2007), he or she absolutely does stand to help or hinder the child's development by virtue of the quality of ongoing communication and coordination maintained with the child's parents about the child.

As Gonzalez-Mena (1992) noted, parents and care providers alike hold deep-seated, very strong views about how children are supposed to be taken care of. Typically, such views remain largely subconscious and nonverbal—until challenged by someone with a conflicting view. Resolving caregiving conflict is vitally important for infants and young children, however. Van IJzendoorn, Tavecchio, Stams, Verhoeven, and Reiling (1998) reported that child well-being suffers when there is poor attunement and support between parents and nonparental caregivers, whereas better communication is associated with greater attunement and better child well-being. Greenman and Stonehouse's (1996) description of what constitutes positive family care provider alliances is especially on point. They emphasized the importance of teamwork; an established set of common goals; shared decision making; sensitivity to each other's perspectives; shared/mutual appreciation for, understanding of, and liking for the child; and the absence of rivalry or competition for the child's affections. A more thoughtful description of a coparenting alliance could not be written. When the Greenman and Stonehouse elements are all operative, any coparenting system can function to serve a child's best interests.

DYADS VERSUS TRIANGLES: THE ISSUE OF LEVEL OF ANALYSIS

Much of what has been described thus far concerns the manner in which families tend to the basic functions that support the healthy development of all children. Every family must have attentive caregivers who tend to the child's basic needs for nutrition, care, shelter, and nurturance. Every family must keep children safe, protecting them from harm that can come from either inside or outside the family. Every family must teach children to learn self-discipline and to abide by the rules of the family and the culture. When accomplished successfully, these functions help children learn to trust, to develop care and compassion for others, and to be industrious.

There is nothing to say that these functions cannot be handled by one single individual, parenting multiple children through time. Millions of children have been raised by just a single hand, one individual who always undertook every function unaided (as is presently true of many children of poor, immigrant single mothers living in urban areas of the United States). In some instances, parents who are completely alone in caring for their children are unable to look to others who might partner in parenting, for every option available presents a legitimate threat to the child's or parent's safety and well-being. Other parents who go it single-handedly make a deliberate, conscious choice to shoulder all responsibility alone. Moreover, in the main, it is still the case that mothers worldwide carry the lion's share of burden and responsibility for the myriad responsibilities that caring for a child demands.

It is this truth that makes the conceptual leap to understanding coparenting most difficult to grasp. Much of the reason that the fields of infant and early childhood mental health have been so slow to embrace the importance and impact of coparenting dynamics in families is precisely because children's mothers are so pivotal in the development of babies and toddlers. Indeed, the cultural model that has developed throughout the world is one in which mothers are implicitly charged with the ultimate responsibility for children's fates, for good or ill (McHale, 2007a, 2007b; McHale & Fivaz-Depeursinge, 1999). The model currently guiding the theory and practice of infant mental health is a decidedly dyadic one, in which the target of intervention is the primary attachment bond that the child has developed with his or her mother. In this model, others can certainly be called on to play a hand as supports for the mother–child dyad, and interventions have increasingly sought to mobilize contributions from fathers or other "support figures" involved in the family. Moreover, father–infant dyads have themselves been a focus of intervention for the past quarter century. Infant mental health professionals do recognize that children also form enduring attachment bonds with their fathers, often even when they do not live together with them. However, even in work with fathers, the focus of family interventions is typically guided by a dyadic, parent-to-child model.

As children age and are referred to clinicians for help with noncompliance and other behavioral problems, interventions begin focusing less exclusively on parents' attunement to children's signals and more intensively on helping the family negotiate child behavior management. Although behavioral parent management trainings are "family friendly" in the sense that most encourage involvement by more than just one parent (or at least sharing materials with others who cannot attend), they maintain a dyadic parent-to-child feel. There is relatively limited attention typically given in treatment manuals to establishing whether coparents disagree with one another about whether the child even has problems, or on ensuring that all of the child's coparents are on the same page before actually beginning treatment modules.

Supporting and strengthening the child's evolving dyadic relationship with his or her mother and/or father is certainly invaluable in helping the parent to become more sensitive and attuned to the child's needs. Without sensitively attuned caregiving, a child is in danger of developing an insecure attachment with the caregiver. Similarly, coaching a parent to respond more effectively to a child's noncompliance can enable the parent to develop the degree of authority and credibility required to enforce structure and limits. However, sensitivity, warmth, supportiveness, and limit setting are all parenting qualities that describe a mother or father acting independently. They are characteristics of dyadic (parent–child) exchanges. Enhancing one parent's behavior does not always have positive ripple effects in improving the coparenting system that evolves among mother, father, and child (McHale, 2007a). This is a key point: The levels of analyses—dyadic in the case of parenting, triadic (or polyadic) in the case of coparenting—are different.

So too are the levels of analyses for coparenting and marital quality. Marital relationships are dyadic. Coparenting relationships are triadic or polyadic. It is certainly true that coparental adjustment is positively affected by good couple relationships in families in which the child's parents are married (see Chapter 2). It is also true that in families in which the parents are married, mother and father enact child-related decisions from the platform of their marital dyad. However, the distinction is that every coparenting exchange and action implicitly or explicitly involves the child, and hence coparenting communications and systems are always, at minimum, triangular in nature. They are constituted both of three individuals and also of three distinct dyadic relationships. Properties of the emergent coparenting system, however, are unique and stand separate from the constituting individuals or subsystems (see Figure 1.1).

Coparenting Systems as Triangles

Much has been written about how triangular emotional systems differ from dyadic ones (Zittoun, Gillespie, Cornish, & Psaltis, 2007). Since the beginnings of the field, triangles have had a central focus in psychoanalytic accounts. Freud (1905/1953) discussed triangles with respect to navigation of the oedipal crisis (Brickman, 1993; Ermann, 1989; Frank, 1988), and triangles have been important in accounts of splitting in the service of ambivalence (Juni, 1995) and of separation-individuation (Henderson, 1982). The three-person emotional system is seen as especially important for preschool-age children in their efforts to manage normal relationship ambivalence (Greenspan, 1982).

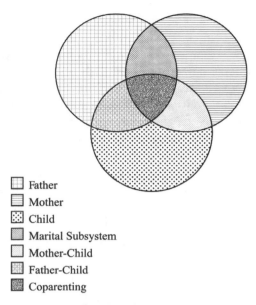

Father
Mother
Child
Marital Subsystem
Mother-Child
Father-Child
Coparenting

Figure 1.1. Coparenting in a one-child nuclear family.

Triangles have also been a central focus of clinicians working from family systems perspectives (Bell & Bell, 1979; Donley, 1993). Bowen (1961, 1972; Kerr & Bowen, 1988) has described emotional triangles as the basic building blocks of families and outlined ways in which a third person can help to stabilize inherently unstable dyads. As Bowen has discussed, however, triangles bring with them relational stresses distinct from those typically described in dyadic frameworks. For example, in situations in which a member of a triangle becomes responsible for or tries to change the relationship of two others, that person shoulders the stress for the others' relationship. Stress within emotional triangles can be a positional phenomenon. When younger, less differentiated family members are overburdened with this role, they can be trapped in problematic relationships that they are ill-equipped to handle (Friedman, 1991).

S. Minuchin (1974) also outlined several ways that triangular dynamics can affect children in families. Coparenting adults may compete for a child's loyalty, and one may succeed in establishing a coalition with the child that excludes other coparents. Coparents can respond to distress in their relationship by deflecting their distress and anxiety and then focusing it on the problems of a child. This can provide short-term relief for the adults' relational distress and artificially bond them together, but such detouring often results in psychosomatic or other emotional problems for the pathologized child, who is then the focal point of the family system as the "identified patient."

S. Minuchin and other family theorists agreed that the identified patient's symptomatology often plays an important role in maintaining family homeostasis, keeping the family system together, and preventing it from fragmenting. This occurs because the problems of the pathologized child provide for a coherent, if dysfunctional, organizing function to the family (S. Minuchin, Rosman, & Baker, 1978).

Fivaz-Depeursinge (2008; see also Chapter 10, this volume) examined the triadic interactions of two-parent nuclear families of very young infants. She uncovered evidence in support of three different kinds of coalitions S. Minuchin found in clinic-referred families: detouring coalitions (with scapegoating or role reversal); triangulation, in which the parents struggle against each other by trying to ally with the child, who is torn between them and takes on the role of a go-between or withdraws; and binding, in which the child is tied to one parent against the other. Although much of the focus in these theoretical accounts has been on the development of pathological coalitions, triangles are not inherently pathological—they are inherent in all family systems and can be either functional or dysfunctional.

Other Coparenting Triangles

Although much of the seminal work on triangles and child development portrays the mother–father–child triangular system, triangles characterize all forms of coparenting systems. Because children form relationships with multiple attachment figures, any coparenting individual can either support the child's attachments to each other person important to the child or undermine that connection. In the Minnesota study of risk and resilience, for example, a number of higher risk infants who had been insecurely attached to their mothers during infancy were later found to be functioning well as toddlers and preschoolers (Sroufe, 2005; Vaughn, Waaters, Egeland, & Sroufe, 1979). When this was the case, increases in social support for the primary caregiver proved to be the strongest factor in predicting improved functioning in kindergarten for those who had been anxiously attached as infants (Sroufe, 2005). Because positive coparenting alliances support not just the child, but also the parent and each parent–child relationship (see Figure 1.1; for reviews, see McHale, 2009; see also Chapter 2, this volume), the supportive influence of an important coparenting adult may have helped steady some of the mother–child attachment relationships in the Minnesota study.

More broadly, the successful reintegration of a child's mother or father into the flow of the child's and family's life after immigration separations, military service, substance abuse treatment, or incarceration may rely on coparents in the family having maintained that person's positive presence in the family home by speaking regularly and positively about them while they were away (Cecil, McHale, & Strozier, 2008). The same can be said about the role played by mothers and fathers in divorced families and in fragile families in which one of the two parents is not coresident. Positive and affirmative regard for the nonresident parent during their separation from the child communicates coparenting solidarity and promotes a sense of enduring family integrity.

On the flip side, day-to-day disparagement of a coparent, undermining of that parent's relationship with the child, and competition for a child's love and affection are characteristics of other coparent–child triangles. Such unresolved dissonance has damaging aftereffects not just on children's relationships with both coparents but also on the children themselves. When any one coparent demeans or belittles another, their criticism erodes the child's own sense of self, for the criticized coparent is also a part of that child. The invisible damage done to children by disparagement and undermining between coparents can be substantial, though it often goes unnoticed. Significant damage can also be done to children's developing attachments when coparents do not work together (Brown, Schoppe-Sullivan, Mangelsdorf, & Neff, 2010; Caldera & Lindsey, 2006).

Problems such as these can occur in any triangular system—in intact and divorced families, between coparents in extended kinship systems, even between parents and day caregivers. Although casting day caregivers as "coparents" would be a mischaracterization because the majority will actually have no permanent place in the child's life and exit by design after a few years, the work of Van IJzendoorn et al. (1998) verified that the emotional system tying caregivers to the child and the child's parents is a centrally important one in early childhood. Care should hence always be taken to properly assess caregivers' emotional involvement with a child and family when mapping the communication and coordination between all those having formative influence in a child's life (see Chapter 7).

COPARENTING AND CHILD DEVELOPMENT

As detailed throughout this book and elsewhere, researchers have succeeded in documenting that coparenting dynamics in families influence and are influenced by children's adjustment (Cook, Schoppe-Sullivan, Buckley, & Davis, 2009; Fivaz-Depeursinge, Frascarolo, Lopes, Dimitrova, & Favez, 2007; McHale, 2007a; McHale & Cowan, 1996), both in two-parent nuclear families and in postdivorce family systems (Ahrons, 2007; Napp-Peters, 2005). Newer work has begun to link child adjustment to the coparenting dynamics of mother–grandmother coparenting systems (Baker, McHale, Strozier, & Cecil, 2010), as well. Clinically, of course, the powerful impact of coparenting in families has been understood and documented by family therapists for more than half a century. What empirical investigations stand to add to the extensive real-life wisdom and advice of clinicians is the documentation of how coparenting dynamics take form and evolve in diverse families through developmental time (McHale, 2007a, 2009). Further research is also needed to elucidate the circumstances that best promote positive coparenting adjustments across the full diversity of functional coparenting structures in all manner of families; the correlates and enduring benefits to children of effective coparenting structures and dynamics in diverse family systems; and the unique beneficial effects coparenting solidarity has in families when parenting and marital or couple relationships falter. From this empirical knowledge base, better informed decisions about serving children's and families' interests will be able to be made.

Coparenting During Infancy

The beneficial effects for children of positive and coordinated coparenting can be expected to differ at different points in the family life cycle. In families with infants who are forming attachments, several issues are important. Infant regulation depends on the consistency of caregiver responsiveness, and most theories of early regulation focus on the development and impact of attunement between mother and baby (Stern, 1985). When other family members have been factored into family equations, their relevance has typically been conceived of as auxiliary. That is, most theorists have conceptualized other family caregivers as important during infancy insofar as they either support mothers in their development of an optimal dyadic regulatory system with their infants or serve as a "backup" resource for babies when mothers' accessibility is compromised as a function of depression, drug dependence, or psychosis. Cross-caregiver consistency has only rarely been studied, though conceptually it might be expected that infants will thrive and have fewer problems developing predictable and consistent rhythms when the different coparenting adults who care for them develop coordinated predictable routines and response systems.

The differences in how adults handle and engage with babies during wakeful alertness and play are likely to be less important than the strategies caregivers use to structure the infant's day and to comfort and soothe the baby when distressed. Unpredictable responses to infant crying, feeding difficulties, middle-of-night awakenings, and other distress signals make it difficult for infants to learn to self-soothe and demand that they exert more energy accommodating to their environment than to developing intrinsic rhythms and capacity for self-regulation. Moreover, given newly emerging evidence about the importance of early experience in supporting the architecture of brain-behavior response systems during times of stress (National Scientific

Council on the Developing Child, 2005), inconsistency in the caregiving environment can potentially have a more lasting legacy. Detrimental effects of both within- and cross-caregiver inconsistency may be most pronounced in families with infants with difficult temperaments, colic, or other forms of behavioral or biological regulation problems.

Though most infant mental health interventions overlook these realities as they target the mother–infant dyad, the Erikson Institute Fussy Baby Network, a preventative intervention program for parents and infants birth to age 1 year, has provided leadership in embracing a coparenting model. Erikson redesigned its home visiting after recognizing that the peak time for infant crying and fussing (4–8 weeks postpartum) is a critical time in early family formation and that coparenting infants with early regulatory difficulties heightens the risk of establishing negative family patterns that frequently endure (Gilkerson, Gray, & Mork, 2005). Parenting Partner Guidelines were designed to prompt home visitors to remain attuned to the role and perspective of all caregivers, present or not, toward establishing positive patterns of consistent responses for difficult to sooth infants (Katch, 2009). Home visitors now determine during the first contact who the important coparents in the baby's life are (see Chapter 7) and encourage inclusion of these individuals in subsequent visits. When discussing soothing strategies, visitors inquire about views of other caregivers and how those individuals might respond to the ideas being considered. Visitors affirm the stress and inevitable areas of agreement and disagreement between coparents and explore how coparents can support one another's efforts with the baby. A major contribution of this groundbreaking, transformational effort is its explicit promulgation of a coparenting framework for intervention from the point of initial home visitor training (cf. P. Minuchin et al., 2007).

Adult–infant interactions are never only top-down; infants are full partners in the triangular systems that evolve in their families and shape their parents' behavior through their patterns of attention, gaze, and affect, even during the earliest months of life. Two research teams (Fivaz-Depeursinge & Corboz-Warnery, 1999; Nadel & Tremblay-Leveau, 1999) initially uncovered infants' precocious capacities for sharing attention between two people at the same time, with Fivaz-Depeursinge and Corboz-Warnery (1999) coining the term *triangular capacity* to describe such social attentional sharing. They found that infants as young as 3 months old not only tracked back-and-forth exchanges between two adult partners but also made triangular bids of their own, bids that functioned to influence the flow of interaction (e.g., sharing protest in order to change a state of affairs, or interest or pleasure as a signal to continue; see Fivaz-Depeursinge & Corboz-Warnery, 1999). In 2008, McHale, Fivaz-Depeursinge, Dickstein, Robertson, and Daley found something equally remarkable—3-month-old infants' triangular capacities are tied to the quality of coparenting within their family. These data suggest that triadic systems in families, like dyadic systems, take shape very early on and that children's development is intertwined with the functioning of the family system. To date, infants' triangular capacities have been studied only in two-parent nuclear families. There will be much of interest in studies of the phenomenon in other family configurations.

Coparenting During the Toddler and Early Childhood Years

In many cultures, a normative developmental shift that can perturb the existing coparenting dynamic in the family occurs as toddlers become increasingly verbal and independent. It is during the toddler years that families must begin to negotiate a balance between fulfilling the child's affectional and bonding needs and setting limits. Family adaptations during this phase of the child's life differ markedly across cultures (Garcia Coll, 1990; LeVine, 1977; Ogbu, 1981). Such adaptations must be understood within the context of the beliefs, values, and goals of different cultures, as all families strive to foster behavioral competencies they believe children will need to survive in their environment. Children's growing mobility and disobedience increase the already important influence of fathers or other family caregivers to help address the increasing demands instigated by the child's growing autonomy and willfulness.

As the coparenting system evolves to accommodate child development, differentiated roles will develop in some families, with caregiving needs handled by one individual or group of individuals and discipline by others. In other families, both caregiving and discipline will typically fall to just one person. In still other families, there will be a more balanced distribution. How children are coparented will depend on cultural norms, family size, child gender, and particular family circumstances. To date, however, few studies have charted comprehensively the variety of roles played and fulfilled by different family caregivers in different cultures with children of different ages.

Kurrien and Vo's (2004) study of families in India affords one interesting glimpse into within-culture variability in the routine cocaregiving environments experienced by young children in that country, though much of the focus of their analysis is on instrumental caregiving (meals, accompanying to and from school, homework, bedtime). Coparents play other important roles, too. Even in cultures in which men assume little or no responsibility for routine caretaking activities, they and other family coparents provide comfort and support in times of stress; promote children's development through shared activities, humor, joint attention, and turn taking; and provide the guidance, modeling, feedback, and encouragement necessary for the learning of new skills. Although not typically recognized as essential contributions to coparenting, especially when coparenting is conceptualized as a division of "labor" (see Chapter 6), the encouragement and promotion of security, sharing of emotions and activities, and scaffolding of complex new skills are arguably the most important jobs any coparenting adult can take on in promoting the developing child's social and emotional development (Hogan, 2007).

Coparenting During Middle Childhood

As children age and their lives come to be increasingly influenced by school, peers, and factors beyond the family itself, coparenting remains as important as ever. Children's development will continue to introduce dynamic new presses for existing coparenting alliances. How effectively coparents work together to respond when children and adolescents encounter difficulties with insensitive teachers or bullying students at school, experience anxiety and contemplate quitting or avoiding extracurricular activities that present challenges, and make acquaintances with questionable peers or seek play dates and sleepovers with children from families that give one or both parents pause can make all the difference in a child's life trajectory (Brody et al., 1994; Feinberg, Kan, & Hetherington, 2007).

There is also evidence that effective coparenting may be especially important in the context of neighborhood and community violence or adversity (Forehand & Jones, 2003; see also Chapter 4, this volume). In the face of competing influences and life challenges, coparents who communicate regularly, airing and resolving their conflicting viewpoints; who provide consistent, sensitive, and coordinated messages to children; and who keep one another (and the child's other coparents) apprised of their contacts with the child around major life issues will stand the greatest chance of maintaining a protective family structure for the child.

One important issue likely to surface at some point during the middle childhood years will be keeping the child's confidence. There are times in the lives of most children and families during which a child differentially seeks out one of his or her coparents to discuss a sensitive topic (Smetana, Villalobos, Rogge, & Tasopoulos-Chan, 2010). Well-functioning coparenting systems respect the child's need for privacy and help maintain the sense of privacy while also maintaining open communication between parents. In other families, however, secrecy becomes endemic and is sometimes even encouraged by parents seeking to fortify their own standing with the child and weaken the child's bonds with other coparents.

In such cases, secrecy can have very negative aftereffects. In many postdivorce family systems, for example, ongoing animosity and rivalry between a child's coparents may lead one or both of the adults to actually encourage a child to keep secrets from the other parent. Unwittingly, however, parents' entrainment of secrecy may prime the child to keep other secrets as well and to not disclose important details about their emotional life to parents (Darling,

Sumsille, Caldwell, & Dowdy, 2006). This is a growing concern with the access and savvy that even very young children now have with respect to computers; encouragement of secrecy exacerbated by a lack of communication, consistency, and support between coparents can combine to have grave consequences for children growing up in an Internet age.

Coparenting During Adolescence

During the adolescent years, as children begin their movement toward sexuality, experimentation, and independence from the family, coparenting alliances are tested once again, perhaps even more intensively than ever before. Some of the more compelling coparenting research of the past decade has involved studies of coparenting and adolescent risk. Baril, Crouter, and McHale (2007), using a path-analytic approach and controlling for earlier problem behaviors, determined that coparenting conflict predicted relative increases in adolescent risky behavior over 2 years and found that coparenting conflict mediated the link between marital love and adolescents' risky behavior 1 year later. Echoing these findings on the salience of coparental functioning for adolescent adjustment, Feinberg, Kan, and Hetherington (2007) found that coparenting conflict predicted as much or more unique variance in parenting and adolescent adjustment as did marital quality and disagreement together. After controlling for stability, coparenting conflict predicted mothers' and fathers' negativity and adolescent antisocial behavior (but not depression). These studies suggested that interventions that focus on coparental relationships in families with adolescents may modify trajectories of adolescent risky behavior.

In summary, children of all ages can be expected to benefit when their parents work well with one another. Benefits come when the adults in children's lives provide adequate protection and safety for them, read their needs effectively and communicate regularly about them, and show sensitivity to and respect for their desire to maintain a meaningful and satisfying connection with each member of their coparenting system. Effective coparenting systems do experience but also resolve dissonance; the best decisions about children often can only be made when there is a sharing and reconciliation of coparents' opposing viewpoints.

The most effective coparents are also likely to be those who possess the capacity to read and respond empathically to the child's needs. Although it is important that coparents support and stand by one another to provide necessary structure for children once major decisions have been discussed and made together, they do not inevitably or mindlessly support one another's day-to-day actions with the child. In any sound system there will be agreed-on checks-and-balances, allowing one adult to step in and take over for another when that person is at wits' end and parenting in a counterproductive or insensitive way. When coparents are interchangeable in this way, the child is far more likely to experience a supportive, responsive, and growth-promoting environment.

SUMMARY AND CONCLUDING POINTS

It is the contention of this chapter that virtually every child will be coparented, and that virtually every family coparents. This is a bold assertion, intended to open the door for a fresh and authentic means of understanding families of all cultures, shapes, and forms. From the perspective advanced in this chapter, the relevant question to ask is not whether a coparenting system has taken shape in a family, but rather what the family's coparenting structure and dynamics look like. In some families, a clearly visible coparenting alliance will develop that is strong, supportive, and constituted of a well-defined membership that remains consistent across developmental time. In others, the system that develops will be more fluid and amorphous, with movement by different coparenting adults into and out of the system. In some families, all coparents will come to the table to weigh in each time significant decisions about the child must be made. In others, a single coparent will wield seemingly unilateral authority and make most major decisions her- or himself without consulting the child's other coparents. What establishes a coparent's place in a family system is the child's connection to that person, the person's enduring commitment to helping care for and protect the child, and the family's recognition and endorsement of the person in that role. The manner and degree of each person's contribution are determined by the family, and the success of the child's coparenting system in supporting his or her development will rest on the quality of coordination, cooperation, and support among the family's coparenting adults.

Sixty years of clinical work by family therapists has established that coparenting systems are critically important for the adjustment of children in clinically referred families. Thirty years of research and clinical experience with postdivorce family systems has established that coparenting is critically important for both the short- and long-term adjustment of children from such families. Fifteen years of empirical research with two-parent nuclear family systems has shed light on the myriad and important ways in which the development of children in nonreferred community samples is affected by the coparenting of their parents. And emerging research, detailed throughout this book and elsewhere, has begun to establish the relevance of coparenting for children's development in other diverse family systems. At present, however, we have not even yet begun to chart the tip of the iceberg, and we have much yet to learn about coparenting and child development in diverse family systems. Such work is and will remain of foundational importance in our efforts to create strong, safe, and healthy socialization environments for all children. It is time to accelerate this work in concert and in earnest.

REFERENCES

Ahrons, C. R. (2007). Family ties after divorce: Long-term implications for children. *Family Process, 46*, 53–65. doi:10.1111/j.1545-5300.2006.00191.x

Baker, J., McHale, J., Strozier, A. & Cecil, D. (2010). Mother-grandmother coparenting relationships in families with incarcerated mothers: A pilot study. *Family Process, 49*, 165–184.

Baril, M. E., Crouter, A. C., & McHale, S. M. (2007). Processes linking adolescent well-being, marital love, and coparenting. *Journal of Family Psychology, 21*, 645–654. doi:10.1037/0893-3200.21.4.645

Bell, L. G., & Bell, D. C. (1979). Triangulation: Pitfall for the developing child. *Group Psychotherapy, Psychodrama & Sociometry, 32*, 150–155.

Bowen, M. (1961). Family psychotherapy. *American Journal of Orthopsychiatry, 31*, 40–60.

Bowen, M. (1972). On the differentiation of self. In J. Framo (Ed.), *A dialogue between family researchers and family therapists* (pp. 111–173). New York, NY: Springer.

Brickman, H. R. (1993). Between the devil and the deep blue sea: The dyad and the triad in psychoanalytic thought. *The International Journal of Psycho-Analysis, 74*, 905–915.

Brody, G. H., Stoneman, Z., Flor, D., McCrary, C., Hastings, L., & Conyers, O. (1994). Financial resources, parent psychological functioning, parent co-caregiving, and early adolescent competence in rural two-parent African-American families. *Child Development, 65*, 590–605. doi:10.2307/1131403

Brooks-Gunn, J., & Furstenberg, F. F. (1986). The children of adolescent mothers: Physical, academic, and psychological outcomes. *Developmental Review, 6*, 224–251. doi:10.1016/0273-2297(86)90013-4

Brown, G. L., Schoppe-Sullivan, S., Mangelsdorf, S., & Neff, C. (2010). Observed and reported supportive coparenting as predictors of infant-mother and infant-father attachment security. *Early Child Development and Care, 180*, 121–137. doi:10.1080/03004430903415015

Caldera, Y. M., & Lindsey, E. W. (2006). Coparenting, mother-infant interaction, and infant-parent attachment relationships in two-parent families. *Journal of Family Psychology, 20*, 275–283. doi:10.1037/0893-3200.20.2.275

Cecil, D., McHale, J., & Strozier, A. (2008). Female inmates, family caregivers, and young children's adjustment: A research agenda and implications for corrections programming. *Journal of Criminal Justice, 36*, 513–521. doi:10.1016/j.jcrimjus.2008.09.002

Cook, C. J., Schoppe-Sullivan, S. J., Buckley, C. K., & Davis, E. F. (2009). Are some children harder to coparent than others? Children's negative emotionality and coparenting relationship quality. *Journal of Family Psychology, 23,* 606–610. doi:10.1037/a0015992

Crosbie-Burnett, M., & Lewis, E. A. (1999). Use of African-American family structures and functioning to address the challenges of European-American postdivorce families. In S. Coontz, M. Parson, & G. Raley (Eds.), *American families: A multicultural reader* (pp. 455–469). London, England: Routledge.

Darling, N., Sumsille, P., Caldwell, L. L., & Dowdy, B. (2006). Predictors of adolescents' disclosure to parents and perceived parental knowledge: Between-and within-person differences. *Journal of Youth and Adolescence, 35,* 659–670. doi: 10.1007/s10964-006-9058-1

Donley, M. G. (1993). Attachment and the emotional unit. *Family Process, 32,* 3–20. doi:10.1111/j.1545-5300.1993.00003.x

Ermann, M. (1989). The triangle as relational form: Developmental dynamics of triangulation process. *Praxis der Psychotherapie und Psychosomatik, 34,* 261–269.

Feinberg, M. E., Kan, M. L., & Hetherington, E. M. (2007). The longitudinal influence of coparenting conflict on parental negativity and adolescent maladjustment. *Journal of Marriage and the Family, 69,* 687–702. doi:10.1111/j.1741-3737. 2007.00400.x

Fivaz-Depeursinge, E. (2008). Infant's triangular communication in "two for one" versus "two against one" family triangles: Case illustrations. *Infant Mental Health Journal, 29,* 189–202. doi:10.1002/imhj.20174

Fivaz-Depeursinge, E., & Corboz-Warnery, A. (1999). *The primary triangle: A developmental systems view of fathers, mothers, and infants.* New York, NY: Basic Books.

Fivaz-Depeursinge, E., Frascarolo, F., Lopes, F., Dimitrova, N., & Favez, N. (2007). Parents-child role reversal in trilogue play. Case studies of trajectories from pregnancy to toddler-hood. *Attachment & Human Development, 9,* 17–31. doi:10.1080/ 14616730601151425

Forehand, R., & Jones, D. J. (2003). Neighborhood violence and coparent conflict: Interactive influence on child psychosocial adjustment. *Journal of Abnormal Child Psychology, 31,* 591–604. doi:10.1023/A:1026206122470

Frank, H. (1988). On the role of the father in psychosomatic illnesses developing during childhood. *Praxis der Psychotherapie und Psychosomatik, 33,* 242–248.

Freud, S. (1953). Three essays on the theory of sexuality. In J. Strachey (Ed. & Trans.), *The standard edition of the complete psychological works of Sigmund Freud* (Vol. 7, pp. 125–243). London, England: Hogarth Press. (Original work published in 1905)

Friedman, E. (1991). Bowen theory and therapy. In A. S. Gurman & D. P. Kniskern (Eds.), *Handbook of family therapy* (Vol. 2, pp. 134–170). New York, NY: Brunner/Mazel.

Garcia Coll, C. T. (1990). Developmental outcome of minority infants: A process-oriented look into our beginnings. *Child Development, 61,* 270–289. doi:10.2307/1131094

Gilkerson, L., Gray, L., & Mork, N. (2005). Fussy babies, worried families, a new service network. *Zero to Three, 25*(3), 34–41.

Gonzalez-Mena, J. (1992). Taking a culturally sensitive approach in infant-toddler programs. *Young Children, 47*(2), 4–9.

Greenman, J., & Stonehouse, A. (1996). *Prime times: A handbook for excellence in infant and toddler care.* St. Paul, MN: Redleaf Press.

Greenspan, S. (1982). The second other. In S. Cath, A. Gurwitt, & J. Ross (Eds.), *Father and child: Developmental and clinical perspectives* (pp. 123–139). Boston, MA: Little Brown.

Henderson, J. (1982). The role of the father in separation-individuation. *Bulletin of the Menninger Clinic, 46,* 231–254.

Hogan, A. E. (2007). *Infant mental health in childcare: Functions of relationships.* Conference call presentation sponsored by FSU Center for Prevention & Early Intervention Policy Infant/Toddler Network, Tallahassee, FL.

Jones, C. W., & Lindblad-Goldberg, M. (2002). Ecosystemic structural family therapy. In F. W. Kaslow, R. F. Massey, & S. D. Massey (Eds.), *Comprehensive handbook of psychotherapy* (Vol. 3, pp. 3–34). New York, NY: Wiley.

Juni, S. (1995). Triangulation as splitting in the service of ambivalence. *Current Psychological Research & Reviews, 14,* 91–111. doi:10.1007/BF02686884

Katch, L. (2009). *Fussy baby network: Parenting partner guidelines.* Unpublished manuscript.

Kerr, M. E., & Bowen, M. (1988). *Family evaluation.* New York, NY: Norton.

Kurrien, R., & Vo, E. D. (2004). Who's in charge? Coparenting in South and Southeast Asian families. *Journal of Adult Development, 11,* 207–219. doi:10.1023/B:JADE.0000035628.42529.e5

LeVine, R. A. (1977). Child rearing as cultural adaptation. In P. H. Leiderman, S. R. Tulkin, & A. Rosenfeld (Eds.), *Culture and infancy: Variations in the human experience* (pp. 15–27). New York, NY: Academic Press.

McHale, J. (2007a). *Charting the bumpy road of coparenthood: Understanding the challenges of family life.* Washington, DC: Zero to Three Press.

McHale, J. (2007b). When infants grow up in multiperson relationship systems. *Infant Mental Health Journal, 28,* 1–23. doi:10.1002/imhj.20142

McHale, J. (2009). Shared child-rearing in nuclear, fragile, and kinship family systems: Evolution, dilemmas, and promise of a coparenting framework. In M. Schulz, M. Pruett, P. Kerig, & R. Parke (Eds.), *Strengthening couple relationships for optimal child development: Lessons from research and intervention* (pp. 77–94). Washington, DC: American Psychological Association.

McHale, J., & Cowan, P. (1996). Understanding how family-level dynamics affect children's development: Studies of two-parent families. *New Directions for Child and Adolescent Development, 74.*

McHale, J., & Fivaz-Depeursinge, E. (1999). Understanding triadic and family group process during infancy and early childhood. *Clinical Child and Family Psychology Review, 2,* 107–127. doi:10.1023/A:1021847714749

McHale, J., Fivaz-Depeursinge, E., Dickstein, S., Robertson, J., & Daley, M. (2008). New evidence for the social embeddedness of infants' early triangular capacities. *Family Process, 47,* 445–463. doi:10.1111/j.1545-5300.2008. 00265.x

McHale, J., Khazan, I., Erera, P., Rotman, T., DeCourcey, W., & McConnell, M. (2002). Coparenting in diverse family systems. In M. Bornstein (Ed.), *Handbook of parenting: Vol. 3. Being and becoming a parent* (2nd ed., pp. 75–107). Mahwah, NJ: Erlbaum.

McHale, J., Lauretti, A., Talbot, J., & Pouquette, C. (2002). Retrospect and prospect in the psychological study of coparenting and family group process. In J. McHale & W. Grolnick (Eds.), *Retrospect and prospect in the psychological study of families* (pp. 127–165). Hillsdale, NJ: Erlbaum.

Minkler, M., & Roe, K. M. (1996). Grandparents as surrogate parents. *Generations, 20,* 34–38.

Minuchin, P., Colapinto, J., & Minuchin, S. (2007). *Working with families of the poor* (2nd ed.). New York, NY: Guilford Press.

Minuchin, S. (1974). *Families and family therapy.* Cambridge, MA: Harvard University Press.

Minuchin, S., Rosman, B., & Baker, L. (1978). *Psychosomatic families: Anorexia nervosa in context.* Cambridge, MA: Harvard University Press.

Nadel, J., & Tremblay-Leveau, H. (1999). Early perception of social contingencies and interpersonal intentionality: Dyadic and triadic paradigms. In P. Rochat (Ed.), *Early social cognition: Understanding others in the first months of life* (pp. 189–212). Mahwah, NJ: Erlbaum.

Napp-Peters, A. (2005). Multi-parent families as "normal" families—segregation and parent-child-alienation after separation and divorce. *Praxis der Kinderpsychologie und Kinderpsychiatrie, 54,* 792–801.

National Scientific Council on the Developing Child. (2005). *Excessive stress disrupts the architecture of the developing brain* (Working Paper No. 3). Retrieved from http://developingchild.harvard.edu/library/reports_and_working_papers/ working_papers/wp3

Ogbu, J. U. (1981). Origins of human competence: A cultural-ecological perspective. *Child Development, 52,* 413–429. doi:10.2307/1129158

Roy, K., & Burton, L. (2007). Mothering through recruitment: Kinscription of nonresidential fathers and father figures in low-income families. *Family Relations, 56,* 24–39. doi:10.1111/j.1741-3729.2007.00437.x

Smetana, J. G., Villalobos, M., Rogge, R. D., & Tasopoulos-Chan, M. (2010). Keeping secrets from parents: Daily variations among poor, urban adolescents. *Journal of Adolescence, 33*, 321–331. doi:10.1016/j.adolescence.2009.04.003

Sroufe, L. A. (2005). Attachment and development: A prospective, longitudinal study from birth to adulthood. *Attachment & Human Development, 7*, 349–367. doi:10.1080/14616730500365928

Stack, C. B. (1974). *All our kin: Strategies for survival in a black urban community.* New York, NY: Harper & Row.

Stern, D. N. (1985). *The interpersonal world of the infant.* New York, NY: Basic Books.

Van IJzendoorn, M. H., Tavecchio, L. W. C., Stams, G. J., Verhoeven, M., & Reiling, E. (1998). Attunement between parents and professional caregivers: A comparison of childrearing attitudes in different child-care settings. *Journal of Marriage and the Family, 60*, 771–781. doi:10.2307/353545

Vaughn, B., Waters, E., Egeland, B., & Sroufe, L. A. (1979). Individual differences in infant-mother attachment at 12 and 18 months: Stability and change in families under stress. *Child Development, 50*, 971–975. doi:10.2307/1129321

Walsh, F. (2006). *Strengthening family resilience* (2nd ed.). New York, NY: Guilford Press.

Wilson, M. N. (1984). Mothers' and grandmothers' perceptions of behavior in three-generational black families. *Child Development, 55*, 1333–1339. doi:10.2307/1130003

Zittoun, T., Gillespie, A., Cornish, F., & Psaltis, C. (2007). The metaphor of the triangle in theories of human development. *Human Development, 50*, 208–229. doi:10.1159/000103361

2

COPARENTING IN TWO-PARENT NUCLEAR FAMILIES

SARAH C. MANGELSDORF, DANIEL J. LAXMAN, AND ALLISON JESSEE

The focus of this chapter is on coparenting in families in which both mothers and fathers are coresident with their children. Coparenting has been conceptualized in a variety of ways since researchers first began discussing the construct of coparenting in studies of these "intact" (nondivorced) families (e.g., Gable, Belsky, & Crnic, 1995; McHale, 1995; McHale, Kuersten, & Lauretti, 1996). Talbot and McHale's (2004) definition of coparenting as "an enterprise undertaken by two or more adults working together to raise a child for whom they share responsibility" (p. 192) is perhaps the most inclusive of these and is the one used to organize this chapter. Generally, there has been agreement among scientists and practitioners about this core element of defining coparenting, though differences have arisen about how best to precisely operationalize coparenting. This chapter reviews major research thrusts in the field of coparenting as the construct has been defined and operationalized, including the development of coparenting, the factors that influence the development of coparenting, and what is known about effects of coparenting processes on children's development.

COPARENTING AND ITS RELATIONSHIP TO MARITAL AND PARENTING SUBSYSTEMS IN THE FAMILY

Conceptually, coparenting is related to, but also distinct from, what has traditionally been called *marital quality*. As McHale (2009) outlined, coparenting is a specific form of triadic (or polyadic) family interaction, and in the assessment of coparenting, clinicians and researchers focus specifically on the beliefs and interactions of partners that pertain to the child and their shared connection to that child. In contrast, clinicians and researchers interested in understanding and evaluating adults' couple relationship quality focus on and assess the partner's sentiments about and dyadic interactions with one another; all couples, including those who are not parents, can be understood in terms of their commitment to and intimate partnered relationship with one another. It is important that coparenting and marital quality both appear to be distinct predictors of child adjustment (Feinberg, Kan, & Hetherington, 2007; Frosch, Mangelsdorf, & McHale, 2000; McHale & Rasmussen, 1998).

The functioning of the coparenting relationship can be largely described by the extent to which parents support or undermine each other's parenting efforts (Belsky, Putnam, & Crnic, 1996; McHale, 1995). However, coparenting is a family dynamic that involves both overt and covert practices. As outlined by McHale (1997), *overt* coparenting occurs when the child is involved in or present during the parent's interactions with one another (e.g., when all family members are physically together), whereas *covert* coparenting occurs when one parent is away and the other parent either supports and reaffirms or deconstructs and fails to reaffirm the coparenting "contract" or alliance that the adults have mutually fashioned together. Children who hear their parents undermine or negate parenting decisions made by the other coparent when that parent is not physically present experience their family's coparenting alliance in a very different way than do children whose parents reinforce and support one another's involvement with and connection to the child, whether that parent is physically present or not. Parents too develop a private sense of whether their partners are supportive coparents, and parents' beliefs about the solidarity of their alliance together as parents have been tied to the adjustment of their young children (Abidin & Brunner, 1995; Floyd & Zmich, 1991). To reiterate, coparenting dynamics in families are revealed by a number of different overt and covert beliefs and practices, which collectively come to define the adults' capacity to work together effectively in the care and upbringing of children.

HISTORY OF COPARENTING RESEARCH

The field of coparenting as we understand it today had two primary fore-bears: a rich clinical literature outlining the intrafamily dynamics of families who had come to the attention of therapists (e.g., Minuchin, 1974) and a series of empirical studies of how adults parented postdivorce (e.g., Maccoby & Mnookin, 1992). Both family therapists and divorce researchers have determined that problems in coparenting (low support, high undermining) could be tied to poorer child outcomes. Furthermore, in a now-classic special issue of *New Directions for Child and Adolescent Development* edited by McHale and Cowan (1996), "Understanding How Family-Level Dynamics Affect Children's Development: Studies of Two-Parent Families," a handful of researchers who had pioneered the study of dynamics and outcomes of coparenting in nonclinical samples of coresident, nondivorced families set the stage for the field of coparenting research.

Since the publication of McHale and Cowan (1996), accumulating evidence has documented that the quality of coparenting between adults is an important predictor of a wide array of important child outcomes in intact families, just as it is in divorced families. Indeed, across children's development, coparenting appears to be more strongly linked to child outcomes than does general marital quality (Abidin & Brunner, 1995; Feinberg, Kan, & Hetherington, 2007; Frosch et al., 2000; McHale & Rasmussen, 1998), and some studies have suggested that coparenting is as strong or stronger a correlate of child functioning as maternal or paternal parenting (Karreman, van Tuijl, van Aken, & Dekovic, 2008). Given the converging evidence indicating that how adults coparent together has important implications for the quality of their children's adjustment, it is imperative to understand the mechanisms underlying variations in coparenting quality. We address these issues next.

CHANGES IN COPARENTING OVER TIME

In this section, we review the existing literature on the developmental course of coparenting, beginning with a discussion of how factors before the birth of the child may influence coparenting and then moving on to discuss coparenting in infancy, the toddler and preschool years, middle childhood, and adolescence.

The Transition to Parenthood and Coparenting During Infancy

Even before their first child is born, men and women are setting the stage for the quality of their subsequent coparenting relationship. Recent investigations have found that understanding parents' beliefs and representations about the family before the birth of a child can help predict later, and sometimes even long-term, coparenting adjustment. McHale and Rotman (2007) found that the degree of difference between spouses' beliefs about parenting before babies were born predicted postbaby coparental adjustment. Not surprisingly, larger differences in parental beliefs predicted lower coparenting solidarity. In a particularly intriguing analysis, Von Klitzing, Simoni, Amsler, and Burgin (1999) found that expectant parents who talked about their future family using dyadic metaphors (baby and me) rather than triadic metaphors invoking the coparent showed more problems with early family adjustment. More recently, Talbot, Baker, and McHale (2009) tied parents' prenatal states of mind with respect to attachment to early patterns of coparenting conflict and cohesion during the first few months of the child's life, with insecurity breeding more problematic adjustment in families.

The changes couples must make from a marital dyad to a family triad require unanticipated emotional work while "making room" for a third person. Parents who struggle to successfully negotiate the adjustments that come with having an infant appear to be more likely to create a coparenting environment that can have negative consequence for their child. In families in which adults find themselves competing for their babies' affection as they become less attuned to the needs of their partners, early patterns of *hostile–competitive* coparenting (i.e., undermining coparenting) sometimes develop. Such dynamics appear to set a stage for negative child outcomes, including problems with attachment during infancy (Caldera & Lindsey, 2006) and toddlerhood (Frosch et al., 2000) and later problems with aggression during the preschool years (McHale & Rasmussen, 1998). Early patterns of coparenting detachment and disengagement also sometimes develop, with untoward outcomes for children. The key point we emphasize here is that even though young infants may not yet consciously understand their family's coparenting processes, early coparenting patterns in many cases appear to exert enduring effects on the infants' development (McHale et al., 1996).

Toddler and Preschool Years

Coparenting interactions during toddlerhood and the preschool years are especially salient for children, who need parents' coordinated support in internalizing the rules and standards that will govern their behavior both at home and at school. Disparaging comments made to the child by one coparent about the other may be especially detrimental to children during these years, whereas supportive coparenting interactions promote feelings of security at the family level (McHale, 1997). Karreman, van Tuijl, van Aken, and Dekovic (2008) suggested that such security may help children develop healthy behavioral and interactional skills and regulate their emotions, whereas hostility between parents can create uncertainty and negative arousal that can affect how the child regulates his or her emotions. Consistent with this hypothesis, McHale et al. (1996) found that 30-month-olds show higher levels of frustration during lab tasks in families in which parents exchanged more negative verbal comments about one another during interactions with the child.

In one intriguing analysis, Belsky, Putnam, and Crnic (1996) found that when parents showed less supportive and more undermining coparenting of their toddlers, children are less inhibited at 3 years than would have been predicted on the basis of their earlier temperamental profile. Belsky and his colleagues interpreted this finding to mean that in face of parental conflict and poor coparenting, children "toughen up" and learn not to show distress when frightened. As a number of researchers have found undermining and hostile coparenting to predict child externalizing behavior, it is also possible that Belsky and his colleagues were actually detecting early signs of disruptive behavior development—greater child disinhibition across time. In support of this possibility, Schoppe, Mangelsdorf, and Frosch (2001) found undermining coparenting at 3 years to predict externalizing behavior problems at 4 years. Studies have also found hostile–withdrawn coparenting to be associated with higher levels of mother-reported oppositional behavior, withdrawal, and anxiety/depression in preschool children (Katz & Low, 2004).

Although the majority of studies on coparenting have focused on negative coparenting dynamics, positive coparenting experiences are also important and strongly supportive of young children's socioemotional development (McHale et al., 1996). High positive engagement between parents during discussions of child-rearing tasks is linked to more secure father–child attachment concurrently (Frosch et al., 2000). In addition, when families display higher levels of warmth and coparenting cooperation during family interactions, preschoolers enact fewer aggressive interactions between characters during doll play and show less behavioral discomfort while watching puppets act out positive and negative family scenarios (McHale, Johnson, & Sinclair, 1999). These effects are evident even after controlling for both mother's and father's parenting. Relatedly, Kolak and Vernon-Feagans (2008) found that warmth and cooperation are significantly related to fewer internalizing and externalizing problems in toddlers, though the concurrent data do now allow determination of whether coparenting caused behavior problems or whether parents made poorer coparenting adjustments when their children started showing high levels of behavior problems.

Middle Childhood

How parents work together remains important for school-age children. Children's experiences at home prepare them for classroom settings, and the behaviors that they observe at home often set the tone for their interactions and behaviors at school (Stright & Neitzel, 2003). Children who see models of support and cooperation at home may carry those interaction strategies over to other relationships, such as those with peers and teachers. Low levels of positive coparenting and high levels of undermining coparenting are both associated with conflicted peer interactions at 5 years (Leary & Katz, 2004). Furthermore, in the same study, hostile–withdrawn coparenting at 5 years predicted lower levels of positive peer conversation and higher levels of conflicted peer interaction 4 years later. In another prospective study, Stright and Neitzel (2003) found that supportive coparenting shown the summer before children entered third grade predicted fewer attention problems, less passivity and dependence, and higher math and reading grades during third grade. This result remained significant, even when controlling for parents' level of rejection. In a sample of African American children, coparenting quality was associated with 9- to 12-year-olds' attention levels and task persistence (Brody & Flor, 1996), and interparental conflict (in the presence of the child) predicted lower levels of self-regulation and academic competency (Brody, Stoneman, & Flor, 1995).

It is interesting that very few researchers have reported gender differences in coparenting–child linkages, though there are a few interesting trends worthy of note. McConnell and Kerig (2002) reported that hostile–competitive coparenting is associated with higher levels of self-reported anxiety and mother-reported behavior problems (both externalizing and internalizing) among 7- to 11-year-old boys, but not girls. In contrast, coparenting patterns characterized by larger parenting discrepancies (substantially different levels of parent–child investment and warmth by the two parents) are associated with mother-reported internalizing problems for girls, but not for boys. In McHale, Johnson, and Sinclair's (1999) study, coparenting problems were more strongly associated with negative family representations and more playground behavior problems in families of boys than families of girls.

On the positive side, Kolak and Vernon-Feagans (2008) found that greater coparental banter (warm, supportive teasing) was associated with fewer externalizing problems among toddler girls, though this association was not found for toddler boys. Theoretically driven hypotheses concerning gendered dynamics in coparenting are certainly worth pursuing; studies to date have suggested that gender differences may be especially likely to consolidate under conditions of couple or marital unhappiness or distress.

Adolescence

Although the research is less extensive, there is good reason to expect that coparenting solidarity should be especially important as children enter adolescence and begin testing limits. In the few studies that have examined coparent–adolescent relationships, coparenting has indeed been associated with outcomes for adolescents. For example, in one important study, Baril, Crouter, and McHale (2007) found that after controlling for earlier behavior problems, coparenting conflict predicted increases in adolescents' risky behaviors over 2 years. In another study, coparenting conflict predicted adolescent antisocial behavior (Feinberg, Kan, & Hetherington, 2007). Interestingly, coparenting conflict predicted as much or more variance in adolescent adjustment as did the combination of marital quality and marital disagreement. Clearly, much more research is needed to explore further the risk-promoting and buffering effects that negative and positive coparenting can play in influencing adolescent adjustment.

Although researchers have not yet begun to examine how coparenting may continue beyond adolescence, coparenting does not end when children reach adulthood. Indeed there is every reason to believe that as young adults navigate the work world, becoming independent and perhaps becoming parents themselves, their parents may continue to coparent in supportive and/or undermining ways. This is an area ripe for future exploration.

Cross-Time Stability of Coparenting

Though coparenting solidarity appears to be important for children across the span of infancy, childhood, and adolescence, very few longitudinal studies have examined the natural evolution of coparenting in families or the degree of stability in coparenting over time. Accurately assessing the stability of coparenting can be challenging because coparenting styles may differ at different phases in the child's life. For example, during the transition to parenthood, the most important aspects of coparenting may be how connected partners are able to remain, whereas during adolescence, the ability to work together to set limits may be more critical (McHale & Rotman, 2007). Thus, coparenting may manifest itself differently throughout the family's development.

Despite a lack of heterotypic continuity, studies that attempted to establish the stability of coparenting across time have suggested that there does appear to be some degree of coherence in family's adaptations. For example, in one longitudinal study of infants from 3 to 30 months of age, McHale and Rotman (2007) found that coparental solidarity (a measure created by using both Conflict and Cohesion indicators at all time periods) was stable from 3 to 12 months and also from 12 to 30 months of infant age (McHale & Rotman, 2007).

Similarly, Schoppe-Sullivan, Mangelsdorf, Frosch, and McHale (2004) found that supportive and undermining coparenting behaviors were stable between 6 months and 3 years. Additionally, an intensive naturalistic study of coparenting exchanges in families' homes revealed that the frequency of supportive coparenting events in families remains relatively stable between 15 and 21 months of infant age, whereas frequency of purely unsupportive coparenting exchanges actually decreases during this period. Frequency of mixed interactions increases, suggesting that couples may find ways to counteract their impulses to disagree about the toddler over time (Gable, Belsky, & Crnic, 1995).

PREDICTORS OF COPARENTING

In this final section of the chapter, we review what is currently known about the factors that play a role in shaping coparenting adjustment. Since the first research documenting the associations between coparenting quality and child adjustment was published (e.g., Belsky, Putnam, & Crnic, 1996; McHale, Kuersten, & Lauretti, 1996), the next logical question to emerge was: What causes individual differences in coparenting? It has been well documented in the parenting literature that one's family of origin may have a profound effect on how one comes to parent as an adult (e.g., Sroufe & Fleeson, 1988). Thus, it is likely that, just as with parenting, there is considerable influence of the family of origin on how an adult coparents. It is certainly plausible that parents may coparent in manners similar to the ways that they were coparented. However, it obviously takes two parents to coparent, and thus the family histories of both members of the couple must be examined to understand the role that families of origin may play in the quality of coparenting. Many predictors of coparenting have been examined to date; some of these predictors or correlates are more demographic in nature, and some more psychological (e.g., family of origin, attachment representations). Our review focuses on family characteristics (family size and child birth order), characteristics of parents (educational attainment, personality, and parenting beliefs and attitudes), characteristics of children (gender, temperament), and characteristics of the marital relationship as they are related to coparenting quality. We also consider the associations between coparenting and variables such as life stress and social support, which may be seen as characteristics both of the parents and of the larger social context.

Family Size and Child Birth Order

It is surprising that data regarding the impact of the number of children in a family on coparenting dynamics and quality are quite sparse.

Conceptually, it might be anticipated that coparents would be forced by necessity to get more organized and to show greater teamwork when having to parent multiple children than when having to parent just one; the exclusive focus by both on a single child, often at the root of triangulation in families (see Chapter 10, this volume), might potentially also give way to more evenly distributed attentions among children as family size increases. Consistent with this latter notion, Lindsey, Caldera, and Colwell (2005) found that mothers with more than one child engaged in less intrusive coparenting (e.g., interfering in the father's interactions with the child) than did mothers with only one child, whereas McHale and colleagues found similarly that parents of second-born infants showed lower levels of joint involvement and structuring during triadic play interactions with the babies than did parents of first born infants (McHale, 2007). Overall, though, studies have generally not documented major effects of birth order or presence of another child on coparenting behavior (e.g., McHale, Kuersten-Hogan, Lauretti, & Rasmussen, 2000). Further research in this area is needed.

Parent Characteristics: Educational Attainment

A few studies have indicated that higher educational attainment by one or both parents may be associated with more harmonious coparenting interactions. For example, Stright and Bales (2003) reported that in a sample of preschool children and their parents, both fathers' and mothers' education level was positively related to supportive coparenting. Van Egeren (2003) also found that fathers who reported higher education levels and socioeconomic status prebirth also reported higher levels of positive coparenting in the 6 months after birth. However, data from Belsky, Crnic, and Gable (1995) indicated that the relationship of most importance may have to do with mother–father educational compatibility. They found that in a sample of families with first-born, 15-month-old sons, it was the difference between spouses' level of education that mattered most, such that parents who had a greater difference in education level showed less supportive coparenting (Belsky et al., 1996). These findings regarding educational attainment and coparenting quality are similar to findings regarding socioeconomic status (SES) and dyadic interaction quality (e.g., Parke & Buriel, 2006). However, the association between SES and coparenting parenting quality is probably not due to education per se but instead to a correlation with a third variable such as life stress. It is well documented that lower SES parents experience much higher levels of stress, which may in turn impede parenting quality (McLoyd, 1998) and also coparenting quality.

Parent Characteristics: Age of Parent

No conclusive findings have established whether parental age affects coparenting quality. Although Van Egeren (2003) reported that mothers reported more positive coparenting experiences in families in which fathers were older, Gable, Belsky, and Crnic (1995) found that fathers who were younger supported their partner in parenting more frequently than did older fathers. Lindsey et al. (2005) found that younger mothers of 1-year-olds were more prone to intrusive, or undermining, coparenting than were older mothers. It would seem likely that coparenting adjustments might have as much to do with parental developmental maturity as with age per se, though this has not been definitively established.

Parent Gender and the Development of the Coparenting Alliance

One central question that has been of interest to researchers is how coparenting alliances are coconstructed. Some writers portray women as the architects of coparenting relationships and note their "gatekeeping" behavior or propensity to consciously or unconsciously include or exclude fathers from actively parenting children. There is some evidence that maternal prebirth characteristics are more predictive of coparenting than are paternal characteristics (Van Egeren, 2003), although work by Talbot et al. (2009) indicated that taking both parents' psychological characteristics into account simultaneously sheds important light on the kinds of early coparenting adaptations they make.

There are also data indicating that during infancy fathers show more positive and supportive coparenting than do mothers (Gable et al., 1995; Gordon & Feldman, 2008; Lindsey et al., 2005) and report being more satisfied with their coparental interactions than do mothers (Van Egeren, 2004). Although this portrayal of mothers as watching guard over babies and of fathers as behaving more supportively than mothers may be characteristic of many families' interactions during infancy, other data have told a different story. For example, Margolin, Gordis, and John (2001) found that in both preschool and preadolescent samples, it was mothers who were judged to be higher on cooperative behavior than fathers. Margolin and colleagues also found that mothers showed more gender-targeted behavior when coparenting; mothers with sons were rated higher on triangulation (i.e., focusing on the child to the exclusion of the father) than were mothers with daughters, whereas fathers were equally likely to show triangulating behavior with sons and daughters. This is somewhat surprising given that in studies of dyadic parent–child interaction, it is often found that mothers act more similarly with sons and daughters than fathers do, and it is fathers' interactional style that differs as a function of child gender (Parke & Buriel, 2006).

Beyond looking for archetypal differences in how mothers and fathers coparent, a second relevant line of inquiry has examined effects of mothers' parenting on fathers, or fathers' parenting on mothers, although this body of work is technically not concerned with gender per se. Schoppe-Sullivan, Brown, Cannon, Mangelsdorf, and Sokolowski (2008) found that when mothers did less gatekeeping (i.e., more encouragement and less criticism) to fathers, coparenting quality was better. They also found that when fathers were more highly involved and more competent at child care, coparenting was better. A similar pattern was found by Gordon and Feldman (2008), who reported that more positive social behavior of each parent when alone with their infant predicted greater coparenting mutuality in triadic interaction.

Parental Personality and Psychological Security and Well-Being

Studies in this area can be organized into two main categories: effects of psychological security and well-being (including depression) and effects of personality characteristics.

Psychological Security and Well-Being

McHale (1995) found that when mothers and fathers reported a stronger sense of feeling cared for and loved by others, the coparenting interactions they coconstructed were more likely to be balanced and marked by more equivalent levels of warmth and involvement directed toward their partner and their baby during triadic play. It should be noted, however, that these findings explained little variance in coparenting compared with marital quality. More recently, Talbot et al. (2009) reported that insecure states of mind with respect to attachment also predicted high coparenting conflict and low coparenting cohesion during early infancy. In this study, states of mind with respect to attachment were as strongly connected to coparenting as was marital adjustment.

Parents' self-esteem and ego resilience are also associated with more optimal coparenting relationships. It is likely that parents who feel more secure about themselves and are less stress reactive are more likely to be able to work flexibly with their partner in coparenting and less likely to critically undermine their partner. For example, Van Egeren (2003) found that fathers married to women with stronger ego development reported better coparenting experiences. Similarly, Lindsey et al. (2005) found that both maternal and paternal self-esteem could be tied to more effective coparenting. Talbot and McHale (2004) found that in families in which fathers were more ego resilient, marital distress was less likely to spill over and disrupt coparenting of infants. Similarly, Elliston, McHale, Talbot, Parmley, and Kuersten-Hogan (2008) observed that fathers who reported having greater ego resilience were less likely to withdraw during child care discussions during early infancy. They also found connections between ego resilience and perceptions of being respected as a parent by their partner. Collectively, these findings suggest that parental adjustment appears to serve as a resource in strengthening coparenting and protecting it from negative effects of marital distress.

Not surprisingly, parental depressive symptoms appear to be a risk factor for negative coparenting dynamics. In Elliston et al.'s (2008) sample, fathers who had shown an increase in depressive symptoms in the months after their child was born were more prone to withdraw during child care discussions at 3 months. Bronte-Tinkew, Scott, Horowitz, and Lilja (2009) found that fathers with more depressive symptoms when their child was 9 months old reported greater conflict over the child with their spouse, less daily discussion of the child, and less support from their spouse a year later. It is possible that depressed fathers withdraw from their role as coparent and as marital partner, and this is evidenced in the lower amount of daily discussion about the child. Further research on relations between depression and coparenting adjustment are needed to disentangle cause and effect in these relationships and to determine whether positive coparenting is a resource for young children in families with a depressed parent.

Parents' Personality Traits

Conclusions concerning particular personality characteristics are far less consistent, and so here we highlight just a few representative studies and findings. Stright and Bales (2003) found that mothers who were less positively adjusted in their personality (more negative scores on each of the Big Five factors) were in more problematic coparenting relationships, whereas those more positively adjusted reported more positive alliances. Talbot and McHale (2004) found both maternal self-control and paternal flexibility to be correlated with coparenting harmony, and Kolak and Volling (2007) found that both mothers and fathers high in negative expressiveness show more coparenting conflict. Finally, one study found that partners more similar to one another in their personality traits might have better coparenting relationships. Belsky, Crnic, and Gable (1995) found that larger differences between parents in extroversion and interpersonal affect were tied to higher levels of unsupportive coparenting.

These studies have provided some interesting leads concerning personality features that may promote or interfere with positive coparenting, though much more research in this area is needed before any conclusions can be drawn with confidence. In several studies (e.g., Kolak & Volling, 2007; Talbot & McHale, 2004), statistical interactions have qualified main effects of coparenting, suggesting that personality traits may exert their effects under certain circumstances or in certain contexts (e.g., high stress, low marital quality).

Parents' Family of Origin Experiences

Although little research has been conducted on how representations of parenting and coparenting from one's family of origin are related to one's own coparenting, Stright and Bales (2003) found that mothers' recollections of observing supportive coparenting in their families of origin were positively related to supportive coparenting in their own families. Van Egeren (2003) noted a similar finding with fathers. Fathers who reported better coparenting in their families of origin reported better coparenting with their own child. This is clearly a promising area for further research.

Parents' Attitudes and Beliefs About Coparenting

As we commented earlier in this chapter, several studies have indicated that how parents are thinking about their coparenting relationships before their babies are born predicts later coparenting adjustment. Van Egeren (2003) found that mothers who were more concerned about child rearing before birth reported having poorer coparenting experiences in the 6 months following birth. Similarly, McHale et al. (2004) and McHale and Rotman (2007) tied mothers' and fathers' negative prenatal outlooks on coparenting to low cooperation and family warmth after the birth of the child. Bronte-Tinkew et al. (2009) found that when fathers reported having wanted the pregnancy, couples reported less conflict over the children, compared with families in which fathers characterized the pregnancy as mistimed or unwanted.

Unrealistic expectancies may also set parents up for later problems with coparenting adjustment. Van Egeren (2003) found that fathers who claimed prenatally to be focusing principally on positive aspects of childbirth and parenting reported greater declines in later coparenting satisfaction. Khazan, McHale, and Decourcey (2008) and Van Egeren (2004) each reported that more significantly violated expectations of mothers about levels of father support predicted less positive coparenting during infancy.

Parents' Prenatal Beliefs About Child Rearing

Lindsey et al. (2005) found that when parents advocate child-rearing practices that are less restrictive and more nurturing, they show less intrusive and more supportive coparenting. Schoppe-Sullivan et al. (2008)

found that more progressive, nontraditional beliefs about father involvement by both men and women also predicted more positive coparenting. When parents' beliefs are contradictory, however, less positive coparenting adjustment sometimes follows. McHale et al. (2004) found that mothers' prenatal reports of greater discrepancies between their own and their husbands' parenting beliefs predicted coparenting difficulties at 3 months postpartum, and McHale and Rotman (2007) established that greater prenatal discrepancies in mothers' and fathers' ideas about parenting predicted less coparenting solidarity at 12 and at 30 months postpartum. Van Egeren (2003) likewise found that when parents disagree about how permissive and protective parents should be, problems follow. Conversely, when fathers' and mothers' beliefs are more congruent, coparenting is more positive (Lindsey et al., 2005). Together, these findings indicate that parents' beliefs about parenting, both alone and when considered in combination with their partners, are important determinants of early coparenting adjustment.

Effects of Child Gender

McHale (1995) reported that marital distress is correlated with hostile–competitive families of boys (but not girls), whereas larger parenting discrepancies exist in maritally distressed families of girls (but not boys). It may be that the form of coparenting distress seen in families differs as a function of child gender, with boys at greater risk of exposure to hostile–competitive dynamics and girls to disengagement by and/or between coparents. The findings of Elliston and colleagues (2008) with families of very young infants are consistent with this father-withdrawal pattern with girls but not boys. Some of the research on father involvement has suggested that as a group, fathers are more invested in relationships with their sons than with their daughters (e.g., Pleck, 1997). Given this, it makes sense that when there is marital distress in couples, fathers of girls may be more willing to withdraw than fathers of boys. However, although these findings suggest that gender differences in coparenting may surface under circumstances in which the couple is experiencing marital distress, there is no real evidence that children's gender directly influences coparenting. Studies have found no mean differences in coparenting quality as a function of child gender when parents interact together with children (e.g., McHale et al., 2000), though a few studies hint that mothers might approach coparenting of boys differently than coparenting of girls. As discussed earlier, Margolin et al. (2001) reported that mothers of boys were rated higher on triangulation than were mothers of girls. By and large, however, the organizing effects of child gender on coparenting appear to be very limited.

Effects of Child Temperament

When studies of coparenting have asked parents to report on their child's temperament, they have generally found more positive coparenting in families with easier children and less positive coparenting in families with more difficult children (Davis, Schoppe-Sullivan, Mangelsdorf, & Brown, 2009; Gordon & Feldman, 2008; Lindsey et al., 2005; McHale & Rotman, 2007; Schoppe-Sullivan, Mangelsdorf, Brown, & Sokolowski, 2007; Van Egeren, 2004). In these studies, child temperament often interacts with some other risk factor, such as marital quality, to predict coparenting, rather than exerting effects in isolation. A particularly intriguing line of research has examined associations between children's effortful control and the quality of coparenting in families. Greater effortful control has been linked to more positive coparenting adjustment in families (Karreman et al., 2008), and effective coparenting appears to prevent children who show low effortful control from developing externalizing behavior problems (Schoppe-Sullivan, Weldon, Davis, & Buckley, 2009). In these studies, however, coparenting is often implicitly depicted as a cause of effortful control rather than effortful control organizing coparenting adjustment. In the longitudinal investigation conducted by Davis et al. (2009), there was evidence of bidirectional associations between child temperament and coparenting such that early infant difficulty was associated with a decrease in supportive coparenting behavior across time, and conversely early supportive coparenting was associated with a decrease in infant difficulty. Future research should continue to explore the complex associations between child temperament and coparenting over time.

Marital Characteristics

Marital quality is undoubtedly the factor that has been linked to coparenting quality more reliably than any other factor examined. Studies have linked low levels of supportive coparenting to such marital indicators as relationship anxiety (Belsky, Crnic, & Gable, 1995), observed distress (McHale, 1995) and hostility (Katz & Gottman, 1996), low self-reported marital quality (Gordon & Feldman, 2008; McHale, 1997), defensiveness during child-related disagreements (Margolin et al., 2001), and low engagement in a marital discussion (Schoppe-Sullivan et al., 2004). Undermining coparenting has been linked to partners' discomfort with closeness and intimacy (Belsky, Crnic, & Gable, 1995), observed marital distress (McHale, 1995), marital hostility and husband withdrawal (Katz & Gottman, 1996), low self-reported marital quality (McHale, 1997), hostility and defensiveness during child-related disagreements (Margolin et al., 2001), and low positive engagement in a marital discussion (Schoppe-Sullivan et al., 2004). Schoppe-Sullivan et al. (2004) reported that the relationship between marital conflict and undermining coparenting is stronger at 3 years than at 6 months. Though most of the studies summarized previously have examined marital and coparenting adjustment at the same point in time, longitudinal studies have confirmed the strong ties between marital quality and later coparenting adjustment (Bonds & Gondoli, 2007; Bronte-Tinkew et al., 2009; McHale et al., 2004; Van Egeren, 2004).

Less is known about the interplay between coparenting and marital adjustment across developmental time. Three studies to date have attempted to clarify this dialectic. Van Egeren (2004) found that as coparenting quality decreased over time, martial quality increased, and vice versa; her interpretation of this puzzling finding was that "one aspect of the couple relationship may be maintained at the expense of the other" (p. 453). Belsky and Hsieh (1998) found that in families in which fathers' reported that levels of love for wives decreased over time, there was a higher proportion of unsupportive coparenting events in the intervening interval than in families in which fathers' love remained high at both earlier and later time points. A parallel finding emerged for mothers, with more unsupportive coparenting in families in which mothers reported higher levels of marital conflict over time. Finally, Schoppe-Sullivan and colleagues (2004) found that coparenting at 6 months postpartum predicted marital quality at 3 years, but not vice versa. The Belsky and Schoppe-Sullivan studies suggested that the quality of early coparenting can either enhance or erode the quality of the marriage over time, though this is an area in need of further investigation.

Stress and Support

Finally, forces outside of the family can have an effect on coparenting adjustment. Because very few studies have examined this issue, we comment on this theme only briefly here. Belsky, Crnic, and Gable (1995) reported that in families experiencing greater stress, spousal differences on a variety of factors (including those outlined earlier) were more likely to show ties to negative coparenting. Lindsey et al. (2005) found that mothers reporting greater social support showed more supportive coparenting. It is likely that any number of factors outside the family, such as work status and strain of parents, positive and negative involvement of extended family and other significant adults, and significant life events may formatively shape coparenting adjustment at different phases of the family life cycle.

CONCLUSION

Like parenting, coparenting in families is multiply determined. Coparenting relationships are more positive when parents report better adjustment, higher self-esteem, and more ego resilience. The quality of the marriage is also predictive of coparenting quality, but research has indicated these are distinct, but related, dimensions. Finally, it is also clear that child temperament, or at least parents' perceptions of child temperament, plays a part in the quality of the coparenting relationship, and the evidence has suggested that these are interactive, rather than direct, effects of temperament. Future research should explore whether research using observational measures of temperament yields similar results.

Other pressing questions exist about whether and how parents' family history and relationship representations relate to coparenting quality, and about stability and change in coparenting across very different developmental periods (e.g., early childhood, middle childhood, and adolescence). Most of the research reviewed in this chapter has focused on largely middle-class, European American samples. Just as studies of parenting have found different patterns of predictors, correlates, and consequences of dimensions of parenting in samples that vary as a function of SES and ethnicity (e.g., Parke & Buriel, 2006), there is every reason to think that different patterns will emerge in coparenting research currently being conducted with more diverse samples. Studies engaging both clinical and nonclinical populations would also advance the field in necessary ways. Finally, greater translation is needed between basic research on coparenting and preventive interventions; understanding the unique importance of coparenting in families of young children is a prerequisite for helping couples develop an alliance that is both more rewarding for them and more beneficial for the social and emotional adjustment of their child.

REFERENCES

Abidin, R. R., & Brunner, J. F. (1995). Development of a parenting alliance inventory. *Journal of Clinical Child Psychology, 24,* 31–40. doi:10.1207/s15374424jccp2401_4

Baril, M. E., Crouter, A. C., & McHale, S. M. (2007). Processes linking adolescent well-being, marital love, and coparenting. *Journal of Family Psychology, 21,* 645–654. doi:10.1037/0893-3200.21.4.645

Belsky, J., Crnic, K., & Gable, S. (1995). The determinants of coparenting in families with toddler boys: Spousal differences in daily hassles. *Child Development, 66,* 629–642. doi:10.2307/1131939

Belsky, J., & Hsieh, K. (1998). Patterns of marital change during the early childhood years: Parent personality, coparenting, and division-of-labor correlates. *Journal of Family Psychology, 12*, 511–528. doi:10.1037/0893-3200.12.4.511

Belsky, J., Putnam, S., & Crnic, K. (1996). Coparenting, parenting, and early emotional development. In J. P. McHale & P. A. Cowan (Eds.), *Understanding how family-level dynamics affect children's development: Studies of two-parent families. New Directions for Child and Adolescent Development, 74*, 45–55. doi:10.1002/cd.23219967405

Bonds, D. D., & Gondoli, D. M. (2007). Examining the process by which marital adjustment affects maternal warmth: The role of coparenting support as a mediator. *Journal of Family Psychology, 21*, 288–296. doi:10.1037/0893-3200.21.2.288

Brody, G. H., & Flor, D. (1996). Coparenting, family interactions, and competence among African American youths. In J. P. McHale & P. A. Cowan (Eds.), *Understanding how family-level dynamics affect children's development: Studies of two-parent families. New Directions for Child and Adolescent Development, 74*, 77–91.

Brody, G. H., Stoneman, Z., & Flor, D. (1995). Linking family processes and academic competence among rural African American Youths. *Journal of Marriage and the Family, 57*, 567–579. doi:10.2307/353913

Bronte-Tinkew, J., Scott, M. E., Horowitz, A., & Lilja, E. (2009). Pregnancy intentions during the transition to parenthood and links to coparenting for first-time fathers of infants. *Parenting, 9*, 1–35. doi:10.1080/15295190802656729

Caldera, Y. M., & Lindsey, E. W. (2006). Coparenting, mother-infant interaction, and infant-parent attachment relationships in two-parent families. *Journal of Family Psychology, 20*, 275–283. doi:10.1037/0893-3200.20.2.275

Davis, E. F., Schoppe-Sullivan, S. J., Mangelsdorf, S. C., & Brown, G. L. (2009). The role of infant temperament in stability and change in coparenting across the first year of life. *Parenting, 9*, 143–159. doi:10.1080/15295190802656836

Elliston, D., McHale, J., Talbot, J., Parmley, M., & Kuersten-Hogan, R. (2008). Withdrawal from coparenting interactions during early infancy. *Family Process, 47*, 481–499. doi:10.1111/j.1545-5300.2008.00267.x

Feinberg, M. E., Kan, M. L., & Hetherington, E. M. (2007). The longitudinal influence of coparenting conflict on parental negativity and adolescent maladjustment. *Journal of Marriage and the Family, 69*, 687–702. doi:10.1111/j.1741-3737.2007.00400.x

Floyd, F. J., & Zmich, D. E. (1991). Marriage and the parenting partnership: Perceptions and interactions of parents with mentally retarded and typically developing children. *Child Development, 62*, 1434–1448. doi:10.2307/1130817

Frosch, C. A., Mangelsdorf, S. C., & McHale, J. L. (2000). Marital behavior and the security of preschooler-parent attachment relationships. *Journal of Family Psychology, 14*, 144–161. doi:10.1037/0893-3200.14.1.144

Gable, S., Belsky, J., & Crnic, K. (1995). Coparenting during the child's 2nd year: A descriptive account. *Journal of Marriage and the Family, 57*, 609–616. doi:10.2307/353916

Gordon, I., & Feldman, R. (2008). Synchrony in the triad: A microlevel process model of coparenting and parent-child interactions. *Family Process, 47*, 465–479. doi:10.1111/j.1545-5300.2008.00266.x

Karreman, A., van Tuijl, C., van Aken, M. A. G., & Dekovic, M. (2008). Parenting, coparenting, and effortful control in preschoolers. *Journal of Family Psychology, 22*, 30–40. doi:10.1037/0893-3200.22.1.30

Katz, L. F., & Gottman, J. M. (1996). Spillover effects of marital conflict: In search of parenting and coparenting mechanisms. *New Directions for Child Development, 74*, 57–76. doi:10.1002/cd.23219967406

Katz, L. F., & Low, S. M. (2004). Marital violence, co-parenting, and family-level processes in relation to children's adjustment. *Journal of Family Psychology, 18*, 372–382. doi:10.1037/0893-3200.18.2.372

Khazan, I., McHale, J. P., & Decourcey, W. (2008). Violated wishes about division of childcare labor predict early coparenting process during stressful and nonstressful family evaluations. *Infant Mental Health Journal, 29*, 343–361. doi:10.1002/imhj.20183

Kolak, A. M., & Vernon-Feagans, L. (2008). Family-level coparenting processes and child gender as moderators of family stress and toddler adjustment. *Infant and Child Development, 17*, 617–638. doi:10.1002/icd.577

Kolak, A. M., & Volling, B. L. (2007). Parental expressiveness as a moderator of coparenting and marital relationship quality. *Family Relations, 56*, 467–478. doi:10.1111/j.1741-3729.2007.00474.x

Leary, A., & Katz, L. F. (2004). Coparenting, family-level processes, and peer outcomes: The moderating role of vagal tone. *Development and Psychopathology, 16*, 593–608. doi:10.1017/S0954579404004687

Lindsey, E. W., Caldera, Y., & Colwell, M. (2005). Correlates of coparenting during infancy. *Family Relations, 54*, 346–359. doi:10.1111/j.1741-3729.2005.00322.x

Maccoby, E. E., & Mnookin, R. H. (1992). *Dividing the child: Social and legal dilemma of Custody*. Cambridge, MA: Harvard University Press.

Margolin, G., Gordis, E. B., & John, R. S. (2001). Coparenting: A link between marital conflict and parenting in two-parent families. *Journal of Family Psychology, 15*, 3–21. doi:10.1037/0893-3200.15.1.3

McConnell, M. C., & Kerig, P. K. (2002). Assessing coparenting in families of school-age children: Validation of the Coparenting and Family Rating System. *Canadian Journal of Behavioural Science, 34*, 44–58. doi:10.1037/h0087154

McHale, J. P. (1995). Coparenting and triadic interactions during infancy: The roles of marital distress and child gender. *Developmental Psychology, 31*, 985–996. doi:10.1037/0012-1649.31.6.985

McHale, J. P. (1997). Overt and covert coparenting processes in the family. *Family Process, 36*, 183–201. doi:10.1111/j.1545-5300.1997.00183.x

McHale, J. P. (2007). When infants grow up in multiperson relationship systems. *Infant Mental Health Journal, 28*, 370–392. doi:10.1002/imhj.20142

McHale, J. P. (2009). Shared child rearing in nuclear, fragile, and kinship family systems: Evolution, dilemmas, and promise of a coparenting framework. In M. S. Schulz, M. K. Pruett, P. K. Kerig & R. D. Parke (Eds.), *Strengthening couple relationships for optimal child development: Lessons from research and intervention* (pp. 77–94). Washington, DC: American Psychological Association.

McHale, J. P., & Cowan, P. A. (Eds.). (1996). Understanding how family-level dynamics affect children's development: Studies of two-parent families [Special issue]. *New Directions for Child and Adolescent Development, 74*.

McHale, J. P., Johnson, D., & Sinclair, R. (1999). Family dynamics, preschoolers' family representation, and preschool peer relations. *Early Education and Development, 10*, 373–401. doi:10.1207/s15566935eed1003_8

McHale, J. P., Kazali, C., Rotman, T., Talbot, J., Carleton, M., & Lieberson, R. (2004). The transition to coparenthood: Parents' prebirth expectations and early coparental adjustment at 3 months postpartum. *Development and Psychopathology, 16*, 711–733. doi:10.1017/S0954579404004742

McHale, J. P., Kuersten, R., & Lauretti, A. (1996). New directions in the study of family-level dynamics during infancy and early childhood. *New Directions for Child and Adolescent Development, 74*, 5–26.

McHale, J. P., Kuersten-Hogan, R., Lauretti, A., & Rasmussen, J. L. (2000). Parental reports of coparenting and observed coparenting behavior during the toddler period. *Journal of Family Psychology, 14*, 220–236.

McHale, J. P., & Rasmussen, J. L. (1998). Coparental and family-level dynamics during infancy: Early family precursors of child and family functioning during preschool. *Development and Psychopathology, 10*, 39–59. doi:10.1017/S0954579498001527

McHale, J. P., & Rotman, T. (2007). Is seeing believing? Expectant parents' outlooks on coparenting and later coparenting solidarity. *Infant Behavior and Development, 30*, 63–81. doi:10.1016/j.infbeh.2006.11.007

McLoyd, V. C. (1998). Socioeconomic disadvantage and child development. *American Psychologist, 53*, 185–204. doi:10.1037/0003-066X.53.2.185

Minuchin, S. (1974). *Families and family therapy*. Oxford, England: Harvard University Press.

Parke, R., & Buriel, R. (2006). Socialization in the family: Ethnic and ecological perspectives. In N. Eisenberg (Ed.), *The handbook of child psychology: Social, emotional, and personality development* (6th ed., Vol. 3, pp. 429–504). New York, NY: Wiley.

Pleck, J. H. (1997). Paternal involvement: Levels, origins, and consequences. In M. E. Lamb (Ed.), *The role of the father in child development* (3rd ed., pp. 66–103). New York, NY: Wiley.

Schoppe-Sullivan, S. J., Brown, G. L., Cannon, E. A., Mangelsdorf, S. C., & Sokolowski, M. S. (2008). Maternal gatekeeping, coparenting quality, and fathering behavior in families with infants. *Journal of Family Psychology, 22*, 389–398. doi:10.1037/0893-3200.22.3.389

Schoppe-Sullivan, S. J., Mangelsdorf, S. C., Brown, G. L., & Sokolowski, M. S. (2007). Goodness-of-fit in family context: Infant temperament, marital quality, and early coparenting behavior. *Infant Behavior and Development, 30*, 82–96. doi:10.1016/j.infbeh.2006.11.008

Schoppe, S. J., Mangelsdorf, S. C., & Frosch, C. A. (2001). Coparenting, family process, and family structure: Implications of preschoolers externalizing behavior. *Journal of Family Psychology, 15*, 526–545. doi:10.1037/0893-3200.15.3.526

Schoppe-Sullivan, S. J., Mangelsdorf, S. C., Frosch, C. A., & McHale, J. L. (2004). Associations between coparenting and marital behavior from infancy to preschool years. *Journal of Family Psychology, 18*, 194–207. doi:10.1037/0893-3200.18.1.194

Schoppe-Sullivan, S. J., Weldon, A. H., Cook, J. C., Davis, E. F., & Buckley, C. K. (2009). Coparenting behavior moderates longitudinal relations between effortful control and preschool children's externalizing behavior. *Journal of Child Psychology and Psychiatry, and Allied Disciplines, 50*, 698–706. doi:10.1111/j.1469-7610.2008.02009.x

Sroufe, L. A., & Fleeson, J. (1988). The coherence of family relationships. In R. A. Hinde & J. Stevenson-Hinde (Eds.), *Relationships within families* (pp. 27–47). Oxford, England: Clarendon Press.

Stright, A. D., & Bales, S. S. (2003). Coparenting quality: Contributions of child and parent characteristics. *Family Relations, 52*, 232–240. doi:10.1111/j.1741-3729.2003.00232.x

Stright, A. D., & Neitzel, C. (2003). Beyond parenting: Coparenting and children's classroom adjustment. *International Journal of Behavioral Development, 27*, 31–40. doi:10.1080/01650250143000580

Talbot, J. A., Baker, J. K., & McHale, J. P. (2009). Sharing the love: Prebirth adult attachment status and coparenting adjustment during early infancy. *Parenting: Science and Practice, 9*, 56–77.

Talbot, J. A., & McHale, J. P. (2004). Individual parental adjustment moderates the relationship between marital and coparenting quality. *Journal of Adult Development, 11*, 191–205. doi:10.1023/B:JADE.0000035627.26870.f8

Van Egeren, L. A. (2003). Prebirth predictors of coparenting experiences in infancy. *Infant Mental Health Journal, 24*, 278–295. doi:10.1002/imhj.10056

Van Egeren, L. A. (2004). The development of the coparenting relationship over the transition to parenthood. *Infant Mental Health Journal, 25*, 453–477. doi:10.1002/imhj.20019

Von Klitzing, K., Simoni, H., Amsler, F., & Burgin, D. (1999). The role of the father in early family interactions. *Infant Mental Health Journal, 20*, 222–237. doi:10.1002/(SICI)1097-0355(199923)20:3<222::AID-IMHJ2>3.0.CO;2-B

3

COPARENTING IN EXTENDED KINSHIP SYSTEMS: AFRICAN AMERICAN, HISPANIC, ASIAN HERITAGE, AND NATIVE AMERICAN FAMILIES

DEBORAH J. JONES AND KRISTIN M. LINDAHL

In the 2008 presidential election, Americans elected the first ethnic minority man to be the president of the United States, a man not only raised by his European American single mother and her parents but also one whose mother-in-law now assists with raising the first daughters. There is perhaps no better symbol of the diversification of the American family in 2010 than the Obama family and no better exemplar of the critical role that extended kinship systems have long played in coparenting in many ethnically diverse families. Although coparenting has received far more attention in the literature on European American families, the relevance of coparenting for ethnically and structurally diverse families, and in particular the role of extended family in coparenting, has not been overlooked (for reviews, see Jones, Zalot, Foster, Sterrett, & Chester, 2007; McHale, Khazan, et al., 2002).

Over the past 50 years, family structure in the United States has undergone considerable change. Only 67% of U.S. children are living with both their biological parents (U.S. Census Bureau, 2006). Increasingly, children are living in diverse family structures, including single-parent households with or without extended kin present, stepfamilies, and cohabitating families. Coincident with these changes in family structure has been a rise in the number of ethnic minority families in the United States. Myopically extending a two-parent conceptualization of coparenting to try to understand coparenting dynamics of African American, Latino/Hispanic, Asian, or Native American families runs the risk of neglecting the influence of the multiple caregivers formatively involved in rearing the child (Kurrien & Vo, 2004). Not only do extended kinship systems provide another layer of babysitting assistance for ethnically diverse parents, but in many cases, extended family members are also active cocaregivers (i.e., coparents) integrally involved in the daily lives of children (Kurrien & Vo, 2004).

Although minority families of various ethnicities in the United States face a similar range of challenges (e.g., poverty, segregation, discrimination), variations in cultural values, beliefs, history, and behavioral traditions are likely to differentially affect the specific child-rearing practices that families adapt to meet these challenges (Varela et al., 2004). However, a theme that cuts across studies of ethnic minority groups in the United States is that they are rooted in a culture that values collectivism, placing the needs of the group before the needs of the individual, rather than individualism (Gaines et al., 1997). Related to collectivism, *familism*—an orientation toward the well-being of one's nuclear and extended family—also is a traditional value intricately interwoven into the culture of many ethnic minority groups in the United States (Gaines et al., 1997). In turn, African, Asian, and Native American groups, as well as Latino groups, not only place a supreme value on the family but also value a definition of *family* that extends beyond the nuclear family to extended family and nonbiological relatives who, through close relationships, are symbolically included within the family structure. Oppression has likely strengthened, rather than weakened, the central role of the nuclear and extended family for ethnic minority groups in the United States (Harrison, Wilson, Pine, Chan, & Buriel, 1995; Hoppe & Heller, 1975), and it is this common value of familism that likely serves as the foundation for the contributions of extended family to child rearing in each of these groups as well (Baca Zinn, & Wells, 2000; Fuller-Thomson & Minkler, 2005; Halgunseth, 2004; Kurrien & Vo, 2004).

In this chapter, readers will find a relatively greater emphasis given to studies of mothers coparenting with extended family members. Though this emphasis reflects the state of the field (for reviews, see Murry, Bynum, Brody, Willert, & Stephens, 2001; Phares, Lopez, Fields, Kamboukos, & Duhig, 2005; Saracho & Spodek, 2008; Chapter 13, this volume), it should not be taken to indicate the unimportance or absenteeism of fathers or the relative unimportance of mothers and fathers coparenting together (Brody, Stoneman, & Flor, 1996; Chuang & Su, 2009; Cowan, Cowan, Pruett, Pruett, & Wong, 2009; Formoso, Gonzalez, Barrera, & Dumka, 2007; Li, 2009; Lindahl & Malik, 1999). Quite the contrary, as several other chapters in this volume attest, the myth of father absence—especially in families of infants and young children—has been challenged, and fresh conceptualizations are now guiding contemporary research and clinical efforts in recent work on mother–father coparenting in minority families.

COPARENTING IN AFRICAN AMERICAN FAMILIES

Consistent with collectivism and familism, the role of extended family and kin in the African American community has been extensively documented in the literature (e.g., Boyd-Franklin, 1989; Franklin, 1997). African societies define the family broadly, consisting of not only the nuclear family but also extended family members such as aunts, uncles, cousins, and grandparents (Johnson & Staples, 2005; Sudarkasa, 1997). African American families tend to also be more "fluid" than European American families, with more frequent changes in individuals residing in the household as well as a greater reliance on extended family for support (for reviews, see Greenwood et al., 1996; Jones et al., 2007).

According to data from the U.S. Census Bureau (2006), 51% of African American youth live in single mother homes (51%), compared with 23% of American youth in general. However, although *single* by a marital status definition (McLoyd, Cauce, Takeuchi, & Wilson, 2000), relatively few truly parent alone. To the contrary, 97% of adult African American single mothers identify another adult or family member (nonmarital coparents) involved in child rearing; such individuals include biological fathers, maternal grandmothers and aunts, and other relatives and friends (Jones, Shaffer, Forehand, Brody, & Armistead, 2003). African American single mothers are also more likely to reside in the home of a grandparent, aunt or uncle, sibling, or nonrelative friend than are European American single mothers or two-parent families (U.S. Census Bureau, 2006). Even when African American single mothers own or rent their own homes, they are more likely than married mothers to invite other family members, as well as nonrelative boarders, to reside with them. Although cohabitation with other adults and family members can be, at least in part, a financial decision, maternal relationships with other adults both in and outside the home serve valuable roles for children.

The role of African American extended family networks has been explicated in several qualitative studies that have used ethnographic methodologies, including immersion within communities, observation of families, and interviews with family members (Trickett & Oliveri, 1997). Such studies have revealed how extended family members in African American single-mother families contribute to child rearing both indirectly, through provision of financial assistance, and directly, through child-rearing activities. One mother in Jarrett and Burton's (1999) ethnographic study portrayed child rearing as a "joint effort" she shared with her own mother, who transported her son to school and cared for him while she was at work (p. 180). Ethnographic studies have also revealed that financial, emotional, and instrumental support to African American single mothers also comes from nonrelatives or fictive kin (Boyd-Franklin, 1989), who provide a place to stay, meals, and financial assistance when necessary (Jefferson, Jarrett, & Allen, 2001). Ethnographic research also highlights the value and roles of men who may or may not be biological relatives as coparents in African American families (Roy & Burton, 2007).

Building on qualitative work, larger scale studies have examined how the relationships that African American mothers have with other adults and family members who assist with child rearing affect maternal and youth adjustment. A primary focus in this area has been on the adjustment of teen mothers (see Chapter 5, this volume), with a few studies also examining the adjustment of the infants and young children. Nearly all of this work has examined the impact of involvement by the child's biological father and/or the child's maternal grandmother (i.e., the teenage mother's mother), despite the fact that other individuals, including paternal relatives, grandfathers, boyfriends, and friends also play child-rearing roles for children of teenage mothers (e.g., Davis, Rhodes, & Hamilton-Leaks, 1997; Gee & Rhodes, 2003). One replicated finding is that a higher degree of child-rearing support from other adults and family members is associated with better outcomes for the teen mother, particularly when the quality of the relationship between the mother and her coparent is more positive (e.g., Gordon, Chase-Lansdale, & Brooks-Gunn, 2004; Voight, Hans, & Bernstein, 1998).

In U.S. multigenerational households in which African American mothers and grandmothers coparent children (Barnett, 2008), it has taken some time to gain a firm consensus on the merits and challenges of the arrangements, especially when mothers are younger (see Chapters 5 and 13, this volume). Some studies have suggested that grandmother involvement is not associated with the adjustment of the teen mother (Davis & Rhodes, 1994), whereas others have suggested that grandmother involvement is associated with better outcomes, including greater psychosocial adjustment, educational attainment, and better parenting (e.g., Davis et al., 1997; Wakschlag, Chase-Lansdale, & Brooks-Gunn, 1996). Still other work has suggested that grandmother involvement may increase stress for teen mothers (Voight et al., 1998). Findings have sometimes also been inconsistent when the association between grandmother involvement and child outcomes has been examined (Black & Nitz, 1996; Leadbeater & Bishop, 1994). As it turns out, however, the quality of the coparenting relationship between the teen mother and her own mother must be taken into account. When a relationship is positive, grandmother involvement is perceived as helpful and associated with better outcomes for teen mothers (Gee & Rhodes, 2003). However, when relationship problems are present, grandmother involvement may be viewed as intrusive and controlling, increasing stress and, in turn, compromising the teen mother's parenting (e.g., Bogat, Caldwell, Guzman, Galasso, & Davidson, 1998; Davis, 2002; see also Chapter 5, this volume, for a more extensive discussion).

Studies of teen mothers, although helpful, may not be directly applicable to the broader range of African American women parenting as single mothers. To date, relatively little is known about effects of child-rearing assistance provided to adult African American single mothers by extended family coparents (for a review, see Jones et al., 2007). In one of the few relevant studies, Jones et al. (2003) asked 28- to 40-year-old single mothers (average age of children = 11 years) to identify who assisted them as child-rearing supports. Only 3% reported that no other adult or family member assisted with child rearing. Among the remaining mothers, most identified the child's maternal grandmother (31%) or biological father (26%) as the most salient support. Others identified a maternal aunt (11%) or one of the child's older sisters (11%), with still others identifying other relatives and nonrelatives such as friends and neighbors. As of yet, however, sample sizes of different subgroups of individuals have been too small to allow a determination of whether the degree of relationship to the mother and child (e.g., grandmother, biological father, friend) in any way moderates the impact of the cocaregiver's involvement and support.

The quality of relationships between African American single mothers and nonmarital coparents is associated with both maternal and child adjustment (Jones et al., 2003; Jones, Dorsey, et al., 2005; see Chapter 4, this volume, for a detailed discussion of coparenting in fragile families). African American single mothers who report experiencing greater conflict about child-rearing issues with nonmarital coparents have children who report greater internalizing and externalizing difficulties, compared with children of mothers who report less conflict, though this link between mother–coparent child-rearing conflict and child adjustment may be mediated by maternal depressive symptoms, as well as compromises in maternal parenting (Jones et al., 2003; Shook, Jones, Dorsey, Forehand, & Brody, 2010). That is, mothers who disagree more with coparents about child rearing report more depressive symptomatology than mothers who disagree less, which appears to in turn negatively affect child outcomes.

Does the quality of African American mothers' coparenting relationships buffer children from risk? In one relevant study, children who faced high levels of neighborhood risk (e.g., gangs, violence, drugs) but whose mothers reported higher quality relationships with nonmarital coparents evidenced fewer adjustment problems than did children who lived in similarly risky neighborhoods but whose mothers reported lower quality relationships (Forehand & Jones, 2003). The quality of the mother–coparent relationship also buffers maternal parenting behavior from neighborhood risk; African American single mothers who reside in riskier neighborhoods appropriately heighten their monitoring behavior in the context of better relationships with nonmarital coparents than in the context of poorer ones (Jones, Forehand, O'Connell, Brody, & Armistead, 2005). Similarly, recent work has suggested that African American single mothers who receive more support for child rearing from their nonmarital coparents evidence more optimal parenting behaviors (i.e., higher levels of monitoring combined with more warmth/support), which, in turn, was associated with greater child competence (Shook et al., 2010).

Given the importance of the quality of the relationships that African American single mothers have with their nonmarital or extended kinship system coparents, a needed next step is to identify factors associated with higher versus lower quality coparenting relationships when the coparenting occurs between mother and members of their extended family systems. Sterrett, Jones, Forehand, and Garai (2010) reported that among African American single mothers, coparenting with nontraditional coparents, neighborhood quality, maternal parenting style, and maternal mental health are all associated with quality of coparenting relationships.

At present, very little is known about how African American fathers negotiate child rearing with extended family members (McAdoo & McAdoo, 2002). Most studies have concerned teen fathers' child-rearing negotiations with their children's mothers and maternal grandmothers. Gavin et al. (2002) found the father's relationship with the mother to be the most robust predictor of his involvement, with relationship quality with the residential maternal grandmother also a predictor. Krishnakumar and Black (2003) found that teen mothers report better relationships with teen fathers if maternal grandmothers report a positive relationship with both parents. Without question, the importance of African American fathers' relationship with maternal grandmothers and other maternal kin is important to consider. Also of importance, however, is the support that African American fathers receive from their own extended family. This has not been a focus of much study, though Haxton and Harknett (2009) determined that compared with African American mothers, African American fathers are less likely to receive financial and housing support from grandparents and other kin as they transition to parenthood. Ultimately, interventions designed to improve coparenting relationships between higher risk African American mothers and fathers (e.g., Fagan, 2008) may be enhanced by taking into consideration the nature and quality of the coparenting relationships likely to evolve between each of the parents and members of their own extended kinship system.

COPARENTING IN HISPANIC AND LATINO FAMILIES

Hispanic Americans presently constitute the largest minority group in the United States (12% of the population; Varela et al., 2004). Certainly, there is significant diversity within the umbrella term *Hispanic/Latino*, and future research may prove it unwise to group together all families of Hispanic or Latino origin when summarizing coparenting research. To date, however, data are quite limited, and no body of work yet exists that would allow researchers to draw firm conclusions about the similarities and differences that likely exist among different Hispanic or Latino cultural groups. Therefore, in the brief review provided in this chapter, we refer to *Hispanic* and *Latino* as a whole, and generalizations to any specific group should be done cautiously.

Hispanic and Latino families are more likely to be first-generation Americans than most other ethnic groups (Goodman & Silverstein, 2006), and three generations living together is common, particularly among immigrants (Bryson & Casper, 1999). For example, among Hispanic and Latino youth, 10% have coresident grandparents, in contrast to 5% of non-Hispanic, European American children (Fields, 2003).

Latino and Hispanic grandparents traditionally have played a pivotal role in assisting not only with essential child-care duties, but also in passing on cultural traditions, values, and language (Silverstein & Chen, 1999). Latino grandparents are more likely to coparent (rather than have custodial care) than are African American grandparents (Goodman & Silverstein, 2002), and those in coparenting situations experience less emotional distress, greater life satisfaction, and fewer health problems than do those who assume custodial care (Goodman & Silverstein, 2006). One explanation for this finding is that such coparenting arrangements are consistent with a cultural ideal—that of close intergenerational relationships and reciprocal contact (Goodman & Silverstein, 2002). Latina grandmothers, because they are traditionally involved in assisting in child care (Baca Zinn & Wells, 2000), also may coparent grandchildren under more routine, less stressful circumstances than grandparents in other groups. In fact, European American grandmothers are more likely than any other group to assume caretaking of grandchildren after crisis-driven circumstances, which may account for their elevated levels of negative affect (Goodman & Silverstein, 2006). Several studies show, however, that the salubrious effects of coparenting for Latina or Hispanic grandmothers are attenuated when the relationship between the grandmother and the mother is compromised (Goodman & Silverstein, 2005; Kalil, Spencer, Spieker, & Gilchrist, 1998).

COPARENTING IN FAMILIES OF ASIAN ANCESTRY

In Asian cultures, as in African American and Hispanic and Latino cultures, there is a deep sense of family, and extended family networks as an integral part of daily life (Kurrien & Vo, 2004). Because of differences in immigration history, culture, and reasons for grandparents to take on caregiving roles, however, the nature of coparenting relationships in Asian families may be unique. The collectivist orientation and strong sense of family within many Asian societies is a distinguishing characteristic of Asian culture; social harmony, family solidarity, and respect for elders are important and organizing influences for many Asian families (McHale, Rao, & Krasnow, 2000). Relatives, especially grandparents, are often treated as surrogate parents. In a qualitative study of five Vietnamese families, Kurrien and Vo (2004) found that the parents perceive their extended family members as fulfilling roles, including teaching, nurturing, and providing discipline and moral instruction. In a study of Chinese American and Korean American grandparents in New York City, Yoon (2009) found 60% of the sample lived with one or both of their grandchildren's parents and grandchildren and 100% ($N = 101$) reported providing care during the day while the parents worked. Grandparents of Asian heritage are less likely than almost any other ethnic group to share in child-care responsibilities because of problems related to drug or alcohol abuse, teenage pregnancy, or child abuse (Yoon, 2009).

Extended family involvement is linked to child well-being in Asian families. Hackett and Hackett (1993) found that coparenting from extended family members promoted psychological well-being, whereas a lack of emotional support was associated with distress. Sonuga-Barke and Mistry (2000) argued that the direct beneficial effect of grandmother involvement on Asian children derives from direct, constructive caretaking provided by grandmothers (as opposed to an indirect effect via providing support to mothers). Related to this point, extended family coparenting in the context of three-generation homes is associated with better socioemotional outcomes for children from contemporary Indian families than for children in nuclear families, as long as the joint family relationships were cohesive (Chakrabarti, Biswas, Chattopadhyay, & Saha, 1998). This study echoes the data we reviewed on African American and Hispanic families, highlighting that it is not just family composition that matters for children's developmental outcomes but also the qualitative nature of the family relationships.

Further evidence of the beneficial effects of extended family coparenting for child functioning comes from Naug (2000), who examined coparenting in urban economically disadvantaged Indian families and found maternal perception of instrumental and emotional support from extended family members to be related to children's cognitive and social development. McHale, Rao, et al. (2000) also examined coparenting in the People's Republic of China and found maternal report of coparenting cohesion to correlate with preschoolers' academic competency and conduct.

The beneficial effects of coparenting in multigenerational living arrangements extend to grandmothers as well as grandchildren, though it is less clear to what extent the benefits extend also to parents. Sonuga-Barke and Mistry (2000), in a study of Asian heritage families living in the United Kingdom, found grandmothers in extended families to have fewer mental health problems than those in nuclear families. The opposite pattern was found for mothers, however, such that mothers from nuclear families reported less depression and anxiety than did mothers from extended families. The authors speculated that when mothers perceived themselves as burdened by being simultaneously a good mother, wife, and daughter-in-law or when they perceived grandmother support as intrusive or overbearing, they experienced detrimental effects. In support of this, Sonuga-Barke, Mistry, and Qureshi (1998) found that when conflict between mothers and grandmothers increased, so did maternal risk for depression and anxiety.

The impact of extended family coparenting on fathering has only recently been investigated in families of Asian heritage. In a study of Hindu mothers in India, Kurrien and Vo (2004) found that though mothers were the primary caretakers for all families, in joint or extended family arrangements, the child-care responsibilities were shared among a variety of females (mother, grandmother, aunt). There was significant variability in fathers' involvement, however. Fathers tended to be more involved in nuclear families, suggesting that extended kin coparenting structures might inhibit fathering for some families.

COPARENTING IN NATIVE AMERICAN FAMILIES

There are more than 550 federally recognized tribes (U.S. Department of the Interior, Bureau of Indian Affairs, 2002). Although it would be naïve to think that there is some "monolithic Native American reality" (Fuller-Thomson & Minkler, 2005), the unique historical contexts of Native American people, including forced relocation to reservations, make exploration of family functioning and coparenting for these families particularly important. To what extent coparenting arrangements vary in conjunction with cultural differences found across different tribes and tribal organizations, however, has not yet been empirically studied.

Elders in Native American families are traditionally revered, and historically grandparents have played a key socialization role in providing care for grandchildren (Fuller-Thomson & Minkler, 2005). In keeping with tradition, Native American grandparents are often quite accustomed to roles that include significant care of grandchildren, and grandparents are often viewed as transmitters of values, customs, and beliefs to their grandchildren (Mutchler, Baker, & Lee, 2007; Schweitzer, 1999). Coparenting also extends outward beyond grandparents because child rearing is perceived to involve the entire extended family, and the child is seen as being born into two relational systems—the birth family and the tribal kin network (Kopera-Frye, 2009).

In addition to cultural tradition and the high value placed on grandparent involvement in child rearing, the challenges faced by many Native American families (especially those living on reservations), including economic distress, poor health (30% do not have health insurance), and substance abuse, also have led to increased grandparent coparenting. With many reservations having unemployment rates above 50% and correspondingly high poverty levels, employment opportunities on site are often limited (Brzuzy, Stromwall, Sharp, Wilson, & Segal, 2000). The rise in women's employment outside the home, and in many cases off the reservation, has led to increased grandparent involvement (Fuller-Thomson & Minkler, 2005).

Navajos constitute 12% of the 2.5 million American Indian population and are the second largest American Indian group in the United States (Hossain & Anziano, 2008). Most Navajos live on or near a reservation, though some do live in urban areas (Hossain & Anziano, 2008). Traditional Navajo society is structured by matrilineal family groups that are organized within an extended family structure. Although all members of the family are involved in child rearing, the grandmother plays a particularly important role in the Navajo culture (Hossain & Anziano, 2008). This coparenting arrangement, however, does not appear to affect paternal involvement as much as it might in other cultural groups (e.g., Hossain, 2001; Hossain & Anziano, 2008).

CONCLUSIONS REGARDING COPARENTING IN EXTENDED FAMILY SYSTEMS

Perhaps most notable when comparing studies of coparenting in intact and divorced European American families with the growing number of studies on coparenting in extended family systems in ethnically diverse families is the difference in the quality and standards of the research methods (see

Murry et al., 2001). First, research on the role of extended family coparents has focused largely on the quality of the mother's relationship with her nonmarital coparent (e.g., Forehand & Jones, 2003; Jones, Dorsey, et al., 2005; Jones, Forehand, et al., 2005), with relatively less attention given to the mental health and well-being of the coparents. The relationship of the children to the nonmarital coparents and the impact of this relationship on youth adjustment has also been the focus of relatively little research attention (for a notable exception, see Sterrett, Jones, & Kincaid, 2009). Accordingly, more work on extended family coparents, as well as their relationships with youth, is necessary to fully understand the role of coparenting in ethnic minority families.

As McHale outlines in Chapter 7 of this volume, studies of coparenting in nuclear families have involved self-reports, interviews, and observation and coding of interactions between parents and children. As McLoyd et al. (2000) noted, this level of methodological rigor is largely missing from most research on ethnically diverse samples, and research specifically on coparenting in extended family systems is no exception. More intensive studies of coparenting in extended family systems using multimethod approaches will increase our confidence in findings and contribute to a richer conceptualization of coparenting in ethnically diverse families.

The research on coparenting in extended family systems has also typically focused on two broad domains of the coparenting relationship: support and conflict regarding child-rearing activities. State-of-the-field coparenting measures, however, include much richer assessments of the coparenting relationship, including division of child-rearing labor and nuanced aspects of the coparent alliance (e.g., Belsky & Hsieh, 1998). For example, coparent communication with and about children is a multidimensional construct, including both overt and covert processes (e.g., McHale, 1997; McHale, Kuersten-Hogan, Lauretti, & Rasmussen, 2000). Future research should attempt to establish the relevance of current coparenting conceptualizations and coding systems for the study of extended family systems so that a richer understanding of how extended family members collectively and successfully coordinate child rearing can be established.

The research on coparenting in extended families has also focused to a large extent on teen and single mothers, particularly in African American families. Less attention, however, has been directed to those arrangements in which extended family members are coparenting with married parents. McHale, Lauretti, Talbot, and Pouquette (2002), drawing on the conceptual work of Sudarkasa (1997), noted that mother–father–grandmother coparenting dynamics in African American families may differ as a function of the family's socioeconomic status. In African American families with the economic means to raise their children in conjugally focused and centered family groups, resident grandmothers may play more of a subsidiary role than they do in low-income families (McHale, Lauretti, et al., 2002). A proper and nuanced understanding of multi-individual coparenting among African, Asian, Native American, and Latino families is hence going to demand careful attention to within-group as well as between-group diversity.

Another topic in need of careful attention is the reasons why coparents get involved in actively rearing children who are not their own (see Chapter 13). Although many extended family members coparent because they are guided to do so by a prevailing cultural ethic, others step into an active coparenting role out of a feeling of obligation (e.g., to compensate for father absence) or in a time of crisis (e.g., because of maternal illness). Sterrett et al. (2010) found that the quality of African American single mothers' relationships with nonmarital coparents was more compromised in families in which mothers engaged in lax parenting. It is hence plausible that when extended family members step into the role of coparents out of necessity, there is a greater likelihood of conflict coming to characterize the coparenting relationship.

Finally, much of the work on coparenting in the extended family systems of diverse families has been cross-sectional or short-term longitudinal in nature. Therefore, we know relatively little about the stability of the extended family coparents who participate in child rearing for ethnically diverse children through time or the ultimate impact of their involvement on children's psychosocial functioning. Perhaps more to the point, a more thorough conceptualization of extended family members' involvement in children's lives requires culturally informed and sensitive means of capturing both the stability and the fluidity of the involvement of extended family coparents over time (Roy & Burton, 2007). The role of these individuals and their opportunity to influence children may change as the children age, and more sophisticated methods will be needed to capture the evolution of extended family coparenting over time.

DIRECTIONS FOR FUTURE RESEARCH

Theoretically driven studies that incorporate richer assessment (i.e., observational methods), include all coparents, and follow the family over time are very much needed. Such studies will contribute greatly to our understanding of the processes by which ethnic minority families successfully negotiate child rearing with their extended family members and the impact such processes have on youth adjustment. Given the well-documented difficulties researchers have had successfully recruiting and retaining fathers in studies of intact families (Phares, 1995), there will unquestionably be logistical barriers to including extended family coparents in future research. This will be especially so if the extended family members participating in coparenting do not live with the family, are at major odds with one or both of the child's biological parents, and/or are involved in caring for multiple children. However, overcoming such barriers is absolutely critical if we are to fully understand the range of potential extrafamilial coparenting influences on youth being raised in ethnically diverse families. In turn, the information garnered from this work will be critical to the development, enhancement, and implementation of family-based prevention and intervention efforts aimed at promoting health and well-being among the growing number of ethnic minority families in the United States.

REFERENCES

Baca Zinn, M., & Wells, B. (2000). Diversity within Latino families: New lessons for family social science. In D. H. Demo, K. R. Allen, & M. A. Fine (Eds.), *Handbook of family diversity* (pp. 252–273). New York, NY: Oxford University Press.

Barnett, M. A. (2008). Mother and grandmother parenting in low-income three-generation rural households. *Journal of Marriage and the Family, 70,* 1241–1257. doi:10.1111/j.1741-3737.2008.00563.x

Belsky, J., & Hsieh, K. H. (1998). Patterns of marital change during the early childhood years: Parent personality, coparenting, and division-of-labor correlates. *Journal of Family Psychology, 12,* 511–528. doi:10.1037/0893-3200.12.4.511

Black, M. M., & Nitz, K. (1996). Grandmother co-residence, parenting, and child development among low income, urban teen mothers. *The Journal of Adolescent Health, 18,* 218–226. doi:10.1016/1054-139X(95)00168-R

Bogat, G., Caldwell, R., Guzman, B., Galasso, L., & Davidson, W. (1998). Structure and stability of maternal support among pregnant and parenting adolescents. *Journal of Community Psychology, 26,* 549–568. doi:10.1002/(SICI)1520-6629 (199811)26:6<549::AID-JCOP3>3.0.CO;2-7

Boyd-Franklin, N. (1989). *Black families in therapy: A multisystems approach.* New York, NY: Guilford Press.

Brody, G., Stoneman, Z., & Flor, D. (1996). Parental religiosity, family processes, and youth competence in rural, two-parent African American families. *Developmental Psychology, 32,* 696–706. doi:10.1037/0012-1649.32.4.696

Bryson, K., & Casper, L. (1999). *Co-resident grandparents and grandchildren* (Current Population Reports, Special Studies, Publication No. P23-198). Washington, DC: U.S. Bureau of the Census.

Brzuzy, S., Stromwall, L., Sharp, P., Wilson, R., & Segal, E. (2000). The vulnerability of American Indian women in the new welfare state. *Affilia: Journal of Women and Social Work, 15,* 193–203.

Chakrabarti, S., Biswas, D., Chattopadhyay, P. K., & Saha, S. (1998). Family size and emotional adjustment in children. *Social Science International, 14,* 11–18.

Chuang, S. S., & Su, Y. (2009). Says who?: Decision making and conflicts among Chinese-Canadian and Mainland Chinese parents of young children. *Sex Roles, 60,* 527–536. doi:10.1007/s11199-008-9537-9

Cowan, P. A., Cowan, C. P., Pruett, M. K., Pruett, K., & Wong, J. J. (2009). Promoting fathers' engagement with children: Preventive interventions for low-income families. *Journal of Marriage and the Family, 71,* 663–679. doi:10.1111/j.1741-3737.2009.00625.x

Davis, A. (2002). Younger and older African American adolescent mothers' relationships with their mothers and female peers. *Journal of Adolescent Research, 17,* 491–508. doi:10.1177/0743558402175004

Davis, A., & Rhodes, J. (1994). African-American mothers and their mothers: An analysis of supportive and problematic interactions. *Journal of Community Psychology, 22,* 12–20. doi:10.1002/1520-6629(199401)22:1<12::AID-JCOP2290220103>3.0.CO;2-7

Davis, A. A., Rhodes, J. E., & Hamilton-Leaks, J. (1997). When both parents may be a source of support and problems: An analysis of pregnant and parenting female African American adolescents' relationships with their mothers and fathers. *Journal of Research on Adolescence, 7,* 331–348. doi:10.1207/s15327795jra0703_5

Fagan, J. (2008). Randomized study of prebirth coparenting intervention with adolescent and young fathers. *Family Relations, 57,* 309–323. doi:10.1111/j.1741-3729.2008.00502.x

Fields, J. (2003). *Children's living arrangements and characteristics: March 2002* (Current Population Reports, Report No. P20-547). Washington, DC: U.S. Census Bureau.

Forehand, R., & Jones, D. J. (2003). Neighborhood violence and coparent conflict: Interactive influence on child psychosocial adjustment. *Journal of Abnormal Child Psychology, 31,* 591–604. doi:10.1023/A:1026206122470

Formoso, D., Gonzalez, N. A., Barrera, M., & Dumka, L. E. (2007). Interparental relations, maternal employment, and fathering in Mexican American families. *Journal of Marriage and the Family, 69,* 26–39. doi:10.1111/j.1741-3737.2006.00341.x

Franklin, J. (1997). African American families: A historical note. In H. P. McAdoo (Ed.), *Black families* (3rd ed., pp. 5–8). Thousand Oaks, CA: Sage.

Fuller-Thomson, E., & Minkler, M. (2005). American Indian/Alaskan Native grandparents raising grandchildren: Findings from the Census 2000 supplementary survey. *Social Work, 50,* 131–139.

Gaines, S. O., Marelich, W. D., Bledsoe, K. L., Steers, W. N., Henderson, M. C., Granrose, C. S., . . . Page, M. S. (1997). Links between race/ethnicity and cultural values as mediated by racial/ethnic identity and moderated by gender. *Journal of Personality and Social Psychology, 72,* 1460–1476. doi:10.1037/0022-3514.72.6.1460

Gavin, L. E., Black, M., Minor, S., Abel, Y., Papas, M., & Bentley, M. (2002). Young, disadvantaged fathers' involvement with their infants: An ecological perspective. *The Journal of Adolescent Health, 31,* 266–276. doi:10.1016/S1054-139X(02)00366-X

Gee, C., & Rhodes, J. (2003). Adolescent mothers' relationship with their biological fathers: Social support, social strain, and relationship continuity. *Journal of Family Psychology, 17,* 370–383. doi:10.1037/0893-3200.17.3.370

Goodman, C. C., & Silverstein, M. (2002). Grandmothers raising grandchildren: Family structure and well-being in culturally diverse families. *The Gerontologist, 42,* 676–689.

Goodman, C., & Silverstein, M. (2005). Latina grandmothers raising grandchildren: Acculturation and psychological well-being. *International Journal of Aging & Human Development, 60,* 305–316. doi:10.2190/NQ2P-4ABR-3U1F-W6G0

Goodman, C., & Silverstein, M. (2006). Grandmothers raising grandchildren: Ethnic and racial differences in well-being among custodial and coparenting families. *Journal of Family Issues, 27,* 1605–1626. doi:10.1177/0192513X06291435

Gordon, R. A., Chase-Lansdale, P., & Brooks-Gunn, J. (2004). Extended households and the life course of young mothers: Understanding the associations using a sample of mothers with premature, low birth weight babies. *Child Development, 75,* 1013–1038. doi:10.1111/j.1467-8624.2004.00723.x

Greenwood, D., Szapocznik, J., McIntosh, S., Antoni, M., Ironson, G., Tejeda, M., . . . Sorhando, L. (1996). African American women, their families, and HIV/AIDS. In R. Resnick & R. Rozensky (Eds.), *Health psychology through the life span: Practice and research opportunities* (pp. 349–359). Washington, DC: American Psychological Association.

Hackett, L., & Hackett, R. (1993). Parental ideas of normal and deviant child behavior: A comparison of two ethnic groups. *The British Journal of Psychiatry, 162,* 353–357. doi:10.1192/bjp.162.3.353

Halgunseth, L. C. (2004). Continuing research on Latino families: El pasado y el future. In M. Coleman & L. H. Ganong (Eds.), *Handbook of contemporary families: Considering the past, contemplating the future* (pp. 333–351). Thousand Oaks, CA: Sage.

Harrison, A. O., Wilson, M. N., Pine, C. J., Chan, S. Q., & Buriel, R. (1995). Family ecologies of ethnic minority children. In P. N. R. Goldberger & J. B. Veroff (Eds.), *The culture and psychology reader* (pp. 292–320). New York, NY: New York University Press.

Haxton, C. L., & Harknett, K. (2009). Racial and gender differences in kin support: A mixed-methods study of African American and Hispanic couples. *Journal of Family Issues, 30,* 1019–1040. doi:10.1177/0192513X09333946

Hoppe, S., & Heller, P. (1975). Alienation, familism, and the utilization of health services by Mexican Americans. *Journal of Health and Social Behavior, 16,* 304–314. doi:10.2307/2136879

Hossain, Z. (2001). Division of household labor and family functioning in off-reservation Navajo Indian families. *Family Relations, 50,* 255–261. doi:10.1111/j.1741-3729.2001.00255.x

Hossain, Z., & Anziano, M. C. (2008). Mothers' and fathers' involvement with school-age children's care and academic activities in Navajo Indian families.

Cultural Diversity & Ethnic Minority Psychology, 14, 109–117. doi:10.1037/1099-9809.14.2.109

Jarrett, R. L., & Burton, L. M. (1999). Dynamic dimensions of family structure in low-income African American families: Emergent themes in qualitative research. *Journal of Comparative Family Studies, 30,* 177–187.

Jefferson, S., Jarrett, R. L., & Allen, T. (2001, November). *If you don't have family, you don't have nobody: The support networks of low-income, African American women.* Poster session presented at the annual meeting of the National Council on Family Relations, Rochester, NY.

Johnson, L., & Staples, R. (2005). *Black families at the crossroads.* San Francisco, CA: Jossey-Bass.

Jones, D., Dorsey, S., Forehand, R., Foster, S., Armistead, L., & Brody, G. (2005). Co-parent support and conflict in African American single mother-headed families: Associations with mother and child adjustment. *Journal of Family Violence, 20,* 141–150. doi:10.1007/s10896-005-3650-0

Jones, D., Forehand, R., O'Connell, C., Brody, G., & Armistead, L. (2005). Neighborhood violence and maternal monitoring in African American single mother-headed families: An examination of the moderating role of social support. *Behavior Therapy, 36,* 25–34. doi:10.1016/S0005-7894(05)80051-6

Jones, D. J., Shaffer, A., Forehand, R., Brody, G., & Armistead, L. P. (2003). Coparent conflict in single mother-headed African-American families: Do parenting skills serve as a mediator or moderator of child psychosocial adjustment. *Behavior Therapy, 34,* 259–272. doi:10.1016/S0005-7894(03)80016-3

Jones, D., Zalot, A., Foster, S., Sterrett, E., & Chester, C. (2007). A review of child-rearing in African American single mother families: The relevance of a coparenting framework. *Journal of Child and Family Studies, 16,* 671–683. doi:10.1007/s10826-006-9115-0

Kalil, A., Spencer, M. S., Spieker, S. J., & Gilchrist, L. D. (1998). Effects of grandmother coresidence and quality of family relationships on depressive symptoms in adolescent mothers. *Family Relations, 47,* 433–441. doi:10.2307/585274

Kopera-Frye, K. (2009). Needs and issues of Latino and Native American nonparental relative caregivers: Strengths and challenges within a cultural context. *Family and Consumer Sciences Research Journal, 37,* 394–410. doi:10.1177/1077727X08329563

Krishnakumar, A., & Black, M. (2003). Family processes within three-generation households and adolescent mothers satisfaction with father involvement. *Journal of Family Psychology, 17,* 488–498. doi:10.1037/0893-3200.17.4.488

Kurrien, R., & Vo, E. D. (2004). Who's in charge? Coparenting in South and Southeastern Asian families. *Journal of Adult Development, 11,* 207–219. doi:10.1023/B:JADE.0000035628.42529.e5

Leadbeater, B. J., & Bishop, S. J. (1994). Predictors of behavior problems in preschool children of inner-city Afro-American and Puerto Rican adolescent mothers. *Child Development, 65,* 638–648. doi:10.2307/1131406

Li, M. (2009). A model parent group for enhancing aggressive children's social competence in Taiwan. *International Journal of Group Psychotherapy, 59*, 407–419. doi:10.1521/ijgp.2009.59.3.407

Lindahl, K. M., & Malik, N. M. (1999). Marital conflict, family processes, and boys' externalizing behavior in Hispanic American and European American families. *Journal of Clinical Child Psychology, 28*, 12–24. doi:10.1207/s15374424jccp2801_2

McAdoo, H. P., & McAdoo, J. L. (2002). The dynamics of African American fathers' family roles. In H. P. McAdoo (Ed.), *Black children: Social, educational, and parental environments* (2nd ed., pp. 3–11). Thousand Oaks, CA: Sage.

McHale, J. (1997). Overt and covert coparenting processes in the family. *Family Process, 36*, 183–210.

McHale, J., Khazan, I., Erera, P., Rotman, T., DeCourcey, W., & McConnell, M. (2002). Coparenting in diverse family systems. In M. H. Bornstein (Ed.), *Handbook of parenting: Vol. 3. Being and becoming a parent* (2nd ed., pp. 75–107). Mahwah, NJ: Erlbaum.

McHale, J. P., Kuersten-Hogan, R., Lauretti, A., & Rasmussen, J. (2000). Parental reports of coparenting and observed coparenting behavior during the toddler period. *Journal of Family Psychology, 14*, 220–236. doi:10.1037/0893-3200.14.2.220

McHale, J., Lauretti, A., Talbot, J., & Pouquette, C. (2002). Retrospect and prospect in the psychological study of coparenting and family group process. In J. McHale & W. Grolnick (Eds.), *Retrospect and prospect in the psychological study of families* (pp. 127–165). Hillside, NJ: Erlbaum.

McHale, J. P., Rao, N., & Krasnow, A. D. (2000). Constructing family climates: Chinese mothers' reports of their co-parenting behavior and preschoolers' adaptation. *International Journal of Behavioral Development, 24*, 111–118. doi:10.1080/016502500383548

McLoyd, V. C., Cauce, A. M., Takeuchi, D., & Wilson, L. (2000). Marital processes and parental socialization in families of color: A decade review of research. *Journal of Marriage and the Family, 62*, 1070–1093. doi:10.1111/j.1741-3737.2000.01070.x

Murry, V. M., Bynum, M., Brody, G., Willert, A., & Stephens, D. (2001). African American single mothers and children in context: A review of studies on risk and resilience. *Clinical Child and Family Psychology Review, 4*, 133–155. doi:10.1023/A:1011381114782

Mutchler, J. E., Baker, L. A., & Lee, S. (2007). Grandparents responsible for grandchildren in Native-American families. *Social Science Quarterly, 88*, 990–1009. doi:10.1111/j.1540-6237.2007.00514.x

Naug, K. (2000). Maternal social networks in an urban slum and its impact on cognitive and social development in children. *Journal of Personality and Clinical Studies, 16*, 53–62.

Phares, V. (1995). Fathers' and mothers' participation in research. *Adolescence, 30*, 593–602.

Phares, V., Lopez, E., Fields, S., Kamboukos, D., & Duhig, A. (2005). Are fathers involved in pediatric psychology research and treatment? *Journal of Pediatric Psychology, 30,* 631–643. doi:10.1093/jpepsy/jsi050

Roy, K., & Burton, L. (2007). Mothering through recruitment: Kinscription of non-residential fathers and father figures in low-income families. *Family Relations, 56,* 24–39. doi:10.1111/j.1741-3729.2007.00437.x

Saracho, O. N., & Spodek, B. (2008). Fathers: The invisible parents. *Early Child Development and Care, 178,* 821–836. doi:10.1080/03004430802352244

Schweitzer, M. M. (1999). *American Indian grandmothers: Traditions and transitions.* Albuquerque: University of New Mexico Press.

Shook, S., Jones, D. J., Dorsey, S., Forehand, R., & Brody, G. (2010). Mother-coparent relationship quality among African American single mother families: The relative roles of conflict and support in youth adjustment. *Journal of Family Psychology, 24,* 243–251.

Silverstein, M., & Chen, X. (1999). The impact of acculturation in Mexican American families on the quality of adult grandchild-grandparent relationships. *Journal of Marriage and the Family, 61,* 188–198. doi:10.2307/353893

Sonuga-Barke, E. J., & Mistry, M. (2000). The effect of extended family living on the mental health of three generations within two Asian communities. *The British Journal of Clinical Psychology, 39,* 129–141. doi:10.1348/014466500163167

Sonuga-Barke, E. J., Mistry, M., & Qureshi, S. (1998). The mental health of Muslim mothers in extended families: The impact of intergenerational disagreement on anxiety and depression. *The British Journal of Clinical Psychology, 37,* 399–408.

Sterrett, E., Jones, D. J., Forehand, R., & Garai, E. (2010). Predictors of coparenting relationship quality in African American single mother families: An ecological model. *The Journal of Black Psychology, 36,* 277–302. doi:10.1177/0095798409353754

Sterrett, E., Jones, D. J., & Kincaid, C. (2009). Psychosocial adjustment of low-income African American youth from single mother homes: The role of youth-coparent relationship quality. *Journal of Clinical Child and Adolescent Psychology, 38,* 427–438.

Sudarkasa, N. (1997). African American families and family values. In H. P. McAdoo (Ed.), *Black families* (3rd ed., pp. 9–40). Thousand Oaks, CA: Sage.

Trickett, E., & Oliveri, M. (1997). Ethnography and sociocultural processes: Introductory comments. *Ethos, 25,* 146–151. doi:10.1525/eth.1997.25.2.146

U.S. Census Bureau. (2006). *Families and living arrangements, 2006* (Current Population Survey Report). Retrieved from http://www.census.gov/newsroom/releases/archives/families_households/cb07-46.html

U.S. Department of the Interior, Bureau of Indian Affairs. (2002). Indian entities recognized and eligible to receive services from the U.S. Bureau of Indian Affairs. *Federal Register, 67,* 46327–46333.

Varela, R. E., Vernberg, E. M., Sanchez-Sosa, J. J., Riveros, A., Mitchell, M., & Mashunkashey, J. (2004). Parenting style of Mexican, Mexican American, and

Caucasian non-Hispanic families: Social context and cultural influences. *Journal of Family Psychology, 18,* 651–657. doi:10.1037/0893-3200.18.4.651

Voight, J., Hans, S., & Bernstein, V. (1998). Support networks of adolescent mothers: Effects on parenting experience and behavior. *Infant Mental Health Journal, 17,* 58–73.

Wakschlag, L., Chase-Lansdale, P., & Brooks-Gunn, J. (1996). Not just "ghosts in the nursery": Contemporaneous intergenerational relationships and parenting in young African-American families. *Child Development, 67,* 2131–2147.

Yoon, S. M. (2009). The characteristics and needs of Asian-American grandparent caregivers: A study of Chinese-American and Korean-American grandparents in New York City. *Journal of Gerontological Social Work, 44,* 75–94. doi:10.1300/J083v44n03_06

4

COPARENTING IN FRAGILE FAMILIES: UNDERSTANDING HOW PARENTS WORK TOGETHER AFTER A NONMARITAL BIRTH

MARCIA J. CARLSON AND ROBIN S. HÖGNÄS

Nonmarital childbearing has increased dramatically in the United States since the early 1960s, rising from 6% of all births in 1960 to 41% in 2008 (Hamilton, Martin, & Ventura, 2010). Whereas similar trends have occurred in many developed nations, the United States stands out in the extent to which such births are associated with socioeconomic disadvantage and relationship instability. This has given rise to a new term, *fragile families*, which we define as unmarried couples who have a child together. The increase in fragile families reflects changes not only in the initial context of births but also in the fundamental nature and patterns of child rearing.

Although much of the recent literature on coparenting has focused on married, coresident parents with children, most unmarried couples will break up within only a few years of a new child's birth (McLanahan, 2009). Therefore, for many unmarried parents, coparenting will occur across households and may be more similar to coparenting among divorced parents than among married parents. However, given the disadvantaged characteristics of unmarried parents, coparenting in this context may be even more complicated than it is after a legal divorce.

In this chapter, we provide an overview of coparenting in fragile families, focusing particularly on what has been learned from the Fragile Families and

Child Wellbeing Study. We begin by identifying key theoretical perspectives related to coparenting generally. Then, we briefly describe the typical characteristics of unmarried parents with children and the nature of their couple relationships over time. Next, we summarize contributions to the coparenting literature from more recent studies focused on unmarried parents (or similar populations), and we present some new data about coparenting among fragile families. Finally, we conclude by suggesting key areas for future research and noting implications for public policy.

THEORETICAL PERSPECTIVES AND PRIOR
EMPIRICAL RESEARCH

As this volume underscores, family systems theory stresses the importance and dynamic nature of various family relationships (mother–father, parent–child, and sibling–sibling) that affect each other and influence individual outcomes (Bronfenbrenner, 1986; P. Minuchin, 1988). Among these dyadic relationships, an important family-level (or triadic) relationship is the one between adults raising a child together (S. Minuchin, 1974). This coparenting relationship is defined as the extent to which parents can effectively work together in rearing their common child and has been identified as a unique construct distinct from both couple relationship quality and parenting behavior (Hayden et al., 1998; McHale, 1995; McHale, Kuersten-Hogan, Lauretti, & Rasmussen, 2000). Coparenting is also differentiated from *parallel parenting*, in which each parent maintains a relationship with their child separate and distinct from that of the other parent (Furstenberg, 1988; Furstenberg & Cherlin, 1991). For parents living together, coparenting strengthens and reinforces the dyadic relationship each parent has with their child. For parents living apart—which is the case for the majority of unmarried parents only a few years after a focal child's birth—coparenting may represent the primary (or only) regular interaction they have with each other as they endeavor to coordinate their parental investments across households (Margolin, Gordis, & John, 2001). Indeed, cooperative parenting may be of greater import when families do not share the unifying context of household residence (Maccoby, Depner, & Mnookin, 1990).

As detailed elsewhere in this volume, an initial focus of coparenting research was on parental relationships following divorce (Ahrons, 1981; Wallerstein & Kelly, 1980); studies indicated benefits to children of cooperative postdivorce coparental relationships and adverse effects of conflicted ones (Maccoby & Mnookin, 1992). Emery, Laumann-Billings, Waldron, Sbarra, and Dillon (2001) determined that mediation, rather than litigation, promoted long-term coparenting by divorced parents, suggesting that attainment of positive coparenting and continued involvement of noncustodial fathers may depend on what happens in the early stages of divorce (Ahrons & Miller, 1993). Positive coparental interactions among divorced parents, though the exception and not the rule, then increase both the father's role in child-rearing decisions and the responsiveness of his fathering (Furstenberg & Nord, 1985; Sobolewski & King, 2005). On the other hand, once coparental relationships become tense, parents may avoid contact with one another in order to minimize conflict (Seltzer, McLanahan, & Hanson, 1998).

More recent research has focused on coparenting among coresident (mostly married) families and how it relates to couples' relationship quality, parenting behavior, and child well-being. This growing literature, published mostly within psychology, is based primarily on small, nonrepresentative samples. Even so, findings underscore the distinct nature of coparenting—vis-à-vis both couple relationship quality and parenting (Hayden et al., 1998)—and suggest that among coresident households, coparenting is linked to both marital behavior and child well-being (for a review, see Chapter 2, this volume); indeed, several studies have indicated that coparenting may mediate between the former and the latter (e.g., Katz & Low, 2004; Margolin, Gordis, & John, 2001). Parents' adjustment is an antecedent to positive coparenting, and cooperative coparenting in two-parent families is linked to more responsive parenting of infant and school-age children by both mothers and fathers, and to better child adjustment (see Chapter 2).

UNMARRIED PARENTS' CHARACTERISTICS AND COUPLE RELATIONSHIPS

Though research on coparenting in married and divorced families may be relevant to unmarried parents in the circumstances of coresiding versus living apart, respectively, unmarried couples are a very different demographic group from couples who are or were legally married and as a whole are much less well understood. This is changing, thanks to the Fragile Families and Child Well-being Study, a birth-cohort study of nearly 5,000 children born in 20 large U.S. cities at the end of the 20th century (see Reichman, Teitler, Garfinkel, & McLanahan, 2001). The study includes an oversample of nonmarital births along with a comparison group of marital births. The mothers, fathers, and children were followed over 5 years after the birth (a 9-year follow-up is nearly complete as of this writing), and the data (when weighted) are representative of births to parents in cities with populations of 200,000 or more in the late 1990s. Detailed descriptions of the Fragile Families respondents appear in other publications (e.g., Carlson & McLanahan, 2010; McLanahan, in press; McLanahan et al., 2003), and so here we briefly summarize the relevant data.

Unmarried parents differ from married (and divorced) parents in ways that have important implications for their long-term economic well-being, their family stability, and—our focus here—their ability to work together as effective coparents. Existing data have indicated that most unmarried parents are in their 20s (with one quarter under age 20 and 16% in their 30s); most have a high school degree or less and are African American or Hispanic. Many parents have children by more than one partner (so-called *multipartnered fertility* or MPF), and a high fraction of fathers have some history of incarceration. This description suggests that limited resources and high complexity in family relationships and parental roles may challenge unmarried parents' ability to coparent cooperatively.

One of the most important findings to emerge from the Fragile Families study is the close connection between unmarried fathers and mothers at the time of their child's birth (McLanahan, 2004); more than four fifths of couples are in romantic relationships at the birth. About half of couples are living together, and a majority of both parents hold positive views of the benefits of marriage and believe their chances of marrying the other parent are "pretty good" or "almost certain." Although women are slightly more distrusting of men than men are of women, the quality of most couple relationships is high, and physical violence is relatively rare. However, longitudinal data reveal that these unmarried relationships are highly unstable and will likely dissolve within only a few years. Not surprisingly, as shown in Table 4.1, couples with greater relational attachment at birth are much more likely to still be together 5 years later; we show married couples at birth for comparison purposes. Of couples cohabiting at birth, 56% remained together 5 years later (28% married, 28% still cohabiting), compared with 77% of couples married at birth who remained married. Of couples in "visiting" relationships (romantically involved but living apart) when the baby was born, 7% got married, 14% were cohabiting, and 6% were still in a visiting relationship at 5 years. Among couples reporting no romantic relationship at birth (either friends or no relationship at all), only a small minority later married or cohabited; fully 90% of such couples were not romantically involved at 5 years. Parents who started off as friends were more likely to be friends at 5 years than those who started off with no relationship, suggesting that a friendly relationship at the outset may contribute to parents being able to work together in rearing their common child later (see Fagan & Palkovitz, 2007). That said, because couples who are friends early on may differ in important (and unobserved) ways from other couples, it is not clear whether being friends contributes in a causal way to later positive coparenting.

With respect to factors that encourage union stability and marriage, research has been consistent with theories about economic incentives to

TABLE 4.1
Relationship Stability, Birth to 5 Years (%)

| Time of birth | 5 years after birth of child (% of row total) | | | | | | |
	Married	Cohabiting	Visiting	Friends	No relationship	n	Total
Married	77	0	0	0	22	1,012	100%
Unmarried	17	19	3	20	42	3,120	100%
Cohabiting	28	28	2	14	29	1,487	100%
Visiting	7	14	6	27	46	1,093	100%
Friends	3	5	1	34	56	254	100%
No relationship	4	6	0	10	81	286	100%
No. of cases (n)	1,292	592	78	760	1,410	4,132	

Note. Figures are weighted by national sampling weights; numbers of cases are unweighted. Relationship status was reported by mothers. Cohabitation at 5 years was defined as living together all or most of the time or some of the time; cohabitation at the time of birth was reported as yes/no.

marry (Becker, 1991; Ellwood & Jencks, 2004) in substantiating that men's earnings, wages, and employment are important for marriage after a nonmarital birth (Gibson-Davis, 2009; Harknett, 2008; Harknett & McLanahan, 2004). Evidence regarding women's economic resources is less clear, though education appears to be the key socioeconomic factor for women that increases the likelihood of marriage (Carlson, McLanahan, & England, 2004; Harknett, 2008). Social psychological theories also describe how culture—defined as widely shared beliefs and practices—affects decisions and behavior surrounding family formation (Axinn & Thornton, 2000; Clarkberg, Stolzenberg, & Waite, 1995; Nock, 1995). Positive attitudes toward and expectations about marriage and religiosity encourage stability (Carlson, McLanahan, & England, 2004; Waller & McLanahan, 2005; Wilcox & Wolfinger, 2007); gender distrust, sexual jealousy (especially by women toward men), and MPF are key deterrents to marriage (Carlson et al., 2004; Edin & Kefalas, 2005; Hill, 2007; Monte, 2007). Finally, married partners' perceptions of the emotional quality of their relationship affects whether they stay together or break up (Cowan, Cowan, Schulz, & Heming, 1994; Gottman, 1994; Karney & Bradbury, 1995), a linkage demonstrated among fragile families as well (Carlson et al., 2004).

There is a growing qualitative literature examining perceived barriers to marriage, which has identified both financial and relationship "prerequisites"; these include having sufficient resources to establish an independent household and afford a wedding celebration and having a relationship free of problems related to substance use, physical violence, or the father's criminal background (Cherlin, 2004; Edin & Kefalas, 2005; Gibson-Davis, Edin, & McLanahan, 2005). In addition to discouraging union formation/stability after a nonmarital birth, these latter factors likely also interfere with parents' ability to work together in rearing their common child, whether or not they remain romantically involved.

COPARENTING AMONG FRAGILE FAMILIES:
WHAT DO WE KNOW FROM RECENT RESEARCH?

A nascent literature has begun to explore the nature, processes, and consequences of coparenting among unmarried parents with children or in related populations. Although there is much to be learned, these new studies have shed some light on the levels and antecedents of coparenting, the link between coparenting and father involvement, and the potential of policy intervention to strengthen coparenting. We summarize key findings in each of these areas in this section.

Levels of Coparenting

Given the relationship instability of unmarried parents, coparenting occurs less frequently in coresidential units than across households. In the Fragile Families study, positive coparenting was assessed at each wave with six items about whether the other parent (a) acts like the father or mother the respondent wants for her or his child, (b) can be trusted to take good care of the child, (c) respects the schedules and rules the respondent makes for the child, (d) supports the respondent in the way he or she wants to raise the child—and whether the respondent (e) can talk with the other parent about problems that come up with the child, and (f) can count on the other parent for help when the respondent needs someone to look after the child.[1] Response choices are *rarely true* (1), *sometimes true* (2), and *always true* (3).[2] The six questions were asked of mothers only if fathers had seen the child since the previous survey. This positive coparenting construct reflects perceptions of how well the parents work together in rearing their common child (i.e., the triadic interaction), as distinguished from the parent–child relationship or the mother–father relationship.

For parents living apart, Carlson, McLanahan, and Brooks-Gunn (2008) found that the average level of coparenting reported by unmarried mothers about nonresident fathers across the six items was moderate (2.3 on the 1-to-3 scale) at Year 1, with only a slight decline to 2.1 at Years 3 and 5. Thus, a typical mother describing how she and the focal father worked together to rear their common child portrayed positive aspects of coparenting as, on average, *sometimes true*. Using data reported by nonresident fathers in the Fragile Families study about coparenting, Bronte-Tinkew and Horowitz (2010) reached a more optimistic conclusion. Aggregating scores from only three of the six items, they found that fathers' reports of positive coparenting averaged 7.5 on a 0-to-9 scale (corresponding to 2.5 on the 3-point scale). The higher scores may be because unmarried (especially nonresident) fathers interviewed in the Fragile Families study (75% at baseline and 85% at least once from birth to Year 5) were more connected to mothers and more involved with their children than fathers not interviewed. Taken together, these data suggest that positive coparenting among unmarried parents who live apart but stay connected remains moderate to high over the first 5 years after a nonmarital birth.

---

[1]These questions were developed by Julien Teitler, Columbia University, for the Fragile Families study.
[2]In the 3- and 5-year surveys, an additional choice of *never* was given; we combine the small number of responses in this category with *rarely true* to yield a consistent 3-point scale across all years.

Antecedents of Coparenting

What enhances (or deters) coparenting in unmarried families? Studies of resident (especially married) fathers portray men's roles as both partner and parent as a "package deal" (Furstenberg & Cherlin, 1991; Schoppe-Sullivan, Brown, Cannon, Mangelsdorf, & Sokolowski, 2008; Townsend, 2002). Although this may be less true for unmarried parents, both the type of relationship parents share after a nonmarital birth (i.e., cohabiting, romantic but living apart, friends, or no relationship) and—independent of relationship type—the quality of the relationship (i.e., supportiveness and ability to communicate effectively) have been linked to greater involvement by unmarried fathers (Fagan & Palkovitz, 2007; Ryan, Kalil, & Ziol-Guest, 2008). In cases in which the "package" comes apart as a result of union dissolution, men frequently lose connection to their child(ren), particularly if the mother repartners and a new man assumes the "father" role (Edin, Tach, & Mincy, 2009; Tach, Mincy, & Edin, 2010). In other words, nonresident fathers desiring a positive coparenting relationship with mothers and involvement with their child may find this difficult to attain, especially in circumstances in which unmarried mothers and fathers have different expectations about how parenting should be shared (Waller, 2002). Indeed, unmarried fathers have reported having less influence than divorced fathers in decision making about their child and experiencing more conflict surrounding attempts to be involved (Insabella, Williams, & Pruett, 2003).

Bronte-Tinkew and Horowitz (2010) found that fathers who lived away from children all 3 years after a nonmarital birth reported lower coparenting if they had previously been incarcerated, had more children with the focal mother, had no romantic involvement with the mother, had a new partner, and had more frequent contact with the child. By contrast, positive coparenting was higher when both parents had some college education, when mothers worked, when fathers had higher income, when fathers provided more informal financial support (e.g., buying things for the child), and when the child was a boy. Thus, it appears that both economic capacities and relationship circumstances are fundamental domains that affect the ability of unmarried parents living apart to cooperate in rearing their common child. Later, we present results of new analyses of factors associated with coparenting in fragile families, both for parents who live together and for a broader sample of parents living apart.

Coparenting and Father Involvement

Understanding the link between coparenting and father involvement after a nonmarital birth is important because fathers' contributions of time and money represent a substantial resource for children and their mothers (Amato

& Gilbreth, 1999; King & Sobolewski, 2006). Because mothers typically have primary responsibility for young children, and most often have custody if and when a parental union dissolves, engaging the father early on in a child's life is implicitly related to coparenting. In fact, particularly during the prenatal period and when the child is very young, it can be difficult to draw proper distinctions among the constructs of couple relationship quality, coparenting, and parental involvement.

Cabrera, Fagan, and Farrie (2008), studying fathers' prenatal involvement (i.e., contributing financially, helping with transportation, and presence at the birth), found that more prenatal involvement predicted higher father engagement in child activities between the ages of 1 and 3 years. However, because there are likely unobserved selection factors affecting both early and later involvement of men as partners and parents, it is not possible to determine whether prenatal involvement had independent causal effects on later outcomes. That said, because a new birth represents an important turning point for couples and perhaps especially for fathers, it may be an opportune window for intervention (Feinberg, 2002). Mothers' support of fathers' new role is important: If both parents share a belief in the importance of fathers' caregiving, the couple is more likely to stay together (Hohmann-Marriott, 2009). For these reasons, recognizing the importance of the mother–father relationship for the family system, for fathers' ties to children, and ultimately for children's well-being is an important direction for both future research and public policy (see Chapters 1 and 6, this volume).

Because most unwed couples break up after only a few years (hence the couple's romantic relationship quality is no longer a salient issue), a key question is how coparenting is linked with father involvement for nonresident fathers. In an analysis of coparenting and father involvement from the Fragile Families study approximately 1, 3, and 5 years after a nonmarital birth, Carlson, McLanahan, and Brooks-Gunn (2008) drew on methods designed to deal with selection (both into nonresident fatherhood and into higher levels of involvement) to evaluate the direction of the association between coparenting and father involvement. Their results provided consistent evidence across three measures of paternal involvement (days of contact, spending 1 or more hours with the child, and frequency of engaging in activities) that supportive coparenting appears to affect fathers' subsequent involvement, whereas early paternal involvement has little effect on future coparenting. Further, using fixed effects regression models that control for all time-invariant individual characteristics and reduce bias because of unobserved heterogeneity across cases (Snijders, 2005), the authors found the effects of coparenting on father involvement to be robust. These conservative "within-person" estimates suggest that when coparenting between couples improves, fathers are likely to become more involved with their children (Carlson et al., 2008). These data underscore that coparenting and father involvement are distinct constructs for nonresident fathers and that intervening to enhance cooperative coparenting could potentially help keep nonresident fathers connected to their children over time.

On a related note, fathers' access to their children and roles in child rearing are highly contingent on mothers' approval and facilitation of their involvement, typically referred to as *gatekeeping* (Ahrons & Miller, 1993; Allen & Hawkins, 1999). Although mothers often facilitate rather than hinder father involvement (Walker & McGraw, 2000), they clearly also make choices about when and how fathers will spend time with the child, particularly when the child is young. Evidence from the Fragile Families study data—including a qualitative follow-up of participants in Oakland (Waller, 2002)—suggests that mothers often take active steps to protect their children from "unhealthy" men (Waller & Swisher, 2006), particularly fathers who have problems with physical violence and substance abuse. Although most unmarried fathers do not present a danger to their children or their children's mothers, it is important for interventions to be sensitive to this concern. Interventions designed to strengthen coparenting among unmarried parents are discussed in greater detail in Chapter 9 of this volume.

NEW EVIDENCE FROM THE FRAGILE FAMILIES STUDY

We now present new analyses of Fragile Families study data examining differences in levels of positive coparenting across groups and multivariate analyses of antecedents across residential and nonresidential contexts.

Variation in Levels of Coparenting

First, we describe levels of positive coparenting across groups. In Table 4.2, we show overall mean scores across the six coparenting items in the Fragile Families study separately for coresident parents and parents living apart at Years 1, 3, and 5. Then, we show means by race, education, poverty status, and MPF.[3]

Among the 52% of unmarried parents living together at Year 1, the average reported level of positive coparenting by mothers is 2.7–2.8 on the 1-to-3 index, indicating very favorable maternal views on coparenting in this context. From Year 1 to Year 3, coparenting assessments decline slightly (but significantly) and then remain steady between Years 3 and 5. Consistent with results in Carlson et al. (2008), maternal reports of positive coparenting are somewhat

---

[3]Although not shown in the table, we evaluated statistically significant differences using one-way comparisons of means using Scheffé tests; we discuss in the text only differences of $p < .05$.

TABLE 4.2
Mean Levels of Coparenting After a Nonmarital Birth (Mothers' Reports)

Parents[a]	Year 1 M	(SD)	Year 3 M	(SD)	Year 5 M	(SD)
Coresident status of parents						
Coresident	2.84	(0.44)	2.74	(0.34)	2.77	(0.33)
Living apart	2.29	(0.66)	2.06	(0.69)	2.12	(0.66)
Coparenting by subgroup						
Mother's race/ethnicity						
White non-Hispanic	2.57	(0.59)	2.34	(0.70)	2.33	(0.64)
African American non-Hispanic	2.61	(0.52)	2.41	(0.61)	2.37	(0.63)
Hispanic	2.63	(0.52)	2.51	(0.58)	2.54	(0.55)
Other non-Hispanic	2.68	(0.49)	2.49	(0.74)	2.44	(0.67)
Mother's education (at time of birth)						
Less than HS	2.58	(0.58)	2.45	(0.62)	2.43	(0.63)
HS degree	2.64	(0.50)	2.44	(0.64)	2.43	(0.61)
Some college	2.65	(0.46)	2.37	(0.62)	2.41	(0.61)
College degree	2.55	(0.63)	2.45	(0.65)	2.33	(0.63)
Mother's poverty status (at time of birth)						
Poor	2.58	(0.57)	2.43	(0.62)	2.41	(0.66)
Not poor	2.64	(0.51)	2.44	(0.65)	2.43	(0.59)
Couple MPF status (at 1 year)						
None (first birth or all children together)	2.65	(0.49)	2.46	(0.63)	2.46	(0.60)
Father only	2.50	(0.59)	2.23	(0.73)	2.25	(0.68)
Mother only	2.70	(0.49)	2.62	(0.45)	2.57	(0.60)
Both parents	2.62	(0.52)	2.45	(0.58)	2.38	(0.57)
Total number of cases (n)	2,496		2,726		2,511	

Note. All figures are weighted by national sampling weights for each year; numbers of cases are unweighted. Coparenting is the average of six items, range = 1–3 (1 = *Never/rarely*, 2 = *Sometimes*, and 3 = *Always*), with higher scores indicating higher coparenting. HS = high school; MPF = multipartnered fertility.
[a]The percentages of parents coresiding at the 1-, 3-, and 5-year surveys were 52%, 45%, and 36%, respectively.

lower when parents live apart—closer to 2 on the 1-to-3 scale. Recall too that coparenting questions are asked only if fathers saw children since the previous survey, meaning that the "worst" nonresident fathers are excluded from these analyses. At Years 1, 3, and 5, 13%, 29%, and 33%, respectively, of nonresident fathers had not seen the child since the previous survey. Therefore, the estimates reported here should be seen as an upper bound (and increasingly so over time), because fathers who do not see the child are presumably not interacting with the mother about the child. The overall picture appears to be that maternal perceptions of coparenting quality decline significantly between Years 1 and 3, then remain steady between Years 3 and 5.

Subgroup analyses reveal striking consistency in levels of coparenting reported by mothers regardless of race/ethnicity, education, and poverty status. Among the very few significant differences is a higher report of coparenting from Hispanic mothers than from non-Hispanic White or non-Hispanic Black mothers at Years 3 and 5 (but not Year 1). This may reflect the important role of family life, or *familism*, within the Hispanic community (Zinn & Pok, 2002). Also of interest, more educated parents do not report more positive coparenting; we find essentially no difference in coparenting as a function of mother's educational attainment. Although most unmarried parents studied had relatively low education (typically a high school degree or less) and few mothers had any college education, the highest educated mothers did not appear to be systematically different from their less-educated counterparts with respect to coparenting. Also, we observed little difference by poverty status at the time of the baby's birth. Although poor mothers had slightly (and significantly) lower levels of coparenting at Year 1, there were no differences over Years 3 and 5.

The most persistent differences in coparenting are observed as a function of couples' MPF status, a common situation among unwed couples. In the Fragile Families study, 59% of unmarried couples (compared with 21% of married couples) already had a child by a prior partner—of the mother, father, or both (Carlson & Furstenberg, 2006). The modal child born outside of marriage thus has at least one half sibling at the start of life. Childbearing across partnerships creates the possibility that parents have divergent interests among their common children and those conceived with other partners. This may diminish their ability to effectively coparent and may also reduce the resources parents invest in a given child.

These data echo research on the complexities that remarriage brings to family life because of the presence of children from previous marriages (Furstenberg & Cherlin, 1991; Ihinger-Tallman, 1988). The lack of clear norms, authority, legal relationships, and habits in stepfamilies with children compared with first families led to the characterization of remarriage as an "incomplete institution" (Cherlin, 1978). Children born outside of marriage likely receive even fewer parental resources and experience less effective coparenting when parents have children by prior partners compared with children born within marriage. This is both because unmarried parents are, on average, more economically disadvantaged than married parents and because of the absence of social legitimacy and paternal obligations established via marriage.

Descriptive statistics in Table 4.2 indicate that parents' ability to cooperatively coparent a focal child appears compromised if fathers—or both fathers and mothers—are also rearing children from prior partnerships. Across all years, the lowest levels of coparenting were reported when the father (only) had a child by another partner. At Years 1 and 3, coparenting was significantly lower when fathers (only) had a child by a prior partner, compared with all other fertility categories; at Year 5, this category was significantly lower than mother (only) and no MPF but did not differ from families in which both parents had a child by another partner. However, when the mother (only) had a child by another partner, coparenting was always higher than father (only) MPF—and sometimes (but not consistently) higher than the no-MPF category or when both parents had MPF.

Because these coparenting measures were reported by mothers, it is not surprising that women's own prior children were perceived as having less influence on how well they could work together with the father of the focal child, whereas his children were perceived as more detrimental. Because children typically live with mothers, these data may suggest that parental obligations to half siblings outside of the focal child's household are more deleterious for coparenting than obligations to half siblings within the household. Work in progress on how MPF affects parental relationships and children's well-being (in behavioral and cognitive domains) has suggested that this result continues to hold up in multivariate analyses—fathers' MPF appears to significantly diminish coparenting among the focal child's biological parents (Carlson, Furstenberg, & McLanahan, 2010), a finding consistent with prior qualitative research among unmarried parents (Waller, 2002).

Antecedents of Coparenting

We now summarize results from random effects models (see Table 4.3) examining factors associated with coparenting following a nonmarital birth for parents living together versus apart. Several variables are significantly associated with coparenting, although again, strikingly, demographic characteristics are not strong predictors of coparenting.

For coresident parents (Model 1), when only demographic and socioeconomic factors are included, only small, marginally significant estimates are found for Hispanic ethnicity and fathers' high school degree—both are positively associated with better coparenting. Mother's age and father's age are

TABLE 4.3
Random Effects Estimates Predicting Coparenting After a Nonmarital Birth

Characteristics	Coresident parents		Parents living apart	
	Model 1	Model 2	Model 1	Model 2
Demographic				
Mothers' race/ethnicity				
(ref = White non-Hispanic)				
Black non-Hispanic	.03	.06**	.16**	.17**
Hispanic	.04+	.05*	.07	.08
Other non-Hispanic	.06	.06	.17	.19+
Father of different race/ethnicity	−.03	−.02	−.07	−.07
Mother foreign born	.04	.02	.11	.10
Father foreign born	−.00	−.03	−.08	−.13+
Mothers' education (ref = less than HS)				
HS degree	.02	.00	−.06	−.04
Some college or more	−.00	−.02	−.12**	−.11*
Fathers' education (ref = less than HS)				
HS degree	.03+	.01	.02	−.00
Some college or more	.03	.00	−.00	−.04
Mother's age (years)	.00+	.00	.01*	.00
Father's age (years)	−.00*	−.00	.00	.01+
Mother lived with both parents at 15	.00	−.00	−.01	.01
Father lived with both parents at 15	−.01	−.01	.06	.03
Mother's self-reported health status	−.02	.00	−.09	−.02
Father's self-reported health status	−.04	−.00	−.01	.04
Social psychological				
Mother's religious attendance		−.01		−.01
Father's religious attendance		.00		.01
Mother substance problem		.09		.09
Father substance problem		−.04		.02
Mother at risk of depression		−.11**		−.21**
Father at risk of depression		−.06*		−.13**
Father ever incarcerated		−.05**		−.11**
Relationship quality and fertility history				
Supportiveness			.27**	.29**
Father hits/slaps			−.09*	−.06
Number of children in mother's household			−.01	.02+
Couple MPF (ref = no MPF)				
Father only			−.03	−.12**
Mother only			.02	.09*
Both parents			.00	−.08
Child				
Child is a boy		−.01		−.02
Child has "difficult" temperament		−.02*		−.03*
Constant	2.73**	2.09**	1.97**	1.31**
No. of unique cases (n)	1,366	1,366	1,164	1,164
No. of observations	2,847	2,847	2,166	2,166

Note. Coparenting is the average of six items reported by mothers with responses ranging from 1 = *Never/rarely* to 3 = *Always,* with higher scores indicating higher quality coparenting. Cases are pooled across Years 1, 3, and 5 after a nonmarital birth based on coresidence status of the biological parents (with each other) at each survey wave. HS = high school; MPF = multipartner fertility.
+*p* < .10. *p* < .05. **p* < .01.

(marginally) statistically significant, although the magnitude is negligible because they each round to zero. Adding the broader array of variables in Model 2 increases the magnitude of the estimates for two race/ethnic variables: Black non-Hispanic and Hispanic mothers report better coparenting than White non-Hispanic mothers. Yet, none of the other demographic factors are statistically significant, and magnitudes are close to zero. We note that parents' risk of depression is associated with lower coparenting, as is fathers' history of incarceration. As expected, couples with more supportive dyadic relationships between them (i.e., communicating and understanding each other) also have better coparenting relationships, whereas fathers' physical violence is associated with lower coparenting. There are no significant differences in coparenting by parents' multipartnered fertility history for coresident couples. As for child factors, there is no difference in coparenting by the focal child's gender, but "difficult" temperament diminishes coparenting, suggesting that parents have a harder time coordinating their efforts when the child is harder to deal with; this underscores a growing emphasis in family research on how children influence family processes (Crouter & Booth, 2003).

Turning to parents living apart (and typically children live with the mother), Black non-Hispanic mothers report significantly higher positive coparenting than White non-Hispanic mothers (Model 1). Because African American couples with children are less likely to live together, parenting while living separately is more normative within the Black community (Mincy & Pouncy, 2007). Surprisingly, mothers with some college education report lower levels of coparenting compared with those with less than a high school degree. This may be because more highly educated mothers have higher expectations about nonresident fathers' involvement, so they assess fathers' coparenting behaviors more critically.

Adding the additional covariates in Model 2 does little to change the estimates for Black non-Hispanic race/ethnicity and some college education. Also, "other" non-Hispanic race becomes marginally significant and positive, indicating that this small group of (mostly Asian) mothers report higher positive coparenting than White mothers. At the same time, being foreign born is now marginally significantly linked with lower levels of coparenting. As with coresident parents, mothers' and fathers' depression and fathers' incarceration are strongly associated with lower positive coparenting. Similarly, when mothers report that there was more supportiveness in the couple relationship when they were still together, coparenting is higher. However, for parents living apart, physical violence is not linked to coparenting. It may be that mothers have separated from violent fathers, thus limiting fathers' contact with mothers (and their children) and limiting coparenting contact (Waller & Swisher, 2006). Compared with couples with no MPF, coparenting is significantly lower when the father (only) has children by a prior partner. By contrast, when the mother (only) has a child by a prior partner, coparenting is reportedly higher; as noted previously, a half sibling living in the household may be less disruptive to coparenting (at least from mothers' perspectives) than a half sibling living elsewhere. As with coresident couples, the focal child's more difficult temperament is linked to slightly lower positive coparenting.

Overall, these estimates suggest that coparenting is typically high for parents subsequent to a nonmarital birth, especially when parents are still romantically involved and living together. Among parents living apart, Black mothers report higher levels of coparenting by nonresident fathers than do other race/ethnic groups, consistent with the greater acceptance of rearing children apart within the Black community (Mincy & Pouncy, 2007). At the same time, fathers' MPF (common among nonresident—and especially Black—fathers) deters coparenting. Regardless of coresidence status, having (or having had) a high-quality couple relationship is linked to maternal reports of higher coparenting; parental depression and paternal incarceration diminish cooperative coparenting.

Limitations of the Fragile Families Study

Although the Fragile Families study has added significant new information to our understanding of coparenting among unmarried parents with children, it is important to keep in mind its limitations. As with all quantitative surveys, response rates and attrition must be noted. By using a hospital-based design, the Fragile Families study was able to attain higher response rates than other similar studies, particularly for fathers, who are typically underrepresented in national surveys (Garfinkel, McLanahan, & Hanson, 1998; Nelson, 2004). At the same time, one quarter of unmarried fathers were not interviewed at the time of the birth, and of unmarried parents interviewed at baseline, 16% of mothers and 19% of fathers were lost to attrition by the 5-year survey. Attrition is not random, and those who drop out are more likely to be racial/ethnic minorities and have lower socioeconomic resources than those who remain. Hence, analyses of supportive coparenting may be overestimated to the extent that parents lost to attrition likely have lower coparenting than those who remain in the study.

A second limitation concerns reliance on maternal reports. Using mothers' reports allows all couples in a given survey wave to be included, even if fathers are not interviewed. However, mothers provide only one perspective on the coparenting relationship, and fathers' views may differ. Mothers also may not convey accurate information about the frequency and content of nonresident fathers' involvement with children (Coley & Morris, 2002; Seltzer & Brandreth, 1995), and the extent of their knowledge is likely correlated with the degree of cooperative coparenting. Also, using maternal reports for both the coparenting and outcome variables (and some covariates) may inflate correlations because the same respondent may over- or underreport positive feelings of all kinds, referred to as *shared method variance* (Marsiglio, Amato, Day, & Lamb, 2000).

Third, as a multidimensional survey designed by an interdisciplinary team, the Fragile Families study covered a wide range of topics but with less detail about any given topic than would typically be found in a study focused primarily on one substantive area. With respect to coparenting, no measures of negative coparenting were included, such as the extent to which mothers and fathers may actively undermine the parenting of one another.

Fourth, although not a limitation of the Fragile Families study per se, survey data generally are inherently inferior to experimental design for discerning causal effects. Therefore, caution must be taken in interpreting findings concerning coparenting (or any measure of interest) as causal; even with the wide array of measures included in the Fragile Families study, there are certainly other unmeasured factors affecting coparenting, its antecedents, and its consequences.

CONCLUSIONS AND IMPLICATIONS

Research on coparenting in fragile families is critically important, as unmarried parents with children typically remain unmarried and break up within only a few years after the child is born. Fragile Families study data reveal that compared with married parents, unmarried parents are more likely to be Black or Hispanic, have low education levels, and have children with more than one partner. Collectively, these and other differences affect parents' relationships with each other, their relationships with their child, and their coparenting relationship vis-à-vis their common child. Coparenting among unmarried couples is a product of social psychological characteristics, such as depression and the quality of parents' relationships, both of which can be related to parents' broader socioeconomic circumstances. For unmarried parents who live apart, the story is complicated by whether the father has a child with another partner.

Although scholars have begun to explore important aspects of coparenting in fragile families, there are many unanswered questions. One such question concerns the extent to which coparenting in fragile families affects children's well-being. Cooperative, low-conflict coparenting relationships have been linked to better child outcomes among coresident (mostly married) and divorced parents (see Chapters 2 and 9, this volume), but we do not yet have sufficient data about this linkage among unmarried families. Second, we need to understand more about how coparenting processes differ in fragile families as a function of parents' race/ethnicity and children's age. Though the "package deal" linking partner and parent roles may be less salient in Black families (Edin, Tach, & Mincy, 2009) in which the "baby father" role is more clearly distinguished from the mother–father romantic relationship (Mincy & Pouncy, 2007), data on variation in coparenting remain scarce, and virtually nothing is known about whether coparenting changes as children's needs and the parenting tasks required over the course of childhood and adolescence change. Third, the complex interrelationship between coparenting, fathering, and child support is not well understood; it may be of value to know whether coparenting is associated with fathers' payment of child support—and whether this operates directly or indirectly.

Finally, with respect to implications for public policy, strengthening couple relationship quality and encouraging marriage were a focus of the Healthy Marriage Initiative funded by the U.S. Deficit Reduction Act of 2005. To the extent that Healthy Marriage efforts succeed in promoting stable marriages, the United States will have fewer children ever living away from their fathers in the first place. Yet, even with genuinely successful interventions that achieve healthy marriages for some, there will likely still be many other unwed couples who break up. To the extent that better coparenting among unmarried parents positively affects child development and well-being, a critical issue in need of further study, policy interventions might usefully focus not only on strengthening the couple's romantic relationship but also on strengthening their ability to work together in rearing their child.

REFERENCES

Ahrons, C. R. (1981). The continuing co-parental relationship between divorced parents. *American Journal of Orthopsychiatry, 51*, 415–428. doi:10.1111/j.1939-0025.1981.tb01390.x

Ahrons, C. R., & Miller, R. B. (1993). The effect of the postdivorce relationship on paternal involvement: A longitudinal analysis. *American Journal of Orthopsychiatry, 63*, 441–450. doi:10.1037/h0079446

Allen, S. M., & Hawkins, A. J. (1999). Maternal gatekeeping: Mothers' beliefs and behaviors that inhibit greater involvement in family work. *Journal of Marriage and the Family, 61*, 199–212. doi:10.2307/353894

Amato, P. R., & Gilbreth, J. G. (1999). Nonresident fathers and children's well-being: A meta-analysis. *Journal of Marriage and the Family, 61*, 557–573. doi:10.2307/353560

Axinn, W. G., & Thornton, A. (2000). The transformation in the meaning of marriage. In L. J. Waite (Ed.), *The ties that bind* (pp. 147–165). New York, NY: Aldine de Gruyter.

Becker, G. S. (1991). *A treatise on the family*. Cambridge, MA: Harvard University Press.

Bronfenbrenner, U. (1986). Ecology of the family as a context for human development: Research perspectives. *Developmental Psychology, 22*, 723–742. doi:10.1037/0012-1649.22.6.723

Bronte-Tinkew, J., & Horowitz, A. (2010). Factors associated with unmarried, nonresident fathers' perceptions of their coparenting. *Journal of Family Issues, 31*, 31–65. doi:10.1177/0192513X09342866

Cabrera, N. J., Fagan, J., & Farrie, D. (2008). Explaining the long reach of fathers' prenatal involvement on later paternal engagement. *Journal of Marriage and the Family, 70*, 1094–1107. doi:10.1111/j.1741-3737.2008.00551.x

Carlson, M. J., & Furstenberg, F. F., Jr. (2006). The prevalence and correlates of multipartnered fertility among urban U.S. parents. *Journal of Marriage and the Family, 68*, 718–732. doi:10.1111/j.1741-3737.2006.00285.x

Carlson, M. J., Furstenberg, F. F., Jr., & McLanahan, S. S. (2010). *Multi-partnered fertility, parental relationships, and child wellbeing*. Unpublished manuscript.

Carlson, M. J., & McLanahan, S. S. (2010). Fathers in fragile families. In M. E. Lamb (Ed.), *The role of the father in child development* (5th ed., pp. 241–269). Hoboken, NJ: Wiley.

Carlson, M. J., McLanahan, S. S., & Brooks-Gunn, J. (2008). Coparenting and nonresident fathers' involvement with young children after a nonmarital birth. *Demography, 45*, 461–488. doi:10.1353/dem.0.0007

Carlson, M., McLanahan, S., & England, P. (2004). Union formation in fragile families. *Demography, 41*, 237–261. doi:10.1353/dem.2004.0012

Cherlin, A. (1978). Remarriage as an incomplete institution. *American Journal of Sociology, 84*, 634–650. doi:10.1086/226830

Cherlin, A. J. (2004). The deinstitutionalization of American marriage. *Journal of Marriage and the Family, 66*, 848–861. doi:10.1111/j.0022-2445.2004.00058.x

Clarkberg, M., Stolzenberg, R. M., & Waite, L. J. (1995). Attitudes, values, and the entrance into cohabitational unions. *Social Forces, 74*, 609–634. doi:10.2307/2580494

Coley, R. L., & Morris, J. E. (2002). Comparing father and mother reports of father involvement among low-income minority fathers. *Journal of Marriage and the Family, 64*, 982–997. doi:10.1111/j.1741-3737.2002.00982.x

Cowan, P. A., Cowan, C. P., Schulz, M. S., & Heming, G. (1994). Prebirth to preschool family factors in children's adaptation to kindergarten. In R. D. Parke & S. G. Kellam (Eds.), *Exploring family relationships with other social contexts* (pp. 75–114). Hillsdale, NJ: Erlbaum.

Crouter, A. C., & Booth, A. (Eds.). (2003). *Children's influence on family dynamics: The neglected side of family relationships*. Mahwah, NJ: Erlbaum.

Edin, K., & Kefalas, M. (2005). *Promises I can keep: Why poor women put motherhood before marriage*. Berkeley: University of California Press.

Edin, K., Tach, L., & Mincy, R. (2009). Claiming fatherhood: Race and the dynamics of paternal involvement among unmarried men. *The Annals of the American Academy of Political and Social Science, 621*, 149–177. doi:10.1177/0002716208325548

Ellwood, D. T., & Jencks, C. (2004). The spread of single-parent families in the United States since 1960. In D. P. Moynihan, T. M. Smeeding, & L. Rainwater (Eds.), *The future of the family* (pp. 25–65). New York, NY: Russell Sage Foundation.

Emery, R. E., Laumann-Billings, L., Waldron, M. C., Sbarra, D. A., & Dillon, P. (2001). Child custody mediation and litigation: Custody, contact, and coparenting 12 years after initial dispute resolution. *Journal of Consulting and Clinical Psychology, 69*, 323–332. doi:10.1037/0022-006X.69.2.323

Fagan, J., & Palkovitz, R. (2007). Unmarried, nonresident fathers' involvement with their infants: A risk and resilience perspective. *Journal of Family Psychology, 21*, 479–489. doi:10.1037/0893-3200.21.3.479

Feinberg, M. E. (2002). Coparenting and the transition to parenthood: A framework for prevention. *Clinical Child and Family Psychology Review, 5*, 173–195. doi:10.1023/A:1019695015110

Furstenberg, F. F., Jr. (1988). Good dads—bad dads: Two faces of fatherhood. In A. J. Cherlin (Ed.), *The changing American family and public policy* (pp. 193–218). Washington, DC: The Urban Institute.

Furstenberg, F. F., & Cherlin, A. (1991). *Divided families: What happens to children when parents part.* Cambridge, MA: Harvard University Press.

Furstenberg, F. F., Jr., & Nord, C. W. (1985). Parenting apart: Patterns of childrearing after marital disruption. *Journal of Marriage and the Family, 47*, 893–904. doi:10.2307/352332

Garfinkel, I., McLanahan, S. S., & Hanson, T. L. (1998). A patchwork portrait of nonresident fathers. In I. Garfinkel, S. S. McLanahan, D. R. Meyer, & J. A. Seltzer (Eds.), *Fathers under fire: The revolution in child support enforcement* (pp. 31–60). New York, NY: Russell Sage Foundation.

Gibson-Davis, C. (2009). Money, marriage, and children: Testing the financial expectations and family formations theory. *Journal of Marriage and the Family, 71*, 146–160. doi:10.1111/j.1741-3737.2008.00586.x

Gibson-Davis, C., Edin, K., & McLanahan, S. (2005). High hopes but even higher expectations: The retreat from marriage among low-income couples. *Journal of Marriage and the Family, 67*, 1301–1312. doi:10.1111/j.1741-3737.2005.00218.x

Gottman, J. M. (1994). *What predicts divorce? The relationship between marital processes and marital outcomes.* Hillsdale, NJ: Erlbaum.

Hamilton, B. E., Martin, J. A., & Ventura, S. J. (2010). *Births: Preliminary data for 2008* (National Vital Statistics Reports, Vol. 58, No. 16). Hyattsville, MD: National Center for Health Statistics.

Harknett, K. (2008). Mate availability and unmarried parent relationships. *Demography, 45*, 555–571. doi:10.1353/dem.0.0012

Harknett, K., & McLanahan, S. S. (2004). Racial and ethnic differences in marriage after the birth of a child. *American Sociological Review, 69*, 790–811. doi:10.1177/000312240406900603

Hayden, L. C., Schiller, M., Dickstein, S., Seifer, R., Sameroff, S., Miller, I., . . . Rasmussen, S. (1998). Levels of family assessment: I. Family, marital, and parent-child interaction. *Journal of Family Psychology, 12*, 7–22. doi:10.1037/0893-3200.12.1.7

Hill, H. D. (2007). Steppin' out: Infidelity and sexual jealousy among unmarried parents. In P. England & K. Edin (Eds.), *Unmarried couples with children* (pp. 104–132). New York, NY: Russell Sage Foundation.

Hohmann-Marriott, B. E. (2009). Father involvement ideals and the union transitions of unmarried parents. *Journal of Family Issues, 30*, 898–920. doi:10.1177/0192513X08327885

Ihinger-Tallman, M. (1988). Research on stepfamilies. *Annual Review of Sociology, 14*, 25–48. doi:10.1146/annurev.so.14.080188.000325

Insabella, G. M., Williams, T., & Pruett, M. K. (2003). Individual and coparenting differences between divorcing and unmarried fathers: Implications for family court services. *Family Court Review, 41*, 290–306. doi:10.1177/1531244503041003003

Karney, B. R., & Bradbury, T. N. (1995). The longitudinal course of marital quality and stability: A review of theory, method, and research. *Psychological Bulletin, 118*, 3–34. doi:10.1037/0033-2909.118.1.3

Katz, L. F., & Low, S. M. (2004). Marital violence, co-parenting, and family-level processes in relation to children's adjustment. *Journal of Family Psychology, 18*, 372–382. doi:10.1037/0893-3200.18.2.372

King, V., & Sobolewski, J. M. (2006). Nonresident fathers' contributions to adolescent well-being. *Journal of Marriage and the Family, 68*, 537–557. doi:10.1111/j.1741-3737.2006.00274.x

Maccoby, E. E., Depner, C. E., & Mnookin, R. H. (1990). Coparenting in the second year after divorce. *Journal of Marriage and the Family, 52*, 141–155. doi:10.2307/352846

Maccoby, E. E., & Mnookin, R. H. (1992). *Dividing the child: Social and legal dilemmas of custody.* Cambridge, MA: Harvard University Press.

Margolin, G., Gordis, E. B., & John, R. S. (2001). Coparenting: A link between marital conflict and parenting in two-parent families. *Journal of Family Psychology, 15*, 3–21. doi:10.1037/0893-3200.15.1.3

Marsiglio, W., Amato, P., Day, R. D., & Lamb, M. E. (2000). Scholarship on fatherhood in the 1990s and beyond. *Journal of Marriage and the Family, 62*, 1173–1191. doi:10.1111/j.1741-3737.2000.01173.x

McHale, J. P. (1995). Coparenting and triadic interactions during infancy: The roles of marital distress and child gender. *Developmental Psychology, 31*, 985–996. doi:10.1037/0012-1649.31.6.985

McHale, J. P., Kuersten-Hogan, R., Lauretti, A., & Rasmussen, J. L. (2000). Parental reports of coparenting and observed coparenting behavior during the toddler period. *Journal of Family Psychology, 14,* 220–236. doi:10.1037/0893-3200. 14.2.220

McLanahan, S. (2004). Fragile families and the marriage agenda. In L. Kowaleski-Jones & N. Wolfinger (Eds.), *Fragile families and the marriage agenda* (pp. 1–22). New York, NY: Springer.

McLanahan, S. (2009). Fragile families and the reproduction of poverty. *The Annals of the American Academy of Political and Social Science, 621,* 111–131. doi:10. 1177/0002716208324862

McLanahan, S. (in press). Family instability and complexity after a nonmarital birth: Outcomes for children in fragile families. In M. J. Carlson & P. England (Eds.), *Social class and changing families in an unequal America.* Stanford, CA: Stanford University Press.

McLanahan, S., Garfinkel, I., Reichman, N., Teitler, J., Carlson, M., & Norland Audigier, C. (2003). *The Fragile Families and Child Wellbeing Study* (Baseline National Report) Princeton, NJ: Princeton University, Center for Research on Child Wellbeing.

Mincy, R. B., & Pouncy, H. (2007). *Baby fathers and American family formation: Low-income, never-married parents in Louisiana before Katrina.* New York, NY: Center for Marriage and Families, Institute for American Values.

Minuchin, P. (1988). Relationships within the family: A systems perspective on development. In R. A. Hinde & J. Stevenson-Hinde (Eds.), *Relationships within families: Mutual influences* (pp. 7–26). New York, NY: Oxford University Press.

Minuchin, S. (1974). *Families and family therapy.* Cambridge, MA: Harvard University Press.

Monte, L. M. (2007). Blended but not the Bradys: Navigating unmarried multiple partner fertility. In P. England & K. Edin (Eds.), *Unmarried couples with children* (pp. 183–203). New York, NY: Russell Sage Foundation.

Nelson, T. J. (2004). Low-income fathers. *Annual Review of Sociology, 30,* 427–451. doi:10.1146/annurev.soc.29.010202.095947

Nock, S. L. (1995). A comparison of marriages and cohabiting relationships. *Journal of Family Issues, 16,* 53–76. doi:10.1177/019251395016001004

Reichman, N., Teitler, J., Garfinkel, I., & McLanahan, S. (2001). Fragile families: Sample and design. *Children and Youth Services Review, 23*(4–5), 303–326. doi:10. 1016/S0190-7409(01)00141-4

Ryan, R. M., Kalil, A., & Ziol-Guest, K. M. (2008). Longitudinal patterns of non-resident fathers' involvement: The role of resources and relations. *Journal of Marriage and the Family, 70,* 962–977. doi:10.1111/j.1741-3737.2008.00539.x

Schoppe-Sullivan, S. J., Brown, G. L., Cannon, E. A., Mangelsdorf, S. C., & Sokolowski, M. S. (2008). Maternal gatekeeping, coparenting quality, and fathering behavior in families with infants. *Journal of Family Psychology, 22,* 389–398. doi:10.1037/0893-3200.22.3.389

Seltzer, J. A., & Brandreth, Y. (1995). What fathers say about involvement with children after separation. In W. Marsiglio (Ed.), *Fatherhood: Contemporary theory, research and social policy* (pp. 166–192). Thousand Oaks, CA: Sage.

Seltzer, J. A., McLanahan, S. S., & Hanson, T. L. (1998). Will child support enforcement increase father-child contact and parental conflict after separation? In I. Garfinkel, S. S. McLanahan, D. R. Meyer, & J. A. Seltzer (Eds.), *Fathers under fire: The revolution in child support enforcement* (pp. 157–190). New York, NY: Russell Sage Foundation.

Snijders, T. A. B. (2005). Fixed and random effects. In B. S. Everitt & D. C. Howell (Eds.), *Encyclopedia of statistics in behavioral science* (Vol. 2, pp. 664–665). Chichester, England: Wiley.

Sobolewski, J. M., & King, V. (2005). The importance of the coparental relationship for nonresident fathers' ties to children. *Journal of Marriage and the Family, 67,* 1196–1212. doi:10.1111/j.1741-3737.2005.00210.x

Tach, L., Mincy, R., & Edin, K. (2010). Parenting as a package deal: Relationships, fertility, and nonresident father involvement among unmarried parents. *Demography, 47,* 181–204. doi:10.1353/dem.0.0096

Townsend, N. W. (2002). *The package deal: Marriage, work and fatherhood in men's lives.* Philadelphia, PA: Temple University Press.

Walker, A. J., & McGraw, L. A. (2000). Who is responsible for responsible fathering? *Journal of Marriage and the Family, 62,* 563–569. doi:10.1111/j.1741-3737. 2000.00563.x

Waller, M. R. (2002). *My baby's father: Unmarried parents and paternal responsibility.* Ithaca, NY: Cornell University Press.

Waller, M. R., & McLanahan, S. S. (2005). "His" and "her" marriage expectations: Determinants and consequences. *Journal of Marriage and the Family, 67,* 53–67. doi:10.1111/j.0022-2445.2005.00005.x

Waller, M. R., & Swisher, R. (2006). Fathers' risk factors in fragile families: Implications for "healthy" relationships and father involvement. *Social Problems, 53,* 392–420. doi:10.1525/sp.2006.53.3.392

Wallerstein, J. S., & Kelly, J. B. (1980). *Surviving the breakup: How children and parents cope with divorce.* New York, NY: Basic Books.

Wilcox, W. B., & Wolfinger, N. H. (2007). Then comes marriage? Religion, race, and marriage in urban America. *Social Science Research, 36,* 569–589. doi:10.1016/ j.ssresearch.2006.02.005

Zinn, M. B., & Pok, A. Y. H. (2002). Tradition and transition in Mexican-origin families. In R. L. Taylor (Ed.), *Minority families in the United States: A multicultural perspective* (pp. 79–100). Upper Saddle River, NJ: Prentice Hall.

5

COPARENTING IN FAMILIES WITH ADOLESCENT MOTHERS

LAURA D. PITTMAN AND REBEKAH LEVINE COLEY

Contrary to public perceptions, adolescent childbearing has declined substantially, dropping a full 50% in the past half century. In 1960, nearly 9% of girls ages 15 to 19 years gave birth in any given year. This rate dropped to just over 4% in 2006, although the years of 2006 and 2007 also saw increases in annual adolescent births, reversing a 15-year trend of declines (Child Trends, 2009). Dramatic differences are also apparent across racial/ethnic groups. Although less than 3% of White adolescent girls ages 15 to 19 gave birth in 2006, more than 6% of African American and more than 8% of Hispanic adolescent girls ages 15 to 19 did. Moreover, although the notable overall declines in adolescent parenthood might seem cause for hope or celebration, a contrasting trend alters this perception. In 1960, only 15% of adolescent births occurred outside of marriage. By 2006, this percentage had increased nearly six-fold, to 84% (Holcombe, Peterson, & Manlove, 2009). Thus, early parenthood today almost always occurs outside the context of a coresident, marital union. Instead, young parents experience a range of family forms, with many young mothers maintaining coresidence with their own parent(s) for at least the first few years after childbirth.

Entering parenthood during adolescence has been considered a significant risk for development of both young mothers and their children (for reviews, see Coley & Chase-Lansdale, 1998; M. R. Moore & Brooks-Gunn, 2002). Although their developmental trajectories vary (e.g., Oxford et al., 2005), on average adolescent mothers differ from those who come from similar backgrounds but delay childbirth. For example, in adulthood, young mothers are more likely to have financial problems and socioeconomic instability, worse mental health, and less stable romantic relationships than those who delay childbearing (Jaffee, 2002). Children of adolescent mothers also have an increased risk of negative outcomes. Although in infancy few differences emerge, in the preschool years, children of adolescent mothers tend to have lower cognitive abilities and more social and behavioral problems than children of older mothers (M. R. Moore & Brooks-Gunn, 2002). These small but consistent differences likely set the stage for a negative pathway through childhood, with multiple untoward consequences seen by young adulthood. For example, children of teenage mothers are more likely to become teenage parents themselves, leave school prematurely, be unemployed, and become involved in the criminal justice system (Jaffee, Caspi, Moffitt, Belsky, & Silva, 2001; Pogarsky, Thornberry, & Lizotte, 2006). Although some of these differences in outcomes can be linked to preexisting conditions associated with early childbearing, the demands and consequences of early parenthood operate in the context of, and work in tandem with, such preexisting characteristics to increase the likelihood of these negative outcomes (Jaffee et al., 2001).

As in all families, the parenting of young mothers is likely a key contributor to the developmental trajectories of their children (see Bornstein, 2002). Yet, adolescent mothers do not function in isolation but are part of a larger family system that works collectively to raise children (Minuchin, 1974; see also Chapters 1, 4, and 13, this volume). McHale, Kuersten-Hogan, and Rao (2004) argued that too often studies examining parenting focus exclusively on mothers, ignoring important aspects of coparenting and family systems. In families with adolescent mothers, the coparenting relationships are often more complicated than in many families with older mothers. Although some biological fathers establish themselves as coparents, more often the young mothers' own parents, especially their mothers, serve in this role. Within the large literature on adolescent mothers, relatively limited attention has been paid to the coparenting roles of fathers and grandmothers, with only a few studies moving beyond a simple acknowledgement of the presence or absence of coparenting figures in the household.

We argue that to truly understand the influence of coparents in adolescent mother families, we need to expand knowledge on the quality and processes within these relationships. Delineating factors leading to positive coparenting relationships and understanding the effects of coparenting on young parents and their children also need attention. In this chapter, we summarize the extant literature on coparenting within adolescent mother families, noting consistent findings, assessing conflicts in the field, and identifying numerous questions in need of further research. We note that almost no research in the field of adolescent parents uses the term *coparenting* or explicitly defines central constructs in the language of coparenting, such as parental alliance, cooperation, or mentoring of parenting skills (e.g., Apfel & Seitz, 1991; Futris & Schoppe-Sullivan, 2007). Rather, much of the literature in this arena focuses on fathers' and grandmothers' coresidence, quality of relationship with young mothers, role as a support person for young mothers, and global involvement in child rearing. In this chapter, we review this broader arena of research on constructs related to coparenting, noting in particular studies that address more targeted aspects of coparenting such as alliances and cooperation.

FATHERS AS COPARENTS

Unmarried young fathers' engagement in coparenting their children born to adolescent mothers has not always been easy to estimate. There is general agreement that a substantial portion of young fathers have limited and sometimes no engagement with their children and their children's mothers and, hence, no involvement in meaningful coparenting. Data have also indicated that among fathers who start off their parenting tenure engaged, a good proportion disengage over the first few years of their child's life. Perhaps in response to these patterns, much research in this field has taken a more simplistic view of family processes, for instance focusing on fathers' contact with their children and continued involvement with mothers. In one of the earliest studies to examine a nationally representative sample of young fathers completed in the early 1980s, Lerman (1993) found that 50% were not married to the child's mother at the time of birth and that among the single fathers, the proportion with no contact with their child nearly tripled between early and middle childhood.

Other longitudinal studies of smaller samples have reported that only about one in 10 young fathers coreside with their children for a decade or more (Furstenberg & Harris, 1993; Howard, Lefever, Borkowski, & Whitman, 2006). A somewhat more optimistic window into father contact is provided by analyses assessing the proportion of young fathers who retain regular contact with their children through the 1st or 2nd decade, either through coresidence or regular visiting. In this case, the proportion of committed fathers has been estimated at between 35% and 55% (Furstenberg & Harris, 1993; Howard et al., 2006). Recent data from the Fragile Families and Child

Wellbeing Study (see Chapter 4) generally echo these findings but also provide important indications that unmarried fathers' engagement with their children may be especially likely and visible during the child s early years.

Other studies that have focused primarily on fathers' support to mothers rather than on direct parenting involvement draw a less positive picture. One such study, which assessed a sample of adolescent mothers during pregnancy and then 3 years later, found that fewer than 20% of adolescent mothers nominated the father of their child as a primary source of social support in emotional and practical realms at both time points; by the follow-up, fathers were nominated as sources of support less frequently than maternal grandmothers, closest friends, or new male partners (Gee & Rhodes, 2003).

Correlates of Young Fathers' Coparenting

Beyond delineating the basic patterns of young fathers' connections to their children, the empirical literature on coparenting also has sought to identify correlates of fathers' engagement. In the 1980s and 1990s, rich qualitative or mixed-methods studies were conducted by Mercer Sullivan (1985, 1989, 1993), Frank Furstenberg (1995), and Elijah Anderson (1993). These detailed portrayals of young fathers identified a number of themes important in understanding the barriers and supports available for coparenting in adolescent parent families. Strengths and supports included family and community pressures and shared expectations for young fathers to be involved with their children and to provide both monetary and emotional support and care. Sullivan (1993) argued that specific expectations regarding the optimal manner of fulfilling fathering responsibilities differed by race/ethnicity. Latino and White communities supported early coresidence and marriage, whereas African American communities were more supportive of young parents retaining separate residences but young fathers contributing regular care and economic support (Sullivan, 1993). Other studies have replicated this pattern, arguing that young African American fathers' engagement with their children appears less contingent on their romantic relationship with the child's mother than in other racial/ethnic groups (Florsheim et al., 2003).

These earlier qualitative studies also identified a variety of barriers to fathers' involvement as coparents, including (a) dissolution of the romantic relationships between parents and intrusive forces of new romantic relationships and multipartner fertility, (b) disruptive forces of extended family, (c) fathers' limited economic resources, and (d) dangers of alternate economic activities such as street crime and drug sales (Furstenberg, 1995; Sullivan, 1985, 1989, 1993; see also Edin & Kefalas, 2005). The importance of these barriers has since been replicated in quantitative studies.

Couple Relationship Quality and Relationship Stability Versus Dissolution

Perhaps the most replicated finding in the study of young parents is that dissolution of the couple's romantic relationship or high relationship conflict at the time of pregnancy and childbirth is the primary force prohibiting young fathers' continued involvement in parenting. A number of short-term longitudinal studies have found that a couple's relationship quality prior to childbirth is related both to the likelihood of fathers' engagement with their children and to the quality of fathers' parenting in the child's early years (Coley & Chase-Lansdale, 1999; Cutrona, Hessling, Bacon, & Russell, 1998; Fagan, Bernd, & Whiteman, 2007; Florsheim et al., 2003; D. R. Moore, Florsheim, & Butner, 2007; for a conflicting view, see Kalil, Ziol-Guest, & Coley, 2005). For example, Florsheim and colleagues found that hostility in adolescent mother–father relationships during pregnancy foreshadowed fathers' hostile parenting, physically punitive parenting, and risk of child abuse behavior with their infants 2 years later (Florsheim & Smith, 2005; D. R. Moore & Florsheim, 2008).

The Role of New Partners and Extended Family

Fewer empirical studies have attended to how other adults, including extended family members and new romantic partners in the lives of young mothers, influence biological fathers' involvement. Qualitative studies have suggested that extended family members, particularly the maternal and paternal grandmothers of the new child, may play a central role in either encouraging or prohibiting the young couple's continued relationship and fathers' involvement in coparenting (Anderson, 1993; Furstenberg, 1995; Sullivan, 1993). Within quantitative studies that have addressed this issue, there have been conflicting results. For example, in studies examining the relationship between young mothers and their own mothers, there have been some suggestions that grandmothers act as gatekeepers and either enable or waylay young fathers' involvement. Some studies have reported support for the hypothesis that coresidence and coparenting by grandmothers are linked with diminished paternal involvement (Gee & Rhodes, 2003; Kalil et al., 2005), although other studies report nonsignificant links (Coley & Chase-Lansdale, 1999).

Findings are more consistent when research focuses on the quality rather than just the quantity of family relationships or fathers' parenting. For instance, greater support from both mothers' and fathers' parents has been linked with more high-quality parenting behaviors among adolescent parents, including lower parenting stress, less physically punitive parenting, and lower risk of child abuse (Fagan et al., 2007; Florsheim et al., 2003). A third focus has been the quality of the grandmother's relationship with the father, with results suggesting that better relationship quality is linked with higher levels of father involvement (Gavin et al., 2002).

In considering this research on a range of family relationships, we note that greater attention is needed to discerning directionality and attending to potential selection effects. For example, one possible process is that high-quality parent relationships may promote fathers' active engagement in coparenting young children; an alternate argument is that fathers who are committed to and involved in coparenting will work harder at maintaining collaborative relationships with mothers and extended family members, particularly when mothers and fathers are not cohabiting or romantically involved (Hernandez, Coley, & Lewin-Bizan, 2006; see also Chapter 4, this volume). Few existing studies have incorporated conceptual models and used data adequate to test complex transactional models such as this with young parents.

In addition to the importance of mother–father relationships and extended family roles, recent data has suggested the potential import of new romantic pairings among adolescent mothers or young fathers, although empirical research in this arena is limited. One study of a predominantly White, rural population of adolescent mothers found that 18 months after the child's birth, young fathers were most likely to remain involved with their child when they retained a romantic relationship with the mother and least likely to remain involved when the mother was in no romantic relationship, with fathers showing moderate continued involvement when the mother had a new romantic partner (Cutrona et al., 1998). Similarly, a study of predominantly adolescent African American mothers found that a new residential partner actually predicted a very small increased likelihood of biological fathers remaining highly involved with their children over the first 3 years (Coley & Chase-Lansdale, 1999). These small quantitative studies are provocative and suggest that the role of new partners is complex and deserving of further study. One possibility is that selection factors may play some role. That is, young parents who can create and maintain new stable romantic relationships may also have better relational skills. Such skills may be what allow them to cooperate in parenting their child together outside of continued romantic relationships, even in the face of new partnerings. Perceptions and motivations of biological fathers in such families are also in need of further study.

Fathers' Economic Resources

Quantitative studies have borne out links hinted at in qualitative studies of fathers' economic and psychosocial resources and their engagement in coparenting with their young children. Adolescent fathers' financial hardship has been linked to lower relationship quality and parenting quality across numerous studies (Coley & Chase-Lansdale, 1999; Danziger & Radin, 1990; Wiemann, Agurcia, Rickert, Berenson, & Volk, 2006). This said, there are also suggestions that this link may be attenuated among African American and Latino youth, perhaps in relation to the more normative experience of economic hardship among minority populations (Florsheim, Moore, Zollinger, MacDonald, & Sumida, 1999).

Fathers' Antisocial Behaviors

Another barrier to fathers' engagement in coparenting is their involvement in criminal activities, drug use/sales, violence, or gangs. Engagement in such activities has been linked with lower father support to adolescent mothers at the time of their child's birth (Wiemann et al., 2006). Research has also shown that conduct disorder and substance use by both fathers and mothers are linked to lower relationship quality and higher likelihood of violence within the couple relationship (D. R. Moore et al., 2007). These findings indicate that parents' antisocial behaviors interfere with healthy parental relationships and quality parenting. Engagement in such behaviors also is associated with poorer child functioning (Jaffee, Moffitt, Caspi, & Taylor, 2003), suggesting that parental engagement in antisocial or criminal activities is detrimental to children's well-being through numerous mechanisms. It is possible, however, that positive parental relationships or parenting behaviors may sometimes mitigate the negative effects of parents' characteristics (Coley, Carrano, & Lewin-Bizan, 2010). For example, Futris and Schoppe-Sullivan (2007) found that a strong parental alliance was particularly important among couples with moderate barriers to fathers' continued involvement in parenting, whereas parental alliance was not important for fathers with very low or very high barriers.

In sum, research has identified a number of economic, psychosocial, and relational factors that may act as supporting or prohibiting forces affecting young fathers' engagement in coparenting. Programs and policies seeking to increase fathers' positive engagement in coparenting must be aware of and attend to such barriers, incorporating mechanisms to support relational strengths while at the same time attending to economic, behavioral, and relational barriers that inhibit fathers' engagement. Research needs to continue to find ways to involve traditionally understudied populations so as to create more generalizable findings; make use of longitudinal, prospective methods; and pay greater attention to directionality and to the risk of bias from unmeasured factors in delineating these complex relationships. Such research, unpacking the complex processes in families, will help to better inform efforts to increase young fathers' positive engagement in coparenting even in the face of contextual stressors and barriers.

Effects of Fathers' Coparenting

In addition to understanding the precursors to young fathers' engagement in coparenting, another theme in the literature concerns the effects of coparenting—that is, whether father engagement in coparenting has beneficial effects for young parents and children. Research is much more limited in this arena. There is a consistent pattern indicating that the collaborative involvement of young fathers in parenting roles has the potential to improve the well-being of adolescent mothers and the functioning of their families, though results in studies to date have been modest in size. For example, Kalil et al. (2005) reported that diminished levels of involvement by fathers in coparenting over the course of a year predicted increased parenting stress among adolescent mothers, though the decreases did not predict changes in maternal depression or mastery. In other work, Gee and Rhodes (2003) found that although fathers' support to mothers did not play a protective role, conflict and stress in the mother–father relationship were important, predicting greater symptoms of maternal depression and anxiety. Also notable in this study was the finding that high support from grandmothers served a buffering role, reducing this linkage.

Longitudinal studies that have followed young families for a decade or more also have noted links with children's development (Howard et al., 2006). Furstenberg and Harris (1993), for instance, noted that although fathers' contact throughout childhood was not strongly linked to children's long-term success, children who maintained close emotional attachments to their fathers showed better economic and psychosocial functioning at the end of adolescence. Very few studies focusing exclusively on adolescent parents have carefully assessed the quality of fathers' coparenting and effects on children's development over time, however, and this represents an important arena for new research.

GRANDMOTHERS AS COPARENTS

In contrast to fathers, who are less likely to coreside or coparent, grandmothers of children born to adolescent mothers show much higher rates of involvement with coparenting across numerous family forms. In fact, the majority of adolescent mothers choose to live with their own mothers, at least while their child is young (Acs & Koball, 2003). Patterns of coresidence appear to differ by race and ethnicity, with African American teen mothers more likely to live with their family of origin than either Hispanic or European American teen mothers (Eshbaugh & Luze, 2007). These differences may help explain why much of the research on grandmother coparenting among adolescent mother families has focused on African Americans. It is important to note that across ethnic groups and living arrangements, grand-mothers often function as coparents, providing significant support to young mothers in the form of material aid, positive feedback, and direct care of children (e.g., Spieker & Bensley, 1994; Contreras, Lopez, Rivera-Mosquera, Raymond-Smith, & Rothstein, 1999).

Coresidence

A substantial body of research has assessed correlates of grand-mothers' coresidence with adolescent mothers and their children. In studies with adult mothers, coresidence of grandmothers in single-parent house-holds is generally positive for children's developmental outcomes, promoting mental health and behavioral adjustment similar to children and adolescents in other two-parent households (see Chapter 4). However, the effect of grandmother coresidence is more ambiguous among families with adolescent mothers.

Many studies have reported that young mothers living with their own mothers show improved educational and occupational outcomes over time compared with those living alone or with partners (e.g., Furstenberg, Brooks-Gunn, & Morgan, 1987; Gordon, Chase-Lansdale, & Brooks-Gunn, 2004). Yet, the benefits of grandmother coresidence do not necessarily trickle down to either mothers' parenting or children's functioning. Some studies have found coresiding young mothers to provide a more nurturing environment for their children than mothers living independently (e.g., Furstenberg et al., 1987; Leadbeater & Bishop, 1994). Yet, in other studies grandmother coresidence has been linked to lower levels of maternal warmth, more problematic parenting, poorer parenting attitudes, and less parenting confidence among young mothers (Black & Nitz, 1996; Chase-Lansdale, Brooks-Gunn, & Zamsky, 1994; East & Felice, 1996).

Similarly, clear patterns have not emerged to indicate whether coresidence with grandmothers is beneficial or harmful to infants and young children of teenage mothers. Some studies have shown evidence of better cognitive and socioemotional functioning among children in mother–grandmother house-holds (e.g., Furstenberg et al., 1987; Leadbeater & Bishop, 1994), whereas other studies have found poorer cognitive and physical development in toddlers of adolescent mothers in multigenerational households (e.g., Black & Nitz, 1996). There are many possible explanations for these mixed findings, including effects of preexisting factors that may lead adolescent mothers to decide to live with their family of origin (Gordon et al., 2004), differences by economic conditions (e.g., Hogan, Hao, & Parish, 1990), or interpersonal factors within the family (Coley & Chase-Lansdale, 1998; Kalil, Spencer, Spieker, & Gilchrist, 1998).

Coparenting

Although coresidence is assumed to be a proxy for mothers and grand-mothers working together in parenting, this assumption may not be warranted. For example, grandmothers who live outside the home are known to provide frequent child care assistance (e.g., Smith, 2000) and may be highly involved in the lives of young mothers and their children. In addition, there is variability in shared caregiving responsibilities between coresiding mothers and grandmothers. In their qualitative study of 119 African American adolescent mothers with 18-month-old children, Apfel and Seitz (1991) found four distinct coparenting arrangements. The supported primary parent model was found in about 20% of these families, in which young mothers clearly had primary responsibility for their young child's care and grandparents provided regular support in the form of visits, financial help, babysitting, and communication. In about 10% of families, grandmothers replaced young mothers as the primary caregiver (parental replacement model). In both of these models, the primary parenting role was fulfilled by one person, the young mother or the grandmother.

Cooperative coparenting was more apparent in the parental supplemental and parental apprentice models. About half of the families in this study fit a parental supplemental model (Apfel & Seitz, 1991), in which grandmothers and young mothers shared responsibilities for caring for the young child, whether grandmothers lived in the home or not (see also Oberlander, Black, & Starr, 2007). Finally, a parental apprentice model was found in about 10% of families, in which grandmothers actively mentored daughters in their development as a parent with the expectation that, with time, young mothers would become the primary parent. Follow-ups with this sample 5 years later found that the parental supplemental model was still common (seen in about one third of families), but the parental apprentice model was no longer present (Apfel & Seitz, 1996).

This research also indicated that grandmother support and coparenting may have long-term benefits for young mothers' parenting. Specifically, when young mothers had either no responsibility or all the responsibility for parenting their infant child, there was a higher likelihood of the child being raised by someone other than their mother when he or she was 12 years old. In fact, by this age, 28% of young mothers were no longer involved in parenting their children (Apfel & Seitz, 1996). Results suggest a curvilinear relationship between grandmothers' coparenting support and young mothers' success as parents. Other studies have found negative associations between grandmother provision of child care and adolescent mothers' parenting. For example, grandmothers who provided more child care had adolescent daughters who were less nurturing toward their children, had lower empathy for their child, and had less understanding of child development and family roles (Culp, Culp, Noland, & Anderson, 2006; East & Felice, 1996; Oyserman, Radin, & Saltz, 1994). Thus, helping young mothers maintain a balance in coparenting with their mothers may be an effective strategy to build their parenting skills and increase their comfort in the parenting role.

The research discussed previously focused on the quantity of support or coparenting provided by grandmothers. Fewer studies have examined directly the quality of grandmothers' parenting with their grandchildren and whether there are substantial similarities between grandmothers' and mothers' parenting quality. Associations have been found between both positive (e.g., nurturance; Oyserman et al., 1994) and negative (e.g., negative affect, authoritarian parenting; Chase-Lansdale et al., 1994) aspects of grandmothers' and young mothers' parenting of young children. Typically, these associations have been interpreted directionally, as grandmothers influencing adolescent mothers' parenting. However, additional research is needed to follow these patterns over time to disentangle the direction of effect. If such studies were to indeed find that grandmothers' parenting influences the mothers' parenting, this may be a possible target for intervention efforts to increase positive parenting.

Grandmothers' parenting also seems to be influenced by coresidence and the young mothers' age. Among families with a younger mother, grandmothers were observed to interact more positively with their 3-year-old grandchild when they lived in the same household compared with those not living with the child. The reverse was true in families with older mothers (Chase-Lansdale et al., 1994). This highlights the complexities in these coparenting relationships and the need to disentangle multiple factors in the family context that may influence how effective such relationships are. One potentially important factor is the quality of the mother–grandmother relationship, which is complex because the grandmother is both a mother to the daughter as well as a coparent.

Support and Conflict in Mother–Grandmother Relationship

As in mother–father coparenting relationships, the quality of the mother–grandmother relationship can be conceptualized in at least two ways: (a) with a broad view toward the overall quality of the mother–grandmother relationship, and (b) with a more narrow view toward the quality of the coparenting relationship. A number of studies have assessed global aspects of adolescent mother–grandmother relationships. Adolescent mothers who perceived their relationship with their own mothers to be more supportive and less conflictual appear to function better both psychologically and in their parenting. Specifically, when young mothers felt their own mothers supported their pregnancy and the decision to become a parent, or when they received more caregiving assistance, they reported better mental health (Barratt, Roach, Morgan, & Colbert, 1996; Shanok & Miller, 2007). Conversely, young mothers who had a high degree of conflict with their own mothers had worse psychological outcomes (Caldwell, Antonucci, & Jackson, 1998; Davis, 2002; Davis & Rhodes, 1994), with conflict in the grandmother–mother relationship being a more significant predictor of mothers' mental health than grandmother support. However, the influence of negative family relationships may vary by living arrangements. Kalil et al. (1998) found that young mothers who reported the lowest level of depressive symptoms were those coresiding with their mothers and reporting positive family cohesion, whereas those who reported the highest level of depressive symptoms were also coresiding with their mothers, but in conditions of more negative family cohesion.

Evidence is accruing that the influence of mother–grandmother relationship quality also extends to the mothers' parenting and grandchildren's outcomes. African American young mothers who experienced supportive mother–grandmother relationships reported more parenting competence, less parenting stress, and fewer negative attitudes that are related to child abuse (Florsheim et al., 2003; Oberlander et al., 2007). Conversely, when the mother-grandmother relationship was more conflictual, young African American mothers with 6-month-old children were found to have lower parenting satisfaction (Hess, Papas, & Black, 2002). In one of the few studies considering the link to children's outcomes, Sommer et al. (2000) found that when pregnant adolescents reported more support from their mothers prenatally, 3 years later their children had better adaptive behaviors, although no differences were found in other aspects of child cognitive and socioemotional outcomes. Thus, having a more supportive, less conflictual mother–grandmother relationship seems to influence how young mothers are faring psychologically, how they are parenting, and perhaps how their children are faring.

Fewer studies have considered how mother–grandmother coparenting quality may influence young mothers. Some have speculated that the shared caregiving evident between many young mothers and grandmothers may lead to conflict regarding parenting practices and discipline (e.g., Coley & Chase-Lansdale, 1998). Yet, this was not found in a sample of African American adolescent mothers, in which the level of conflict between young mothers and grandmothers did not differ on the basis of whether they shared caregiving (Oberlander et al., 2007). However, specific conflict over child-rearing issues has been linked to parenting stress when children were 6, 12, or 24 months old (Spencer, Kalil, Larson, Spieker, & Gilchrist, 2002). Similarly, mothers who reported greater disagreements over parenting also had higher levels of depressive symptoms (Kalil et al., 1998). How aspects of the coparenting alliance between mothers and grandmothers (e.g., cooperation, conflict) are linked to specific parenting and child outcomes has not been explored, and this is a promising area for future research. Results suggest that interventions targeting improving the quality of the global relationship as well as the parenting alliance between mothers and grandmothers would increase adolescent mothers' mental health and, subsequently, parenting and children's development.

Mothers' Individuation and Autonomy

As stated earlier, the relationship between adolescent mothers and their own mothers goes beyond their shared roles as caregivers. As adolescent mothers are still maturing, their mothers are still actively parenting them. Key milestones of adolescence include establishing one's identity and becoming an autonomous adult (Erikson, 1963). Adolescent mothers are likely to struggle with these milestones because they have transitioned early to an adult role while still needing to rely on their mothers for extensive support. Young mothers whose own mothers are able to balance respecting their daughter's growing autonomy while providing help in the area of parenting are more effective as parents of infants and preschool-age children (Hess et al., 2002; Pittman, Wakschlag, Chase-Lansdale, & Brooks-Gunn, in press). Similarly, adolescent mothers who successfully negotiate identity development and are able to psychologically separate from their family of origin appear to be more effective in their parenting and to have infants with more advanced mental development (Aiello & Lancaster, 2007). Overall, grandmothers who support young mothers' independence while remaining emotionally available appear to facilitate their daughters' assumption of their adult roles including that of a parent. Helping grandmothers find this balance would be a key way to improve this coparent relationship.

Influences on the Grandmother

Few studies have considered the impact of young mothers' pregnancy and resulting parenthood on grandmothers. Burton and Bengston (1985) found that African American grandmothers who transitioned early to this role had significantly more discomfort than those who transitioned on time, primarily because of the increased parenting obligations related to both their own children and their grandchildren. Similarly, Sadler and Clemmens (2004) interviewed young grandmothers who were living with their daughters and found themes of identity confusion, experiences of increased stress in early grandparenthood, as well as limited coping resources, but also considerable pride and joy in grandchildren. Grandmothers who provided more direct care to children of their adolescent daughters reported more stress and less marital satisfaction (Culp et al., 2006). Like grandparents who become custodial parents to their grandchildren, these grandmothers appear to have worse mental and physical health and experience more stress related to their multiple roles (Minkler & Fuller-Thomson, 1999).

It is unclear what relational factors contribute to grandmothers' well-being in families with adolescent mothers. Like young mothers, grandmothers may benefit from a more positive mother–grandmother relationship. The majority of grandmothers placed their daughters within their social support network and reported positive reciprocal relationships with them, perceiving more support and less conflict over child-rearing issues than their daughters perceived (Caldwell et al., 1998). Yet, Sadler and Clemmens (2004) reported multiple domains in which grandmothers reported conflict in their relationship with their daughters, including child-rearing decisions, time with friends, household chores, and teens' choices and priorities. In the Caldwell et al. (1998) report, grandmothers who perceived greater conflict, but not less support, in their relationships with their daughters reported more depressive symptoms. More studies examining factors linked to grandmothers' mental health may also help explain differences in their effectiveness as a coparent.

Grandfathers

Although most research has focused on the influence and role of grandmothers in coparenting alliances, grandfathers are also present in many multigenerational households with young mothers. Perhaps because traditionally women take on the role of child rearing, however, most studies have not considered how grandfathers contribute to the family system. The few studies that have suggest that there is value in examining the role grandfathers play in these families. Davis, Rhodes, and Hamilton-Leaks (1997) identified approximately a quarter of a larger sample of adolescents who had both grandmother and grandfather figures as part of their support network. In this subgroup, the support of both grandmothers and grandfathers each uniquely predicted lower levels of depression in young mothers. In addition, paternal support seemed to be influential even when the grandfather was not living with the young mother. In another study, young mothers were found to be more nurturing toward their child when living in grandfather–grandmother-present homes compared with grandmother-only homes (Oyserman et al., 1994). Furthermore, in grandfather-present homes, young mothers' nurturance was more strongly associated with the grandfathers' than the grandmothers' nurturance toward the baby. The roles that grandfathers may play in multicoparent relationships alongside both mothers and grandmothers (see Chapter 1) should be considered both in interventions targeting adolescent mothers and in future research studies.

LIMITATIONS AND FUTURE DIRECTIONS

Although there is a sizable literature base on adolescent parents and a fair number of studies including information on fathers and grandmothers, we argue that the empirical knowledge base on coparenting among these families is still extremely limited. As addressed previously, research that looks at the quality of coparenting relationships within both mother–father and mother–grandmother pairs is relatively rare. Indeed, to our knowledge there are no standardized instruments for assessing aspects of coparenting within this population. Existing studies have hence relied on a broad range of measures, nearly all incorporating a very small number of questions with limited psychometric information to assess data quality. One of the few exceptions is Baker, McHale, Strozier, and Cecil's (2010) report of an intergenerational coparenting rating system developed for use with incarcerated mothers.

On a related note, most existing research in this field has relied principally or solely on the reports of young mothers. Needed are studies that systematically include both fathers' and grandparents' reports on their experiences and perceptions and that use a range of data collection methods including observational and interview-based approaches. When these alternate methods are used, patterns of findings can vary by reporter (Baker et al., 2010). Multimethod efforts will allow researchers to determine how data from various sources are associated both with each other and with child outcomes. Such advances in study methodology will promote a better understanding of how coparenting affects adolescent mothers and their children.

A related concern is that much of the research in this area has been based on small, nonrepresentative samples, limiting generalizability as well as statistical power. As noted in Chapter 4, research on young fathers has been especially prone to suffer from low response rates and thus the attendant limitations of selection bias and limited generalizability (see also Coley, 2001). Further, because many studies have focused on just one ethnic group, most often African Americans, we remain limited in our understanding of how universal patterns of findings may be. In addition, as is the case with most of the literature on coparenting in the general population (McHale et al., 2004), almost no research on coparenting within adolescent mother families has examined young mothers and their families beyond the first few years after the child's birth (for exceptions, see Furstenberg, 1995; Furstenberg & Harris, 1993).

As Apfel and Seitz documented (1996), coparenting patterns are likely to shift over the course of the mothers' and children's development. Although the sheer prevalence of multigenerational households, particularly in low-income and minority families, suggests that grandparents are likely to continue to be involved in the life of these young families (Lugalia & Overturf, 2004), the way coparenting is negotiated may change over time. Such changes would likely vary both as a function of earlier experiences with the coparenting alliance as well as children's changing developmental needs (see Chapter 1). Normatively, only about half of young fathers remain intensively involved in parenting over time, and new romantic partners may move in and out of coparenting roles with mothers. Relatedly, some young mothers develop increased parenting competence over time and later move away from coparenting with their own mothers. Other mothers maintain the status quo, while still others continue to move further away from a parenting role over time. For these reasons, large-scale longitudinal studies using strong measures of multiple aspects of the family system are needed if we are to truly begin to understand coparenting in families with young mothers over time.

Finally, very little research has carefully assessed the development of children in adolescent mother families, carefully attending to how coparental relationships with fathers and grandparents can most effectively promote children's healthy developmental trajectories. Hence, much remains to be learned, though collectively the research findings we have reviewed provide evidence that targeting the development of healthy coparenting relationships with fathers and/or grandparents stands to be a promising avenue for intervention efforts. Strengthening coparenting alliances may help adolescent mothers to more effectively fulfill their role as parent and thereby influence positive developmental trajectories in their children.

REFERENCES

Acs, G., & Koball, H. (2003, June). *TANF and the status of teen mothers under age 18* (Report No. A-62 in Series, New Federalism: Issues and Options for States). Washington, DC: The Urban Institute. Retrieved from http://www.urban.org/publications/310796.html.

Aiello, R., & Lancaster, S. (2007). Influence of adolescent maternal characteristics on infant development. *Infant Mental Health Journal, 28,* 496–516. doi:10.1002/imhj.20150

Anderson, E. (1993). Sex codes and family life among poor inner-city youths. In R. I. Lerman & T. J. Ooms (Eds.), *Young unwed fathers: Changing roles and emerging policies* (pp. 74–98). Philadelphia, PA: Temple University Press.

Apfel, N. H., & Seitz, V. (1991). Four models of adolescent mother-grandmother relationships in Black inner-city families. *Family Relations, 40,* 421–429. doi:10.2307/584899

Apfel, N., & Seitz, V. (1996). African American adolescent mothers, their families, and their daughters: A longitudinal perspective over twelve years. In B. J. R. Leadbeater & N. Way (Eds.), *Urban girls: Resisting stereotypes, creating identities* (pp. 149–170). New York, NY: New York University Press.

Baker, J. K., McHale, J., Strozier, A., & Cecil, D. K. (2010). Mother-grandmother coparenting relationships in families with incarcerated mothers: A pilot investigation. *Family Process, 49,* 165–184.

Barratt, M. S., Roach, M. A., Morgan, K. M., & Colbert, K. K. (1996). Adjustment to motherhood by single adolescents. *Family Relations: Journal of Applied Family and Child Studies, 45,* 209–215.

Black, M. M., & Nitz, K. (1996). Grandmother co-residence, parenting, and child development among low income, urban teen mothers. *The Journal of Adolescent Health, 18,* 218–226. doi:10.1016/1054-139X(95)00168-R

Bornstein, M. H. (Ed.). (2002). *Handbook of parenting* (2nd ed.). Mahwah, NJ: Erlbaum.

Burton, L. M., & Bengston, V. L. (1985). Black grandmothers: Issues of timing and continuity of roles. In V. L. Bengston & J. Robertson (Eds.), *Grandparenthood* (pp. 61–77). Beverly Hills, CA: Sage.

Caldwell, C. H., Antonucci, T. C., & Jackson, J. S. (1998). Supportive/conflictual family relations and depressive symptomatology: Teenage mother and grandmother perspectives. *Family Relations: Interdisciplinary Journal of Applied Family Studies, 47,* 395–402.

Chase-Lansdale, P. L., Brooks-Gunn, J., & Zamsky, E. S. (1994). Young African-American multigenerational families in poverty: Quality of mothering and grandmothering. *Child Development, 65,* 373–393. doi:10.2307/1131390

Child Trends. (2009, September). *Facts at a glance. A fact sheet reporting national, state and city trends in teen childbearing* (Publication 2009-25). Washington DC: Author. Retrieved from http://www.childtrends.org/Files//Child_Trends-2009_08_31_FG_Edition.pdf

Coley, R. L. (2001). (In)visible men: Emerging research on low-income, unmarried, and minority fathers. *American Psychologist, 56,* 743–753. doi:10.1037/0003-066X.56.9.743

Coley, R. L., Carrano, J., & Lewin-Bizan, S. (2010). *Unpacking links between fathers' antisocial behaviors and children's behavior problems: Direct, indirect, and synergistic effects with harsh parenting.* Unpublished manuscript.

Coley, R. L., & Chase-Lansdale, P. L. (1998). Adolescent pregnancy and parenthood: Recent evidence and future directions. *American Psychologist, 53,* 152–166. doi:10.1037/0003-066X.53.2.152

Coley, R. L., & Chase-Lansdale, P. L. (1999). Stability and change in paternal involvement among urban African American fathers. *Journal of Family Psychology, 13,* 416–435. doi:10.1037/0893-3200.13.3.416

Contreras, J. M., Lopez, I. R., Rivera-Mosquera, E. T., Raymond-Smith, L., & Rothstein, K. (1999). Social support and adjustment among Puerto Rican adolescent mothers: The moderating effect of acculturation. *Journal of Family Psychology, 13,* 228–243. doi:10.1037/0893-3200.13.2.228

Culp, A. M., Culp, R. E., Noland, D., & Anderson, J. W. (2006). Stress, marital satisfaction, and child care provision by mothers of adolescent mothers: Considerations to make when providing services. *Children and Youth Services Review, 28,* 673–681. doi:10.1016/j.childyouth.2005.06.009

Cutrona, C. E., Hessling, R. M., Bacon, P. L., & Russell, D. W. (1998). Predictors and correlates of continuing involvement with the baby's father among adolescent mothers. *Journal of Family Psychology, 12,* 369–387. doi:10.1037/0893-3200.12.3.369

Danziger, S. K., & Radin, N. (1990). Absent does not equal uninvolved: Predictors of fathering in teen mother families. *Journal of Marriage and the Family, 52,* 636–642. doi:10.2307/352930

Davis, A. A. (2002). Younger and older African American adolescent mothers' relationships with their mothers and female peers. *Journal of Adolescent Research, 17,* 491–508. doi:10.1177/0743558402175004

Davis, A. A., & Rhodes, J. E. (1994). African-American teenage mothers and their mothers: An analysis of supportive and problematic interactions. *Journal of Community Psychology, 22,* 12–20. doi:10.1002/1520-6629(199401)22:1<12::AID-JCOP2290220103>3.0.CO;2-7

Davis, A. A., Rhodes, J. E., & Hamilton-Leaks, J. (1997). When both parents may be a source of support and problems: An analysis of pregnant and parenting female African American adolescents' relationships with their mothers and fathers. *Journal of Research on Adolescence, 7,* 331–348. doi:10.1207/s15327795jra0703_5

East, P. L., & Felice, M. E. (1996). *Adolescent pregnancy and parenting: Findings from a racially diverse sample.* Mahwah, NJ: Erlbaum.

Edin, K., & Kefalas, M. (2005). *Promises I can keep: Why poor women put motherhood before marriage.* Berkeley, CA: University of California Press.

Erikson, E. H. (1963). *Childhood and society* (2nd ed.). New York, NY: Norton.

Eshbaugh, E. M., & Luze, G. J. (2007). Adolescent and adult low-income mothers: How do needs and resources differ? *Journal of Community Psychology, 35,* 1037–1052. doi:10.1002/jcop.20210

Fagan, J., Bernd, E., & Whiteman, V. (2007). Adolescent fathers' parenting stress, social support, and involvement with infants. *Journal of Research on Adolescence, 17,* 1–22. doi:10.1111/j.1532-7795.2007.00510.x

Florsheim, P., Moore, D., Zollinger, L., MacDonald, J., & Sumida, E. (1999). The transition to parenthood among adolescent fathers and their partners: Does antisocial behavior predict problems in parenting? *Applied Developmental Science, 3,* 178–191. doi:10.1207/s1532480xads0303_4

Florsheim, P., & Smith, A. (2005). Expectant adolescent couples' relations and subsequent parenting behavior. *Infant Mental Health Journal, 26,* 533–548. doi:10.1002/imhj.20076

Florsheim, P., Sumida, E., McCann, C., Winstanley, M., Fukui, R., Seefeldt, T., & Moore, D. (2003). The transition to parenthood among young African American and Latino couples: Relational predictors of risk for parental dysfunction. *Journal of Family Psychology, 17,* 65–79. doi:10.1037/0893-3200.17.1.65

Furstenberg, F. F. (1995). Fathering in the inner city: Paternal participation and public policy. In W. Marsiglio (Ed.), *Fatherhood: Contemporary theory, research, and social policy* (pp. 119–147). Thousand Oaks, CA: Sage.

Furstenberg, F. F., Brooks-Gunn, J., & Morgan, S. P. (1987). *Adolescent mothers in later life*. Cambridge, MA: Cambridge University Press. doi:10.1017/CBO9780511752810

Furstenberg, F. F., & Harris, K. M. (1993). When and why fathers matter: Impacts of father involvement on the children of adolescent mothers. In R. I. Lerman & T. J. Ooms (Eds.), *Young unwed fathers: Changing roles and emerging policies* (pp. 117–138). Philadelphia, PA: Temple University Press.

Futris, T. G., & Schoppe-Sullivan, S. J. (2007). Mothers' perceptions of barriers, parenting alliance, and adolescent fathers' engagement with their children. *Family Relations, 56,* 258–269. doi:10.1111/j.1741-3729.2007.00457.x

Gavin, L. E., Black, M. M., Minor, S., Abel, Y., Papas, M. A., & Bentley, M. E. (2002). Young, disadvantaged fathers' involvement with their infants: An ecological perspective. *The Journal of Adolescent Health, 31,* 266–276. doi:10.1016/S1054-139X(02)00366-X

Gee, C. B., & Rhodes, J. E. (2003). Adolescent mothers' relationship with their children's biological fathers: Social support, social strain and relationship continuity. *Journal of Family Psychology, 17,* 370–383. doi:10.1037/0893-3200.17.3.370

Gordon, R. A., Chase-Lansdale, P., & Brooks-Gunn, J. (2004). Extended households and the life course of young mothers: Understanding the associations using a sample of mothers with premature, low birth weight babies. *Child Development, 75,* 1013–1038. doi:10.1111/j.1467-8624.2004.00723.x

Hernandez, D., Coley, R. L., & Lewin-Bizan, S. (2006, March). *Father involvement and parental relationship quality among new parents: A reciprocal relationship?* Paper presented at the Population Association of America meetings, Los Angeles, CA.

Hess, C. R., Papas, M. A., & Black, M. M. (2002). Resilience among African American adolescent mothers: Predictors of positive parenting in early infancy. *Journal of Pediatric Psychology, 27,* 619–629. doi:10.1093/jpepsy/27.7.619

Hogan, D. P., Hao, L.-X., & Parish, W. L. (1990). Race, kin networks, and assistance to mother-headed families. *Social Forces, 68,* 797–812. doi:10.2307/2579354

Holcombe, E., Peterson, K., & Manlove, J. (2009, March). *Ten reasons to still keep the focus on teen childbearing* (Publication 2009-10). Washington, DC: Child Trends. Retrieved from http://www.childtrends.org/Files/Child_Trends-2009_04_01_RB_KeepingFocus.pdf

Howard, K. S., Lefever, J. E. B., Borkowski, J. G., & Whitman, T. L. (2006). Fathers' influence in the lives of children with adolescent mothers. *Journal of Family Psychology, 20,* 468–476. doi:10.1037/0893-3200.20.3.468

Jaffee, S. R. (2002). Pathways to adversity in young adulthood among early child bearers. *Journal of Family Psychology, 16,* 38–49. doi:10.1037/0893-3200.16.1.38

Jaffee, S., Caspi, A., Moffitt, T. E., Belsky, J., & Silva, P. (2001). Why are children born to teen mothers at risk for adverse outcomes in young adulthood? Results from a 20-year longitudinal study. *Development and Psychopathology, 13*, 377–397. doi:10.1017/S0954579401002103

Jaffee, S. R., Moffitt, T. E., Caspi, A., & Taylor, A. (2003). Life with (or without) father: The benefits of living with two biological parents depend on the father's antisocial behavior. *Child Development, 74*, 109–126. doi:10.1111/1467-8624.t01-1-00524

Kalil, A., Spencer, M. S., Spieker, S. J., & Gilchrist, L. D. (1998). Effects of grandmother coresidence and quality of family relationships on depressive symptoms in adolescent mothers. *Family Relations: Interdisciplinary Journal of Applied Family Studies, 47*, 433–441.

Kalil, A., Ziol-Guest, K. M., & Coley, R. L. (2005). Perceptions of father involvement patterns in teenage-mother families: Predictors and links to mothers' psychological adjustment. *Family Relations, 54*, 197–211. doi:10.1111/j.0197-6664.2005.00016.x

Leadbeater, B. J., & Bishop, S. J. (1994). Predictors of behavior problems in preschool children of inner-city Afro-American and Puerto Rican adolescent mothers. *Child Development, 65*, 638–648. doi:10.2307/1131406

Lerman, R. I. (1993). A national profile of young unwed fathers. In R. I. Lerman & T. J. Ooms (Eds.), *Young unwed fathers: Changing roles and emerging policies* (pp. 27–51). Philadelphia, PA: Temple University Press.

Lugalia, T. A., & Overturf, J. (2004). *Children and the households they live in: 2000* (Report No. CENSR-14). Washington, DC: U.S. Census Bureau.

McHale, J. P., Kuersten-Hogan, R., & Rao, N. (2004). Growing points for coparenting theory and research. *Journal of Adult Development, 11*, 221–234. doi:10.1023/B:JADE.0000035629.29960.ed

Minkler, M., & Fuller-Thomson, E. (1999). The health of grandparents raising grandchildren: Results of a national study. *American Journal of Public Health, 89*, 1384–1389. doi:10.2105/AJPH.89.9.1384

Minuchin, S. (1974). *Families and family therapy*. Cambridge, MA: Harvard University Press.

Moore, M. R., & Brooks-Gunn, J. (2002). Adolescent parenthood. In M. H. Bornstein (Ed.), *Handbook of parenting: Vol. 3. Being and becoming a parent* (2nd ed., pp. 173–214). Mahwah, NJ: Erlbaum.

Moore, D. R., & Florsheim, P. (2008). Interpartner conflict and child abuse risk among African American and Latino adolescent parenting couples. *Child Abuse & Neglect, 32*, 463–475. doi:10.1016/j.chiabu.2007.05.006

Moore, D. R., Florsheim, P., & Butner, J. (2007). Interpersonal behavior, psychopathology, and relationship outcomes among adolescent mothers and their partners. *Journal of Clinical Child and Adolescent Psychology, 36*, 541–556. doi:10.1080/15374410701662709

Oberlander, S. E., Black, M. M., & Starr, R. H., Jr. (2007). African American adolescent mothers and grandmothers: A multigenerational approach to parenting. *American Journal of Community Psychology, 39*, 37–46. doi:10.1007/s10464-007-9087-2

Oxford, M. L., Gilchrist, L. D., Lohr, M. J., Gillmore, M. R., Morrison, D. M., & Spieker, S. J. (2005). Life course heterogeneity in the transition from adolescence to adulthood among adolescent mothers. *Journal of Research on Adolescence, 15*, 479–504. doi:10.1111/j.1532-7795.2005.00108.x

Oyserman, D., Radin, N., & Saltz, E. (1994). Predictors of nurturant parenting in teen mothers living in three generational families. *Child Psychiatry and Human Development, 24*, 215–230. doi:10.1007/BF02353198

Pittman, L. D., Wakschlag, L. S., Chase-Lansdale, P. L., & Brooks-Gunn, J. (in press). "Mama, I'm a person, too!": Individuation and young African-American mothers' parenting competence. In P. Kerig, M. Schulz, & S. Hauser (Eds.), *Adolescence and beyond: Family processes and development*. Oxford, England: Oxford University Press.

Pogarsky, G., Thornberry, T. P., & Lizotte, A. J. (2006). Developmental outcomes for children of young mothers. *Journal of Marriage and the Family, 68*, 332–344. doi:10.1111/j.1741-3737.2006.00256.x

Sadler, L. S., & Clemmens, D. A. (2004). Ambivalent grandmothers raising teen daughters and their babies. *Journal of Family Nursing, 10*, 211–231. doi:10.1177/1074840704263984

Shanok, A. F., & Miller, L. (2007). Stepping up to motherhood among inner-city teens. *Psychology of Women Quarterly, 31*, 252–261. doi:10.1111/j.1471-6402.2007.00368.x

Smith, K. (2000). *Who's minding the kids? Child care arrangements: Fall 1995* (Current Population Reports, Series P-28, Special Censuses). Washington, DC: U.S. Census Bureau.

Sommer, K. S., Whitman, T. L., Borkowski, J. G., Gondoli, D. M., Burke, J., Maxwell, S. E., & Weed, K. (2000). Prenatal maternal predictors of cognitive and emotional delays in children of adolescent mothers. *Adolescence, 35*, 87–112.

Spencer, M. S., Kalil, A., Larson, N. C., Spieker, S. J., & Gilchrist, L. D. (2002). Multigenerational coresidence and childrearing conflict: Links to parenting stress in teenage mothers across the first two years postpartum. *Applied Developmental Science, 6*, 157–170. doi:10.1207/S1532480XADS0603_5

Spieker, S., & Bensley, L. (1994). Roles of living arrangements and grandmother social support in adolescent mothering and infant attachment. *Developmental Psychology, 30*, 102–111. doi:10.1037/0012-1649.30.1.102

Sullivan, M. L. (1985). *Teen fathers in the inner city: An exploratory ethnographic study*. New York, NY: Ford Foundation.

Sullivan, M. L. (1989). Absent fathers in the inner city. *AAPSS Annals, 501,* 48–58.

Sullivan, M. L. (1993). Young fathers and parenting in two inner-city neighborhoods. In R. I. Lerman & T. J. Ooms (Eds.), *Young unwed fathers: Changing roles and emerging policies* (pp. 52–73). Philadelphia, PA: Temple University Press.

Wiemann, C. M., Agurcia, C. A., Rickert, V. I., Berenson, A. B., & Volk, R. J. (2006). Absent fathers as providers: Race/ethnic difference in support for adolescent mothers. *Child & Adolescent Social Work Journal, 23*(5-6), 617–634. doi:10.1007/s10560-006-0078-1

6

COPARENTING AMONG LESBIAN AND GAY COUPLES

CHARLOTTE J. PATTERSON AND RACHEL H. FARR

Parenting is highly valued by most American adults, regardless of whether they are heterosexual, lesbian, or gay (Gates, Badgett, Macomber, & Chambers, 2007; Riskind & Patterson, 2010). Many adults find being a parent to be the most rewarding part of their adult lives, but parenting also brings with it many challenges. Coordinating successfully with another person to meet children's evolving social and emotional needs—while at the same time pursuing one's own individual goals, maintaining an adult romantic relationship, and providing economic and material support for a family—is a tall order for any parent. Even the most well-prepared parents discover that they must make many unanticipated decisions when parenting together (here termed *coparenting*; C. P. Cowan & Cowan, 1988, 1990; McHale et al., 2002).

In this chapter, our focus is on coparenting and family decisions made by lesbian and gay couples. We acknowledge that the study of coparenting is a broad and complex area. Given that relatively little research is available on other forms of coparenting among lesbian and gay couples, however, we focus here on decisions about how the couple will complete various family and household tasks. Thus, although we acknowledge the significance of other aspects of coparenting, our central focus here is on division of labor.

How are the tasks of parenting accomplished by couples who parent together? Heterosexual couples in the contemporary United States tend to use patterns that involve gender-based specialization (Coltrane, 2000; P. A. Cowan & Cowan, 1992). As is well known, what is today called a "traditional" pattern of dividing labor is that the husband/father specializes in paid employment, which he usually pursues outside the home, and the wife/mother specializes in unpaid employment at home, such as household work and child care. Although these particular specialized divisions of labor have not characterized families for much of history, cultural expectations about these patterns have become very strong.

This type of gendered specialization in division of labor, though well established, has been decreasing in frequency in recent years. It is most pronounced among families in which the wife/mother does not participate in the labor force, and it is least pronounced in families in which both wife/mother and husband/father work full time at professional careers (Demo & Acock, 1993). Because the numbers of families in which both parents are employed in the labor market has been growing, it is not surprising that specialization has decreased to some degree. Certainly, there are heterosexual couples in which nontraditional divisions of labor do occur (Deutsch, 1999; Ehrensaft, 1990). Overall, however, most heterosexual couples adhere, at least to some degree, to specialized divisions of labor (Grych, 2002; Hochschild, 1989; McHale et al., 2002).

The degree to which traditional, specialized divisions of labor occur in families may vary as a function of the family's position in the life course. Especially during the early years of marriage, before becoming parents, heterosexual couples may use divisions of labor that are relatively nonspecialized. The transition to parenthood, however, often involves a shift to more specialized divisions of labor (P. A. Cowan & Cowan, 1992). After the arrival of a baby, the wife/mother may be very involved in feeding and caring for the infant, whereas the husband/father may focus more intently on earning money to support the newly expanded family. With a preoccupied husband and more work at home, the heterosexual wife/mother may feel less satisfied than her husband by their new division of labor (Hackel & Ruble, 1992; Ruble, Fleming, Hackel, & Stangor, 1988). Yet, for perceived lack of better alternatives, couples often continue to use traditional gender-specialized divisions of labor.

Many observers seem to expect that even same-sex couples will show these traditional, gendered patterns of dividing labor. Same-sex parenting couples often report hearing questions such as the following: Which one of you is the husband? Which of you is the mother? How do you get the dishes done? How will your son ever learn to throw a football? Such questions are based on conventional ideas about division of labor and presume that even same-sex couples must somehow specialize, placing one member of the couple in the "husband/father role" and the other in the "wife/mother role."

Data from empirical research suggest, however, that division of labor among lesbian and gay couples proceeds differently in many respects than it does among heterosexual couples (Kurdek, 1993; Patterson, 2002, 2009a, 2009b; Peplau & Fingerhut, 2007). Instead of specializing, same-sex couples have more often been found to share the labor involved in parenting and in maintaining other aspects of their lives together in a relatively equal fashion. In short, it appears that division of labor is often characterized by specialized patterns among heterosexual couples and by shared patterns among lesbian and gay couples.

In what follows, we examine the evidence for shared patterns of division of labor among lesbian mothers. Next, we examine the newer and less extensive studies of division of labor among gay fathers. We then examine associations between child outcomes and modes of dividing labor in families. In the final two sections, we explore the limitations of research to date, asking to what extent these should affect our conclusions, and then end with comments about future directions for research.

DIVISION OF LABOR AMONG LESBIAN MOTHERS

To highlight the nature of research on division of labor among couples who are also lesbian mothers, we begin by describing in some detail one particular study, including its methodology and results (Patterson, Sutfin, & Fulcher, 2004). We then outline ways in which this investigation is representative of the research literature on division of labor among lesbian and gay parenting couples and ways in which it differs from others. In so doing, we extract some general conclusions about research on division of labor among lesbian couples who are parenting young children.

Atlantic Coast Families Study: Participants, Materials, and Procedure

The study we feature was based on data collected for the Atlantic Coast Families Study (Fulcher, Sutfin, & Patterson, 2008; Sutfin, Fulcher, Bowles, & Patterson, 2008), in which Patterson and her colleagues (2004) studied division of labor among lesbian and heterosexual parenting couples. This was a study of 66 upper middle-class families living in the mid-Atlantic region of the United States, half headed by lesbian couples and half headed by heterosexual couples. All participants were parents of young children. All were intact families into which the children had been born or adopted at birth or early in infancy. On average, at the time of assessment, the parents were 41 years of age, and the children were 5 years old.

Families were recruited through churches, day care centers, parenting support groups, and word of mouth. When a parent expressed interest in participation, a researcher contacted the parents by telephone, described the study, reviewed criteria for eligibility, and answered any questions. Once a family agreed to participate, a date and time were set for two researchers to visit the family home. During the home visit, parents were interviewed about demographic information and asked to fill out questionnaires about division of labor and other matters; children were also interviewed, but these data are not featured here (see Fulcher et al., 2008; Sutfin et al., 2008, for more detailed information).

Parental division of labor was assessed using a version of the Who Does What? instrument (C. P. Cowan & Cowan, 1990) appropriate for families of preschoolers, with minor adjustments in wording made so that the instrument would be more appropriate for lesbian as well as for heterosexual parents. The Who Does What? instrument was administered via paper and pencil to each member of every participating couple. Both parents reported the percentage of each of 13 household and 20 child-care tasks that they typically performed ("real" involvement scale) or would ideally perform ("ideal" involvement scale), on a scale ranging from 1 (*I do it all*) to 9 (*My partner/spouse does it all*). A score of 5 on the real involvement scale meant (*We do it equally*), and a score of 5 on the ideal involvement scale meant (*Ideally, we would do it equally*). Finally, partners reported how competent they felt performing each of the tasks, using a scale that ranged from 1 (*not very competent*) to 9 (*very competent*). Items for household tasks included planning and preparing meals, cleaning the house, paying bills, taking out the garbage, and doing laundry; those for child care included feeding, dressing, bathing, choosing toys, and visiting playgrounds. Parents' responses to the items were averaged to create real and ideal household work and child-care scores, as well as scores for competence on both household work and child care.

To assess satisfaction with couple relationships, we used the Locke-Wallace Marital Adjustment Test (Locke & Wallace, 1959). This is a 15-item self-report instrument designed to measure marital adjustment of spouses in heterosexual marriages. Minor semantic adjustments were required to make this test suitable for use with lesbian as well as with heterosexual couples (Chan, Raboy, & Patterson, 1998; Patterson, 1995). Possible scores range from 2 to 158, with higher scores indicating greater satisfaction.

We also collected demographic information about parental age, race, education, employment status (including job titles and hours per week of work time), and individual and household income. In addition, we collected demographic information (e.g., age, sex, race) about children in each family (for further details, see Patterson et al., 2004).

Using information about each parent's occupation, we coded each occupation for prestige. Each occupation was assigned a prestige score, as indicated by the Duncan Socioeconomic Index Scale (Duncan, 1991). Possible scores on the scale ranged from 0 to 100, with higher scores reflecting greater occupational prestige.

Atlantic Coast Families Study: Results

Data from this investigation indicated that lesbian couples reported dividing child care—tasks such as feeding, bathing, and dressing—more evenly than did heterosexual couples and also that, on average, they were more likely to prefer this arrangement (Patterson et al., 2004). There were significant effects of parental sexual orientation on parents' reports of their real responsibilities and also on their ideal preferences for division of labor for child care. Although lesbian couples reported that they split child care evenly, heterosexual couples reported that mothers did more child care than fathers. In addition, lesbian parents reported that they ideally wanted an equal distribution of child care with each parent doing about half of the work. Heterosexual mothers reported, however, that they would ideally do somewhat more than half of the child care, and heterosexual fathers reported that they would ideally like to do somewhat less than half of the child care.

Although they divided child care differently, lesbian and heterosexual couples reported dividing household labor in similar ways, with each partner doing about half the work. In contrast to the findings concerning child care, there were no differences between the groups in division of either real or ideal household work. Both lesbian and heterosexual couples described themselves as sharing the tasks involved in household labor about evenly.

We also studied participants' feelings of competence in performing tasks associated with child care. Results for both lesbian and heterosexual couples revealed no differences between lesbian and heterosexual couples, or between parents within couples, in this regard. Most parents described themselves as very competent in performing child-care tasks.

We calculated the number of hours per week that each adult participant spent, on average, in paid employment. We also added the work hours for both parents in each couple together, to yield a total amount of time spent on paid work per week by that couple. These data revealed that both lesbian and heterosexual couples spent roughly the same total amount of time on paid work each week. Interestingly, however, the hours were allocated differently in the two couple types. Among heterosexual couples, fathers worked more hours per week in paid employment than did mothers. Among lesbian couples, however, both mothers tended to work about equal numbers of hours. In short, lesbian mothers appeared to share the burdens of paid employment, but heterosexual fathers worked longer hours than did heterosexual mothers.

We also studied income and occupational prestige among lesbian and heterosexual parents. On average, parents in this sample reported relatively high prestige occupations and substantial incomes. There were, however, some differences among the groups. Given that lesbian mothers worked more hours per week than did heterosexual mothers, and given that heterosexual fathers worked more hours per week than did lesbian mothers, it was not surprising that their incomes also differed. Heterosexual fathers earned more than lesbian mothers, and lesbian mothers earned more than heterosexual mothers. The prestige of occupations pursued by heterosexual fathers did not differ from that of occupations pursued by lesbian mothers. Heterosexual mothers, however, held jobs that were lower in prestige than those held by fathers or by lesbian mothers. Thus, when we calculated discrepancies between occupational prestige scores within couples, there were greater discrepancies among heterosexual couples than among lesbian couples. In short, although educational attainment and household incomes were similar among lesbian and heterosexual couples, discrepancies between partners in occupational prestige were greater among heterosexual than among lesbian couples. This finding provided another example of greater specialization among heterosexual than among lesbian couples.

Discussion

It is not difficult to summarize the findings from the Atlantic Coast Families Study (Patterson et al., 2004). Among heterosexual couples, mothers reported doing more of the unpaid child care than did fathers. Fathers, however, reported working longer hours at more prestigious jobs, and earning more money than did mothers. In short, heterosexual couples said that they divided labor by specializing—fathers in paid employment and mothers in unpaid child care. They also said that this was the division of labor that they preferred. Among lesbian couples, on the other hand, mothers reported sharing both child care and paid employment in a relatively equal fashion. Mothers in lesbian couples reported working in jobs that were similar in prestige and earning similar incomes. They also said that this was the division of labor that they wanted. In short, the lesbian couples reported that they divided labor by sharing it. Although lesbian and heterosexual couples were attempting to divide the very same labor, they did it in different ways (Patterson et al., 2004).

How representative are the results from this study of the literature on division of labor among lesbian parenting couples? An important distinction to consider in this regard is that between primary parenting couple families and stepparent families. Primary parenting couple families are those with children who have been born or adopted in the context of the parenting couple's current relationship (Johnson & O'Connor, 2002). In the context of lesbian and gay parenting, these are families in which children have been born or adopted after the parent or parents have come out. Stepparent families are those with children who were born or adopted in the context of one partner's previous relationship. In the context of lesbian and gay parenting, these are families in which children have been born or adopted in the context of a previous relationship, usually before a parent has come out. The data collected by Patterson et al. (2004) were all from primary parenting couple families. This is a significant fact because divisions of labor in stepparent families may differ dramatically from those in primary parenting couple families, with the biological parent taking much more responsibility than the stepparent for care of children (Crosbie-Burnett & Helmbrecht, 1993; Hare & Richards, 1993; Moore, 2008).

The main outlines of the Patterson et al. (2004) findings have been reported many times by researchers working with lesbian and heterosexual primary parenting couple families. For example, among researchers using quantitative methods, similar results have been reported by Brewaeys, Ponjaert, Van Hall, and Golombok (1997); Chan, Brooks, Raboy, and Patterson (1998); Ciano-Boyce and Shelley-Sireci (2002); Goldberg and Perry-Jenkins (2007); Solomon, Rothblum, and Balsam (2005); and Tasker and Golombok (1998). Among those who have used qualitative methods, similar results have been reported by Bennett (2003), Dunne (2000), and Sullivan (1996). When primary parenting couples were asked about their divisions of labor, heterosexual couples were likely to report specializing, and lesbian couples were likely to report sharing in a relatively equal fashion. This difference was most pronounced in the comparisons of divisions of labor for child care, on the one hand, and paid employment, on the other.

One aspect of the findings that has varied from one study to another is the extent to which lesbian mothers have reported that division of labor involved in child care is exactly equal versus slightly skewed toward the biological mother doing more child care than the nonbiological mother. One early report found that biological mothers were described as doing more child care than their partners (Patterson, 1995). In another study, Ciano-Boyce and Shelley-Sireci (2002) found that lesbian adoptive couples reported more egalitarian divisions of labor than did lesbian couples with biological children. Biological mothers reported doing more child care than nonbiological mothers, and heterosexual adoptive couples had the most traditional or specialized divisions of labor.

More recently, Goldberg and Perry-Jenkins (2007) also reported that, in primary parenting couples, the biological mother was described as doing more child care than the nonbiological mother. It may be relevant to note that Goldberg and Perry-Jenkins collected data within a few months of the child's birth, and many biological mothers were breastfeeding their infants. This fact suggests that the age of children should be considered in discussions of division of labor because the care that infants need (e.g., breastfeeding) often differs from that needed by children and adolescents (e.g., help with homework). The characteristics of labor to be divided clearly change over the course of child development. Whether biological mothers in lesbian parenting couples do or do not perform, on average, somewhat more child care than nonbiological mothers does not obscure the clear finding that most lesbian parenting couples report sharing child care to a greater degree than do heterosexual couples.

Of course, all the findings represent average figures derived from groups of families. Thus, comparisons of average levels of sharing or specializing between groups may obscure the degree of within-group variability that may also exist. It is probably the case that within every sample there are some lesbian couples who specialize and some heterosexual couples who do not. Thus, even though average figures may differ between groups, there may be individuals within each group who diverge from the central tendency. The extent of such within-group variability is, as yet, unknown.

An intriguing feature of Patterson and colleagues' (2004) study, not shared by many other studies, is that these authors collected information about actual paid work hours per week for each adult and also about the prestige of occupations pursued by each adult in each household. Estimates about the amount of time spent by each parent in paid employment seem somewhat more immune from reporting biases than do some other items. Similarly, parents were asked to give the name and a brief description of their occupation, and these were later coded to yield estimates of occupational prestige; these scores also seem to be less susceptible than some to biases in reporting. Thus, the use of multiple methods by Patterson and her colleagues (2004) would seem to strengthen confidence in their findings.

DIVISION OF LABOR AMONG GAY FATHERS

The clear generalization emerging from research with lesbian and heterosexual couples is that lesbian couples are more likely to report that they divide child care by sharing it equally, and heterosexual couples are more likely to report that one of them specializes in child care. To what extent is this true also of gay male couples with children? Much less research has focused on this question (Biblarz & Stacey, 2010; Silverstein & Auerbach, 1999), but the available data suggest that relatively equal patterns of sharing characterize not only lesbian couples who are parenting young children but also gay male parenting couples (Patterson, 2004).

The first study of this question was conducted by McPherson (1993), whose dissertation explored division of labor, satisfaction with division of labor, and satisfaction with couple relationships among 28 gay and 27 heterosexual couples who were parenting young children. Consistent with the findings from lesbian parenting couples, McPherson found that gay primary parenting couples reported a more even division of responsibilities for child care than did heterosexual couples. Gay couples also reported greater satisfaction with their division of child-care tasks than did heterosexual couples. Finally, gay couples also reported greater satisfaction with their couple relationships than did heterosexual couples, especially in the areas of cohesion and expression of affection. This latter finding has not always been replicated in other studies; for example, Kurdek (2005) found that gay and heterosexual couples reported relatively equal levels of satisfaction with their romantic relationships.

Johnson and O'Connor (2002) also studied division of labor among gay men as well as lesbian parenting couples in planned gay and lesbian parent families. In this study, 19 gay couples and 66 lesbian couples responded to questions about division of labor. Gay couples reported sharing child care but not housework. Lesbian couples, on the other hand, shared housework but tended to specialize when it came to child care. Lesbian women reported that mothers who were biologically related to their children were more likely to do the tasks involved in child care. This study included children who represented a wide range of ages.

More recently, Farr, Forssell, and Patterson (2009) studied 29 gay, 27 lesbian, and 50 heterosexual adoptive parenting couples, each of whom was rearing at least one young child. This study was distinguished by its use of a systematic sampling frame to recruit families from participating adoption agencies. Using the Cowans' Who Does What? instrument, these authors studied division of labor among each of the three couple types. They found that heterosexual couples reported specialized patterns of child care, but both gay and lesbian couples reported shared patterns of child care. Thus, results from this group of families are new in that they are drawn from adoptive families, and they are also consistent with those from earlier research in identifying more egalitarian divisions of labor for child care among gay and lesbian couples than among heterosexual couples.

Overall, the scant data on division of labor among gay fathers have yielded converging results. Much like lesbian couples, gay men who are involved in primary parenting couples have reported sharing child-care labor. Moreover, gay fathers also expressed a preference for equal sharing of child care, just as lesbian mothers have (Farr et al., 2009). These results raise intriguing questions about the implications of equal sharing for children.

Farr and her colleagues (2009) also considered within-group variation in the division of child care among gay, lesbian, and heterosexual adoptive parenting couples. These authors calculated an absolute difference score between partners for each item on the Who Does What? instrument. For example, if one partner listed a 9 (*We do this equally*) on an item and the other partner listed a 1 (*We do this equally*) on the same item, this was an absolute difference score of 8. If one partner listed a 5 (*I do it all*) and the other listed a 4 (*My partner/spouse does it all*), this was an absolute difference score of 1. An average of the absolute difference scores for all childcare items was calculated to create a score for overall degree of specialization in each couple. As expected, Farr et al. (2009) found that lesbian and gay couples reported little overall specialization (i.e., their overall specialization scores were small), but heterosexual couples reported considerably more specialization.

DIVISION OF LABOR AND CHILD OUTCOMES IN FAMILIES HEADED BY SAME-SEX COUPLES

Given the overall clarity of findings with regard to reports about division of labor for child care among same-sex versus heterosexual couples, it is worth asking what implications these findings may have for children growing up in these homes. To what extent are children's adjustment and development linked to aspects of coparenting such as division of labor? To date, there have been only three studies of this issue among lesbian and gay parents and their children.

In the first of these studies, Patterson (1995) evaluated the links between division of labor among 26 lesbian primary parenting couple families and adjustment among their children. Most children in this sample had been conceived using donor insemination. The children were between 4 and 9 years old, with a mean age of 6 years. Results showed that parents were more satisfied with their divisions of labor and that children were more well-adjusted when child care was more evenly divided between the mothers. These findings raised the possibility that shared divisions of labor for child care might, in themselves, be beneficial for children. It is, however, worth noting that in this study both mothers reported that sharing child care was also their preferred or "ideal" mode of dividing this work. Because the mothers were both sharing child care and achieving their ideal pattern, it was unclear which was more important or whether a third variable might be involved.

In a subsequent study, Chan, Brooks, et al. (1998) also evaluated associations between division of labor among 30 lesbian and 16 heterosexual primary parenting couple families, and among their 5- to 11-year-old children. All families had been clients of a single sperm bank, so that in both lesbian and heterosexual parent families, one parent was biologically related to the child and one was not. Among lesbian nonbiological mothers, those who were more satisfied with division of labor were also more satisfied with their couple relationships, and their children had fewer behavior problems (i.e., were more well-adjusted). It is important that the effect of division of labor on children's adjustment was mediated by parental relationship satisfaction. Thus, in the Chan, Brooks, et al. (1998) study, it was clearly the impact of division of labor on relationship satisfaction, rather than division of labor in itself, that was related to child behavior.

Farr, Forssell, and Patterson (2009) also studied associations between child adjustment and parents' divisions of labor in adoptive families led by lesbian, gay, and heterosexual couples. These authors reported no association between children's behavioral adjustment and the degree to which couples reported specializing in terms of child care. However, there were significant associations between children's adjustment and couples' reported levels of satisfaction with their divisions of child-care labor, such that parents who reported greater discrepancies between their real and preferred arrangements also described their children as having more behavior problems. Parents who reported less favorable couple relationship adjustment also described their children as having more behavior problems. It was also the case that parents who reported more specialization and greater discrepancies between their real and ideal divisions of labor also reported less couple relationship satisfaction. Thus, as Chan, Brooks, et al. (1998) found, couples' relationship satisfaction and their satisfaction with their divisions of labor were more clearly linked with child outcomes than were the ways in which couples divided daily tasks.

Overall, then, existing research has begun to explore possible links between division of labor and child adjustment, but much remains to be learned. The information that is available suggests that it is parents' feelings about their arrangements rather than the specifics of their actual divisions of labor that are most closely associated with outcomes for children. Further research is needed to clarify any associations between division of labor and child adjustment, and to examine any pathways through which such associations may be established. Indeed a variety of other important coparenting dynamics beyond division of labor, yet to be studied in gay and lesbian families, may be important mediators in such pathways.

ISSUES IN RESEARCH ON DIVISION OF LABOR AMONG SAME-SEX COUPLES

Many researchers have asked couples to describe their divisions of labor, and most have reported that, on average, lesbian and gay couples describe relatively egalitarian or shared patterns, whereas heterosexual couples, on average, describe more specialized arrangements. There is also consensus that heterosexual couples prefer more specialized arrangements overall, whereas lesbian and gay couples express preferences for more egalitarian patterns overall. Fewer researchers have inquired about the implications, if any, of these decisions for children who are growing up in different types of households, and the findings about children are less clear. This work has all been conducted in the tradition of quantitative research that has dominated academic research in psychology for many years.

A challenge to these conclusions about division of labor among lesbian, gay, and heterosexual couples has arisen from sociological research in the qualitative tradition. Most notably, Carrington (1999) argued that lesbian and gay couples often go to considerable lengths to describe their divisions of labor as egalitarian, even when there is clear evidence to the contrary. In making this argument, Carrington drew on Hochschild's concept of *family myths* (Hochschild, 1989, p. 19). These are family stories designed to preserve a socially acceptable view of the family, even in the absence of supporting evidence. In these terms, Carrington argued that an egalitarian division of labor is a family myth among many lesbian and gay couples. Although they want to be seen as egalitarian in their divisions of labor, Carrington argued, lesbian and gay couples are "neither as egalitarian as they would like to believe nor as we would prefer that others believe" (p. 11). In short, Carrington suggested that quantitative researchers have mistaken family myths about lesbian and gay couples' divisions of labor for true stories.

Working in a qualitative tradition, Carrington conducted lengthy interviews with 26 lesbian couples and 26 gay couples, and conducted week-long field observations with eight of these families (Carrington, 1999). Of the full group of 52 families, only five reported having children at home, and some of these were in joint custody arrangements (i.e., were in the focal home only part of the time). Only three of the children were described as old enough to talk with the researcher (Carrington, 1999, p. 251). It is therefore understandable that questions about division of labor for child care in this study were both few in number and limited in nature (Carrington, 1999, p. 240). Thus, it is clear that no firm conclusions about division of labor in child care can be reached on the basis of information collected by Carrington.

Even though Carrington's (1999) study does not allow clear conclusions about how couples divide the tasks involved in caring for children, it nevertheless presents many interesting ideas about the nature of unpaid family and household labor, as well as about the ways in which couples divide labor and describe their arrangements. One such idea is that couples tend to think too narrowly about what constitutes family labor and, in this way, often render invisible many important contributions that are made by one or the other of them. For instance, Carrington wrote extensively about the character of work involved in feeding a couple or family. In addition to the common definition of this work that involves planning, shopping, cooking, and cleaning, Carrington emphasized additional "hidden" forms of work, such as finding new recipes, learning new food preparation techniques, and remembering family members' food preferences. Most couples do not notice the work involved in hidden forms of feeding work, he argued, so they do not include these when they describe their divisions of labor. Similarly, a couple or family must somehow accomplish tasks that Carrington described under the heading of "kin work," such as making telephone calls, purchasing gifts, and keeping the family calendar. Though often overlooked, these tasks require attention and effort. Despite the importance of such tasks, Carrington (1999) argued that they were rarely included in couples' descriptions of their arrangements. Thus, Carrington suggested that prevailing views of what is included under the heading of "family labor" should be enlarged.

Carrington's point is an important one. If many invisible or hidden tasks are overlooked in a couple's accounts of their activities, then descriptions of their division of labor may be inaccurate. If couples are motivated to overlook certain kinds of labor (e.g., "remembering family food preferences is not really work"), then inaccuracies are more likely, especially when information is collected using quantitative survey assessments. A superficial story that "we split housework about equally" may thus persist "even in the face of obvious empirical observations to the contrary" (Carrington, 1999, p. 177).

Carrington (1999) thus raised the possibility that earlier quantitative research on couples' divisions of labor has relied too heavily on data that may be misleading and superficial. Lacking in the thick description and detailed elaboration that is characteristic of qualitative work, quantitative research on same-sex couples' divisions of labor may therefore be seen as providing only a partial look at the complex realities of family lives. For instance, if much family work goes unacknowledged, this could leave one member of a couple feeling unappreciated and could ultimately work against the creation and maintenance of an effective parenting alliance. Exploration of this and other possibilities is a task for future research.

Some reservations about the work of Carrington (1999) in this context should, however, be considered. Carrington's study did not involve many families with children, and for this reason could not address questions about the division of responsibilities for child care. The families interviewed were mostly from the middle and upper middle classes, and they all lived in the San Francisco Bay Area. The interviews were all conducted by a single researcher. Moreover, the processes under study may be affected in important ways by the presence or absence of children in a household. No heterosexual couples were involved in the study, so no comparisons between lesbian and gay, and heterosexual couples could be offered. In short, Carrington raised many intriguing questions about division of labor among lesbian and gay couples that should be considered in future studies of lesbian and gay parenting, but his own research did not resolve them.

DIRECTIONS FOR FURTHER RESEARCH

Research on coparenting in families headed by lesbian and gay parents has begun, but many important directions for further research can be identified. For the most part, the research to date has focused on issues related to division of labor. Even in this area, questions have emerged about the best interpretation of existing findings. In addition to clarifying issues relevant to division of labor, future research is needed to explore a wider array of coparenting concerns.

In the area of division of labor, an important direction for future research is to use a wider array of research methodologies in the study of lesbian and gay parents and their children. The C. P. Cowan and Cowan (1990) Who Does What? instrument has been widely used, and it continues to provide valuable information. Other methods, such as observational and diary methods, could also be appropriate in this area, as would qualitative interview methods like those championed by Carrington (1999). By bringing to bear a wider array of methodological tools, a more comprehensive understanding of division of labor among lesbian and gay parents will be obtained.

Another important direction for research is to investigate a broader array of topics within the broad field of coparenting. For example, one creative line of research in studies of coparenting in heterosexual families has focused on the emotional dynamics of the mother–father–child triangle (see Chapter 10, this volume). The degree of cooperation between parents, the overall level of cohesion in the family, and the degree of engagement in family activities by both parents have all proven to be important features of coparenting relationships in heterosexual parenting families that would be valuable topics for study in understanding the interpersonal dynamics of gay and lesbian families (McHale et al., 2002). There would be great value in undertaking such work, especially because lesbian and gay parenting couples may be especially likely to enjoy one another's company and find it easy to cooperate with one another in the context of activities with their child (McPherson, 1993). More complex approaches to assessment could be successful in highlighting the special strengths of lesbian and gay parent families, as well as revealing their limitations.

Another important direction for research with lesbian-mother and gay-father families could focus on transformations in coparenting after separation of the primary parenting couple. Although some of the issues and dynamics involved in heterosexual couples' parenting together after divorce have been studied (see Chapter 11, this volume), attention has not yet been devoted to the study of such matters in the families of same-sex couples. As a result, little is known about how same-sex couples attempt to provide for the needs of their children on the dissolution of their couple relationships. What are the special issues for same-sex couples and their children, whose familial relationships may not enjoy protection of law (Patterson, 2009b), and how do parents ensure the continuity of significant family ties for children, even in the face of discontinuity in adult relationships? How are new same-sex partners integrated into caregiving routines and emotional support systems for children? These and many other questions about coparenting under stressful circumstances remain to be addressed in future research.

In future work, it could be valuable to distinguish more carefully than in previous research between those who conceived or adopted children in the context of heterosexual marriages, on the one hand, and those who had children in the context of preexisting lesbian or gay identities, on the other. The coparenting issues are certainly not the same in the two cases. If a gay couple is parenting a child who was born to one of the men in the context of an earlier heterosexual relationship, then the other man in the couple might be in an informal stepfather role; in these cases, the bulk of the child care can be expected to fall on the shoulders of the original father. If a child was adopted by a gay couple after they had been together for a few years, however, then the issue of division of labor may be quite different. In this case, the two fathers are likely to share child care more evenly (Farr et al., 2009). Similar arguments could be made for families formed by lesbian women before coming out versus after coming out, in the context of preexisting sexual minority identities. Modes of family formation may be very much linked with divisions of labor, as well as other coparenting dynamics, and research should acknowledge these possibilities (Moore, 2008).

Another direction for future work is to investigate more closely the adaptations of lesbian and gay parented families in different contexts. As yet, we know little about the impact of socioeconomic, religious, racial, or political factors on coparenting in sexual minority communities. By the same token, we know little about how urban versus rural variations in employment and social networks may affect coparenting strategies in sexual minority communities. Cross-cultural studies are also as yet very rare (for an exception, see Bos, Gartrell, van Balen, Peyser, & Sandfort, 2008).

Another important avenue for exploration is the ways in which coparenting may be structured or channeled by the legal or policy environments in which same-sex couples live (Herek, 2006; Patterson, 2009b). For example, the freedom to give up paid employment and specialize in unpaid family work may be more available to parents whose relationships have the legal protections afforded by marriage (see Patterson et al., 2004). To protect the interests of all, should the couple's relationship dissolve, same-sex couples may sometimes be forced by legal and policy environments that do not recognize their relationships to share both paid and unpaid labor. If legal and policy environments are critical in this way, then different divisions of labor should be observed for same-sex couples living in jurisdictions that vary in their recognition of same-sex couples. These and related questions could be intriguing subjects of future research.

Finally, another important direction for research in this area is to explore the associations between variations in coparenting, on the one hand, and in child adjustment, on the other. To what degree is children's development affected by variations in coparenting strategies or by parents' emotional responses to such variations? To what degree does the impact of coparenting on children depend on children's developmental level and circumstances? And to what extent is any impact of actual coparenting strategies dependent on other variables, such as couples' overall relationship quality? All these are important questions for further research.

As more and more lesbian and gay couples set out to have children in the context of already-established nonheterosexual identities (Tornello & Patterson, 2010), the topic of coparenting among same-sex couples gains both in interest and in importance. The results of this work will be significant for debates about gender and sexual orientation in parenting (Biblarz & Stacey, 2010; Silverstein & Auerbach, 1999). The data that are available thus far suggest that this will prove to be a rich and interesting terrain for study. Indeed, as more and more lesbian and gay adults become parents, it will be more and more important to understand their distinctive approaches to the tasks that are involved.

REFERENCES

Bennett, S. (2003). Is there a primary mom? Parental perceptions of attachment bond hierarchies within lesbian adoptive families. *Child and Adolescent Social Work Journal, 20,* 159–173.

Biblarz, T. J., & Stacey, J. (2010). How does the gender of parents matter? *Journal of Marriage and the Family, 72,* 3–22. doi:10.1111/j.1741-3737.2009.00678.x

Bos, H. M. W., Gartrell, N. K., van Balen, F., Peyser, H., & Sandfort, T. G. M. (2008). Children in planned lesbian families: A cross-cultural comparison between the

United States and the Netherlands. *American Journal of Orthopsychiatry, 78*, 211–219. doi:10.1037/a0012711

Brewaeys, A., Ponjaert, I., Van Hall, E. V., & Golombok, S. (1997). Donor insemination: Child development and family functioning. *Human Reproduction, 12*, 1349–1259.

Carrington, C. (1999). *No place like home: Relationships and family life among lesbians and gay men.* Chicago, IL: University of Chicago Press.

Chan, R. W., Brooks, R. C., Raboy, B., & Patterson, C. J. (1998). Division of labor among lesbian and heterosexual parents: Associations with children's adjustment. *Journal of Family Psychology, 12*, 402–419. doi:10.1037/0893-3200.12.3.402

Chan, R. W., Raboy, B., & Patterson, C. J. (1998). Psychosocial adjustment among children conceived via donor insemination by lesbian and heterosexual mothers. *Child Development, 69*, 443–457.

Ciano-Boyce, C., & Shelley-Sireci, L. (2003). Who is mommy tonight? Lesbian parenting issues. *Journal of Homosexuality, 43*, 1–13. doi:10.1300/J082v43n02_01

Coltrane, S. (2000). Research on household labor: Modeling and measuring the social embeddedness of routine family work. *Journal of Marriage and the Family, 62*, 1208–1233. doi:10.1111/j.1741-3737.2000.01208.x

Cowan, C. P., & Cowan, P. A. (1988). Who does what when partners become parents: Implications for men, women and marriage. *Marriage & Family Review, 12*, 105–131. doi:10.1300/J002v12n03_07

Cowan, C. P., & Cowan, P. A. (1990). Who does what? In J. Touliatos, B. F. Perlmutter, & M. A. Straus (Eds.), *Handbook of family measurement techniques* (pp. 447–448). Beverly Hills, CA: Sage.

Cowan, P. A., & Cowan, C. P. (1992). *When partners become parents: The big life change for couples.* New York, NY: Basic Books.

Crosbie-Burnett, M., & Helmbrecht, L. (1993). A descriptive study of gay male stepfamilies. *Family Relations, 42*, 256–262. doi:10.2307/585554

Demo, D. H., & Acock, A. C. (1993). Family diversity and the division of domestic labor: How much have things really changed? *Family Relations, 42*, 323–331. doi:10.2307/585562

Deutsch, F. M. (1999). *Halving it all: How equally shared parenting works.* Cambridge, MA: Harvard University Press.

Duncan, O. D. (1991). Socioeconomic index. In D. C. Miller (Ed.), *Handbook of research design and social measurement* (5th ed., pp. 331–333). Newbury Park, CA: Sage.

Dunne, G. A. (2000). Opting into motherhood: Lesbians blurring the boundaries and transforming the meaning of parenthood and kinship. *Gender and Society, 14*, 11–35.

Ehrensaft, D. (1990). *Parenting together: Men and women sharing the care of their children.* Urbana: University of Illinois Press.

Farr, R. H., Forssell, S. L., & Patterson, C. J. (2009, May). *Parental sexual orientation, gender, and division of labor among adoptive parenting couples.* Poster presented at the annual meeting of the Association for Psychological Science, San Francisco, CA.

Fulcher, M., Sutfin, E. L., & Patterson, C. J. (2008). Individual differences in gender development: Associations with parental sexual orientation, attitudes, and division of labor. *Sex Roles, 58,* 330–341. doi:10.1007/s11199-007-9348-4

Gates, G. J., Badgett, M. V. L., Macomber, J., & Chambers, K. (2007). *Adoption and foster care by gay and lesbian parents in the United States.* Los Angeles: The Williams Institute, UCLA School of Law.

Goldberg, A. E., & Perry-Jenkins, M. (2007). The division of labor and perceptions of parental roles: Lesbian couples across the transition to parenthood. *Journal of Social and Personal Relationships, 24,* 297–318. doi:10.1177/0265407507075415

Grych, J. H. (2002). Marital relationships and parenting. In M. H. Bornstein (Ed.), *Handbook of parenting: Vol. 4. Social conditions and applied parenting* (pp. 203–225). Mahwah NJ: Erlbaum.

Hackel, L. S., & Ruble, D. N. (1992). Changes in the marital relationship after the first baby is born: Predicting the impact of expectancy disconfirmation. *Journal of Personality and Social Psychology, 62,* 944–957. doi:10.1037/0022-3514.62.6.944

Hare, J., & Richards, L. (1993). Children raised by lesbian couples: Does context of birth affect father and partner involvement? *Family Relations, 42,* 249–255. doi:10.2307/585553

Herek, G. M. (2006). Legal recognition of same-sex relationships in the United States: A social science perspective. *American Psychologist, 61,* 607–621. doi:10.1037/0003-066X.61.6.607

Hochschild, A. R. (1989). *The second shift: Working parents and the revolution at home.* New York, NY: Viking Penguin.

Johnson, S. M., & O'Connor, E. (2002). *The gay baby boom: The psychology of gay parenthood.* New York, NY: New York University Press.

Kurdek, L. (1993). The allocation of household labor in homosexual and heterosexual cohabiting couples. *Journal of Social Issues, 49,* 127–139. doi:10.1111/j.1540-4560.1993.tb01172.x

Kurdek, L. A. (2005). What do we know about gay and lesbian couples? *Current Directions in Psychological Science, 14,* 251–254.

Locke, H., & Wallace, K. (1959). Short marital adjustment and prediction tests: Their reliability and validity. *Marriage and Family Living, 21,* 251–255. doi:10.2307/348022

McHale, J., Khazan, I., Erera, P., Rotman, T., DeCourcey, W., & McConnell, M. (2002). Coparenting in diverse family systems. In M. H. Bornstein (Ed.), *Handbook of parenting: Vol. 3. Being and becoming a parent* (pp. 75–107). Mahwah NJ: Erlbaum.

McPherson, D. (1993). *Gay parenting couples: Parenting arrangements, arrangement satisfaction, and relationship satisfaction.* Unpublished doctoral dissertation, Pacific Graduate School of Psychology, Palo Alto, CA.

Moore, M. R. (2008). Gendered power relations among women: A study of household decision making in Black lesbian stepfamilies. *American Sociological Review, 73,* 335–356. doi:10.1177/000312240807300208

Patterson, C. J. (1995). Families of the lesbian baby boom: Parents' division of labor and children's adjustment. *Developmental Psychology, 31,* 115–123. doi:10.1037/0012-1649.31.1.115

Patterson, C. J. (2002). Lesbian and gay parenthood. In M. H. Bornstein (Ed.), *Handbook of parenting: Vol. 3. Being and becoming a parent* (2nd ed., pp. 317–338). Hillsdale, NJ: Erlbaum.

Patterson, C. J. (2004). Gay fathers. In M. E. Lamb (Ed.), *The role of the father in child development* (4th ed., pp. 397–416). New York, NY: Wiley.

Patterson, C. J. (2009a). Children of lesbian and gay parents: Psychology, law, and policy. *American Psychologist, 64,* 727–736. doi:10.1037/0003-066X.64.8.727

Patterson, C. J. (2009b). Lesbian and gay parents and their children: A social science perspective. In D. A. Hope (Ed.), *Nebraska Symposium on Motivation: Vol. 54. Contemporary perspectives on lesbian, gay and bisexual identities* (pp. 141–182). New York, NY: Springer.

Patterson, C. J., Sutfin, E. L., & Fulcher, M. (2004). Division of labor among lesbian and heterosexual parenting couples: Correlates of specialized versus shared patterns. *Journal of Adult Development, 11,* 179–189. doi:10.1023/B:JADE.00000 35626.90331.47

Peplau, L. A., & Fingerhut, A. (2007). The close relationships of lesbians and gay men. *Annual Review of Psychology, 58,* 10.1–10.20.

Riskind, R. G., & Patterson, C. J. (2010). Parenting intentions and desires among childless lesbian, gay, and heterosexual individuals. *Journal of Family Psychology, 24,* 78–81. doi:10.1037/a0017941

Ruble, D. N., Fleming, A. S., Hackel, L. S., & Stangor, C. (1988). Changes in the marital relationship during the transition to first time motherhood: Effects of violated expectations concerning division of household labor. *Journal of Personality and Social Psychology, 55,* 78–87. doi:10.1037/0022-3514.55.1.78

Silverstein, L. B., & Auerbach, C. F. (1999). Deconstructing the essential father. *American Psychologist, 54,* 397–407. doi:10.1037/0003-066X.54.6.397

Solomon, S. E., Rothblum, E. D., and Balsam, K. F. (2005). Money, housework, sex, and conflict: Same-sex couples in civil unions, those not in civil unions, and heterosexual married siblings. *Sex Roles, 52,* 561–575.

Sullivan, M. (1996). Rozzie and Harriet? Gender and family patterns of lesbian parents. *Gender & Society, 10,* 747–767. doi:10.1177/089124396010006005

Sutfin, E. L., Fulcher, M., Bowles, R. P., & Patterson, C. J. (2008). How lesbian and heterosexual parents convey attitudes about gender to their children: The role of gendered environments. *Sex Roles, 58*, 501–513. doi:10.1007/s11199-007-9368-0

Tasker, F. L., & Golombok, S. (1998). The role of co-mothers in planned lesbian-led families. In G. A. Dunne (Ed.), *Living difference: Lesbian perspectives on work and family life* (pp. 49–68). New York, NY: Harrington Park Press.

Tornello, S. L., & Patterson, C. J. (2010). *Gay fathers' pathways to parenthood: Is there a generational shift?* Unpublished manuscript, University of Virginia, Charlottesville.

II

APPLICATIONS: ASSESSMENT AND INTERVENTIONS TO PROMOTE COPARENTING

7

ASSESSING COPARENTING

JAMES P. McHALE

The focus of this chapter is on assessing coparenting relationships in families. It covers issues relevant to clinicians seeking to identify and mobilize family strengths to enable healthier family functioning, but it also includes commentary relevant to researchers seeking to validly assess and examine the role that coparenting dynamics play in the adjustment of family members. Material draws on both the theory and practice of clinicians and on the methods, procedures, and tools of researchers. The aim is to help researchers become better grounded in measurement and in the real-life complexities of coparenting in the families they study and to help clinicians already very familiar with the lives of the people they serve become better versed in evaluating what they are doing. Many readers may already be guided in their work by family-centered principles in assessment, conferencing, and decision making pioneered by S. and P. Minuchin and their colleagues. However, the call to explicitly conceptualize and evaluate coparenting dynamics in all work with children and families offers a different, albeit complementary, angle on aims of family-centered assessments. For readers not as familiar with the assessment of family-level dynamics, this chapter provides both a conceptual framework for assessing coparenting and suggestions about important processes, tools, and clinical considerations central in approaching any such assessment.

This chapter takes as a starting point a stance articulated in Chapter 1: that from infancy to early adulthood, virtually every child will be coparented, episodically or continuously. Throughout this book, contributors illustrate how an informed understanding of the coparenting structure and dynamics of any family provides unique insight into how the family functions—an insight quite different from the insights that come from evaluating parents' psychological well-being, parenting competency, or marital health (McHale & Fivaz-Depeursinge, 1999, 2010). The key distinction is that coparent–child emotional systems are triangular in nature (Fivaz-Depeursinge & Corboz-Warnery, 1999; P. Minuchin, 1985; Talbot & McHale, 2004). From early infancy forward, children meaningfully shape the three-person dynamic that evolves between them and their coparents (Fivaz-Depeursinge, Frascarolo, Lopes, Dimitrova, & Favez, 2007; McHale, Fivaz-Depeursinge, Dickstein, Robertson, & Daley, 2008), and the same two parenting adults do not coparent their different children in the same way (McHale, 2007a). Recognizing that coparenting formulations will always demand a reading of, at minimum, a three-person emotional relationship system is a prerequisite for sound, maximally useful assessment by the clinician or researcher.

BASIC CONSIDERATIONS IN COPARENTING ASSESSMENT

In approaching the assessment of coparenting structures and dynamics in families, clinicians and researchers must be cognizant of three basic issues: the conceptual lens that they bring in their efforts to understand the family, personal views that assessors bring that can color the process, and cultural variations that provide deeper meaning to patterns and processes that the assessment appears to uncover. These considerations are considered in turn.

Conceptual Lenses

Perception is not a passive process. It is an active drawing of distinctions. Observers are primed to "see" through the lens of the conceptual models in which they were trained. In the case of understanding families, this lens is frequently one of individual dynamics, pathology, and dysfunction. When assessments and interpretations of family functioning are organized by individual pathology models, evaluators see the goal of assessment as thoroughly cataloguing past and current mental health issues and individual parenting deficits. The kinds of questions family members get asked and the relational stance the assessor takes with the family can create a skewed view of the family and its strengths. It can also prompt family members to take on a guarded instead of an open and collaborative stance (Kaplan & Girard, 1994). A valid family assessment is most likely to proceed from an empathic connection and "joining" with families (S. Minuchin, 1974). Moreover, families—especially those who have had to cope with crises—are far more likely to collaborate meaningfully with assessments that center on learning about the family's strengths, successes, and resilience. When this is the focus, evaluators often draw quite different conclusions about the family and its functioning. In short, our conceptual models affect our views of families, their views of us, and the relationships that are developed from first point of contact throughout the assessment process.

A second kind of lens that can skew how families are viewed is the endemic dyadic framework that guides virtually all clinical work with infants and younger children (McHale, 2007b). A dyadic rather than triadic lens leads evaluators to view coparents principally as subsidiary or auxiliary to a mother–child dyad, with questions asked focusing on whether there are others who coparent with mother, rather than on how the family's coparenting alliance is configured and how it operates. It is certainly important to understand the nuances of dyadic mother–infant and mother–child relationships. It is also equally important that evaluators understand how coparenting is structured and carried out in the family. These are not competing conceptualizations and sets of questions. They are different levels of analysis, and each is fundamentally important to address.

Finally, for frontline professionals who work with multicrisis families, the conceptual lens brought to bear can often be quite constraining. Chapter 12 discusses the work of P. Minuchin, Colapinto, and Minuchin (2007), who chronicled how well-entrenched bureaucratic structures lead not just the officials who manage child welfare and other systems, but also the professionals who work within those systems, to adopt and maintain "identified client"/specific problem mind-sets. The client is always the child or the parent, but never the family constellation. As P. Minuchin and colleagues illustrated, changing organizational frameworks is a slow, time-consuming process and is possible only if working from a family-oriented, systemic orientation.

Personal Views

Personal views can also sully the validity of coparenting assessments. Evaluators unwittingly telegraph subtle reactions during interactions with families. For example, many frontline professionals who work with multicrisis families come to view men principally in terms of their negligence and absenteeism or their violence potential. Although professionals often bemoan men's refusal or aversion to engage, men's reluctance may owe to professionals' views as much as it causes them. When assessors communicate discomfort or negative views about men to fathers (and to mothers), they evoke suspicion and defensiveness, instigating interactions that can come to be colored by mutual mistrust and even antagonism.

This family-assessor dialectic is also of concern to research teams hoping to validly evaluate coparenting dynamics. Researchers are taught to control problematic "noise" by standardizing protocols and procedures. Unfortunately, pristine following of standardized instructions and protocols without meaningful human connection is off-putting and bizarre to families at best, and runs great risk of yielding meaningless data at worst. Because coparenting data are most often collected by paraprofessional or student research assistant data collectors, it is vital that such individuals be knowledgeable about and comfortable working with families, and skilled in interviewing, observing, and posing questions. Coparenting observations, interviews, and questionnaires yield valid data only insofar as families are working with able researchers. Although it is usually important that evaluators remain blind to the overall hypotheses of research studies, it is also important that they understand how the information they are gathering, within the context of a standardized protocol, will ultimately be used and interpreted to gain an accurate read of the family and its coparenting alliance.

Cultural Variations

Finally, competent assessments of coparenting must proceed from a knowledge and understanding of norms and mores of diverse cultures. Without such an understanding, the conceptual and personal biases assessors bring to their work may be further exacerbated by unrecognized cultural biases. Take, for example, the developmental milestones that "independence-minded" European Americans commonly use to establish whether children are developing as they should. In many other cultures, families maintain a much more casual attitude about prompt attainment of milestones. In a great many cultures, there are also family routines and practices that carry over into the preschool and early school years (cosleeping, hand-feeding, brushing of teeth, routine cleanup aid to fully toilet-trained children following bowel movements) that Westerners could view as infantilizing and inappropriate beyond the toddler years. Discipline practices are also known to vary markedly from culture to culture, and some cultures are more intensively confrontive of child behaviors than are others.

Sensitivity to cultural issues does not only involve understanding normative cultural variations in family practices. Other issues related to cultural values and to minority groups' adaptations to marginalization can also affect the validity of family assessments. For example, people of different ethnic backgrounds vary in how they seek assistance and in how they view researchers and helping professionals. In some segments of the African American community, there is a strong ethic that mental illness, personal struggles, and need for help should be dealt with privately (Amankwaa, 2003). This ethic complicates research seeking to understand how postpartum depression affects African American families (Miranda, Gross, Persons, & Hahn, 1998; Oquendo, Lizardi, Greewald, Weissman, & Mann, 2004; Rich-Edwards et al., 2006; Segre, Losch, & O'Hara, 2006). Relatedly, in segments of the African American community and among many immigrant communities in which corruption and oppression were widespread in countries of origin, there is often a wariness about involvement with health-related interventions or research initiatives subsidized by government agencies—quite reasonable, on the basis of past histories. Joining and creating authentic partnerships with families in any assessment process is hence especially pertinent and poignant in work with families not of Western European descent.

Race and ethnicity are not the lone issues of importance. Much of what researchers know (or think they know) about adaptive coparenting is a result of studies enrolling only select groups of families. As McHale et al. (2002) highlighted, most observationally based longitudinal studies of coparenting hinge on the goodwill of motivated volunteer participant families; far less is known about families unlikely to enroll in longitudinal research projects—perhaps the majority of all families. Pleck (2008) made a similar point about coparenting in immigrant families—the problem is not just with the paucity of research that has involved these families, but with the selective nature of those who eventually do participate once entry into communities of interest is made. As another example, the Fragile Families and Wellbeing Study, which was unusually successful in recruiting historically understudied families, nonetheless had a significantly different attrition rate of noncoresident fathers. As discussed in Chapter 4, Fragile Families study data rely heavily on maternal reports of father involvement, typically only weakly related to paternal report, especially in families in which there is distress in the coparental partnership. And when men do enroll in coparenting studies, they—along with other family members such as maternal grandmothers (see Chapter 5)—do not always willingly disclose coparenting difficulties or distress, especially if their level of contact and rapport with the researchers is minimal. Taken together, these factors raise questions about how much we truly currently know about adaptive coparenting structures and processes. The rest of this chapter must be read with these caveats in mind, and future research must take seriously these principles if the utility of currently available coparenting assessment instruments and procedures is to be strengthened and enhanced.

ELEMENTS OF A SOUND ASSESSMENT PROCESS

Any essential "read" of the family's coparenting alliance starts by establishing the identities and involvement of all the important parenting adults in the child's life. This is followed by an evaluation of how the family's unique coparental alliance functions with regard to (a) the mutual involvement and engagement by major coparents, (b) the presence and extent of active solidarity and collaboration between these individuals, and (c) the presence and extent of unresolved coparenting dissonance between them. For interventionists, the aim of a coparenting assessment is not just to describe coparenting strengths and areas of need but also to analyze why the coparental alliance is currently functioning as it is. A thorough description of the assessment process in social work (which would involve a narrative social history of the child and family to assist the family team, caseworker, and court, together with a chronology of child welfare actions and interactions with the family) is beyond the scope of this chapter; interested readers are directed to P. Minuchin et al. (2007) for state-of-the-field coverage of fundamental principles in working with families and social service systems. The principal focus here is on coparenting assessment per se.

Establishing Who Is Involved

As several authors in this volume note, most of the research base we can currently call on to understand and evaluate coparenting is built on studies of heterosexual two-parent family systems in which the key coparenting figures are the child's mother and father. But as P. Minuchin and colleagues (2007) explicated, a true family-oriented approach requires identifying all relevant people in the family network, accepting unconventional family shapes. To be sure, in countless two-parent gay, lesbian, and heterosexual families, it will suffice simply to evaluate the coparental alliance between the two adults; if they provide all or nearly all of their children's care and socialization, understanding and resolving problematic coparental functioning between just the two of them will be key in improving their children's adjustment.

Having said this, in many other ostensibly two-parent family systems there will be other central coparenting adults in the child's life. Grandparents and extended kin are coresident and actively coparent in millions of households. Biological fathers are sometimes involved in the lives of children for whom they were sperm donors. In situations in which both parents work, day care providers frequently spend as much or more waking time with infants and toddlers than do the child's parents. Although these individuals are obviously not "parents" in any literal sense, major child problems can ensue if their socialization practices are incompatible with those of the child's parents (see Chapter 1). Family members are the ones who know best who matters to children in their day-to-day lives—and conversely, whose potential parenting involvement could threaten safety in the family. When matters are unclear, interventionists can look to family boundaries to help establish who the child's significant coparents actually are (cf. Chapter 11).

For researchers, circumstances are different, and efforts to validly study coparenting in diverse families can often be quite problematic. Researchers are beholden to internal review boards and federal sponsors who demand specificity about who will be "in" and who will be "out" of a research protocol. Not uncommonly, a research protocol authorizing contact with just one subset of a family's functional coparents leads to incomplete and artificial portrayals of the family's coparenting system and how it functions. For example, in a family in which a nonresident father spends significant segments of time with a toddler-age child, is the biological mother–father coparenting system the correct "unit of assessment" and analysis? As outlined in several chapters, maternal grandmothers coparent in many fragile families, and they can exert important "gatekeeping" effects in enabling or blocking father access, ultimately shaping children's emotional connections to their fathers for good or for ill. Researchers must be positioned to operate from a sufficiently flexible study protocol if they are to accurately capture and portray coparenting dynamics in such family systems.

In other fragile families in which both parents remain connected to their children in parallel parenting arrangements, "other mothers" (fathers' new partners; cf. Burton & Hardaway, 2009) often also play a significant parenting role for children. The same circumstance is true in postdivorce coparenting structures, in which children have meaningful contact not just with biological parents but with each parent's new partner. Indeed, as Chapter 12 argues, even for children in nonkin foster situations, quality of coordination between the temporary foster family and the child's natal family has consequences. Although the relationship system in such families is unique given the two families' triangulation with legal and child welfare systems (P. Minuchin et al., 2007), from a child-centered vantage the involvement and emotional connections among all parties are important to understand.

Genograms and ecomaps are the tools used most often by family-oriented clinicians to help envision members of a family in relation to one another across multiple generations; historically, genograms have been used to help detect repeated patterns in families (McGoldrick, Gerson, & Shellenberger, 1999). Adaptations of conventional genogram format have accommodated diverse cultures along cultural variables of ethnicity, gender, immigration, social class, and spirituality, among others (Milewski-Hertlein, 2001; Thomas, 1998; Watts-Jones, 1997). Ecomaps illuminate social networks of individuals or families and the nature of the bonds within networks (Hartman, 1995).

Although knowing the extent and nature of adults' social networks is some use in clarifying membership in coparental alliances, an ecomap completed for a coparent is insufficient for understanding coparenting. A second, more important, ecomap should also be drawn asking the coparents to trace important connections from the perspective of the infant or young child. Although traditionally this step has seldom been taken, it remains the best means of assuring that all important coparenting individuals in a child's life get properly accounted for in assessments.

Assessing Coparenting Quality

Once principals are correctly identified, how the family's coparental alliance operates is evaluated. For clinicians, this evaluation is part of a formal assessment process describing strengths, needs, and particular concerns. Key areas to investigate are degree of mutual involvement, solidarity, and unresolved dissonance. Using these topics as "headings" in coparenting evaluations assures a focus on relevant coparenting themes within the context of a broader based assessment that also addresses domestic violence, mental illness, and substance abuse. A thorough coparenting assessment would involve both individual interviews and observations of family group interactions. It would seek to accurately pinpoint dynamics, assets, and problems related to coparenting; view coparental involvement, solidarity, and unresolved dissonance from the child's perspective; and recognize that coparenting dynamics will differ for different children in the family. A truly child-centered perspective will approach questions about coparenting quality separately for each sibling in a family.

Mutual Involvement/Engagement

From initial interviews, a preliminary determination is made about how well each parent manages to maintain active, ongoing involvement with the child; give input on major parenting issues and decisions; and increase degree of participation when situations call for heightened effort to best support the child. Developmental considerations are obviously important here; critical levels of participation required for a nonresident father coparenting a baby in the process of developing attachments may differ from critical levels for an adolescent. This said, regardless of child age the ideal family ethic should be respectful, enabling shared access to and involvement with the child. This strength should be so noted in an evaluation when it is already the case.

More often, however, physical or emotional absenting by an important coparent does occur at least episodically. Such absenting can lead to (but also result from) another parent's heightened emotional investment in the child. The relevant dynamic should be noted. In still other families, assessors will find either substantial exclusion of or disengagement by one or more of the child's important coparents, such as when a parent is away from the child for lengthy periods because of obligations to children from other relationships and partners, immigration, incarceration, prolonged military service, or other major life challenges. In such families, information about coparenting is typically obtained from a residential parent. Unfortunately, any single informant's report can create a distorted impression of levels of investment by other coparents, and so the perspectives of all involved coparents are important to seek even when considerable effort is involved in doing so. Moreover, any time two or more coparents are available to take part in assessments, observations of the triad or multiperson family group are uniquely instructive. Such observations substantiate (or call into question) one informant's characterization of others' levels of involvement. They also help to provide specific and useful insights into the family's particular dynamics regarding coparenting detachment or exclusion (McHale & Fivaz-Depeursinge, 2010).

Active Solidarity and Collaboration

Understanding a family's strengths involves gathering information about the degree to which the central coparenting adults trust, support, validate, and cooperate with each other. There are two issues: how trusting and supportive coparents are of one another and how well and regularly they communicate about the child. That is, it is possible for parents to trust that the child is safe and well cared for in the hands of the coparent but not to talk regularly together about the child. This situation is actually quite common, and so proper assessment will examine both the overall level of solidarity between coparents and the extent to which there are functional lines of communication about child-related issues and concerns. From a family strengths perspective, it is especially important to take note of positive functioning in these realms, wherever and in whatever form they exist.

In no family does each coparenting adult exhibit unconditional validation of and experience unconditional support from each other coparent; frustration and annoyance about how a coparent deals with the child are common, as are feelings of disqualification and sometimes disrespect. Such sentiments, even if not expressed openly, must be attended to because they can dampen the solidarity of an alliance. The assessor must also establish how connected and supportive the coparents remain when all is not going well.

Many parents express mixed sentiments about the involvement of grandparents (appreciating their accessibility but bemoaning their practices and/or dreading their criticism). Others yearn for greater grandparental interest and involvement. For their part, grandparents recruited into playing very active roles are often torn, wishing for greater responsibility by the parent but failing to give voice to their wish for fear of letting go of the child. Such dynamics are not always easy to access by interview, and so again observation may be an indispensable adjunct in an assessment of coparenting solidarity and collaboration.

Unfortunately, in many families coparenting solidarity will be nonexistent. Evaluators may find chaotic situations in which it is unclear who can even be counted on to care for the child, or families in which the adults communicate pervasive feelings of isolation, exclusion, invalidation, and/or nonsupport. Although absence of solidarity and collaboration are common in postdivorce family systems, emotional disconnection, with or without overt conflict, is also all too common in nuclear, fragile, and extended kinship families. Documenting a lack of validation, support, and communication helps frame the family's needs and identify targets for change.

Unresolved Coparenting Dissonance

Finally, a determination is made about the extent of significant, unresolved incompatibility in coparents' views about the child's difficulties and/or about how best to parent the child. Dissonance itself is not always bad; it can actually be growth promoting in the longer run when resolved satisfactorily. Further, absence of dissonance can signify a maladaptive and rigid adherence to family structures that may not serve the child well. This said, a pivotal issue in any assessment is whether the child is at the center of ongoing and unproductive child-related conflict (Kerig, 1995). Degree of unresolved dissonance in families can be noted as minimal, identifiable, or substantial. Recall that fathers or grandmothers can be less inclined than mothers to describe coparenting friction during initial or one-time interviews (McHale, 2007a; see also Chapter 5, this volume). For this reason, both direct observations of triangular interactions involving the coparents and child and separate one-on-one assessments with skilled interviewers are valuable in assessing coparenting dissonance.

ASSESSMENT TOOLS: OBSERVATIONAL, INTERVIEW, AND SELF-REPORT SURVEY DATA

It should go without saying that no single form, tool, or observation can ever provide the necessary degree of insight into a family's coparenting structures and dynamics. Individual instruments, at best, are useful in drawing attention to particular areas of strength, need, and functioning. Thorough assessments engage both child and family in face-to-face meetings and as full partners in the process. They include all individuals necessary to evaluate and understand the family coparenting alliance. Assessing individuals or dyads separately and trying to "piece together" the information yields a completely different picture of the family and its dynamics than assessments of the full family group (McHale, Kuersten-Hogan, Lauretti, & Rasmussen, 2000). Assessments should be guided by cultural understanding; attend to substance abuse and domestic violence in family functioning; produce a "big picture," long-term view of coparental functioning; and in the case of clinical assessment, be used to craft the best possible child and family plan. Following is a brief review of paradigms and instruments that evaluate one or more aspects of coparental functioning. Further information can be found in McHale and Fivaz-Depeursinge (2010).

Observations

This section focuses explicitly on triadic and family group observations that include and involve coparents and child(ren). Readers interested in learning about observational assessments of problem-solving styles during dyadic coparenting discussions can consult articles by Baker, McHale, Strozier, and Cecil (2010) and Elliston, McHale, Talbot, Parmley, and Kuersten-Hogan (2008). The reason the focus here is on family groups is that the entire point of taking time to observationally assess coparenting at all is to accurately understand the invisible family structures that may be maintaining the child's referral problem. During family-level interactions, adults' behavior with one another and with the child provides useful insights into family resources and problems, family hierarchy (who takes charge, whether leadership is ultimately shared), and roles of the different adults and of the child in the family's dynamics. For the most valid assessment, all of a family's central members, including very young infants, should be involved; even 3-month-olds are recruited into and actively shape the coparenting process (Fivaz-Depeursinge & Favez, 2006; Fivaz-Depeursinge, Lopes, Python, & Favez, 2009; McHale et al., 2008). Likewise, involvement of a grandparent or kin caregiver who had been absent during an initial assessment session often reveals a different sequence pattern or alliance structure than that initially seen.

Observation of triads and groups are an indispensable staple in the work of family practitioners trained in S. Minuchin's (1974) structural family theory. S. Minuchin gave special credence to the behavioral sequences and interactions observed during contacts with families. Such interactions reveal much of what clinicians need to know about family communication patterns, boundaries, rules, and hierarchies, and what family members do during assessments can be as important as what they say. Family therapists take pains during early contacts with families to listen to and take stock of the family's account of their problems, to obtain information about how the family has already tried to deal with the problem, and to encourage enactments that, when allowed to proceed without the interventions of the therapist, reveal prototypical family patterns. From these assessments, preliminary hypotheses about structural and communication problems in families can be made.

For researchers, observation of triads and groups presents unique challenges. Only during the mid-1990s did child development researchers begin systematically examining coparenting cooperation, interference, and disconnection during triadic interactions (McHale & Cowan, 1996; McHale & Fivaz-Depeursinge, 2010; Kerig & Lindahl, 2000; see also Chapters 1, 2, 10, and 12, this volume). Valid assessments of coparenting demand discipline and grounding to track the subtle but often very meaningful behaviors exhibited by three or more people in interaction together, and there are also measurement and analysis issues to contend with. Moreover, researchers see observations as costly and expensive, and many try to work around these costs and challenges by relying on paper-and-pencil reports. Unfortunately, when the aim is to understand the latent structures and dynamics of families, so much of what is important is missed if there is exclusive reliance on individual self-reports.

From a research standpoint, tasks chosen for triadic interactions are also critical. The nature of tasks chosen affects the likelihood of detecting behavior indicative of different family strengths and areas of need. In most published studies of coparenting, researchers have typically selected semistructured teaching, play, or family discussion observations to elicit and identify coparenting dynamics (see Chapter 2). Some choose tasks allowing family members to move freely about a room. Others enforce more stringent seating expectations. Some structured observations such as the Lausanne Trilogue Play (see Chapter 10) are especially well suited for capturing coparenting dynamics in families with infants.

It is probably most ideal, especially with young children, to ask a family to stay seated for some interactions and be mobile for others. Sometimes a seemingly less dominant coparent will become more active when structures are removed. Other times he or she will remain in the shadow of another coparent regardless of the nature of the task. Similarly, coparents who appear confident, connected, and engaged while playing with a young child may appear more troubled during separations or if asked to set limits. Adults' behavior with a child during triadic interactions can also be compared with their behavior during dyadic (one parent–child only) assessments that use a parallel teaching/play format. Inconsistencies in behavior across contexts can be very revealing. In families with distressed coparenting alliances, parenting behavior deteriorates as adults move from parenting children in a one-on-one dyadic context to parenting in a triadic context. By contrast, the parenting of adults in nondistressed alliances stays more consistent from dyadic to triadic settings (Lauretti & McHale, 2009).

Again, because most observational studies of coparenting have primarily enrolled middle class European American families, caution is advised in interpreting observational data from other family systems (e.g., fragile families, kinship families, gay and lesbian families, foster families, blended families) and cultures. Norms derived from assessment of families in majority cultures cannot be blithely transferred to minority families or diverse family structures, as several chapters in this volume attest. At the time of this book's publication, observation, description, and empirical scoring of coparenting among different cultural groups have not received sufficient attention to offer definitive commentary on the validity of formal observational scoring systems. Some newer work has begun examining coparenting dynamics in mother–grandmother–child triangles (see Chapter 12; McHale, Salman, Strozier, & Cecil, 2011), and this work promises to be of significant value to those working with coparenting in three-generational family systems.

Finally, although thorough coverage is beyond the scope of this chapter, the purpose of assessment in clinical work is of course to guide intervention (McHale & Irace, 2010). Observed coparenting interactions can be videotaped during assessments and examined between sessions to aid the clinician in identifying problematic coalitions and boundaries within the system. These can then be addressed during subsequent interventions with the family, sometimes even using review of the video footage as a tool. Chapter 10 of this volume provides more detailed coverage on use of videotapes and interactive guidance in therapeutic interventions to strengthen coparenting.

Coparenting Interviews

Interviews with coparents are indispensible in coparenting assessments. They provide succinct, relevant information about how the adults function and reveal concerns harbored by parents not always accessible from observational data. A number of formal interview protocols for a variety of family circumstances have been published in the empirical literature (Maccoby, Depner, & Mnookin, 1990; McHale, Kazali, et al., 2004; Pleck & Stueve, 2001; Strozier, Armstrong, Skuza, Cecil, & McHale, 2011; von Klitzing & Burgin, 2005), but no one favored instrument or protocol has become a gold standard for clinical assessments. Interviews used for research purposes often involve creative qualitative analyses in search of themes such as extent of the "I-ness" as opposed to the "we-ness" of interviews (Pleck & Stueve, 2001), presumably signifying the interviewee's fallback propensity to think exclusively (me and my child) or inclusively (my coparent, my child, and I) about their shared child (von Klitzing & Burgin, 2005).

Interviews in the hands of frontline professionals have a more practical function. They are used to establish who the different coparents are; how much time each adult ordinarily spends with the child in a typical week, when, and in what contexts (alone or as a family); and which people get involved in which ways in looking after and socializing the child. From this point, they can be used to query individual parenting practices—what interviewees see as their own and as each of their coparents' strengths, and what they would want to change about both their own parenting and that of each coparent. It is important to ask what clients believe their coparents do well. It is telling when someone is unable to identify any of their coparent's special contributions in parenting the shared child.

The clinician needs to determine what has gone well in how parenting has been shared between the coparenting adults and what circumstances are most in need of change to provide a healthier parenting environment. Clients can be asked about their major disputes concerning what is best for the child and how these differences might be affecting the child. McHale and Fivaz-Depeursinge (2010) provided a summary of important general guidelines for interviews and questions that can be posed about specific coparenting processes and dynamics. Such details are helpful in planning coparenting interventions. Frontline professionals are also referred to the work of P. Minuchin and colleagues (2007) for extensive case examples of ways to talk with both coparents and with children about coparenting in family group settings.

Self-Report Questionnaire Surveys

Though used most often in research settings, the constructs that surveys assess are of interest and can also be of some use in coparenting assessments. Following is a brief review of such measures.

Parent-Report Surveys Used to Assess Coparenting Alliances in Nuclear, Fragile, and Multigenerational Family Systems

Standardized instruments and/or select survey questions are usually used to assess whether and how parents support one another in their roles. For example, in the Fragile Families and Wellbeing Study (see Chapter 4, this volume), mothers were asked to rate whether children's fathers often, sometimes, or never acted as appropriate role models for children; could be trusted to take care of the child; respected the mother's schedule and rules; supported the mother in raising the child; talked with her about problems with parenting; and could be counted on for help. Among survey instruments, the first was the Quality of Coparenting Communication Scale (Ahrons, 1981), an 11-item parent-report measure that assesses quantity and quality of coparents' ongoing communication about the child. Initially designed for divorced couples, the scale has since been used in studies with nuclear families (e.g., McHale, 1997) and mother–grandmother coparenting teams (Dorsey, Forehand, & Brody, 2007).

Other instruments include a 20-item Parenting Alliance Inventory (PAI; Abidin & Brunner, 1995) that queries the degree of support adults feel from one another in their coparenting alliance; a 17-item Coparenting Scale (McHale, 1997), on which parents rate the frequency of their overt and covert behavior strengthening or undermining their coparenting alliance; and a 13-item Measure of Coparenting Alliance (Dumka, Prost, & Barrera, 2002) comprising items from the PAI and items capturing respect of the coparent, constructive communication, and sharing responsibility for child-drearing tasks. Sharing of child-rearing tasks is also the explicit target of Cowan and Cowan's widely used Who Does What? measure (see Chapter 6). Alone, these surveys are all of limited clinical utility, but within the context of a more thorough evaluation designed to identify both coparenting assets and coparenting problems or liabilities, they can help crystallize problems for later follow-up.

Child-Report Surveys on Perceptions of Coparenting Alliances

A few instruments also assess children's perceptions of their parents' coparenting alliance. The Children's Perception of Interparental Conflict Scale (CPIC; Grych, Seid, & Fincham, 1992) is a widely used 49-item questionnaire that assesses 10 dimensions of interparental conflict: frequency, intensity, content, resolution, threat, coping efficacy, content (child related vs. non–child related), triangulation, stability, and self-blame. An adolescent version of the instrument also exists (Bickham & Fiese, 1997). The Co-Parenting Behavior Questionnaire is an 86-item questionnaire that assesses postdivorce parent–child and coparent interactions (Mullet & Stolberg, 1999). Among its 12 subscales, four capture interparent interaction factors (parental respect and cooperation, parental communication, parental conflict, and triangulation). For very young children, projective assessments, such as the Family Doll Placement technique (McHale, Neugebauer, Radin, & Schwartz, 1999), can provide useful information about children's family perceptions. In general, children's perceptions of the coparental structure and dynamics of their family, although often overlooked, are an important component of thorough coparenting and family assessments.

Parent Reports of Coparenting in Their Family of Origin

Measures of adult recollections of coparenting in the origin family have been designed and used principally for research purposes. None have extensive research or field use to document their validity. Instruments include a 12-item questionnaire (Stright & Bales, 2003) on which respondents rate the existence of supportive and unsupportive coparenting in their families of origin; a Parental Disagreement on Expectations of the Child Scale (Scheck, 1979), with 12 items that ask about coparenting of mother and father during childhood and focus on consensus between the two about child-rearing issues; and an adaptation of McHale's (1997) Coparenting Scale used in a study by Corcione, Lovell, and McHale (1997; described in McHale, Kuersten, & Lauretti, 1996) on which unmarried adolescents described recollections of interadult cooperation, conflict, and disparagement from childhood. In this study, 18- to 20-year-olds recalling greater coparenting conflict were more likely than other adolescents to have already selected names for their future children and to express a preference for having multiple sons when they one day had children.

As of now, little attention has gone into development of psychometrically sound measures of recalled coparenting during childhood for people who grew up in families headed by coparents besides mothers and fathers (stepparents, same-sex parents, kinship caregivers). Such measures may be of growing utility in efforts to strengthen the coparenting relationships of partnered and unpartnered expectant parents (McHale, 2009; see also Chapters 8 and 9). What adults "know" about relationship functioning—on the basis of attachment as well as coparenting histories (Talbot, Baker, & McHale, 2009)—unquestionably shapes their early adaptations as new coparents themselves. This is significant because, at least in nuclear family systems, early coparenting structures and adaptations once in place tend to persist across developmental time (McHale & Rotman, 2007).

Surveying Postdivorce Family Systems

Functional coparenting relationships affect the mental health of both parents and children in postdivorce families (see Chapter 11). Clinicians and researchers must be able to evaluate parents' propensities to entangle or shield their shared child from ongoing conflict; support and value the child's relationship with the coparent(s); and make shared rather than unilateral decisions with the coparent about the child's education, activities, and mental health concerns. Measures used with postdivorce couples include Ahrons' (1981) Quality of Coparenting Communication Scale and Abidin and Brunner's (1995) PAI. There have also been adaptations of existing instruments, such as Cookston and colleagues (2007) adaptation of CPIC frequency, intensity, and resolution of interparental conflict items for administration to adults. Although clinicians may find formal surveys useful in work with postdivorce couples, they can also ask directly about key parent behaviors that telegraph how the coparenting alliance is functioning (McHale & Fivaz-Depeursinge,

2010). Parents' responses to these queries are of great aid in conceptualizing dynamics of the coparenting relationship, and once again children's perceptions will add immeasurably to the formulation.

In summary, self-report survey data can be useful in the context of a comprehensive, culturally informed coparenting evaluation. Because a central aim of coparenting assessments is to identify divergence in coparents' views of the child and what is best for the child, comparing reports of child behavior by each coparent on formal survey checklists such as the well-validated Infant-Toddler Social and Emotional Assessment or Child Behavior Checklist can illuminate how differently two coparents see the same child. Adults in families exhibiting coparenting distress often differ notably in whether they see their child as having problems that are cause for concern (McHale, 2007a). In other words, if coparenting problems exist, coparents do not always even agree on whether their child is exhibiting problems at all. Knowing how each adult perceives the child is hence centrally important in conducting coparenting assessments, and self-report survey measures can be a useful means of facilitating this conversation with families. When time or resources are limited, parents can also be asked directly where their views resonate or clash with those of coparents and how they believe this affects the child.

CONCLUSION

The aim of this chapter was to provide a general introduction to the assessment process and the most common means of evaluating coparenting in families. Coparenting assessments augment in necessary ways, but do not replace, responsible assessments of parenting competency, risk, and other core principles of ethical assessment practice (Göpfert, Webster, & Nelki, 2004). Because the whole point of conducting assessments at all is to gain an accurate read of the family and its central coparenting dynamics, I have emphasized the importance of thoughtfully conducting assessments in partnership with families. For clinicians, coparenting should be part of intake assessments with any child seen; the best-laid formulation and case plan are often doomed to fail without the engagement and cooperation of all principals involved. It is centrally important to integrate all individuals with whom the child has emotional connections in this assessment. It is also critical to understand ways that patterns of coordination and support, miscoordination and chaotic unpredictability, or criticism and disparagement of episodically absent coparenting figures affect the child's social and emotional adaptation and well-being.

For researchers, I reiterate the complex, multifaceted nature of coparenting relations and the folly of seeking "quick and dirty" indicators of coparental functioning. I also underscore the reality that valid assessments of the coparenting relationship will always rest on the talents of the frontline researchers who work with families to gather such information, not just on the skills of those trained in formal coding systems to divine core themes from narrative or observational records. Finally, I reiterate how far we have to go in designing culturally relevant instruments respectful of the various functional coparenting systems described throughout this volume. We hence have a useful foundation, but much, much work yet to do.

REFERENCES

Abidin, R. R., & Brunner, J. F. (1995). Development of a parenting alliance inventory. *Journal of Clinical Child Psychology, 24*, 31–40. doi:10.1207/s15374424jccp2401_4

Ahrons, C. R. (1981). The continuing coparental relationship between divorced spouses. *American Journal of Orthopsychiatry, 51*, 415–428. doi:10.1111/j.1939-0025.1981.tb01390.x

Amankwaa, L. C. (2003). Postpartum depression among African-American women. *Issues in Mental Health Nursing, 24*, 297–316. doi:10.1080/01612840305283

Baker, J., McHale, J., Strozier, A., & Cecil, D. (2010). The nature of mother-grandmother coparenting alliances in families with incarcerated mothers. *Family Process, 49*, 165–184.

Bickham, N. L., & Fiese, B. H. (1997). Extension of the Children's Perceptions of Interparental Conflict Scale for use with late adolescents. *Journal of Family Psychology, 11*, 246–250. doi:10.1037/0893-3200.11.2.246

Burton, L. M., & Hardaway, C. (2009, April). *Low-income mothers as "other mothers" to their romantic partners' children: A multi-partnered fertility perspective on co-parenting.* Paper presented at the annual meeting of the Society for Research in Child Development, Denver, CO.

Cookston, J. T., Braver, S. L., Griffin, W., deLusé, S. R., & Miles, J. C. (2007). Effects of the Dads for Life intervention on interparental conflict and co-parenting in the two years after divorce. *Family Process, 46*, 123–137. doi:10.1111/j.1545-5300.2006.00196.x

Corcione, C., Lovell, S., & McHale, J. (1997, April). *Individual differences in toddlers' responses to antagonistic coparental exchanges during family play.* Paper presented at the annual meeting of the Society for Research in Child Development, Washington DC.

Dorsey, S., Forehand, R., & Brody, G. (2007). Coparenting conflict and parenting behavior in economically disadvantaged single parent African American families: The role of maternal psychological distress. *Journal of Family Violence, 22*, 621–630. doi:10.1007/s10896-007-9114-y

Dumka, L., Prost, J., & Barrera, M., Jr. (2002). The parental relationship and adolescent conduct problems in Mexican American and European American families. *Journal of Couple & Relationship Therapy, 1*, 37–57. doi:10.1300/J398v01n04_02

Elliston, D., McHale, J., Talbot, J., Parmley, M., & Kuersten-Hogan, R. (2008). Withdrawal from coparenting interactions during early infancy. *Family Process, 47*, 481–499. doi:10.1111/j.1545-5300.2008.00267.x

Fivaz-Depeursinge, E., & Corboz-Warnery, A. (1999). *The primary triangle: A developmental systems view of mothers, fathers, and infants.* New York, NY: Basic Books.

Fivaz-Depeursinge, E., & Favez, N. (2006). Exploring triangulation in infancy: Two contrasted cases. *Family Process, 45*, 3–18. doi:10.1111/j.1545-5300.2006.00077.x

Fivaz-Depeursinge, E., Frascarolo, F., Lopes, F., Dimitrova, N., & Favez, N. (2007). Parents-child role reversal in trilogue play: Case studies of trajectories from pregnancy to toddlerhood. *Attachment & Human Development, 9*, 17–31. doi:10.1080/14616730601151425

Fivaz-Depeursinge, E., Lopes, F., Python, M., & Favez, N. (2009). Coparenting and toddler's interactive styles in family coalitions. *Family Process, 48*, 500–516. doi:10.1111/j.1545-5300.2009.01298.x

Göpfert, M., Webster, J., & Nelki, J. (2004). Formulation and assessment of parenting. In M. Göpfert, J. Webster, & M. V. Seeman (Eds.), *Parental psychiatric disorder: Distressed parents and their families* (pp. 93–111). Cambridge, England: Cambridge University Press. doi:10.1017/CBO9780511543838.009

Grych, J. H., Seid, M., & Fincham, F. D. (1992). Assessing marital conflict from the child's perspective: The Children's Perception of Interparental Conflict Scale. *Child Development, 63*, 558–572. doi:10.2307/1131346

Hartman, C. R. (1995). The interparental relationship and family routines as predictors of child behavioral disorders among divorced mother-custody families. *Dissertation Abstracts International: Section B. Sciences and Engineering, 56*, 34–76.

Kaplan, L., & Girard, J. L. (1994). *High-risk families: A handbook for practitioners.* New York, NY: Lexington Books.

Kerig, P. K. (1995). Triangles in the family circle: Effects of family structure on marriage, parenting, and child adjustment. *Journal of Family Psychology, 9*, 28–43. doi:10.1037/0893-3200.9.1.28

Kerig, P. K., & Lindahl, K. M. (2000). *Family observational coding systems: Resources for systemic research.* Mahwah, NJ: Erlbaum.

Lauretti, A., & McHale, J. (2009). Shifting patterns of parenting styles between dyadic and family settings: The role of marital distress. In M. Russo & A. De Luca (Eds.), *Psychology of family relationships* (pp. 99–113). New York, NY: Nova Science.

Maccoby, E. E., Depner, C. E., & Mnookin, R. H. (1990). Coparenting in the second year after divorce. *Journal of Marriage and the Family, 52*, 141–155. doi:10.2307/352846

McGoldrick, M., Gerson, R., & Shellenberger, S. (1999). *Genograms: Assessment and intervention.* New York, NY: Norton.

McHale, J. P. (1997). Overt and covert coparenting processes in the family. *Family Process, 36*, 183–201. doi:10.1111/j.1545-5300.1997.00183.x

McHale, J. (2007a). *Charting the bumpy road of coparenthood: Understanding the challenges of family life*. Washington, DC: Zero to Three Press.

McHale, J. P. (2007b). When infants grow up in multiperson relationship systems. *Infant Mental Health Journal, 28*, 370–392. doi:10.1002/imhj.20142

McHale, J. (2009). Shared child-rearing in nuclear, fragile, and kinship family systems: Evolution, dilemmas, and promise of a coparenting framework. In M. Schulz, M. Pruett, P. Kerig, & R. Parke (Eds.), *Strengthening couple relationships for optimal child development: Lessons from research and intervention* (pp. 77–94). Washington, DC: American Psychological Association.

McHale, J., & Cowan, P. (Eds.). (1996). Understanding how family-level dynamics affect children's development: Studies of two-parent families [Special issue]. *New Directions for Child and Adolescent Development, 74*.

McHale, J. P., & Fivaz-Depeursinge, E. (1999). Understanding triadic and family group interactions during infancy and toddler hood. *Clinical Child and Family Psychology Review, 2*, 107–127. doi:10.1023/A:1021847714749

McHale, J., & Fivaz-Depeursinge, E. (2010). Principles of effective coparenting and its assessment in infancy and early childhood. In S. Tyano, M. Keren, H. Herrman, & J. Cox (Eds.), *Parenting and mental health: A bridge between infant and adult psychiatry* (pp. 383–397). London, England: Wiley.

McHale, J. P., Fivaz-Depeursinge, E., Dickstein, S., Robertson, J., & Daley, M. (2008). New evidence for the social embeddedness of infants' early triangular capacities. *Family Process, 47*, 445–463. PMCID: PMC2761722.

McHale, J. P., & Irace, K. (2010). Focused coparenting consultation: Helping parents coordinate to support children. *In Practice, 30*, 164–170.

McHale, J. P., Kazali, C., Rotman, T., Talbot, J., Carleton, M., & Lieberson, R. (2004). The transition to coparenthood: Parents' prebirth expectations and early coparental adjustment at 3 months postpartum. *Development and Psychopathology, 16*, 711–733. doi:10.1017/S0954579404004742

McHale, J., Khazan, I., Erera, P., Rotman, T., DeCourcey, W., & McConnell, M. (2002). Coparenting in diverse family systems. In M. H. Bornstein (Ed.), *Handbook of parenting: Vol. 3. Being and becoming a parent* (2nd ed., pp. 75–107). Mahwah, NJ: Erlbaum.

McHale, J. P., Kuersten, R., & Lauretti, A. (1996). New directions in the study of family-level dynamics during infancy and early childhood. In J. P. McHale & P. A. Cowan (Eds.), *Understanding how family-level dynamics affect children's development: Studies of two-parent families. Directions for Child and Adolescent Development, 74*, 5–26. doi:10.1002/cd.23219967403

McHale, J. P., Kuersten-Hogan, R., Lauretti, A., & Rasmussen, J. L. (2000). Parental reports of coparenting and observed coparenting behavior during the toddler period. *Journal of Family Psychology, 14*, 220–236. doi:10.1037/0893-3200.14.2.220

McHale, J., Neugebauer, A., Radin, A., & Schwartz, A. (1999). Preschoolers' characterizations of multiple family relationships during family doll play. *Journal of Clinical Child Psychology, 28*, 256–268. doi:10.1207/s15374424jccp2802_12

McHale, J. P., & Rotman, T. (2007). Is seeing believing? Expectant parents' outlooks on coparenting and later coparenting solidarity. *Infant Behavior and Development, 30,* 63–81. doi:10.1016/j.infbeh.2006.11.007

McHale, J., Salman, S., Strozier, A., & Cecil, D. (2011, April). *Away but not forgotten: Mother–grandmother–preschooler triadic interactions upon mother's return home following incarceration.* Paper presented at the meetings of the Society for Research in Child Development, Montreal, Quebec, Canada.

Milewski-Hertlein, K. A. (2001). The use of a socially constructed genogram in clinical practice. *The American Journal of Family Therapy, 29,* 23–38. doi:10.1080/01926180125996

Minuchin, P. (1985). Families and individual development: Provocations from the field of family therapy. *Child Development, 56,* 289–302. doi:10.2307/1129720

Minuchin, P., Colapinto, J., & Minuchin, S. (2007). *Working with families of the poor.* New York, NY: Guilford Press.

Minuchin, S. (1974). *Families and family therapy.* Oxford, England: Harvard University Press.

Miranda, J., Gross, J. J., Persons, J. B., & Hahn, J. (1998). Mood matters: Negative mood induction activates dysfunctional attitudes in women vulnerable to depression. *Cognitive Therapy and Research, 22,* 363–376. doi:10.1023/A:1018709212986

Mullet, E. K., & Stolberg, A. (1999). The development of the Co-Parenting Behaviors Questionnaire: An instrument for children of divorce. *Journal of Divorce & Remarriage, 31,* 115–137.

Oquendo, M. A., Lizardi, D., Greenwald, S., Weissman, M., & Mann, J. J. (2004). Rates of lifetime suicide attempt and rates of lifetime major depression in different ethnic groups in the United States. *Acta Psychiatrica Scandinavica, 110,* 446–451. doi:10.1111/j.1600-0447.2004.00404.x

Pleck, J. H. (2008). Studying immigrant fathering: Methodological and conceptual challenges. In S. S. Chuang & R. P. Moreno (Eds.), *On new shores* (pp. 257–287). Lanham, MD: Lexington Books.

Pleck, J. H., & Stueve, J. L. (2001). Time and paternal involvement. In K. Daly (Ed.), *Minding the time in family experience: Emerging perspectives and issues* (pp. 205–226). Oxford, England: Elsevier Science.

Rich-Edwards, J. W., Kleinman, K., Abrams, A., Harlow, B. L., McLaughlin, T. J., Joffe, H., & Gillman, M. W. (2006). Sociodemographic predictors of antenatal and postpartum depressive symptoms among women in a medical group practice. *Journal of Epidemiology and Community Health, 60,* 221–227. doi:10.1136/jech.2005.039370

Scheck, D. C. (1979). Two measures of parental consistency. *Psychology: A Quarterly Journal of Human Behavior, 16,* 37–39.

Segre, L. S., Losch, M. E., & O'Hara, M. W. (2006). Race/ethnicity and perinatal depressed mood. *Journal of Reproductive and Infant Psychology, 24,* 99–106. doi:10.1080/02646830600643908

Stright, A. D., & Bales, S. S. (2003). Coparenting quality: Contributions of child and parent characteristics. *Family Relations, 52*, 232–240. doi:10.1111/j.1741-3729.2003.00232.x

Strozier, A., Armstrong, M., Skuza, S., Cecil, D. & McHale, J. (2011). Coparenting in kinship families with an incarcerated mother: A qualitative study. *Families in Society, 92*, 55–61.

Talbot, J. A., Baker, J. K., & McHale, J. P. (2009). Sharing the love: Prebirth adult attachment status and coparenting adjustment during early infancy. *Parenting: Science and Practice, 9*, 56–77. doi:10.1080/15295190802656760

Talbot, J. A., & McHale, J. P. (2004). Individual parental adjustment moderates the relationship between marital and coparenting quality. *Journal of Adult Development, 11*, 191–205. doi:10.1023/B:JADE.0000035627.26870.f8

Thomas, A. J. (1998). Understanding culture and worldview in family systems: Use of the multicultural genogram. *The Family Journal, 6*, 24–32. doi:10.1177/1066480798061005

Watts-Jones, D. (1997). Toward an African American genogram. *Family Process, 36*, 375–383. doi:10.1111/j.1545-5300.1997.00375.x

von Klitzing, K., & Burgin, D. (2005). Parental capacities for triadic relationships during pregnancy: Early predictors of children's behavioral and representational functioning at preschool age. *Infant Mental Health Journal, 26*, 19–39.

8

COPARENTING INTERVENTIONS FOR EXPECTING PARENTS

MARK E. FEINBERG AND KARI-LYN SAKUMA

Parenthood, with its associated and ongoing changes in roles, relationships, routines, responsibilities, identities, and task demands (Fish, Stifter, & Belsky, 1993; Levy-Shiff, Dimitrovsky, Shulman, & Har-Even, 1998), represents a paradigmatic life change with potentially serious consequences. For example, new parents are at risk of elevated levels of stress and depression (NICHD Early Child Care Research Network, 1999). Despite some controversy, the bulk of evidence suggests that parenthood also tends to strain couples' relations with each other (Lawrence, Rothman, Cobb, Rothman, & Bradbury, 2008). These early strains for parents and their relationships are coincident with the child's earliest years, when children are perhaps most vulnerable and helpless and rely on parents for nurturing, safety, and support.

Despite the fact that an abundance of research has been carried out on risk factors in the family that affect child outcomes, the number of effective and widely disseminated family-focused preventions is limited. For example, of the four family-focused prevention programs among the "model" programs designated by Blueprints for Violence Prevention, three are actually closer to treatment or therapy than prevention. Nurse-Family Partnership (a home visiting program; Olds et al., 1998) is the only family-focused program among the empirically based Blueprints that is a true prevention program. However, Nurse-Family Partnership and most other prenatal and early childhood interventions focus on mothers and babies—despite the fact researchers have known for decades that the relationship between the parents is strongly associated with parenting and children's well-being (Emery, 1982).

Scholarly work on coparenting provides a powerful conceptual framework for integrating the two prominent areas of family-focused prevention: parenting interventions and couple relationship programs. Although there have been striking advances in the basic science underlying these two areas of study, the interventions developed for these subsystems have not been well integrated (Sanders, Markie-Dadds, & Nicholson, 1997). By helping to integrate intervention capabilities for these two areas, the framework provided by the conceptualization of coparenting may lead to more powerful and perhaps more easily disseminable prevention programs.

In this chapter, *coparenting, coparenting relationship,* and *coparenting alliance* are used interchangeably to refer at a general level to the ways that parents (or other adults who have taken on parental responsibilities for a child—e.g., a grandparent, stepparent, aunt) relate to each other in their parenting roles and coordinate their parenting activities. Elsewhere, we have described four overlapping constructs that together appear to represent the domains of coparenting that researchers have examined: agreement between parents on child-rearing goals and approaches; division of child-rearing labor; support vs. undermining of the other parent, including emotional and evaluative attributions, attitudes, comments, and actions; and mutual regulation of family norms and interactions. We use coparenting relationship *quality* to refer to the texture of a particular coparenting relationship, mainly along these four dimensions, which can be evaluated as positive or negative depending on whether the coparenting arrangements and behaviors in the family support or undermine harmony in family relationships and well-being among each of the family members. Given the documented importance of the coparenting alliance for both the well-being of individual family members and the quality of other family relationships, a number of researchers have begun to explore how best to support positive, cooperative coparenting relationships. The logic of prevention science (Hawkins, Catalano, & Miller, 1992), in which intervention applied before problems have developed is preferred to intervention after maladaptive behavioral patterns have emerged, has led several teams to focus on helping expectant parents develop positive coparenting alliances around the time of birth.

Our aims in this chapter are to briefly describe selected conceptual and theoretical considerations related to targeting the coparenting relationship in prevention programs around birth, highlight some the current innovative coparenting interventions for expectant parents, and discuss limitations and future directions.

CONCEPTUAL ISSUES

The prevention science model begins with the identification of a public health problem and then reviews evidence to determine malleable risk or protective factors for that problem. Given the focus of this volume, however, we are reversing this procedure by describing what outcomes may be addressed by targeting coparenting. We then address the issue of the causal influence of coparenting and the strategic design of coparenting-focused interventions.

Targeted Outcomes

Although equifinality is to be expected in prevention work, the wide range of outcomes that may be enhanced through an intervention focused on coparenting may be unique. For example, theory and research discussed in this volume suggest that coparenting is linked concurrently, and in some studies longitudinally, with parental depression and stress; overall couple relationship quality; father involvement; parenting quality; security in the parent–child relationship; and child adjustment—including externalizing behavior problems, internalizing symptoms, peer relations, and perhaps academic achievement. Here we discuss a select few of these potential outcomes.

Parent Adjustment

Enhancing the quality of the coparenting relationship has the potential to promote several dimensions of parents' adjustment in the transition to parenthood period. For example, positive coparenting support and low levels of coparenting disagreement are likely to decrease parental stress. Several possible mechanisms may be involved. First, friction in the coparenting relationship itself is stressful, contributing to a parent's overall level of stress. Second, coparenting in which there is a high level of coordination and validation provides support for each parent. Third, to the degree that the division of labor arrangements is satisfactory or close to expectations, parents (especially mothers) may feel a reduced sense of being overwhelmed. Fourth, a supportive coparent may affirm that parenting in the transition period is relatively stressful, which helps reduce expectations about being the ideal parent and diminish experienced stress.

In addition, we view coparenting support as the most proximal and powerful concurrent environmental influence on perceived parental efficacy, which represents the parent's sense of being able to competently and effectively respond to the child's needs (Teti, O'Connell, & Reiner, 1996). In the stress-coping framework, parental efficacy corresponds to a "secondary appraisal" or assessment of one's ability to manage a stressor or one's reaction to it (Lerman & Glanz, 1997). A parent with a sense of low efficacy may experience helplessness and anxiety when faced with difficult or ambiguous infant signals. Coparenting support serves to bolster a parent's sense of performing the new parenting role adequately and competently, leading to greater confidence in the ability to handle difficult situations (Frank, Jacobson, & Hole, 1986). Coparental support, by reducing stress and helplessness and enhancing confidence, would be expected to decrease parental depression and anxiety.

Couple Relationship Quality

The fact that a majority of families undergoing divorce include a child under 6 years of age (Whiteside & Becker, 2000) would seem to indicate that the early childhood years are stressful for parents' relationships. Although not all couples experience marital deterioration, two thirds of mothers report declines in marital satisfaction after the first child's birth (Shapiro, Gottman, & Carrere, 2000; see also S. M. McHale & Huston, 1985). Researchers have actively debated the existence and extent of a decline in couple relationship quality after the birth of a first child, with findings available to support a range of positions. The issue is difficult to draw conclusions about because couples who have children may be different from couples who do not, and infertility—one reason some couples do not have children—may have consequences for couple relationship quality as well. Yet the preponderance of evidence, and the most rigorous studies, tend to support the presence of some decline in relationship quality for many couples (Lawrence, Rothman, Cobb, Rothman, & Bradbury, 2008; Twenge, Campbell, & Foster, 2003).

The potential of a coparenting-focused intervention to buffer relationship quality from such a decline is supported by longitudinal evidence that coparenting is associated with couple relationship outcomes (Belsky & Hsieh, 1998; Schoppe, Mangelsdorf, Frosch, & McHale, 2001). Further research is needed on the processes involved. It may be that where coparenting is positive but the couple relationship is negative (P. A. Cowan & McHale, 1996), parents have successfully rallied together for the good of their children. This process may designate the coparenting sphere as a nonhostile area, which provides the basis for positive experiences and the retention of positive interactions. The maintenance of a positive coparenting relationship may sustain an incentive for repairing dyadic negativity. Of course, it is also possible that parents who maintain positive coparenting in the face of couple negativity may possess individual or couple strengths that eventually also serve to enhance the couple relationship. Examination of the effects of a coparenting intervention may help test this alternative account.

Father Involvement

Fathers' influence on child well-being has largely been understudied, but interest in the role of fathers has grown over the past 20 years as research has highlighted the influence of their parenting on children—especially on children's externalizing behavior (DeKlyen, Speltz, & Greenberg, 1998; Parke, Cassidy, Burks, Carson, & Boyum, 1992; Stocker & Youngblade, 1999). More recently, researchers have discovered that fatherhood may have positive effects on the life trajectories of individual fathers (Eggebeen & Knoester, 2001). As researchers move to incorporate fathers into early family interventions, an understanding of the coparenting relationship during the transition to parenthood will be essential.

Longitudinal studies have found that fathers' sensitivity to their infants' needs is linked to infant secure attachment (Notaro & Volling, 1999); toddlers' ability to self-regulate negative affect (Davidov & Grusec, 2006); and controlling for mothers' influence, later cognitive and language development at preschool ages (Black, Dubowitz, & Starr, 1999). Positive early interactions between fathers and infants may reduce the risk of later childhood externalizing behavior (Trautmann-Villalba, Gschwendt, Schmidt, & Laucht, 2006), especially when mothers suffer from depression (Chang, Halpern, & Kaufman, 2007). Interventions that only target father involvement have had limited success (P. A. Cowan, Cowan, Pruett, & Pruett, 2009). However, coparenting-focused interventions at the transition to parenthood may be uniquely poised to foster positive father involvement by addressing one important obstacle, especially among low-income, young, and/or unmarried parents: mother support for father involvement. A strong predictor of the father–child relationship is the quality of the father–mother relationship, regardless of whether the parents have ever been married, separated, or divorced (P. A. Cowan, Cowan, Cohen, Pruett, & Pruett, 2008).

Parenting and Child Outcomes

The quality of family relationships in the early years of a child's life is developmentally crucial. Even among relatively well-off, apparently low-risk families, distress during this period is tied to later negative outcomes for children (C. P. Cowan & Cowan, 1992). We posit that coparenting quality influences parenting quality both directly and indirectly, through parental adjustment. Where parents express a mutual commitment to table their own conflicts and prioritize the child's needs when all three are together, the result is likely to be a greater attentiveness to the child's cues and needs. Similarly, to the extent that parents are not engaged in competitive behavior for the child's attention, they will interact in a more sensitive way toward the child (Ihinger-Tallman, Pasley, & Beuhler, 1995). Finally, to the degree that the coparenting relationship provides a forum in which the parents can process their infant's cues and their own reactions to parent–child interactions, as well as problem solve difficulties, their level of insight, comfort, and confidence as parents is likely to increase in the presence of a positive coparenting relationship.

Coparenting quality may also indirectly influence positive parenting practices such as parental sensitivity/warmth and competent child behavioral management (e.g., consistent and firm but not harsh limit setting; Feinberg & Pettit, 2003) through enhanced self-efficacy and lower parental depression. In fact, one of the seminal discussions of the coparenting alliance focused on how this alliance supported the psychological health of each parent (Weissman & Cohen, 1985). Parents who feel supported by their coparent may feel more confident as a parent and experience fewer feelings of helplessness. Empirical work has documented several links in the indirect pathway. Studies have suggested that parental efficacy mediates the relationship between parental emotional distress and lack of sensitive parenting (Gondoli & Silverberg, 1997; Teti, O'Connell, & Reiner, 1996); abundant research has linked parental depression to disruptions in parenting sensitivity and responsivity (Halligan, Murray, Martins, & Cooper, 2007). Thus, coparental support that enhances parental efficacy and reduces parental depression would be expected to improve sensitive parenting as well.

The hypothesized causal influence of coparenting on parenting may be an important pathway for the effect of coparenting quality on child outcomes, although direct paths are possible here too. For example, research has suggested that coparenting has a moderately strong influence on externalizing behavior problems. The associations of coparenting with internalizing problems may be smaller than for externalizing behaviors (Buehler, Anthony, Krishnakumar, & Stone, 1997). However, researchers' capacity to detect early internalizing problems may be more limited than for early externalizing problems. Still, coparenting difficulties as reflected by interparental conflict and child-rearing disagreement have been linked to concurrent and later internalizing problems in children (Kerig, 1998; Jouriles et al., 1991; Shaw, Keenan, Vondra, Delliquadri, & Giovannelli, 1997).

Coparenting as a Causal Risk Factor

Following the logic of the prevention science model, we seek to target a risk factor that is a causal influence on outcomes, not just a statistical risk factor that is a mere marker or correlate of individual and family problems.

The previous descriptions support the hypothesis that coparenting is a causal influence on individual and family outcomes, and there is some empirical evidence to support the claim of causality. One important issue is to determine whether the quality of a couple's romantic relationship or the coparenting dimension of the relationship is a more proximate and causal influence on, in particular, parenting and child outcomes. Our reading of the evidence suggests that coparenting appears to be the proximate and causal influence. For example, research has indicated that the coparenting relationship is more closely related to parenting than other aspects of the couple relationship. When the general couple relationship and coparenting are compared in the same study, coparenting often is found to be of greater significance (Bearss & Eyberg, 1998; Feinberg, Kan, & Hetherington, 2007). In addition, some research has found that coparenting mediates the relationship between the couple relationship and parenting both cross-sectionally and longitudinally (Floyd, Gilliom, & Costigan, 1998; Gonzales, Pitts, Hill, & Roosa, 2000). Moreover, research indicating that coparenting influences marital relations (Hetherington et al., 1999) but not vice versa (Schoppe, Mangelsdorf, Frosch, & McHale, 2001) has suggested that an intervention targeting coparenting would be more appropriate than general marriage enhancement if the ultimate goal is to improve parenting and child adjustment. Given this evidence, we agree with Margolin that the quality of the couple relationship may be a marker of problems, but that the quality of the coparenting relationship is more likely to be a causal influence on individual and family difficulties (Margolin, Gordis, & John, 2001).

Strategic Intervention Development

In addition to targeting malleable risk factors that lead to important public health problems, successful prevention programs also are designed with various strategic elements. One important strategic decision relates to the timing of the intervention. Prevention scientists often focus on life transitions because potential participants may be motivated to engage in programs when faced with the uncertainty of a transition, such as school entry, marriage, parenthood, and divorce. Expectant and new parents are relatively open to education and support as they create an "emergent family system." Moreover, although there is a wide range of experience across the transition to parenthood, research has supported the view that new parents experience a high level of stress and strain (Antonucci & Mikus, 1988), which continues beyond the initial months postpartum (Shapiro, Gottman, & Carrere, 2000). The Cowans have argued persuasively that the stresses and vulnerability of even "low-risk" couples have been underestimated: Parents who are married, have fairly good relationships, and are well off in socioeconomic terms experience difficult strains as they enter parenthood and create an "emergent family system" (C. P. Cowan & Cowan, 1992). Thus, the majority of new parents are motivated to find ways to alleviate potential stressors and, perhaps most important, to maximize their child's well-being.

A second reason why intervening at the transition to parenthood holds promise is because this is the period in which the parents construct their own unique version of coparenting. The coparenting relationship may be more fluid and malleable during its emergence and early development than later, when relationship patterns, family rituals, and implicit agreements have crystallized. Yet the expectations and perceptions parents hold both before and soon after birth have implications for longer term coparenting dynamics (J. P. McHale & Rotman, 2007).

Prevention programs that are able to move beyond the testing stage and become widely disseminated also include strategic design elements that foster adoption by implementers (e.g., health systems, schools, agencies) and attract sustainable funding. For example, adoption is facilitated if the program fits the self-perceived mission of an implementing institution, addresses perceived needs, and is consonant with prevailing cultural values.

OVERVIEW OF INTERVENTIONS

Given the relatively recent emergence of coparenting as a topic of study, it is not surprising that most of the current interventions focusing on the coparenting relationship are still in the early stages of development and testing. This section summarizes the breadth of these current intervention programs as well as other family programs important in contributing to this area.

Becoming a Family Project

One of the earliest and best-known studies to examine the effects of a couple relationship-focused prevention program delivered at the transition to parenthood was the Becoming a Family Project developed by Phil and Carolyn Cowan (C. P. Cowan & Cowan, 1992, 1995). The intervention consisted of weekly group counseling meetings for 12 weeks prior to childbirth and 12 weeks after childbirth. The program aimed to reduce disappointments and distress related to parenting and couple relationships and increase marital satisfaction for couples. The group meetings functioned as a social support mechanism, allowing couples to share their experiences and adjust what they viewed as normal, with trained facilitators providing some thematic guidance and direction in fostering couple sharing and mutual support. Results of the study (N = 72 couples) showed promise for this type of program: There were fewer negative changes in both couple sexual relationships and levels of role satisfaction for program participants compared with control participants, and program fathers identified with their role as a parent to a greater extent than did control fathers (C. P. Cowan & Cowan, 1995). The authors reanalyzed the data a decade later with more sophisticated analytic techniques that incorporated multiple data points extending from 3 months prebirth to 5.5 years postbirth (Schulz, Cowan, & Cowan, 2006). The results showed that across the transition to parenthood, parents assigned to the intervention declined from their initial level of marital satisfaction by only 4% compared with 14% among those in the control condition. Although the results showed the promise of this type of intervention, the program did not lend itself to widespread replication because of its intensive nature and the high level of training of the facilitators.

The Cowans have continued to break ground, developing and testing programs for couples in which a child is transitioning to school and programs to support increased father involvement. For example, in the Supporting Father Involvement Study (P. A. Cowan, Cowan, Pruett, & Pruett, 2009), the Cowans tested whether a father-only program or a couples program would be more effective than a control condition for enhancing father's involvement with children as well as family relationships. Although these programs were not developed for expecting parents, the results have strong implications for other coparenting programs. The study population was primarily from low socioeconomic strata, over two thirds Mexican American, and had at least one child between birth and 7 years of age. The father-only and couple intervention consisted of 16 weekly meetings, during which participants discussed how they felt about themselves, what they wanted to change, and parenting principles. The program included information and exercises relating to parenting styles, communication, and seeking social support. Compared with the control group, both father-only and couples group participants showed positive increases in fathers' engagement with children and involvement in daily child-care tasks 18 months after baseline. However, the couple group participants showed greater declines in parental stress, and couple relationship satisfaction remained stable for both mothers and fathers compared with declining satisfaction in the control group participants. This is one of the few studies that have compared a prevention program delivered to one parent versus both as a couple, and the results suggested that broader impact on the family is obtained when both parents are involved.

Family Foundations Project

The Family Foundations (FF) project was based on an integrative review of the literature on coparenting and early parenting and the consequent emerging theoretical model (Feinberg, 2003). FF was developed as a universal program for parents at all levels of risk, to be implemented within the framework of local childbirth education (CBE) services in the community or local hospital. The strategic rationale for intervening through CBE programs was noted by Belsky and Pensky (1988): CBE is delivered in a universal framework, the public generally views CBE positively (Doering, Entwisle, & Quinlan, 1980), and the location of CBE within local hospitals or other health care offices provides a sustainable institutional niche.

The initial trial of FF ($N = 169$ couples) compared couples randomized to the eight-session program with control couples. The study confirmed that CBE was an appropriate context. Positive response from CBE educators to FF is consonant with reported shifts in the perinatal education field—specifically, toward an expanded role for perinatal educators encompassing preventive approaches facilitating the transition to parenthood (Polomeno, 2000).

Intervention Effects: Parent Report

To assess short-term intervention effects of targeted program mediators, we asked parents to complete questionnaires at pretest during a home visit and again at posttest via a mail-in questionnaire when children were approximately 6 months old. Intent-to-treat analyses with missing data imputation demonstrated significant positive effects of the program at posttest on coparenting relationship quality, maternal depression (Center for Epidemiologic Studies Depression Scale; Radloff, 1977), dysfunctional parent–child interaction (Parental Stress Index; Abidin, 1997), and infant attention capacity and soothability (Infant Behavior Questionnaire; Gartstein & Rothbart, 2003; Feinberg & Kan, 2008). At child age 1 year, parents in the intervention condition demonstrated significantly lower levels of coparental competition and triangulation behaviors than did control parents. Intervention mothers demonstrated significantly greater inclusion of fathers into triadic interaction than did control mothers. There were also significant intervention effects on both parents' positivity toward the child and lower levels of parental negativity among intervention fathers than control fathers. Moreover, intervention children demonstrated significantly higher levels of self-soothing than did control children.

In a single model, we assessed intervention group differences in posttest levels (i.e., Wave 2) as well as change from posttest through child age 1 year (Wave 3) and 3 years (Wave 4). Final results indicated significant overall intervention effects for measures of coparenting and two aspects of parent adjustment: parental efficacy and parent depression (a marginal effect was also found for parental stress, $p = .057$). There was no evidence of moderation by parent gender. For each of these measures, results indicated that an intervention effect was established at posttest that neither increased nor waned to a significant degree by child age 3 years. A significant, moderate effect of FF on parenting Overreactivity (i.e., harsh reactivity) and Laxness was found, with intervention condition parents reporting significantly less likelihood of utilizing corporal punishment.

Finally, results indicated a significant, moderate program effect on child social competence but not on emotional competence at age 3 years. Data also yielded a strong and significant intervention impact on boys' total behavioral problems, with significant impact on both the Externalizing and Internalizing indices (Child Behavior Checklist; Achenbach & Rescorla, 2000). There were no significant effects for girls' problem behavior. We are currently exploring whether this could be a result of gender differences in developmental timing of problem behaviors, or perhaps the result of a stronger impact of the program on families of boys. The latter interpretation would be consistent with some research indicating that fathers are more involved in the early parenting of boys than girls, which could lead to increased opportunity for coparental conflict among parents of boys.

Summary

FF shows promise both because of the results from the pilot study and because of its development within the context of an institutional niche available in most communities. The integration with CBE would position FF as a nonstigmatizing, universal intervention that could be delivered to a large proportion of first-time parents. Moreover, implementation of FF by local hospitals would require minimal need for new expenditures on overhead or recruitment because the administrative structures and recruitment channels already exist. As such, if FF's intervention impact is replicated and further study demonstrates downstream impact on children's adjustment, the approach may represent a cost-effective approach to promoting public health. As a universal intervention for couples, however, FF may not reach high-risk, young, and/or uncommitted new parents.

Young Parenthood Program

The development of coparenting-focused support programs may be particularly important for young, unmarried mothers and fathers: Young fathers are at risk of becoming aggressive or disengaged from their children when the romantic liaison with their coparenting partner dissolves, and young mothers are at risk of becoming depressed and overwhelmed. The Young Parenthood Program (YPP) is a flexible, 10-week couples-focused prevention program delivered by a trained counselor to individual couples (Florsheim et al., 2010). The YPP is designed to help young mothers and fathers develop perspectives and interpersonal skills that will contribute to supportive coparenting, develop ways to contain hostility, and enhance parenting competence.

The rationale for recruiting young fathers prior to childbirth and in collaboration with their partners is based on the principle that targeting risk factors early in development is the best way to prevent problems from either occurring or becoming crystallized, and targeting at-risk parents is the best way to interrupt the cross-generational transmission of problems. The program is intended to be delivered through clinics providing prenatal services and school-based programs for pregnant adolescents.

The YPP draws on the principles of attachment theory and family systems theory insofar as the program is designed to increase the security and warmth of the child's social environment by helping young parents to develop a stable, supportive alliance (C. P. Cowan & Cowan, 1992). The program's 10 sessions are divided into five phases. Early sessions focus on building rapport and educating the couple about how their relationship is relevant to their child's development. Counselors focus on the child's need for a secure base and a safe home environment. The second phase of the program is designed to help partners clarify and identify how personal goals relate to their partner's (personal) goals, their relationship goals, and their respective roles as parents. The third phase targets relational competencies and communication skills (reflective listening, clear expression of needs, communicating acceptance, providing reassurance and support, deescalation of conflict). This phase is designed to improve the couple's ability to function as a partnership, regardless of their relationship status. For those couples who appear to be at risk of intimate partner violence (IPV), this phase includes psychoeducational content addressing the psychological risks associated with IPV and teaching strategies for avoiding it. The fourth phase of the program is designed to help the couple renegotiate roles and find adaptive ways to enlist the support of their extended families and community. Counselors also discuss family planning issues to help increase the likelihood that both parents will wait 3 or more years before having another child. The final phase of the program focuses on concerns about parenting and is tailored to the particular challenges of each couple. During this phase, sessions focus on reinforcing individual and relationship strengths, as these strengths relate to parenting.

Initial tests conducted to determine the efficacy of the YPP on the basis of a small sample of pregnant adolescents (mean age = 16 years) and their partners (mean age = 18 years) revealed that couples who participated in the YPP ($n = 40$) had higher levels of coparenting relational competence (coded from interviews) and were significantly less likely to be engaged in IPV at 2 to 3 months after birth than were control couples ($n = 44$). Although the research team is continuing to analyze the data, these results indicate that engaging couples together in a program that includes a focus on coparenting as well as on communication, the couple relationship, and parenting can have a positive impact on unmarried, young couples.

Couple and Coparent Mechanisms

Prevention research often serves two masters. On the one hand, a specific theory guides the selection of primary targets of the intervention. Assessing whether changing these proximal intervention targets affects ultimate outcomes serves as an experimental test of the theory. On the other hand, program developers would like to maximize the impact of an intervention. Thus, in addition to targeting a single proximal construct (e.g., coparenting), a program may also impact child outcomes through targeting other constructs directly (e.g., parent mood or parenting competence). But targeting multiple constructs dilutes the ability to test any single theoretical proposition. One possible way to serve both masters is to design a study in which multiple intervention targets are compared with each other.

Brian Doss (2004) has begun a study comparing a control condition with two parallel brief counseling approaches with expectant adult couples; one approach focuses on enhancing coparenting, whereas the other focuses on the couple relationship. Both the couple and coparenting relationship versions comprise two counseling sessions with the couple before birth and two after birth. The couple intervention helps couples identify ways to retain positive influences and reduce negative stressors in their relationships. The coparent intervention focuses on exploring each partner's hopes and expectations for their child and their coparenting relationship, and then on developing a workable coparent plan.

This study is poised to answer very interesting questions about whether an improved coparenting relationship will buoy the couple relationship, as well as the question of whether an enhanced couple relationship will support more positive coparenting. Asking these questions in the framework of the experimental design, which provides the greatest purchase on causal directionality, will require the brief interventions to be effective in "moving the needle" (i.e., enhancing the targeted proximal construct). In addition, Doss aims to examine the direct causal effects of couple relationship and coparenting relationships, separately, on infant functioning. Capturing the dynamic processes and understanding the causal relationships associated with child outcomes will contribute to theories surrounding family dynamics and, of course, feedback into the tailoring of interventions (Doss, 2004).

Building Strong Families and the Healthy Marriage Initiative

In discussing coparenting-focused programs targeting the transition to parenthood, it would be a mistake to ignore the large Building Strong Families (BSF) project initiated by the Administration for Children and Families, U.S. Department of Health and Human Services, and the Healthy Marriage

Initiative. This large social experiment (over 5,000 couples enrolled at eight sites) has attracted significant attention. Although this project did not support coparenting interventions per se, the focus on stable home environments and the building of supportive couple relationships are relevant to reducing negative effects on child development. BSF consisted of first supporting the development of three programs by established couple relations researchers and then testing the programs in a multisite randomized trial (each site implemented one of the programs, with random assignment of couples to the program or control conditions).

There were many critics of the Healthy Marriage approach, and their concerns have been published elsewhere (see Huston & Melz, 2004). Nonetheless, the sheer magnitude of the BSF project and its focus on interparental relations deserve consideration here. In important ways, BSF's magnitude may have been premature; insufficient work has been done showing the potential of such programs to attract low-income individuals. In fact, after enrolling in the study, a large proportion of BSF participants in the intervention conditions did not participate in many program sessions. Moreover, BSF jumped into a huge experiment without the benefit of smaller efficacy trials to show that the BSF programs held promise in changing outcomes.

In any case, results at 15 months after baseline indicated that in general the BSF programs did not have a significant impact on outcomes. When outcomes were assessed separately by site, six sites showed generally null findings. One site showed several positive albeit small effects. This site had higher attendance rates at program sessions than at other sites, presumably because participants were paid for attendance at that site. And one site unfortunately showed several iatrogenic effects (i.e., worse outcomes in the intervention condition than in the control condition), including increased relationship violence among those in the intervention condition.

Analyses of BSF impact by subgroups indicated an overall positive effect across sites on couple relationship quality but not on relationship status (i.e., continued romantic involvement, marriage, fidelity) for two groups: African American couples and couples who entered the study at higher levels of relationship quality. On the other hand, BSF had a significant negative impact on the relationship status of three groups: couples in which one or both partners were not African American, couples in which both partners were 21 years or over, and couples in which a partner had a child with another individual. Given the number of these significant findings (five) out of the total of subgroup analyses (60), these results should be considered quite tentative because the rate of significant findings (8%) is only slightly higher than chance (5%). Although one would like to draw as much knowledge as possible from this large and expensive study, it would be too bold to draw any but the most tentative conclusions from these subgroup findings.

Thus, the BSF study has yielded little positive news about the potential of couple programs to impact interparental relations, parent adjustment, and child well-being for low-income families. Given that the programs developed for the BSF trial did not focus on coparenting, the null results should not be interpreted as indicating that attractive and effective interventions focusing on coparenting could not be developed for this population.

FUTURE DIRECTIONS

Although the work on enhancing coparenting among new parents has just begun, we believe certain lessons can be drawn from this brief overview. The first lesson from the early evidence is that enhancing coparenting appears to be possible, and it may have the expected impact on other aspects of individual and family well-being.

Second, the prevention science model of piloting programs before moving to trials, and conducting efficacy studies before effectiveness studies, may help to avoid major problems later. Although this process takes more time and requires a bit more patience, it yields more effective programs that have a better chance of dissemination. We also note that it is important to target causal risk factors for negative outcomes—rather than risk markers or correlates of negative outcomes. We believe that the available evidence suggests that the coparenting relationship plays a more proximal and possibly causal role in fostering positive parenting and child outcomes than the general couple relationship. Moreover, the coparenting relationship may be more malleable than the overall couple relationship, and a focus on coparenting may be more appealing to new parents than a focus on their own couple relationship.

Third, different approaches will need to be developed to address coparenting support among parents based on myriad factors. Only a few of these factors have been addressed in some way by the programs and studies described previously, including age (adolescent parents), family history and individual risk, poverty, and marital status. Other factors that may require attention include ethnicity and culture, romantic involvement status of the couple, and sexual orientation. There is a need for further basic research to identify themes and patterns of coparenting among different cultures and among gay and lesbian couples, in order for intervention developers to sensitively and effectively design supportive prevention programs and practices for such couples. In general, the development of methods to support families through the transition to parenthood and beyond, specifically by focusing on the quality and form of coparenting relations, has just begun.

REFERENCES

Abidin, R. R. (1997). Parenting Stress Index: A measure of the parent-child system. In C. P. Zalaquett & R. J. Wood (Eds.), *Evaluating stress: A book of resources* (pp. 277–291). Lanham, MD: Scarecrow Education.

Achenbach, T. M., & Rescorla, L. A. (2000). *Manual for ASEBA preschool forms & profiles*. Burlington: University of Vermont, Research Center for Children, Youth, & Families.

Antonucci, T. C., & Mikus, K. (1988). The power of parenthood: Personality and attitudinal changes during the transition to parenthood. In G. Y. Michaels & W. A. Goldberg (Eds.), *The transition to parenthood: Current theory and research. Cambridge studies in social and emotional development* (pp. 62–84). New York, NY: Cambridge University Press.

Bearss, K. E., & Eyberg, S. (1998). A test of the parenting alliance theory. *Early Education and Development, 9*, 179–185. doi:10.1207/s15566935eed0902_5

Belsky, J., & Hsieh, K.-H. (1998). Patterns of marital change during the early childhood years: Parent personality, coparenting, and division-of-labor correlates. *Journal of Family Psychology, 12*, 511–528. doi:10.1037/0893-3200.12.4.511

Belsky, J., & Pensky, E. (1988). Marital change across the transition to parenthood. *Marriage & Family Review, 12*(3–4), 133–156. doi:10.1300/J002v12n03_08

Black, M. M., Dubowitz, H., & Starr, R. H. (1999). African-American fathers in low income, urban families: Development and behavior of their 3-year-old children. *Child Development, 70*, 967–978. doi:10.1111/1467-8624.00070

Buehler, C., Anthony, C., Krishnakumar, A., & Stone, G. (1997). Interparental conflict and youth problem behaviors: A meta-analysis. *Journal of Child and Family Studies, 6*, 233–247. doi:10.1023/A:1025006909538

Chang, J. J., Halpern, C. T., & Kaufman, J. S. (2007). Maternal depressive symptoms, father's involvement, and the trajectories of child problem behaviors in a US national sample. *Archives of Pediatrics & Adolescent Medicine, 161*, 697–703. doi:10.1001/archpedi.161.7.697

Cowan, C. P., & Cowan, P. A. (1992). *When partners become parents: The big life change for couples*. New York, NY: Basic Books.

Cowan, C. P., & Cowan, P. A. (1995). Interventions to ease the transition to parenthood: Why they are needed and what they can do. *Family Relations: Journal of Applied Family and Child Studies, 44*, 412–423.

Cowan, P. A., Cowan, C. P., Cohen, N., Pruett, M. K., & Pruett, K. (2008). Supporting fathers' engagement with their kids. In J. D. Berrick & N. Gilbert (Eds.), *Raising children: Emerging needs, modern risks, and social responses* (pp. 44–80). New York, NY: Oxford University Press.

Cowan, P. A., Cowan, C. P., Pruett, M. K., & Pruett, K. (2009). Promoting fathers' engagement with children: Preventive interventions for low-income families. *Journal of Marriage and the Family, 71*, 663–679. doi:10.1111/j.1741-3737.2009.00625.x

Cowan, P. A., & McHale, J. P. (1996). Coparenting in a family context: Emerging achievements, current dilemmas and future directions. *New Directions for Child and Adolescent Development, 74,* 93–106.

Davidov, M., & Grusec, J. E. (2006). Untangling the links of parental responsiveness to distress and warmth to child outcomes. *Child Development, 77,* 44–58. doi:10.1111/j.1467-8624.2006.00855.x

DeKlyen, M., Speltz, M. L., & Greenberg, M. T. (1998). Fathering and early onset conduct problems: Positive and negative parenting, father-son attachment, and the marital context. *Clinical Child and Family Psychology Review, 1,* 3–21. doi:10.1023/A:1021844214633

Doering, S. G., Entwisle, D. R., & Quinlan, D. (1980). Modeling the quality of women's birth experience. *Journal of Health and Social Behavior, 21,* 12–21. doi:10.2307/2136690

Doss, B. (2004). *Research trial proposal.* Unpublished manuscript.

Eggebeen, D. J., & Knoester, C. (2001). Does fatherhood matter for men? *Journal of Marriage and the Family, 63,* 381–393. doi:10.1111/j.1741-3737.2001. 00381.x

Emery, R. E. (1982). Interparental conflict and the children of discord and divorce. *Psychological Bulletin, 92,* 310–330. doi:10.1037/0033-2909.92.2.310

Feinberg, M. (2003). The internal structure and ecological context of coparenting: A framework for research and intervention. *Parenting: Science and Practice, 3,* 95–131. doi:10.1207/S15327922PAR0302_01

Feinberg, M. E., & Kan, M. L. (2008). Establishing family foundations: Intervention effects on coparenting, parent/infant well-being, and parent-child relations. *Journal of Family Psychology, 22,* 253–263. doi:10.1037/0893-3200. 22.2.253

Feinberg, M. E., Kan, M. L., & Hetherington, E. M. (2007). The longitudinal influence of coparenting conflict on parental negativity and adolescent maladjustment. *Journal of Marriage and the Family, 69,* 687–702. doi:10.1111/ j.1741-3737.2007.00400.x

Feinberg, M. E., & Pettit, G. (2003). Promoting positive parenting. In T. Gullotta & M. Bloom (Eds.), *Encyclopedia of primary prevention and health promotion* (pp. 795–803). New York, NY: Kluwer/Plenum Academic Press.

Fish, M., Stifter, C. A., & Belsky, J. (1993). Early patterns of mother-infant dyadic interaction: Infant, mother, and family demographic antecedents. *Infant Behavior and Development, 16,* 1–18. doi:10.1016/0163-6383(93)80025-4

Florsheim, P., Burrow-Sanchez, J., Minami, T., Heavin, S., Hudak, C., & McArther, L. (2010). *The Young Parenthood Program: Co-parenting counseling for pregnant adolescents and young expectant fathers.* Manuscript in preparation.

Floyd, F. J., Gilliom, L. A., & Costigan, C. L. (1998). Marriage and the parenting alliance: Longitudinal prediction of change in parenting perceptions and behaviors. *Child Development, 69,* 1461–1479. doi:10.2307/1132278

Frank, S., Jacobson, S., & Hole, C. B. (1986). Psychological predictors of parents' sense of confidence and control and self- versus child-focused gratifications. *Developmental Psychology, 22*, 348–355. doi:10.1037/0012-1649.22.3.348

Gartstein, M. A., & Rothbart, M. K. (2003). Studying infant temperament via the revised infant behavior questionnaire. *Infant Behavior and Development, 26*, 64–86. doi:10.1016/S0163-6383(02)00169-8

Gondoli, D. M., & Silverberg, S. B. (1997). Maternal emotional distress and diminished responsiveness: The mediating role of parenting efficacy and parental perspective taking. *Developmental Psychology, 33*, 861–868. doi:10.1037/0012-1649.33.5.861

Gonzales, N. A., Pitts, S. C., Hill, N. E., & Roosa, M. W. (2000). A mediational model of the impact of interparental conflict on child adjustment in a multi-ethnic, low-income sample. *Journal of Family Psychology, 14*, 365–379. doi:10.1037/0893-3200.14.3.365

Halligan, S. L., Murray, L., Martins, C., & Cooper, P. J. (2007). Maternal depression and psychiatric outcomes in adolescent offspring: A 13-year longitudinal study. *Journal of Affective Disorders, 97*(1–3), 145–154. doi:10.1016/j.jad.2006.06.010

Hawkins, J. D., Catalano, R. F., & Miller, J. Y. (1992). Risk and protective factors for alcohol and other drug problems in adolescence and early adulthood: Implications for substance abuse prevention. *Psychological Bulletin, 112*, 64–105. doi:10.1037/0033-2909.112.1.64

Hetherington, E. M., Henderson, S. H., Reiss, D., Anderson, E. R., Bridges, M., Chan, R. W., . . . Taylor, L. C. (1999). Adolescent siblings in stepfamilies: Family functioning and adolescent adjustment. *Monographs of the Society for Research in Child Development, 64*(4, Serial No. 222).

Huston, T. L., & Melz, H. (2004). The case for (promoting) marriage: The devil is in the details. *Journal of Marriage and the Family, 66*, 943–958. doi:10.1111/j.0022-2445.2004.00064.x

Ihinger-Tallman, M., Pasley, K., & Beuhler, C. (1995). Developing a middle-range theory of father involvement postdivorce. In W. Marsiglio (Ed.), *Fatherhood: Contemporary theory, research, and social policy* (Sage Series on Men and Masculinity; pp. 57–77). Thousand Oaks, CA: Sage.

Jouriles, E. N., Murphy, C. M., Farris, A. M., Smith, D. A., Richters, J. E., & Waters, E. (1991). Marital adjustment, parental disagreements about child rearing, and behavior problems in boys: Increasing the specificity of the marital assessment. *Child Development, 62*, 1424–1433. doi:10.2307/1130816

Kerig, P. K. (1998). Moderators and mediators of the effects of interparental conflict on children's adjustment. *Journal of Abnormal Child Psychology, 26*, 199–212. doi:10.1023/A:1022672201957

Lawrence, E., Rothman, A. D., Cobb, R. J., Rothman, M. T., & Bradbury, T. N. (2008). Marital satisfaction across the transition to parenthood. *Journal of Family Psychology, 22*, 41–50. doi:10.1037/0893-3200.22.1.41

Lerman, C., & Glanz, K. (1997). Stress, coping, and health behavior. In K. Glanz, F. M. Lewis, & B. K. Rimer (Eds.), *Health behavior and health education* (pp. 113–138). San Francisco, CA: Jossey-Bass.

Levy-Shiff, R., Dimitrovsky, L., Shulman, S., & Har-Even, D. (1998). Cognitive appraisals, coping strategies, and support resources as correlates of parenting and infant development. *Developmental Psychology, 34,* 1417–1427. doi:10.1037/0012-1649.34.6.1417

Margolin, G., Gordis, E. B., & John, R. S. (2001). Coparenting: A link between marital conflict and parenting in two-parent families. *Journal of Family Psychology, 15,* 3–21. doi:10.1037/0893-3200.15.1.3

McHale, J. P., & Rotman, T. (2007). Is seeing believing? Expectant parents' outlooks on coparenting and later coparenting solidarity. *Infant Behavior and Development, 30,* 63–81. doi:10.1016/j.infbeh.2006.11.007

McHale, S. M., & Huston, T. L. (1985). The effect of the transition to parenthood on the marriage relationship. *Journal of Family Issues, 6,* 409–433. doi:10.1177/019251385006004002

NICHD Early Child Care Research Network. (1999). Chronicity of maternal depressive symptoms, maternal sensitivity, and child functioning at 36 months. *Developmental Psychology, 35,* 1297–1310. doi:10.1037/0012-1649.35.5.1297

Notaro, P. C., & Volling, B. L. (1999). Parental responsiveness and infant–parent attachment: A replication study with fathers and mothers. *Infant Behavior and Development, 22,* 345–352. doi:10.1016/S0163-6383(99)00012-0

Olds, D., Henderson, C. R., Jr., Cole, R., Eckenrode, J., Kitzman, H., Luckey, D., . . . Powers, J. (1998). Long-term effects of nurse home visitation on children's criminal and antisocial behavior: 15-year follow-up of a randomized controlled trial. *JAMA, 280,* 1238–1244. doi:10.1001/jama.280.14.1238

Parke, R. D., Cassidy, J., Burks, V. M., Carson, J. L., & Boyum, L. (1992). Familial contribution to peer competence among young children: The role of interactive and affective processes. In R. D. Parke & G. W. Ladd (Eds.), *Family–peer relationships: Modes of linkage* (pp. 107–134). Hillsdale, NJ: Erlbaum.

Polomeno, V. (2000). The Polomeno family intervention framework for perinatal education: Preparing couples for the transition to parenthood. *Journal of Perinatal Education, 9,* 31–48. doi:10.1624/105812400X87482

Radloff, L. S. (1977). The CES-D scale: A self-report depression scale for research in the general population. *Applied Psychological Measurement, 1,* 385–401. doi:10.1177/014662167700100306

Sanders, M. R., Markie-Dadds, C., & Nicholson, J. M. (1997). Concurrent interventions for marital and children's problems. In W. K. Halford & H. Markman (Eds.), *Clinical handbook of marriage and couples interventions* (pp. 509–535). New York, NY: Wiley.

Schoppe, S. J., Mangelsdorf, S. C., Frosch, C. A., & McHale, J. P. (2001, May). *Coparenting and marital behavior at 6 months and 3 years: Related or separate constructs?*

Paper presented at the biennial conference of the Society for Research in Child Development, Minneapolis, MN.

Schulz, M. S., Cowan, C. P., & Cowan, P. A. (2006). Promoting healthy beginnings: A randomized controlled trial of a preventive intervention to preserve marital quality during the transition to parenthood. *Journal of Consulting and Clinical Psychology, 74*, 20–31. doi:10.1037/0022-006X.74.1.20

Shapiro, A. F., Gottman, J. M., & Carrere, S. (2000). The baby and the marriage: Identifying factors that buffer against decline in marital satisfaction after the first baby arrives. *Journal of Family Psychology, 14*, 59–70. doi:10.1037/0893-3200.14.1.59

Shaw, D. S., Keenan, K., Vondra, J. I., Delliquadri, E., & Giovannelli, J. (1997). Antecedents of preschool children's internalizing problems: A longitudinal study of low-income families. *Journal of the American Academy of Child and Adolescent Psychiatry, 36*, 1760–1767. doi:10.1097/00004583-199712000-00025

Stocker, C. M., & Youngblade, L. (1999). Marital conflict and parental hostility: Links with children's sibling and peer relationships. *Journal of Family Psychology, 13*, 598–609. doi:10.1037/0893-3200.13.4.598

Teti, D. M., O'Connell, M. A., & Reiner, C. D. (1996). Parenting sensitivity, parental depression and child health: The mediational role of parental self-efficacy. *Early Development & Parenting, 5*, 237–250. doi:10.1002/(SICI)1099-0917(199612)5:4<237::AID-EDP136>3.0.CO;2-5

Trautmann-Villalba, P., Gschwendt, M., Schmidt, M. H., & Laucht, M. (2006). Father-infant interaction patterns as precursors of children's later externalizing behavior problems: A longitudinal study over 11 years. *European Archives of Psychiatry and Clinical Neuroscience, 256*, 344–349. doi:10.1007/s00406-006-0642-x

Twenge, J. M., Campbell, W. K., & Foster, C. A. (2003). Parenthood and marital satisfaction: A meta-analytic review. *Journal of Marriage and the Family, 65*, 574–583. doi:10.1111/j.1741-3737.2003.00574.x

Weissman, S., & Cohen, R. S. (1985). The parenting alliance and adolescence. *Adolescent Psychiatry, 12*, 24–45.

Whiteside, M. F., & Becker, B. J. (2000). Parental factors and the young child's post-divorce adjustment: A meta-analysis with implications for parenting arrangements. *Journal of Family Psychology, 14*, 5–26. doi:10.1037/0893-3200.14.1.5

9

COPARENTING INTERVENTIONS FOR UNMARRIED PARENTS

FRANCESCA ADLER-BAEDER AND KAREN A. SHIRER

Successful interventions to address coparenting relationships of unmarried parents have the potential for enhancing the home environments of a significant and growing number of children in the United States. The past 40 years have seen considerable increases in the rates of children living in single-parent homes as a result of nonmarital childbirth. In 1976, 17% of single mother households were headed by a never-married mother; in 2009, this rose to 44.8% (U.S. Census Bureau, 2010). In 2007, 39.7% of all births were to unmarried women, up from 18.4% in 1980 (Hamilton, Martin, & Ventura, 2010; Martin et al., 2009). Increases have been most dramatic among low-income and ethnic minority women. In 2007, 51.3% of births to Hispanic women, 65.2% of births to Native American mothers, and 71.6% of children born to African American mothers were nonmarital births (Martin et al., 2009). Research has also indicated that over 70% of mothers who have their first child out of wedlock will go on to have all their children born nonmaritally (Seltzer, 2000).

Many never-married parents make heroic efforts to parent their children well and succeed in doing so. However, these children as a group are at greater risk for a number of negative outcomes, such as delinquent behaviors, academic difficulties, substance abuse, teen pregnancy, and depression and other psychological dysfunction (e.g., McLanahan & Sandefur, 1994). Although the etiology of negative child outcomes is incredibly complex, it is clear that factors related to economic hardship and lack of support for the parent and children are important predictors (Rutter, 2001). In addition, these elements are felt disproportionately among minority and low-income populations, indicating a critical social justice issue (Ooms, 2002).

The risk of negative effects for children is reduced when there is coparenting cooperation, regular instrumental and expressive support, and regular involvement from the noncustodial parent (e.g., Lamb, 2004; McHale, Johnson, & Sinclair, 1999; Schoppe, Mangelsdorf, & Frosch, 2001). Studies have shown that the quality of unmarried parents' coparenting relationships is critically important and impacts the quality of mothers' parenting and fathers' parenting (Dorsey, Forehand, & Brody, 2007; Feinberg, Kan, & Hetherington, 2007; Waller & Swisher, 2006), as well as ongoing father involvement (Carlson, McLanahan, & Brooks-Gunn, 2008; Sobolewski & King, 2005). In addition, in low-income communities and among minority families, particularly African American families, coparenting is a system of relationships, encompassing dyadic and polyadic relationships with kin (Crosbie-Burnett & Lewis, 1993; Roy & Burton, 2007). The quality of these kin coparent relationships with the custodial parent, as well as the relationship between kin coparents and the noncustodial biological parent, has implications for the quality of parenting, parent involvement, and children's well-being (Adler-Baeder & Abell, 2003; Aronson, Whitehead, & Baber, 2003; Kalil, Ziol-Guest, & Coley, 2005; Krishnakumar & Black, 2003).

Research has shown that over 80% of unmarried expectant fathers are romantically involved with the mother prenatally and are present at their child's birth; however, the numbers of these couples who enter into and maintain a committed relationship or marriage are low. By the child's first birthday, the majority of coparents are not romantically involved (McLanahan et al., 2003). Intervention efforts to promote cooperation and connection between coparents may hence be wisest during the prenatal and early postnatal periods. Though evidence is as yet scarce, some preliminary indicators have suggested that such efforts are beneficial for the family, regardless of whether the parents sustain a committed couple relationship or marriage (Carlson et al., 2008; Fagan, 2008).

As noted elsewhere in this volume, opportunities began to emerge in 2002 for federally funded projects that focused on enhancing the adult relationships in low-income and culturally diverse families (Brotherson & Duncan, 2004). Because both relationship/marriage education and fatherhood program initiatives are conceptualized as child-centered initiatives (Brotherson & Duncan, 2004), a natural and necessary convergence is in addressing the critical coparenting relationship, as it is a factor affecting parent involvement, parent–child relationship quality, and ultimately child outcomes. Out of these initiatives, interventions targeting the coparenting relationship of unmarried parents emerged. Some recent efforts target young unmarried fathers and emphasize skills training for the coparenting relationship as a catalyst for enhanced father involvement (Vosler & Robertson, 1998). Efficacy tests of these coparenting interventions have just begun (Fagan, 2008). Several implementers of relationship/marriage education community-based demonstration programs have taken a more comprehensive approach from the start (Ooms & Wilson, 2004), anticipating the value of addressing cooperative coparenting and the relational skills helpful for a coparenting alliance of nonromantically involved parents, including those with children beyond infancy. Either in addition to or instead of skills training in couple dynamics, depending on the make-up of the group, interventions for unmarried parents address the coparenting relationship as distinct from a couple relationship. As in the father-focused interventions, participants discuss the value for children of two-parent and multiparent involvement, the detrimental effects on children of acrimonious coparenting relationships, and the value of support for each other in their parenting roles. They also discuss and practice skills related to cooperation and conflict management around child rearing and shared parenting experiences. At this time, relatively few studies have examined coparenting interventions for unmarried parents, so this chapter is necessarily more descriptive and speculative than some of the others.

In this chapter, we articulate a framework and basic assumptions recommended for programming approaches to coparenting interventions targeting unmarried, low-resource parents. We summarize features of existing programs and the results of the relatively few summative evaluations. Finally, we emphasize suggestions for the further development of coparenting interventions for unmarried parents—an important underserved population—and the research needed to inform practices and policies to support these efforts.

THEORETICAL FRAMEWORK FOR COPARENTING INTERVENTIONS FOR UNMARRIED PARENTS

Here we outline some basic assumptions underlying effective interventions to promote coparenting. First, a risk and resiliency perspective in program design suggests that outcomes are based on the interaction of risk and protective factors (Jenson & Fraser, 2005). We assume that individuals all begin their life's journey with high hopes for their own and their family's future. However, some individuals are more at risk because of barriers that limit access to important economic, social, and human resources. With this view of risk, outreach programs and resources are conceptualized as agents of empowerment for marginalized populations of parents and function as protective or promotive factors (Sameroff & Gutman, 2004) to support resiliency and positive outcomes in the context of risks.

Second, an ecological systems approach (Minuchin, 1988) suggests that positively intervening in a system at one point can benefit functioning in other areas of the system. Empirical evidence points to the coparenting dyad as a distinct microsystem and as a particularly important intervention point in the family system, promoting father involvement and child outcomes (McHale, 2007). Coparenting interventions are therefore designed to address this relationship as distinct from a couple relationship, and they differ from traditional relationship/marital interventions that assume a romantic link between parents. Coparenting focuses on the parental work of child rearing and includes the coordination between coparents of their parenting, the manner in which they either support or undermine each other, and the management of conflict and communication between coparents (McHale et al., 2002).

Third, enhanced connections to resources are especially important for fragile and distressed families (Sorensen, Mincy, & Halpern, 2000) and increase the likelihood of parents' involvement with each other and of fathers' involvement with their children (Fagan, 2008; Kalil et al., 2005). Therefore, it is assumed that coordinated and innovative efforts to promote access to research-based coparenting information to at least one member of the family will result in increased individual, relational, and family strengths among low-resource families.

Another important assumption concerns agency for change. Most family-focused programs and interventions center exclusively on skills and targeted behaviors and hold implicit assumptions that participants have a developed sense of agency for change. This may not be true for young parents (Pajares & Urdan, 2006), those with limited access to resources, or those who have experienced oppression and discrimination (Rutter, 2001). Empowered, self-efficacious individuals are more likely to involve themselves in healthy relationships and believe that they both deserve and can maintain healthy adult relationships. Therefore, a conceptual framework for coparenting intervention for low-resource unmarried parents does well to assume that cognitive elements of individual empowerment, positive self-concept, and sense of self-efficacy will need to be promoted and addressed in the program. This will help strengthen the confidence needed to overcome personal life challenges and influence the use of positive behaviors.

To date, most of what we know about coparenting relationships among adult unmarried parents has come from programs serving African American, low-income communities (Adler-Baeder et al., 2004; Cox & Shirer, 2009;

Dion, 2005; Fagan, 2008; Shirer, Adler-Baeder, Contreras, & Spicer, 2004; Shirer, Contreras, Chen, & London, 2009). This work has been guided by the use of ecocultural theory (Phenice, Griffore, Hakoyama, & Silvey, 2009) and the examination of assumptions regarding definitions of the family. The traditional definition of the "immediate family" in the United States has been influenced by the culture of European American families. This dominant culture normed the "patri-focal" system of law that defines the family based on the legal status of the adults (Weitzman, 1981).

Shaped by their sociohistorical context, African American families operate as a "pedi-focal" family system centered on the children (Crosbie-Burnett & Lewis, 1993) and have created an "ecocultural niche" (Hille, 2006, as cited in Phenice et al., 2009) characterized by a communal philosophy, permeability of family boundaries, movement of children among households, and shared parenting among multiple parents, including both kin and fictive kin (Staples, 1981). Developed in part during slavery as a coping response to the forced removal of parents, particularly fathers, from their families, this pedifocal operation of family is a strength that can promote resource sharing and the continued responsibility for dependent children regardless of changes in relationships among adults. It also carries the assumption that polyadic coparenting systems are included in the family and shift over time, and multiple parents share responsibility for parenting the children. This has implications for whom to include in coparenting interventions. Consideration of cultural history and norms is an essential element of intervention design and implementation in work with minority populations.

DEVELOPING AND IMPLEMENTING COPARENTING PROGRAMS FOR UNMARRIED PARENTS

In this section, we highlight features of early efforts used to enhance coparenting in families of unmarried parents. One approach tested the efficacy of a coparenting intervention for young fathers utilizing a popular prebirth intervention curriculum (Minnesota Early Learning Design, 1997, as cited in Fagan, 2008). Another effort designed a relationship education program targeting a broad range of unmarried coparents. This latter work began with the development of a publicly available curriculum (Shirer, Adler-Baeder, Contreras, Chen, & London, 2007) using an empowerment model of program development (Dumka, Roosa, Michaels, & Suh, 1995; Phenice et al., 2009; Pruett, Cowan, Cowan, & Pruett, 2009; Small & Uttal, 2005). Both potential program participants and deliverers were engaged in program and curriculum design and refinement. This section gives a general overview of methods and features of these interventions, drawing on information from previously unpublished formative evaluation and from published program implementation descriptions.

Program Content

Content features information on essential elements of healthy coparenting relationships (Fagan, 2008; Shirer et al., 2004) and is based on the research distinguishing these dyadic processes from couple dyadic processes. Specific topics across the two curricula include (a) discussions of the value of intentionally strengthening and building solidarity in coparenting relationships, (b) practice in a future-oriented goal-setting approach to parenting and coparenting, (c) practice in self-care, stress management, and empowerment (e.g., positive assertiveness) skills, (d) skill building in good decision making, (e) discussions of characteristics of unhealthy adult relationships and domestic violence, (f) discussions of the value of father involvement and family stability for children's well-being, (g) practice in effective communication patterns used in coparenting, (h) skills practice in anger and conflict management used in coparenting situations, and (i) skill building in managing multiparental dynamics.

Curricular materials for participants (e.g., handouts, slides for presentations) are written for low literacy levels. Hands-on activities and physical movement (e.g., walking around the room to post work/ideas/responses on flipchart paper) can be critical content elements. For example, men as well as women report enthusiasm for the creation of a "memory book" that parents personalize for their family and use to document their experiences in one program (Shirer et al., 2004). A coparenting "contract" is another tangible and enduring element in the other coparenting program (Fagan, 2008).

Target Participants

Theoretically, there are different ways to approach family systems and affect the coparenting relationship. One approach to coparenting enhancement for unmarried parents targets fathers only, such as the initial study of this type of intervention that recruited only unmarried fathers under 25 years of age (Fagan, 2008). Another community-based coparenting intervention strategy with unmarried parents takes an "all welcome" approach (e.g., Adler-Baeder et al., 2004; Cox & Shirer, 2009). This strategy results in diverse groupings of parents. Some come singly (mostly women), some bring a romantic partner, some bring a coparenting partner or partners (e.g., grandparent, sister), and some come with both a romantic partner and parenting partner.

Program Structure

A typical program structure for emergent coparenting interventions for unmarried parents is a university–community networked design, in which a university department partners with local grass-roots organizations embedded in communities (e.g., Adler-Baeder et al., 2004; Cox & Shirer, 2009). Such local organizations have established mechanisms for reaching targeted populations and are collaboratively connected to other organizations and agencies in their areas that provide complementary human services and/or can serve as referral sources for the coparenting programs. With a networked structure, resources (e.g., joint trainings, joint technical assistance meetings, marketing products, evaluation methods) and lessons learned are shared across locations. Such an approach can reduce the duplication of effort and cost involved when organizations implement programs in isolation and allow for more effective infusion of the intervention into existing family programs and services.

Addressing Domestic Violence

Critically important, coparenting interventions associated with healthy relationship/marriage education programs included input early on from representatives of domestic violence (DV) advocacy agencies, and these collaborations are ongoing (Ooms et al., 2006). Discussions center on the importance of ensuring safety for program participants and the use of DV agency guidance in developing, implementing, and refining interventions for couples and coparents. In many programs, DV agency representatives guide development of protocols for safe screening and referral, and review self-identification information. Program content is reviewed for unintended messages that can put victims at further risk. "Cross-trainings" for program staff and DV service staff can be offered so that there is a clear understanding among DV staff of curriculum and program content and goals, and a clear understanding among program educators of recommended DV protocols.

Class Structure

Interventions seem best offered as voluntary, educational, group sessions that have more of a "gathering" than a class feel, because individuals may not have had a positive experience in school settings (Cox & Shirer, 2009). Many program facilitators do not use the term *intervention*, perceiving that it implies dysfunction has occurred. Research and practice fields also sometimes use the term differently; community educators prefer to describe programs as *prevention* and *education*. Classes are offered at a variety of locales—on-site at community agencies, at churches, in schools, and in community centers—on the basis of an assessment of where target participants will feel most comfortable. In work to date, sessions have typically numbered from five to 12, with class times averaging 1.5 hours (e.g., Adler-Baeder et al., 2004; Cox & Shirer, 2009; Fagan, 2008).

It is suggested that programs serving minority fathers use a male team of facilitators, such as a minority male professional and a minority male former participant (Fagan, 2008). Programs that target a broader population of coparents may find it best to use a male/female team of facilitators, ideally including at least one of whom identifies as an ethnic minority (Adler-Baeder et al., 2004; Cox & Shirer, 2009). Because many facilitators' main previous experience is with parenting education (i.e., emphasizing the parent–child relationship dynamic), they can be apprehensive about facilitating classes focused on the coparenting relationship (i.e., emphasizing the adult dyadic dynamics related to the coparenting alliance). Grasping the link between healthy adult relationships (i.e., couple and coparenting) in the family and healthy children and hearing positive responses from participants in their initial classes have helped promote facilitators' motivation and energy for providing the program and have enhanced their success as recruiters (Shirer et al., 2004, 2009).

Recruitment and Retention

For both university-based (Fagan, 2008) and community-based recruitment efforts (e.g., Adler-Baeder et al., 2010; Cox & Shirer, 2009), success in recruitment and retention appears to stem from having a positive history in the community. In fact, many coparenting program participants had prior experience participating in other programs that agencies had offered (Adler-Baeder et al., 2004). Community-based recruiters find recruiting fathers to be especially challenging. Men have explained in focus groups their reluctance to ask for help and their need to remain strong and to demonstrate an ability to handle things themselves (Shirer et al., 2009). They have suggested that men who participate in coparenting programs can play an important role in recruitment by encouraging other men they know to participate. Further, they have suggested that for African American men, an endorsement by a religious leader in their community may be important. Male educators have reported having minimal difficulty recruiting mothers once a father is "on board" but having more difficulty recruiting in reverse (Adler-Baeder et al., 2004; Shirer et al., 2009). However, Fagan's (2008) program targeting young fathers initially screened 501 couples, on the basis of recruitment of young unmarried women in prenatal clinics. Of these, 101 fathers completed either a coparenting or comparison intervention, indicating some success in recruiting fathers through initial contact with mothers.

Efforts to connect to and inform other community stakeholders about the intervention (i.e., community saturation) can also enhance program recruitment. Many participants cite marketing tools (e.g., billboards, public service announcements, community events, and presentations) as their connection to the program (Shirer et al., 2009). Programs also find that recruitment efforts are more successful when focused on the benefits for the child and parent, which is seen as less intimidating than a focus on the coparenting relationship (Adler-Baeder et al., 2004; Shirer et al., 2009).

Finally, practical supports and incentives to initiate and retain parent participation in a multisession program are seen as critical (Adler-Baeder et al., 2004; Ooms & Wilson, 2004). When child care, meals, a comfortable program location, and per-session financial incentives are provided, parents are more likely to attend and complete a voluntary community program (Adler-Baeder et al., 2004; Shirer et al., 2009). It is important that participants have noted that incentives are helpful in bringing them into the program but are not the only elements important for retention. The skill of and connection to the facilitator and to the other group participants are often reasons cited for staying in the program (Shirer et al., 2009).

ASSESSING BENEFITS OF INTERVENTIONS FOR UNMARRIED PARENTS

Although scholars have noted the value of offering coparenting interventions for unmarried parents for over a decade (e.g., Vosler & Robertson, 1998), efforts in summative evaluation are in a very early stage of development. Participants in the few studies that exist have been predominantly minority, with less than $25,000 a year household income and usually with children under the age of 5 years. Participants in the Fagan fatherhood program were all in the program prior to their child's birth, with follow-up at 3-months postbirth (Fagan, 2008). In programs that have recruited for multi-coparent attendance, the majority of participants have attended singly and have predominantly been women. Retention rates across projects are high, particularly for a voluntary educational program, ranging from 73% to 92%. Several studies used a quasi-experimental design (Adler-Baeder et al., 2004; Cox & Shirer, 2009; Fagan, 2008); others focused on initial implementation and did not recruit a control group, and they provide only initial indications of program outcomes that influence coparenting (e.g., Calligas, Adler-Baeder, Smith, Ketring, & Bradford, 2008). Sample sizes have ranged from 85 in an early pilot project to over 1,000.

Self-report survey methods that have been used include assessments of communication, conflict level, parental involvement, coparenting quality (i.e., support, alliance), parental efficacy, individual empowerment, and family harmony. Individual studies have used all or a smaller selection of these measures. Immediate postprogram indicators of perceived benefit in individual and coparenting dimensions have been documented (e.g., Adler-Baeder et al., 2004, 2010; Cox & Shirer, 2009; Fagan, 2008; Shirer et al., 2004, 2009). In studies with quasi-experimental designs, treatment effects have been found in key targeted areas, particularly coparenting behaviors (Adler-Baeder et al., 2004; Cox & Shirer, 2009; Fagan, 2008). In studies of outcomes (i.e., participant group only), comparisons of participant ratings from pre to post on targeted individual and dyadic measures showed statistically significant changes in a desirable direction in each targeted outcome area. Most effect sizes reported were in the moderate range (Calligas et al., 2008). This is notable given that effect sizes considered small (e.g., 0.25) can be interpreted as "meaningful" differences for an educational intervention (Wolf, 1986).

Initial examinations of moderators of program change indicate the value of attendance together as coparents (Adler-Baeder et al., 2010; Calligas et al., 2008). In one study (Calligas et al., 2008), race moderated program change in parental involvement. European American parents reported significantly greater levels of parental involvement than did African American parents at Time 1 and even greater levels at Time 2. However, in interpreting the finding it is important to consider cultural context. The involvement measure assessed amount of caretaking in several areas. If caretaking activities are spread across multiple coparents, as is common in African American families (Crosbie-Burnett & Lewis, 1993), any given parent in such a polyadic system may show lower levels of involvement than a parent in a two-person coparenting situation. In another study, father residence moderated mothers' reports of father involvement (Fagan, 2008), such that mothers who were coresident with fathers reported significant improvement in father engagement postprogram.

Qualitative data from facilitators and parents also provide useful insights about what elements of programming staff and parents like (Shirer et al., 2009). Such data can be of use to others developing similar interventions. Facilitators have expressed both enjoyment and comfort offering the curricula cited previously and judge program content on coparenting strategies to be relevant and important to the target audience because many participants are not in a couple relationship. From participant responses, they recommended presenting a nonthreatening, fun, educational environment. They emphasized the value of talking about unhealthy and unsafe relationships and suggested that all curricula contain this information. They also recommended including skills for navigating blended family (i.e., stepfamily) relationships because many coparents are balancing former relationships (i.e., coparenting relationships) with new couple and step-parenting relationships. Facilitators noted that participants often desire longer term programs and/or ongoing "support" meetings to deal with issues that arise in their coparenting relationships, and they see value in allowing participants to build a support network with fellow participants to reinforce learning for each other.

Interviews and written qualitative responses from parents confirm curriculum learning objectives (Shirer et al., 2004, 2009). Parents in the broadly offered programs have consistently noted that they developed an enhanced awareness of the importance of healthy coparenting relationships and father involvement. They described specific ways in which their coparenting relationships are more cooperative and respectful and note their continued commitment to work on the relationship. Mothers often emphasized their commitment to removing barriers to father's involvement. Fathers and mothers noted their enhanced individual strengths (e.g., stress-management skills, anger-management skills, communication skills), useful in building a stronger coparenting alliance.

Although some very preliminary evidence exists that interventions for unmarried parents that focus on the coparenting relationship apart from the couple relationship may be beneficial, it is entirely too early to draw conclusions. Much more focused and widespread use of these coparenting interventions—as stand-alone programs or hybrid relationship/coparenting education—is needed. Intervention researchers can provide an important contribution by directing efforts toward the continued development of distinct programs and research in this area.

SUGGESTIONS FOR FURTHER DEVELOPMENT OF PROGRAMS FOR UNMARRIED PARENTS

Community-based coparenting interventions for unmarried parents of young children represent a potentially valuable service for a growing number of families. Although coparenting interventions overall are still in early development compared with other areas of family life education, programming for this population of coparents has received comparatively less focused attention and support. It is important to note that most existing programs were developed in the context of a federally funded initiative principally focused on healthy marriages and stable families. Required assessments for most funded programs centered on the quality of the couple relationship. Although unmarried coparents, particularly prenatally and early postnatally, potentially benefit as a couple from relationship skills training, and many move toward committed relationships (e.g., Higginbotham & Adler-Baeder, 2008), the reality is that many coparents interested in these types of programs attend and report no romantic relationship with their young child's other parent and are interested primarily in information to benefit current coparenting relationships.

Diverse, complex family situations in which marriage is not a viable or desired option can be recognized and expected in the planning and design of these interventions. In these situations, information specific to healthy coparenting is distinguished and emphasized, and information relevant to couple relationships can be presented as useful for subsequent couple relationships. A targeted coparenting intervention, as well as an inclusive approach to relationship education (i.e., content focused on healthy couple dynamics as well as content focused on healthy coparenting dynamics), serves a broader population of fragile families and is consistent with an ecocultural approach to intervention, which suggests that interventions should be formed to meet the needs of community members in their current context (Phenice et al., 2009).

A second source of support for unmarried parents who are coparenting has been federal agency departments that focus on at-risk youth and responsible fatherhood. Though little data exist, programs targeting the increased involvement of unmarried fathers could benefit from a focus on the coparenting relationship in addition to caretaking, father–child relationships, and job skills training. And there is evidence from at least one fatherhood program study designed for lower income, mostly married couples that involvement of both mother and father can enhance fatherhood program goals (Cowan, Cowan, Pruett, Pruett, & Wong, 2009). In short, we are learning that the thoughtful implementation of coparenting interventions for unmarried parents creates an important intersection between fatherhood and healthy relationship initiatives.

Much remains to be learned regarding methods and benefits of coparenting interventions for ethnically diverse, unmarried coparents. The majority of research in this area to date has been early formative evaluation studies, using participatory adaptive research methods (Small & Uttal, 2005) to gain an understanding of relevant program content, methods for recruitment and retention, and characteristics of successful community partnerships in the targeted communities. Support of efficacy trials of coparenting interventions for unmarried parents has been essentially nonexistent. Relevant to this, we note from our work that researchers may face resistance from community partners in implementing a randomized, control group design either because a program is still in its initial demonstration phase or because of concerns with withholding a potentially beneficial program from interested participants. Involvement of community partners in planning research methods is recommended, as cooperation of all involved is key to successful intervention research (Small & Uttal, 2005).

Regarding future implementation, in our preprogram participation focus groups, some men made a distinction between parenting, which they viewed as child focused, and coparenting, seen as focused on the other parent(s) (Shirer et al., 2009). This suggests a concept of coparenting consistent with conceptualizations of parenting alliances (i.e., support between adults for parenting), which was in line with planned program content on the benefits to children of healthy coparenting relationships, the value of support for each other in their parenting roles, and the skills related to cooperation and conflict management around childrearing and shared parenting experiences. Women, we noted, were more likely to talk about parenting and coparenting in similar ways and to consider coparenting as parallel and tandem, a child-focused activity, and an element of their parenting. This view is similar to a shared parenting conceptualization of coparenting, centered on division of labor. In other words, for some women, the idea of actively working on the adult interactions in the coparenting relationship was a novel idea and not what they expected a "coparenting" class to focus on. In future work, it will be important for researchers, program implementers, and participants to establish shared definitions of *coparent* and *coparenting* (McHale et al., 2002; see also Chapter 5, this volume).

Another suggestion for future work is the critical assessment of methods for gathering important data and the match between intervention and method design. Although many programs have sought to include multiple coparents, surveys typically collect information from respondents on just one coparent. In the future, adapting measures to allow for completion with multiple referent coparents in mind and using observational assessments of multi-coparent models of interaction would enhance understanding of distinctions among specific dyads (Van Egeren & Hawkins, 2004), as well as allow for the examinations of influences between dyads. Assessments over time will enhance the understanding of the dynamic nature of coparenting quality and the shifting of roles and responsibilities among coparents in the family system described in qualitative studies (Adler-Baeder & Abell, 2003). This more detailed developmental tracking of the intervention's impact in the broad coparenting system over time will be meaningful for program design and adjustment.

In addition to the interplay among coparenting dyads, links between the quality of the coparenting relationship and the quality of couple relationships are well-documented both for parents in relationships with one another (see Chapter 2, this volume) and for parents in a couple relationship with one person and coparent relationship(s) with another (Ganong & Coleman, 2004).

Results from examinations of directions of influence carry implications for approaches in intervention.

We encourage the continued focus on cognitions as well as behaviors in programming. It may be helpful to first focus on promotion of agency and self-efficacy; enhanced value for a future-oriented, intentional approach to parenting and family relationships; and value for involvement of the other biological parent. Then skill building can be targeted. Although early research has shown a treatment effect for coparenting behaviors and quality, it may be unrealistic to expect substantial behavioral and relational quality changes after participation in a short-term educational program. Rather, appropriate goals may center on raising awareness and launching desired behavioral change through enhanced efficacy. Including assessments that tap changes in awareness, efficacy, and intent can be useful. If only behavioral and relational quality assessments are used, important shifts in the change process may be missed.

It is also important to examine changes among participants and family systems within the context of program elements. From the more distal aspects of community saturation, to the more proximal aspects of site characteristics, class characteristics, and facilitator characteristics, information regarding key predictors of program impact will be useful in understanding the intervention process. In other words, it is more helpful to focus on "why does it work?" and "how does it work best and for whom?" than simply "does it work?" (Small & Uttal, 2005).

For community-based programs in which an inclusive approach has been utilized, most coparents who have attended together have been the two biological parents, but we have also noted increasing numbers of kin coparents. Clearly, an opportunity exists within intervention research to further explore the interplay among coparents and coparenting roles and to examine the comparative benefits different program participation patterns have for individuals and families. Both theory and basic research have suggested that involvement of kin coparents and biological parents will lead to enhanced efficacy of the program, as kin coparents have been shown to serve as barriers to parent involvement and to contribute to conflict between biological parents (Kalil et al., 2005). Future work involving comparison treatment groups can examine whether this is indeed the case and whether attendance of multiple coparents together or apart is more beneficial. Again, it is important to consider the broader context in this research, as coparenting systems operate within ecocultural niches, and what is true for one community context may not be true for others.

These delivery variations await empirical study, and program facilitators will likely be supportive of these and other intervention trials examining the effects of class composition. Although many facilitators have agreed with an "all come" approach, they recommend that interested participants be grouped by similarity of situation—as much as is practically possible (Adler-Baeder et al., 2004). Facilitators often find it difficult to manage the logistics of class discussion and activities when participants are in very different situations (e.g., attending as a couple, attending as coparents, attending singly, or attending with a kin coparent). Although class participants understand that different needs are being met and some program content is more salient to their family situation than others, facilitators feel participation and retention would be enhanced by a more tailored approach. Similarly, some participants in focus groups suggest male-only and female-only groups, citing a need for differences in salient topics (Shirer et al., 2009). As more detailed intervention studies emerge, it may also become clearer whether program content that is based on gender and type of coparenting relationship and coparenting system is needed. In addition, past participants and facilitators have each suggested longer, ongoing programs or periodic "booster" sessions. Benefits of longer term versus shorter term participation remain untested.

CONCLUSION

In this chapter, we highlighted the experiences of arguably the most overlooked coparents for intervention: adults who have a young child together but who may not be romantically linked. Studies of fragile families and new parents have pointed to the prenatal and early postnatal period as critical for developing relational strength and positive coparenting expectancies (McHale & Rotman, 2007; McLanahan et al., 2003) and have emphasized the "enduring frameworks" for coparenting established during this time (McHale et al., 2004). This suggests that interventions for new and expecting unmarried parents have the most chance for success, and some early evidence in support of this assumption exists (Fagan, 2008). However, a great many unmarried parents with older children do not fit these parameters. Have they "missed the boat" for helpful intervention? Emerging information from work with nonromantically linked parents and families with children beyond infant age suggests not, indicating the salience and perceived benefit of programming that facilitates the enhancement of individual, interpersonal, and coparenting skills.

In summary, we recommend use of a risk and resiliency approach embedded in an ecological systems framework that considers intervention as a promotive factor (Sameroff & Gutman, 2004) for individual and family well-being and use of an ecocultural perspective of family dynamics. For work with a population that is underrepresented in research, it is especially important to use a participatory research approach that involves multiple "experts" in the process of developing and refining programs for unmarried parents within targeted communities. Current information available from the few interventions providing coparenting training to unmarried parents can be helpful, and continuing to share lessons learned can be valuable across communities. We emphasize again that the development and empirical validation of these programs are in the beginning stages, and there is much more work to be done.

Embracing an iterative and dynamic approach, the goal is not necessarily development of a singular model for rigid replication. The hope is for flexible, effective, culturally relevant programs for low-income, ethnically diverse unmarried parents in a variety of family situations that will result in enhanced self-efficacy and empowerment; enhanced interpersonal skills; effective coparenting relationship systems; continued positive involvement of parents; and, ultimately, positive adult and child outcomes.

REFERENCES

Adler-Baeder, F., & Abell, E. (2003, November). *Intragenerational and intergenerational coparenting among low-income unmarried mothers.* Paper presented at the National Council on Family Relations Annual Conference, Vancouver, British Columbia, Canada.

Adler-Baeder, F., Bradford, A., Skuban, E., Lucier-Greer, M., Ketring, S., & Smith, T. (2010). Demographic predictors of relationship and marriage education participants' pre- and post-program relational and individual functioning. *Journal of Couple & Relationship Therapy, 9,* 113–132. doi:10.1080/15332691003694885

Adler-Baeder, F., Lippert, L., Pflieger, J., Higginbotham, B., Armstrong, S., & Long, A. (2004). *Evaluating a marriage education program for low-resource families: The Family Connections in Alabama project.* Auburn, AL: Auburn University.

Aronson, R. E., Whitehead, T. L., & Baber, W. L. (2003). Challenges to masculine transformation among urban low-income African American males. *American Journal of Public Health, 93,* 732–741. doi:10.2105/AJPH.93.5.732

Brotherson, S., & Duncan, W. (2004). Rebinding the ties that bind: Government efforts to preserve and promote marriage. *Family Relations, 53,* 459–468. doi:10.1111/j.0197-6664.2004.00054.x

Calligas, A., Adler-Baeder, F., Smith, T., Ketring, S., & Bradford, A. (2008, November). *The effects of marriage education on parenting quality: Examining change by participant characteristics.* Paper presented at the annual conference of the National Council on Family Relations, Little Rock, AR.

Carlson, M. J., McLanahan, S. S., & Brooks-Gunn, J. (2008). Coparenting and nonresident fathers' involvement with young children after a nonmarital birth. *Demography, 45,* 461–488. doi:10.1353/dem.0.0007

Cowan, P. A., Cowan, C. P., Pruett, M. K., Pruett, K., & Wong, J. J. (2009). Promoting fathers' engagement with children: Preventive interventions for low-income families. *Journal of Marriage and the Family*, *71*, 663–679. doi:10.1111/j.1741-3737.2009.00625.x

Cox, R., & Shirer, L. (2009). Caring For My Family: A pilot study of relationship and marriage education program for low-income parents. *Journal of Couple & Relationship Therapy*, *8*, 343–364. doi:10.1080/15332690903246127

Crosbie-Burnett, M., & Lewis, E. (1993). Use of African-American family structures and functioning to address the challenges of European-American post-divorce families. *Family Relations*, *42*, 243–248. doi:10.2307/585552

Dion, R. M. (2005). Healthy marriage programs: Learning what works. *The Future of Children*, *15*, 139–156. doi:10.1353/foc.2005.0016

Dorsey, S., Forehand, R., & Brody, G. (2007). Co-parenting conflict and parenting behavior in economically disadvantaged single parent African-American families: The role of maternal psychological distress. *Journal of Family Violence*, *22*, 621–630. doi:10.1007/s10896-007-9114-y

Dumka, L., Roosa, M., Michaels, M., & Suh, K. (1995). Using research and theory to develop prevention programs for high risk families. *Family Relations*, *44*, 78–86. doi:10.2307/584744

Fagan, J. (2008). Randomized study of a prebirth coparenting intervention and adolescent and young fathers. *Family Relations*, *57*, 309–323. doi:10.1111/j.1741-3729.2008.00502.x

Feinberg, M. E., Kan, M. L., & Hetherington, E. M. (2007). The longitudinal influence of conflict on parental negativity and adolescent maladjustment. *Journal of Marriage and the Family*, *69*, 687–702. doi:10.1111/j.1741-3737.2007.00400.x

Ganong, L., & Coleman, M. (2004). *Stepfamily relationships: Development, dynamics, and interventions.* New York, NY: Kluwer Academic.

Hamilton, B. E., Martin, J. A., & Ventura, S. J. (2010). *Births: Preliminary data 2007* (National Vital Statistics Reports, Vol. 57, No. 12). Hyattsville, MD: National Center for Health Statistics.

Higginbotham, B., & Adler-Baeder, F. (2008). The Smart Steps: Embrace the Journey program: Enhancing relational skills and relationship quality in remarriages and stepfamilies. *The Forum for Family and Consumer Issues*, *13*(3). Available at http://ncsu.edu/ffci/publications/2008/v13-n3-2008-winter/higginbotham-adler.php

Hille, J. (2006). *Eco-cultural theory in the research of trans-national families and their daily life* (Eurodiv Paper.33.2006, Fondazione En Enrico Matteri Series). Milan, Italy: Fondazione Eni Enrico Mattei.

Jenson, J., & Fraser, M. (2005). *Social policy for children & families: A risk and resiliency perspective.* Thousand Oaks, CA: Sage.

Kalil, A., Ziol-Guest, K., & Coley. R. (2005). Perceptions of father involvement patterns in teenage-mother families: Predictors and links to mothers' psychological adjustment. *Family Relations*, *54*, 197–211.

Krishnakumar, A., & Black, M. (2003). Family processes within three-generation households and adolescent mothers' satisfaction with father involvement. *Journal of Family Psychology*, *17*, 488–498. doi:10.1037/0893-3200.17.4.488

Lamb, M. (2004). *The role of the father in child development.* New York, NY: Wiley.

Martin, J. A., Hamilton, B. E., Sutton, P. D., Ventura, M. A., Menacker, F., Kirmeyer, S., & Mathews, T. J. (2009). *Births: Final data for 2006* (National Vital Statistics Reports, Vol. 57, No. 7). Hyattsville, MD: National Center for Health Statistics.

McHale, J. (2007). *Charting the bumpy road of coparenthood: Understanding the challenges of family life.* Washington, DC: Zero to Three Press.

McHale, J., Johnson, D., & Sinclair, R. (1999). Family dynamics, preschoolers' family representations, and preschool peer relationships. *Early Education and Development, 10,* 373–401. doi:10.1207/s15566935eed1003_8

McHale, J. P., Kazali, C., Rotman, T., Talbot, J., Carleton, M., & Lieberson, R. (2004). The transition to coparenthood: Parents' prebirth expectations and early coparental adjustment at 3 months postpartum. *Development and Psychopathology, 16,* 711–733. doi:10.1017/S0954579404004742

McHale, J., Khazan, I., Erera, P., Rotman, T., DeCourcey, W., & McConnell, M. (2002). Coparenting in diverse family systems. In M. Bornstein (Ed.), *Handbook of parenting: Vol. 3. Being and becoming parents* (pp. 75–107). Mahwah, NJ: Erlbaum.

McHale, J. P., & Rotman, T. (2007). Is seeing believing? Expectant parents' outlooks on coparenting and later coparenting solidarity. *Infant Behavior and Development, 30,* 63–81. doi:10.1016/j.infbeh.2006.11.007

McLanahan, S., Garfinkel, I., Reichman, N., Teitler, J., Carlson, M., & Audigier, C. (2003). *The Fragile Families and Child Wellbeing Study: Baseline national report.* Princeton, NJ: Center for Research on Child Wellbeing, Princeton University.

McLanahan, S., & Sandefur, G. (1994). *Growing up with a single parent: What hurts, what helps.* Cambridge, MA: Harvard University Press.

Minnesota Early Learning Design. (1997). *MELD for Young Dads curriculum: The other people in your life.* Minneapolis, MN: Author.

Minuchin, P. (1988). Relationships within the family: A systems perspective on development. In R. Hinde & J. Stephenson-Hinde (Eds.), *Relationships within families: Mutual influences* (pp. 7–26). New York, NY: Oxford University Press.

Ooms, T. (2002). Strengthening couples and marriage in low-income communities. In A. J. Hawkins, L. D. Wardle, & D. O. Coolidge (Eds.), *Revitalizing the institution of marriage for the twenty-first century: An agenda for strengthening marriage* (pp. 79–100). Westport, CT: Praeger.

Ooms, T., Boggess, J., Menard, A., Myrick, M., Roberts, P., Tweedie, J., & Wilson, P. (2006). *Building bridges between healthy marriage, responsible fatherhood, and domestic violence programs.* Washington, DC: Center for Law and Social Policy.

Ooms, T., & Wilson, P. (2004). The challenges of offering relationship and marriage education to low-income populations. *Family Relations, 53,* 440–447. doi:10.1111/j.0197-6664.2004.00052.x

Pajares, F., & Urdan, T. (2006). *Self-efficacy beliefs of adolescents.* Charlotte, NC: Information Age.

Phenice, L., Griffore, R., Hakoyama, M., & Silvey, L. (2009). Ecocultural adaptive research: A synthesis of ecocultural theory, participatory research, and adaptive designs. *Family and Consumer Sciences Research Journal, 37*, 298–309. doi:10.1177/1077727X08330683

Pruett, M., Cowan, C., Cowan, P., & Pruett, K. (2009). Lessons learned from the supporting father involvement study: A cross-cultural preventive intervention for low-income families with young children. *Journal of Social Service Research, 35*, 163–179. doi:10.1080/01488370802678942

Roy, K., & Burton, L. (2007). Mothering through recruitment: Kinscription of non-residential fathers and father figures in low-income families. *Family Relations, 56*, 24–39. doi:10.1111/j.1741-3729.2007.00437.x

Rutter, M. (2001). Psychosocial adversity: Risk, resilience, and recovery. In J. M. Richman & M. W. Fraser (Eds.), *The context of youth violence: Resilience, risk, and protection* (pp. 13–41). Westport, CT: Praeger.

Sameroff, A., & Gutman, L. (2004). Contribution of risk research to the design of interventions. In P. Allen-Meares & M. Fraser (Eds.), *Intervention with children and adolescents: An interdisciplinary approach* (pp. 9–26). Boston, MA: Allyn & Bacon.

Schoppe, S. J., Mangelsdorf, S., & Frosch, C. (2001). Coparenting, family process, and family structure: Implications for preschoolers' externalizing behavior problems. *Journal of Family Psychology, 15*, 526–545. doi:10.1037/0893-3200.15.3.526

Seltzer, J. A. (2000). Families formed outside of marriage. *Journal of Marriage and the Family, 62*, 1247–1268. doi:10.1111/j.1741-3737.2000.01247.x

Shirer, K., Adler-Baeder, F., Contreras, D., Chen, G., & London, E. (2007). *Together We Can: A curriculum to improve co-parenting relationships of single parents.* Retrieved from http://www.togetherwecan.fcs.msue.msu.edu/

Shirer, K., Adler-Baeder, F., Contreras, D., & Spicer, J. (2004). Preparing unmarried new parents to make healthy decisions about marriage, father involvement and family formation. In *Vision 2004: What is the future of marriage?* Minneapolis, MN: National Council on Family Relations.

Shirer, K., & Contreras, D., Chen, G., & London, E. (2009, April). *It's not about getting them married: The case for coparenting education for parents and caregivers in low-income families.* Paper presented at the Society for Research in Child Development annual conference, Denver, CO.

Small, S., & Uttal, L. (2005). Action-oriented research: Strategies for engaged research. *Journal of Marriage and the Family, 67*, 936–948. doi:10.1111/j.1741-3737.2005.00185.x

Sobolewski, J. M., & King, V. (2005). The importance of the co-parental relationship for nonresident fathers' ties to children. *Journal of Marriage and the Family, 67*, 1196–1212. doi:10.1111/j.1741-3737.2005.00210.x

Sorensen, E., Mincy, R., & Halpern, A. (2000). *Redirecting welfare policy toward building strong families.* Washington, DC: The Urban Institute.

Staples, R. (1981). The black American family. In C. Mendel & R. Haberstein (Eds.), *Ethnic families in America* (2nd ed., pp. 217–244). New York, NY: Elsevier.

U.S. Census Bureau. (2010). *America's families living arrangements: 2009* (Current Population Survey, Annual Social and Economic Supplement, Table FG6). Retrieved from http://www.census.gov/population/www/socdemo/hh-fam/cps2009.html

Van Egeren, L. A., & Hawkins, D. P. (2004). Coming to terms with co-parenting: Implications of definition and measurement. *Journal of Adult Development, 11,* 165–178. doi:10.1023/B:JADE.0000035625.74672.0b

Vosler, N. R., & Robertson, J. G. (1998). Nonmarital co-parenting: Knowledge building for practice. *Families in Society, 79,* 149–159.

Waller, M., & Swisher, R. (2006). Fathers' risk factors in fragile families: Implications for "healthy" relationships and father involvement. *Social Problems, 53,* 392–420. doi:10.1525/sp.2006.53.3.392

Weitzman, L. J. (1981). The economics of divorce: Social and economic consequences of property, alimony, and child support awards. *UCLA Law Review, 28,* 1183–1268.

Wolf, F. M. (1986). *Meta-analysis: Quantitative methods for research synthesis* (Sage University Series: Quantitative applications in the social sciences, Series No. 59). Beverly Hills, CA: Sage.

10

COPARENTING IN FAMILY–INFANT TRIADS: THE USE OF OBSERVATION IN SYSTEMIC INTERVENTIONS

FRANCE FRASCAROLO, ELISABETH FIVAZ, AND NICOLAS FAVEZ

With the relative recency of the fields of coparenting theory and research, clinical interventions specifically designed to influence the functioning of coparenting alliances have not been systematically studied. However, coparenting interventions have been central in the venerable field of familial approaches—therapeutic interventions that concurrently involve multiple individuals connected by biological, legal, or emotional ties. Family and systemic approaches are effective for a wide variety of clinical issues, ranging from substance addictions in adolescents to behavioral disorders in children and adolescents (Fonagy, Target, Cottrell, Phillips, & Kurtz, 2002). Surprisingly, however, family-based interventions with the young family in the weeks, months, and years after the birth of a new child are scarce, both at the level of therapeutic conceptualization and at the level of specific interventions. In family-based interventions with infants, therapeutic efforts have historically tended to the mother–child relationship only (Favez, Frascarolo, Keren, & Fivaz-Depeursinge, 2009; see also Chapter 1, this volume). Approaches that target coparenting—the ways that parents work together in their roles as parents (McHale, 1995)—are virtually nonexistent. Such approaches, at their best, would blend principles of treatment and prevention, guiding early coparenting alliances in a positive direction and trajectory.

Although there is only sparse research on the effectiveness of coparenting-directed approaches evaluated in randomized clinical trials, a creative clinical and research literature on the relevance of such an approach exists. Our aim in this chapter is to summarize what we currently know about these approaches.

RELEVANT LINES OF RESEARCH ON COPARENTING-RELATED INTERVENTIONS

Interventions targeting coparenting can be classified in three major categories:

1. Historically, coordination both between the parents and among other intrafamilial relationships has been the purview of structural family therapy approaches (S. Minuchin, 1974). Structural therapies successfully address a variety of socioaffective problems that affect one or several members of the family. Though these therapies are not specifically framed as focusing on infancy or on coparenting, coparenting is virtually always a key consideration addressed when there is more than one family caregiver (S. Minuchin, 1974; S. Minuchin, Nichols, & Lee, 2006; Szapocznik & Kurtines, 1989).
2. Coparenting is the explicit target of interventions with postdivorce couples in efforts to promote parental unity toward the child and prevent problems in child adjustment. Although all research and intervention programs have been concerned with young children or adolescents (Emery & Wyer, 1987; Emery, Laumann-Billings, Waldron, Sbarra, & Dillon, 2001; Leek, 1992), most interventions have involved the two coparenting adults but not the children (for a more comprehensive review of this work, see Chapter 9).
3. Coparenting interventions framed as primary or secondary prevention programs for both resident and nonresident mothers and fathers have been designed so as to avoid difficulties during life-transforming events, such as a new child's birth. In such interventions, usually designed for couples but sometimes accepting participation by just one parent (see Chapter 9), mutual coparental involvement and support are addressed, with the goal of making parental adjustment and parenting easier. As with interventions designed for postdivorce families, these interventions typically target the coparenting adults only, rather than taking a triangular or full-family approach.

Next, we provide a brief review of this relevant literature; complementary and more in-depth coverage can be found in other chapters of this volume. We then shift the focus to our own body of work to describe how it is possible to assess coparenting alliances through observation using the Lausanne family model and to illustrate potential uses of this model for the design of coparenting-related interventions.

EFFECTIVENESS OF COPARENTING-RELATED INTERVENTIONS

As outlined elsewhere in this volume, several interventions have been conceived specifically to modify coparental interactions, mainly in divorced families or in families at risk. Several years ago, Feinberg (2002) drew on existing theoretical frameworks to offer a model of coparenting comprising the following four related components, any of which could serve as a target of intervention:

- support versus undermining in the parental role: each parent's supportiveness of one another;
- child-rearing disagreement: shared or nonshared values about important child-related issues (e.g., education, moral values, religious upbringing);
- division of labor: distribution of duties between the parents and partners' perceptions of equity in this distribution; and
- management of family interactions: parents' comanagement of (a) interparental conflict, (b) alliance versus coalition/triangulation of the child in the coparental relationship, and (c) balance of involvement of parents during triadic interactions.

These four components provide a useful framework for both assessing coparental functioning and identifying intervention goals.

Structural Family Approaches

Salvador Minuchin's (1974) structural family approach focused on present-day, here-and-now family interaction and functioning. Although the family's past remained important, Minuchin's stance was that what was most important about the past was reenacted in present transactions. As Chapter 1 outlines, important contributions of structural family theory relevant to coparenting are concepts of family structure, boundaries, and subsystems. Minuchin described ways in which children are triangulated in family systems, such as when a coalition between one parent and the child develops and excludes the other parent. Minuchin also believed that child behavior problems played a functional role in keeping the family together (S. Minuchin, Rosman, & Baker, 1978; see also Chapter 1, this volume). In his therapeutic practice Minuchin worked to reconfigure nonadaptive family coalitions directly with in-session enactments to help introduce, promote, and support change. For a more detailed review of the relevant literature and a summary of integrative models using classic structural family therapy as their base, see McHale and Sullivan (2008).

Interventions With Divorced Families

A second group of interventions, designed for postdivorce families, has been developed to promote the coparenting relationship between parents and to minimize undermining, child-related conflict, and triangulation of the child (Baris & Garrity, 1997; Emery & Wyer, 1987; Mitcham-Smith & Henry, 2007; for a comprehensive review, see Chapter 11, this volume). Interventions using mediation (instead of litigation) and aiming to increase paternal involvement and improve cooperation between parents enhance the likelihood that both parents will still be involved in the child's education 12 years later—reversing trends for noncustodial fathers to progressively lose contact and influence with their children over time (Emery, Laumann-Billings, Waldron, Sbarra, & Dillon, 2001). Taking a look at "successful" families, Sbarra and Emery (2005) documented a curious paradoxical effect: Greater coparental cooperation came with a heightened attendant risk of fathers developing depressive disorders.

Specific themes covered in these intervention programs have been described by Lee and Hunsley (2006; see also Chapter 11, this volume). Overall, converging data support the effectiveness of interventions in increasing paternal investment and coparental coordination and in reducing interparental conflict relative to control groups. Interested readers can consult, for example, the forgiveness intervention model of Bonach (2009), the directed coparenting intervention of Garber (2004), and the Dads for Life program of Cookston, Braver, Griffin, De Lusé, and Miles (2007).

Preventive Interventions With Couples

In preventive efforts with higher risk families (including families in precarious socioeconomic situations), emphasis has been placed on strengthening coparental support. Psychoeducative approaches have received the most systematic study. The recent Supporting Father Involvement project (Cowan, Cowan, Pruett & Pruett, 2007) showed that in families with children birth to 7 years of age, enhancing the relationship between the father and the child's mother both enhanced the conjugal relationship and decreased stress related to parenting while increasing paternal involvement in coparenting 9 months after the intervention had ended. The Family Foundation program for primiparous parents (Feinberg, Jones, Kan, & Goslin, 2010; Feinberg & Kan, 2008; see also Chapter 8, this volume), explicitly focused on coparenting, also offered group sessions before and up to 6 months postbirth. This project likewise showed beneficial effects of the psychoeducational intervention. Families who followed the program showed better adjustment than did those in a control group. Benefits were seen not just in coparental coordination but also in parenting, the marital relationship, and child self-regulation at 1 year postpartum (see Chapter 8).

Similar results were found in the Minnesota Early Learning Design program (Fagan, 2008). This program targeted coparenting of younger parents (under the age of 25) and demonstrated increases in paternal involvement relative to a control group. Other programs that have been more specifically designed to focus on parenting outcomes rather than on coparenting per se have reported kindred increases in paternal involvement when they have included a "partner support" dimension (e.g., Sanders' [1999] Positive Parenting program). Finally, interventions with never married, nonresidential mothers and fathers, although newer, likewise support positive benefits of specifically targeting the parents' coparenting alliance (for a detailed review, see Chapter 9).

In examining the bodies of literature summarized previously, two prominent outcomes receive the greatest attention. The first is increased paternal involvement, and the second is increases in the support mothers give fathers in their parental tasks. In other words, fathers are frequently the targets in intervention models, with their engagement sought through improvements in the relational dynamic of the couple in conflict.

There are some parallels in this view of coparenting in families reminiscent of conceptualizations of conjugal conflict (for a review, see Gottman, 1998). That is, many conceptualizations describe how tensions between partners can trigger father withdrawal, which heightens the mother's dissatisfaction and engages the couple in a negative spiral (e.g., see Elliston, McHale, Talbot, Parmley, & Kuersten-Hogan, 2008). This is an important family dynamic and trajectory, but circumstances can also be more complex than this. For example, Allen and Hawkins (1999) introduced the concept of *maternal gatekeeping* to describe how mothers encourage (or discourage) fathers' involvement with the child; paternal commitment hence appears to depend to some extent on how much mothers encourage their participation. The mother's encouragement, in turn, is related to her perception of the father's parenting skills (Fagan & Barnett, 2003; McBride et al., 2005). So, although there is unquestionably bidirectional influence between the two parents over time (Van Egeren & Hawkins, 2004), it may be important to take maternal perceptions into account if interventions aim to increase paternal involvement and improve coparental cooperation (see Chapter 9).

Though interventionists agree that supporting father involvement in coparenting, promoting solidarity, and minimizing conflict are important aims of any coparenting intervention, there has been limited attention to the assessment of these important family dimensions (see Chapter 7). In the following section, we outline the use of observation as a key tool both in understanding the family's coparenting dynamics and identifying targets of intervention.

ASSESSMENT AS A FIRST STEP IN INTERVENTION

As structural family theories (S. Minuchin, 1974) would suggest, the interactive patterns of coparenting take shape very early, signaled even before birth, and once established continue in a coherent fashion during the first years (Favez, Frascarolo, Carneiro, et al., 2006; McHale & Rotman, 2007). For this reason, it is important to recognize potentially problematic situations and to intervene early. Thoughtful assessments of early coparenting patterns are not just an essential prelude to intervention—they can be seen as the initial stage of the intervention itself. Below, we describe the methodologies we have designed to observe, assess, and intervene with coparenting relationships in families of both infants and older children.

When working with very young children and their family, it is especially appropriate to use the family's interactions as a point of entry to the system. Time-limited but intensive observation and assessment of the family as an interacting group reveal core principles of the family's functioning (McHale & Alberts, 2003; P. Minuchin, 1985). Core coparental interactions "nested" in the family interactions are the central target of two different observation paradigms we have designed for family assessment: the Lausanne Trilogue Play (LTP) and the Picnic Game (PNG).

The Lausanne Trilogue Play

The LTP situation, described in extensive detail by Fivaz-Depeursinge and Corboz-Warnery (1999), allows the systematic observation of family interactions in a three-way relationship between the father, the mother, and the very young child. The implicit goal of any trilogue play is for the three members of the family to share moments of pleasure. In the LTP, the child's parents are invited to play with their son or daughter according to a prescribed scenario as follows:

1. One parent plays with the infant while the other parent is the third party.
2. The parents reverse roles.

3. The three partners play together.
4. The parents interact with each other, placing the infant in the role of the third party (2 + 1).

The parents sit on chairs arranged in a triangle, at a distance facilitating dialogue. In its most controlled use, the infant or young child sits in a reclining chair that can be oriented toward one parent, toward the other, and between the two (Favez, Frascarolo, & Fivaz-Depeursinge, 2006). The setting is adapted to the age; thus, after 12 months, the parents and child sit around a small round table and three sets of three objects are provided, such as three socks, spoons, and little animals. The entire play is videotaped to be used later by the therapist or researcher.

Variations of the situation can be adapted for specific assessments. A prenatal version of the LTP enables a role-play of how expecting parents will cooperate and support each other during their first encounter with their baby, simulated by a doll (Carneiro, Corboz-Warnery, & Fivaz-Depeursinge, 2006). The LTP can also include more than one child, seated around a table, becoming the Lausanne Family Play (LFP). The theme of play can be adapted to the age of the children, such as building something together with blocks, in early childhood; planning for a holiday, in late childhood; or discussing rules about outings during adolescence.

The Picnic Game

As a complement to the LTP, a less structured scenario evoking daily chores and routines can be a useful adjunct (McHale & Fivaz-Depeursinge, 2010). We developed the PNG, a pretend meal simulation, to evoke family interactions that may not be revealed in standard clinical contexts. In the PNG (Frascarolo & Favez, 2005), the family is asked to join together for a pretend picnic. This situation simultaneously allows assessment of the family's capacity to play for fun (an implicit aim of the game) while also providing insights into the adults' coordination of structural features of the play, such as setting a table, tidying up at the end, and requiring the children to respect the spatial limits defined for the game. The two aspects, "game" and "daily chores," are complementary and make the observations very rich.

As we have developed the paradigm, family members are provided a carpeted space of 4 meters × 4 meters (delimiting the space they can use), along with a bench, a table, chairs, toys, and a toy tea set. The instructions invite them to play a picnic for about a quarter of an hour and to tidy up when they are finished. This situation, videotaped in its entirety, can accommodate families with children of any age and any number of people (including babies and grandparents). In the case of parents who are divorced or living apart, it may be preferable to propose that they enact a meal in a restaurant.

COPARENTING ASSESSMENT

The LTP, the LFP, and the PNG allow assessment not just of global family functioning and coparenting, the pivot of the family (McHale, 2007), but also of all other subsystems within the context of the family. In the LTP, certain aspects of the marital system are clearly seen during Part 4; the relationships between each parent and one (LTP) or more (LFP, PNG) children are also in evidence, along with the relationships between siblings (PNG, LFP).

We have dedicated significant effort during the past several years to studying how coparenting is revealed in the LTP, with a focus on how parents cooperate to achieve the implicit goals of the task. We developed a Family Alliance Assessment Scale (unpublished) to aid in these efforts; though developed for research purposes, the systematic evaluation of the interactions has informed our understanding of key features of the family process of interest for clinicians. Specifically, we have determined that during the first two parts of the LTP, the resonating and supportive attitude of the participant observer parent and that parent's ability to refrain from interfering are signs of harmonious coparenting. By contrast, a lack of interest or a propensity to interfere in the dyadic interaction between the baby and the other parent indicate a "poor" coparenting alliance or a competitive one, respectively. In Part 3, when the parents are invited to play jointly with their infant, their ability to play in a coordinated way is a sign of a supportive coparenting. When both try to capture the infant's attention in divergent ways, the coparenting tends toward competitiveness, and the child is often in the middle of this tug-of-war. Coparenting is also considered to be poor if one parent cannot leave any "space" for the other. Part 4 of the LTP provides a small window into the marital relationship and, especially relevant to the thrust of this chapter, also provides insights into the coparental alliance. Because both partners are still seated near and remain "in charge" of their son or daughter, aspects of coparenting are evinced by the degree of agreement between the parents in handling their child as they engage. In this way, the articulation between the marital and the coparenting units is in evidence.

We have also elaborated a system for assessing coalitions in the LTP. Its focus is on distorted intergenerational boundaries between parents and toddlers, and on specific kinds of coalitions. In the first kind, which we call *binding*, one parent allies with the child against the other, so that the other parent is excluded and the child cut off from the latter. In the second form, which we call *triangulation*, the parents compete for the child's attention, so that the child is caught in between them. Finally, in the third kind, which we call *detouring*, the parents turn "against" the child, diverting their tension onto him, and putting him in the position of a victim, decoy, or scapegoat. The evaluation system also assesses the position the child adopts in response to the coparenting style, in particular withdrawal or role reversal (Fivaz-Depeursinge, Lopes, Python, & Favez, 2009). As outlined previously, these concepts build on the seminal work of S. Minuchin while providing a level of systematicity that facilitates both the clinical and research process.

In the PNG coding system, we developed a specific coparenting scale. The key observations for clinicians are: Do parents work together and support each other in their parental tasks? Or do they work in parallel? Are competition or hostility observable? We draw attention to the presence or absence of hostility, conflicts, competition, disparagement, or parental coalition. We also note mutual supportive cooperation with friendly agreement, the former not excluding the latter one. Finally, we take note of distribution of leadership, family warmth, and limit setting.

To illustrate the richness of the data available to clinicians when structured observations are used to assess coparenting, we now provide three different PNG vignettes, each involving a family with a 3-month-old baby. Different types of coparenting are evident in each. The first family is one in which observations revealed two parents fully centered on and attuned to their baby daughter, Julie, throughout the session. Each time one parent interacted with Julie, it was with the complicity of the other parent, without rivalry. There was also evidence during the session that the mother also valued and supported the father, as revealed through several of her comments. Finally, we observed numerous mother–father–baby interactions that revealed cooperative coparenting.

> The mother sits Julie in front of her on her knee and puts her bib back on while the father places his hand as a supporting backrest. Then he caresses his daughter. There are mother–baby exchanges, and then Julie turns toward her father. There is a pleasant exchange approved by the mother, who holds her daughter looking directly at her husband before sitting her back in front of her. The mother then asks the father if he wants to take his daughter on his knee. The father answers, speaking to his daughter: "Do you want to play horsey on daddy's knee?" But the baby is more interested in a rattle she is holding, so the parents talk instead about what she is doing. The mother hands the bag of toys to the father and suggests he should amuse her. The father takes out another toy and plays about with it. Then the father takes his daughter beside him and goes on playing. The mother watches. From time to time, the father puts Julie in front of her mother to begin a short dialogue between them.

In a second family, the interaction is not as well coordinated. We observe some brief instances of competition for the attention of the child, Terry. However, despite the tendency of the mother to turn the baby toward herself (resulting in some exclusion of the father), she also periodically includes the father in her talk, though she does so while remaining riveted on the baby. In this family, we judged coparenting as neither competitive nor supportive but as "poor."

> The father takes out the toy tea set while the mother shows the toys to Terry. Then the mother turns the baby in front of her and shows him the rattle. The mother gets up again and puts down the bag that the toys were in. As she does this, the father orients the baby carrier toward him. But when the mother comes back, she lifts a saucepan and says to the baby, "Look what mummy did." She puts the saucepan beneath the baby's nose to smell and says, "What daddy made smells good," then orients Terry back toward her. She takes a plate out, hands it to her husband, and says in baby talk, "We're feeding daddy. Eat up, daddy." As she enacts these actions, however, she keeps her gaze on Terry. The mother makes herself some coffee while talking to the baby about it: "A little coffee for mummy." The mother gives coffee to the father, again without looking at him, as she talks to her son: "Daddy is going to have his coffee."

In the third family, both parents are involved and centered on their daughter, Sally. Each of the parents tries to capture her attention, with the mother's attempts being most intense. She turns Sally toward herself most of the time and interferes when an interaction takes place between the father and the baby. The coparenting strikes us as especially competitive, and unlike Terry's family, no mother–father exchanges are observable. In fact, the parents never look at one another during the entire game (about half an hour).

> The mother turns the baby carrier toward her so the father finds himself at right angles to the mother–baby axis. The parents watch Sally, and each talks to her about something different. The father plays with the teddy bear and the mother asks Sally if her finger tastes good. The father says, "You want to get out of there, you are fed up being in there." The mother says, "Yes, you are fed up and we'll take you out." She takes Sally out of the carrier and holds her upright in front of the father, but as she bends, her head is interposed between father and daughter. The father says, "You like that; you like standing up." The mother goes further and says, "What are you going to do in a month . . . you are going to go swimming!" The father says again, "You like standing up." Then, as the father plays at lifting his daughter at arm's length, the mother shakes the rattle close to her head and calls to her directly, interfering in the father's game.

The three previous examples, although similar in some respects, also illustrate important between-family differences. They illustrate how the PNG can elicit behaviors that allow an assessment of different coparenting styles reflecting cooperative, poor, and competitive alliances. Having such information about characteristics of the coparenting alliance, both its difficulties and its resources, helps clarify aims of the intervention. Although assessment is necessary for intervention, intervention can take place directly in the assessment situation, as the case that follows illustrates.

ASSESSMENT AND TRIAL INTERVENTION IN A SYSTEMS CONSULTATION: CASE ILLUSTRATION IN THE LTP

In this section, we describe a systems consultation with a clinical case. Systems consultations are one-time sessions (possibly repeatable) in which a therapist asks a consultant (in our case a researcher/therapist) for assistance in identifying or clarifying a situation and in considering different intervention options (Wynne, McDaniel, & Weber, 1986).

Observation and assessment situations, such as the LTP and the PNG, are designed for interventions in several ways. First, the experiences partners have as they negotiate these tasks can in some cases enhance their development. Second, the formalized video feedback that follows the session is a powerful way to promote the family experience of their three-way relationships and to heighten their awareness of both positive and negative interactive patterns (Rusconi-Serpa, Sancho Rossignol, & McDonough, 2009). Third, the information stemming from the situation may be used to construct family-specific metaphors or to prescribe rituals to be carried out at home between sessions. Finally, trial interventions by a consultant during the situation—brief, nonverbal maneuvers used by the consultant to trigger change in the family's interaction patterns—can adjust the family's interactive behaviors and give parents opportunities to enact alternative, nonproblematic behaviors and experience their benefits. Consistent with the conceptual position articulated by Stern (1995), we maintain that effective trial interventions, even though they are directed at interactive patterns, will also come to have an impact on the partners' representations and on their intersubjective experience of threesome interactions.

The trial intervention in the clinical case illustration that follows is one of many we have used in our family consultations. For instance, one method we use to help parents who are having trouble engaging their baby in play is to create a vocal or holding "envelope." This can be accomplished by talking softly to the adult(s) or by holding them by the shoulders, both techniques we have found to facilitate change in the interaction (Fivaz-Depeursinge et al., 2004). Given this new context, sensing that the parents are soothed, the baby is emboldened to engage with them. The baby's gaze at the parents then triggers the parents' intuitive parenting behaviors (their repertoire of specific caretaking responses, e.g., use of dialogue distance or baby talk; see Papousek & Papousek, 1987). The result is the reestablishment of an intuitively driven, natural engagement.

Trial interventions often transform unproductive experiences into productive ones. They may enhance the therapeutic alliance, facilitate insight, or generate "moments of meeting" in which new meanings can emerge thanks to new levels of intersubjective sharing (Stern, 2004). Finally, they create opportunities to test the family's current readiness to change. Implicit trial interventions have also proven to be especially useful in working with parents who were not ready to reflect on their interactions at times of acute crises during psychiatric illness (for other examples, see Fivaz-Depeursinge, Corboz-Warnery, & Keren, 2004).

Clinical Case Illustration

Felix, 6 years old, and his parents were brought to the center by a colleague who worked with the spouses in couple therapy. The therapist and the parents asked for an assessment of family interactions to help with problems they were having with the child.

Prepared by their therapist to play and be videotaped together, the family members set out to do the LTP with a doll-play storytelling. Globally, the content of the story was extremely creative and colorful. However, within the context of the LTP and the "roles" ascribed to each of its four parts, the interactions lacked coordination regarding roles, and we observed serious problems in coparenting.

It was the mother who started out the story with Felix, artfully helping him to choose the characters and set the scene. However, the father kept leaning forward on the table, as if he were an active partner (see Figure 10.1, Panel A); his failure to keep to his role of observer in Part 1 was exemplified by the short distance he kept from the mother–child dyad. The mother progressively let him take over, without a clear transition between Parts 1 and 2. The father and son continued the story, enacting rich and exciting scenes but forgetting about moving to the third part, in spite of the mother's repeated signals. The mother alternated between leaning back in an observer position, with expressions that signaled her growing sense of being excluded, and engaging but unnoticed by both the father and the son. She finally gained entrance but simply went along with their dyadic game. As Part 3 progressed, she was again the one who reminded the father of the instruction to proceed to a dialogue between the two of them, but again her reminders were to no avail. Totally consumed by his son, the father kept reorienting to Felix rather than to the mother. The son, for his part, kept requesting the father's attention—in our framework, thereby also failing to accept a role of third party (see Figure 10.1, Panel B). At one point, when the father, prompted by the mother, turned away from him momentarily, Felix stood up, caught his parents by the hands and tried to move them away. The diversion continued

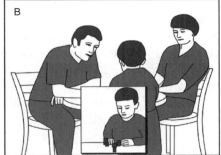
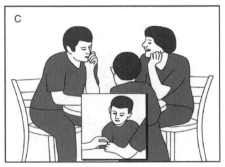

Figure 10.1. Body formations during the four contexts of the Lausanne Trilogue Play. Everyone is included, but displays of third party roles are problematic. A: During mother–child play, father leans in as if active partner. B: During father–child play, mother moves in (not shown) and out to signal to proceed to next context are ignored. C: During three-together play, the three partners are active and appropriately display it. D: During father–mother dialogue, father orients toward son, and son is not on his own. E: As father–mother dialogue continues, child tries to remove parents from setting.

with Felix returning to his chair, the father orienting toward and pleading with him—and the mother pleading with the father. In none of the four configurations did we observe a single moment of threesome affect sharing, although we saw several such moments in the twosomes.

For those unfamiliar with our body of work on the LTP, we underscore that significant difficulties in keeping to "prescribed" LTP roles are typical of problematic coparenting. They reflect a lack of cooperation between parents unable to coordinate to appropriately frame the child's behavior. The boundary between the parents' dyad and the child is breached in favor of a transgenerational coalition, in this case a binding one between the father and son against the mother (Fivaz-Depeursinge, Lopes, Python, & Favez, 2009; S. Minuchin, 1974). These difficulties are frequently observed in families with child behavior problems, such as those described for Felix.

In our work, the consultant watches the interaction from behind a one-way mirror. In this case, she felt a trial intervention was indicated. From her experience watching families in the LTP, she knew that it was unlikely a successful mother–father dialogue would ever result, given the family's distorted and confusing body formation. Though the father was explicitly intent on engaging in dialogue with the mother, he was implicitly remaining directly connected to Felix. This made it impossible for the parents to maintain a dialogue that drew a clear boundary between their dyad and the child. Indeed, to the clinician, the nonverbal context of the family members' body formations revealed more about the family's (covert) dynamics than anything the parents might have said about them.

Rather than explaining this to the adults, the consultant chose instead to attempt change by implicit means. She felt the family members had sufficient flexibility and playfulness to play along with her and that to surprise them with an intervention would be advantageous. This also provided an opportune way to test readiness for change at that time. After the mother's third unsuccessful attempt to reengage the father in dialogue with her, the research consultant reentered the room and asked for permission to try something. The parents, intrigued, gracefully accepted, while the child watched attentively.

First, she approached the father, firmly took him by the shoulders, and moved him to change his body orientation from being turned toward Felix to orienting toward the mother (see Figure 10.2, Panel A). Second, she approached the mother, gently holding her by the shoulders and helping her to further orient toward the father (see Figure 10.2, Panel B). Throughout the intervention, the parents and the consultant joked together, whereas Felix watched the scene in silent fascination. Finally, she asked them to continue their dialogue in this new formation. The mother asked, "What about?" and the consultant replied, "Just go on with what you had begun . . . like what you are going to do tonight, something that concerns the two of you."

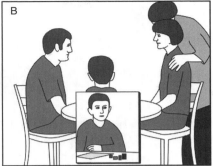

Figure 10.2. Trial intervention by consultant. A: Consultant orients father toward mother; child watches, intrigued. B: Consultant orients mother toward father; child watches, intrigued.

After a moment of hesitation, they resumed their conversation. But soon the father actually turned away from Felix—perhaps to counter an impulse to turn toward him. The consultant who had remained close by stopped him: "No! not too far." Father exclaimed, "Oh, not a wall here!" acknowledging the space between him and his son (along with his understanding of a boundary that was not too tight). Mother replied, "The wall is here," indicating the space between herself and the father. And the child chimed in, "There are walls everywhere here!" In our view, this was a moment of sharing of a new meaning among the three members of the family and the consultant.

The parents resumed their dialogue. The consultant remained vigilant and had to stop the father twice again from turning toward his son, even though Felix had begun drawing silently and was no longer seeking the father's attention. After a while, the consultant thanked the family for their graceful collaboration. Then the therapist reentered the room. He explained that the parents were very concerned about their son, as Felix insisted on sleeping with his parents, was undisciplined both at home and at school, and had no friends. His parents wondered whether he was hyperactive. However, the father was not nearly as concerned as the mother, because he had been like his son as a child and had easily grown out of it.

The parents came back 2 weeks later for a video-feedback session with the therapist. They reported much progress with Felix's behavior—he was sleeping on his own and was reportedly more disciplined at school. They were intrigued with the LTP situation and felt that there was something to it. They watched the videotape with the therapist and the consultant, who took pains not to engage in an intellectual discussion but rather to stay attuned to the feelings the parents had experienced as they displayed the different body formation contexts. The parents gained insight into the meaning of the implicit, nonverbal, affective context and readily understood the importance of using this intuitive knowledge in situations in which they needed to provide together a consistent affective framing for their child in defining limits.

Comments

Use of a trial intervention must be called for by particular family dynamics and should be carefully selected. Such interventions draw on the legacy of structural family therapy and rely largely on nonverbal interaction. They are also consistent with recent theories on the importance of implicit relational knowledge (Lyons-Ruth et al., 1998). The power of such interventions is in modifying the context in which the partners interact at a moment when they appear ready to change. Later, video feedback is an essential tool in helping to anchor the change.

DISCUSSION AND CONCLUSION

As McHale et al. (2004) outlined, early coparenting dynamics take shape in ways anticipated by prenatal functioning and, once established, remain remarkably stable through early childhood (Favez, Frascarolo, & Fivaz-Depeursinge, 2006; McHale & Rotman, 2007)—a circumstance demanding dedicated clinical efforts targeting coparental functioning. Although Feinberg's (2002) model suggests various potential targets for intervention, our focus has been on the management of family interactions, among which conflict and triangulation are particularly meaningful.

As we have illustrated, coparenting can be assessed for both clinical purposes and research purposes using both structured observation situations, such as the LTP, and more open-ended situations, such as the PNG. Such assessments can be carried out very early, even with infants as young as 3 months old. Whereas the LTP focuses on family triangles—father–mother–child triads, mother–grandmother–child triads, or coparent–child triads in gay and lesbian families—the LFP and PNG more flexibly allow observation of families with several children, and the PNG even enables inclusion of other important supplementary adults, such as grandparents.

Assessments of coparenting within triads or family groups afford different kinds of information than can be gleaned from dyadic child-related problem-solving discussions between the parents or interviews with adults about their coparenting alliance. Because these forms of data are also valuable in case conceptualization, we believe it advisable to complement observational family-level instruments with other methods (for a review, see McHale & Fivaz-Depeursinge, 2010; see also Chapter 7, this volume).

We believe there to be great advantage in using these relatively structured but "clinically friendly" family-level observational methods in both preventive interventions and in family psychotherapy research. As we have argued, targeting interaction as a point of entry in clinical work with families of infants and young children makes very good sense. Moreover, making use of standardized procedures introduces a degree of systematicity to assessments and affords the possibility of reevaluations in later sessions, allowing for measurement of change. Videotaping is also indispensible, allowing parents to have a double perspective on their functioning and lending itself to research efforts. Finally, therapeutic benefits can take place within the assessment procedure, provided care is taken to create a "good enough holding environment."

In closing, we advocate for the use of direct coparenting observation whenever working with families. Such information about the coparenting alliance is unparalleled when the goal is understanding and supporting adaptive alliances to optimally support child development.

REFERENCES

Allen, S., & Hawkins, A. (1999). Maternal gatekeeping: Mothers' beliefs and behaviors that inhibit greater father involvement in family work. *Journal of Marriage and the Family*, *61*, 199–212. doi:10.2307/353894

Baris, M., & Garrity, C. (1997). Coparenting post-divorce: Helping parents negotiate and maintain low-conflicts separation. In K. Halford & H. Markman (Eds.), *Clinical handbook of marriage and couples interventions* (pp. 619–649). Hoboken, NJ: Wiley.

Bonach, K. (2009). Empirical support for the application of the Forgiveness Intervention Model to postdivorce coparenting. *Journal of Divorce & Remarriage*, *50*, 38–54. doi:10.1080/10502550802365631

Carneiro, C., Corboz-Warnery, A., & Fivaz-Depeursinge, E. (2006). The prenatal Lausanne trilogue play: A new observational assessment tool of the prenatal coparenting alliance. *Infant Mental Health Journal*, *27*, 207–228. doi:10.1002/imhj.20089

Cookston, J., Braver, S., Griffin, W., De Lusé, S., & Miles, J. (2007). Effects of the Dads for Life Intervention on interparental conflict and coparenting in the two years after divorce. *Family Process*, *46*, 123–137. doi:10.1111/j.1545-5300.2006.00196.x

Cowan, C. P., Cowan, P. A., Pruett, M. K., & Pruett, K. (2007). An approach to preventing coparenting conflict and divorce in low-income families: Strengthening couple relationships and fostering fathers' involvement. *Family Process*, *46*, 109–121. doi:10.1111/j.1545-5300.2006.00195.x

Elliston, D., McHale, J., Talbot, J., Parmley, M., & Kuersten-Hogan, R. (2008). Withdrawal from coparenting interactions during early infancy. *Family Process, 47*, 481–499. doi:10.1111/j.1545-5300.2008.00267.x

Emery, R. E., Laumann-Billings, L., Waldron, M., Sbarra, D., & Dillon, P. (2001). Child custody mediation and litigation: Custody, contact and coparenting 12 years after initial dispute resolution. *Journal of Consulting and Clinical Psychology, 69*, 323–332. doi:10.1037/0022-006X.69.2.323

Emery, R. E., & Wyer, M. M. (1987). Child custody mediation and litigation: An experimental evaluation of the experience of parents. *Journal of Consulting and Clinical Psychology, 55*, 179–186. doi:10.1037/0022-006X.55.2.179

Fagan, J. (2008). Randomized study of a prebirth coparenting intervention with adolescents and young fathers. *Family Relations, 57*, 309–323. doi:10.1111/j.1741-3729.2008.00502.x

Fagan, J., & Barnett, M. (2003). The relationship between maternal gatekeeping, paternal competence, mothers' attitude about the father role, and father involvement. *Journal of Family Issues, 24*, 1020–1043. doi:10.1177/0192513X03256397

Favez, N., Frascarolo, F., Carneiro, C., Montfort, V., Corboz-Warnery, A., & Fivaz-Depeursinge, E. (2006). The development of the family alliance from pregnancy to toddlerhood and children outcomes at 18 months. *Infant and Child Development, 15*, 59–73. doi:10.1002/icd.430

Favez, N., Frascarolo, F., & Fivaz-Depeursinge, E. (2006). Family alliance stability and change from pregnancy to toddlerhood and marital correlates. *Swiss Journal of Psychology, 65*, 213–220. doi:10.1024/1421-0185.65.4.213

Favez, N., Frascarolo, F., Keren, M., & Fivaz-Depeursinge, E. (2009). Principles of family therapy in infancy. In C. Zeanah (Ed.), *Handbook of infant mental health* (3rd ed., pp. 468–484). New York, NY: Guilford.

Feinberg, M. E. (2002). Coparenting and the transition to parenthood: A framework for prevention. *Clinical Child and Family Psychology Review, 5*, 173–195. doi:10.1023/A:1019695015110

Feinberg, M. E., Jones, D. E., Kan, M. L., & Goslin, M. C. (2010). Effects of Family Foundations on parents and children: 3.5 years after baseline. *Journal of Family Psychology, 24*, 532–542.

Feinberg, M. E., & Kan, M. L. (2008). Establishing Family Foundations: Intervention effects on coparenting, parent/infant well-being, and parent-child relations. *Journal of Family Psychology, 22*, 253–263. doi:10.1037/0893-3200.22.2.253

Fivaz-Depeursinge, E., & Corboz-Warnery, A. (1999). *The primary triangle: A developmental systems view of mothers, fathers and infants.* New York, NY: Basic Books.

Fivaz-Depeursinge, E., Corboz-Warnery, A., & Keren, M. (2004). The primary triangle: Treating infants in their families. In A. J. Sameroff, S. C. McDonough, & K. L. Rosenblum (Eds.), *Treating parent-infant problems: Strategies for intervention* (pp. 123–151). New York, NY: Guilford Press.

Fivaz-Depeursinge, E., Lopes, F., Python, M., & Favez, N. (2009). Co-parenting and toddler's interactive styles in family coalitions. *Family Process, 48*, 500–516. doi:10.1111/j.1545-5300.2009.01298.x

Fonagy, P., Target, M., Cottrell, D., Phillips, J., & Kurtz, Z. (2002). *What works for whom? A critical review of treatments for children and adolescents*. New York, NY: Guilford Press.

Frascarolo, F., & Favez, N. (2005). Une nouvelle situation pour évaluer le fonctionnement familial: Le Jeu du Pique-Nique [A new situation to assess the family functioning: The Picnic Game]. *Devenir, 17*, 141–151. doi:10.3917/dev.052.0141

Garber, B. (2004). Directed Coparenting Intervention: Conducting child-centered interventions in parallel with highly conflicted co-parents. *Professional Psychology, Research and Practice, 35*, 55–64. doi:10.1037/0735-7028.35.1.55

Gottman, J. M. (1998). Psychology and the study of marital processes. *Annual Review of Psychology, 49*, 169–197. doi:10.1146/annurev.psych.49.1.169

Lee, C., & Hunsley, J. (2006). Addressing coparenting in the delivery of psychological services to children. *Cognitive and Behavioral Practice, 13*, 53–61. doi:10.1016/j.cbpra.2005.05.001

Leek, D. (1992). Shared parenting support program. *The American Journal of Forensic Psychology, 10*, 49–64.

Lyons-Ruth, K., Bruschweiler-Stern, N., Harrison, A. M., Nahum, J. P., Sander, L., Stern, D. N., & Tronick, E. T. (1998). Implicit relational knowing: Its role in development and psychoanalytic treatment. *Infant Mental Health Journal, 19*, 282–289. doi:10.1002/(SICI)1097-0355(199823)19:3<282::AID-IMHJ3>3.0.CO;2-O

McBride, B., Brown, G., Bost, K., Shin, N., Vaughn, B., & Korth, B. (2005). Paternal identity, maternal gatekeeping, and father involvement. *Family Relations, 54*, 360–372. doi:10.1111/j.1741-3729.2005.00323.x

McHale, J. P. (1995). Coparenting and triadic interactions during infancy: The roles of marital distress and child gender. *Developmental Psychology, 31*, 985–996. doi:10.1037/0012-1649.31.6.985

McHale, J. (2007). *Charting the bumpy road of coparenthood: Understanding the challenges of family life*. Washington, DC: Zero to Three.

McHale, J., & Alberts, A. (2003). Thinking three: Coparenting and family-level considerations for infant mental health professionals. *Signal, 11*, 1–11.

McHale, J., & Fivaz-Depeursinge, E. (2010). Principles of effective coparenting and its assessment in infancy and early childhood. In S. Tyano, M. Keren, H. Herman, & J. Cox (Eds.), *Parenting and mental health: A bridge between infant and adult psychiatry* (pp. 357–372). London, England: Wiley.

McHale, J. P., Khazali, C., Rotman, T., Talbot, J., Carleton, M., & Lieberson, R. (2004). The transition to co-parenthood: Parents' prebirth expectations and early coparental adjustment at 3 months postpartum. *Development and Psychopathology, 16*, 711–733. doi:10.1017/S0954579404004742

McHale, J., & Rotman, T. (2007). Is seeing believing? Expectant parents' outlooks on coparenting and later coparenting solidarity. *Infant Behavior and Development, 30,* 63–81.

McHale, J., & Sullivan, M. (2008). Family systems. In M. Hersen & A. M. Gross (Eds.), *Handbook of clinical psychology: Vol. 2. Children and adolescents* (pp. 192–226). Hoboken, NJ: Wiley.

Minuchin, P. (1985). Families and individual development: Provocations from the field of family therapy. *Child Development, 56,* 289–302. doi:10.2307/1129720

Minuchin, S. (1974). *Families and family therapy.* Cambridge, MA: Harvard University Press.

Minuchin, S., Nichols, M. P., & Lee, W. Y. (2006). *Assessing families and couples: From symptom to system.* Boston, MA: Allyn & Bacon.

Minuchin, S., Rosman, B. L., & Baker, L. (1978). *Psychosomatic families: Anorexia nervosa in context.* Cambridge, MA: Harvard University Press.

Mitcham-Smith, M., & Henry, W. (2007). High-conflict divorce solutions: Parenting coordination as an innovative coparenting intervention. *The Family Journal, 15,* 368–373. doi:10.1177/1066480707303751

Papousek, H., & Papousek, M. (1987). Intuitive parenting: A dialectic counterpart to the infant's integrative competence. In J. D. Osofsky (Ed.), *Handbook of infant development* (2nd ed., pp. 669–720). New York, NY: Wiley.

Rusconi-Serpa, S., Sancho Rossignol, A., & McDonough, S. C. (2009). Video feedback in parent-infant treatments. *Child and Adolescent Psychiatric Clinics of North America, 18,* 735–751. doi:10.1016/j.chc.2009.02.009

Sanders, M. (1999). Triple-P positive parenting program: Towards an empirically-validated multilevel parenting and family support strategy for the prevention of behavior and emotional problem in children. *Clinical Child and Family Psychology Review, 2,* 71–90.

Sbarra, D. A., & Emery, R. E. (2005). Coparenting conflict, nonacceptance and depression among divorced adults: Results from a 12-year follow-up study of child custody mediation using multiple imputation. *American Journal of Orthopsychiatry, 75,* 63–75. doi:10.1037/0002-9432.75.1.63

Stern, D. N. (1995). Self/other differentiation in the domain of intimate socio-affective interaction: Some considerations. In P. Rochat (Ed.), *The self in infancy: Theory and research* (pp. 419–429). Amsterdam, the Netherlands: Elsevier.

Stern, D. N. (2004). *The present moment in psychotherapy and everyday life.* New York, NY: Norton.

Szapocznik, J., & Kurtines, W. (1989). *Breakthroughs in family therapy with drug abusing problem youth.* New York, NY: Springer.

Van Egeren, L. A., & Hawkins, D. P. (2004). Coming to terms with coparenting. Implications of definition and measurement. *Journal of Adult Development, 11,* 165–178. doi:10.1023/B:JADE.0000035625.74672.0b

Wynne, L., McDaniel, S., & Weber, T. (1986). *Systems consultation: A new perspective for family therapy.* New York, NY: Guilford Press.

11

COPARENTING AFTER DIVORCE: PAVING PATHWAYS FOR PARENTAL COOPERATION, CONFLICT RESOLUTION, AND REDEFINED FAMILY ROLES

MARSHA KLINE PRUETT AND TRACY DONSKY

As this volume attests, coparenting is a concept that has recently enjoyed far more attention than in previous decades. Research with married families, long influenced by theories about attachment and the primacy of the maternal role in parenting, has focused primarily on the role of the mother–child relationship in promoting healthy child development. Fathers, traditionally less involved in childrearing, were also less of a focal point for understanding pathways to children's development. In fact, as of the mid-1960s, the index to the *Handbook of Child Psychology* did not have a single reference to fathers (Nash, 1965). Mothers were given the credit and shouldered the blame for how children "turned out" (see Chapter 1, this volume). Similarly, in separating families, mothers typically obtained sole or primary legal and physical custody of children. Fathers were often relegated to secondary parent status, and many dropped out of their children's lives altogether (Fabricius & Hall, 2000; Kelly & Emery, 2003). Over the past 40 years, however, there has been a dramatic shift in family structures and the role of parents. These changes have impacted married and divorcing families alike.

In this chapter, we begin with a brief historical review of the evolution of coparenting among divorcing spouses, describing its similarities and dissimilarities to coparenting in intact marriages. After conceptualizing the working relationship between former partners or spouses who choose to coparent, we follow with a discussion of interventions that have emerged in the service of supporting separated parents' successful navigation of the complexities inherent in sharing responsibilities for child rearing while remaining logistically and emotionally separated. We end with a brief discussion of data showing how coparenting operates differently for divorcing mothers and fathers.

EVOLUTION OF COPARENTING IN SEPARATED AND DIVORCING FAMILIES

Trends toward explicit discussions about joint custody and shared parenting in divorcing families emerged in the late 1970s ("One Child, Two Homes," 1979) and continued to gather momentum over the following decades. In the 1990s, mothers joined the workforce in increasing numbers and did so earlier in their children's lives across economic strata, whereas fathers became increasingly involved in hands-on child-care activities and functions (P. A. Cowan, Cowan, Cohen, Pruett, & Pruett, 2008; Sayer, Bianchi, & Robinson, 2004). In tandem with these cultural shifts, researchers began to tout the critical role that fathers play in children's development as it became clear that children with sensitive and committed fathers benefited cognitively, socially, and emotionally from that involvement (Lamb, 2000; Thomas & Forehand, 1993; see also K. D. Pruett, 2000).

Concurrently, there was a dramatic increase in statutory joint custody provisions in most states. The shift in child custody determinations, bolstered by research showing that children of divorce long for more contact with fathers throughout childhood (Emery, 2004; Marquadt, 2006; Wallerstein, Lewis, & Blakeslee, 2000), prompted the widespread use of statutorily prescribed parenting plans for divorcing spouses. Parenting plans specify each parent's entitlements to decision making and residential arrangements, thereby ensuring (in theory and often in practice) the nonresidential parent's (usually the father) time with his children. This development in family law helped solidify unmarried and divorced fathers' role in their children's lives; fathers more often stayed involved and to a greater extent than in decades prior. The number of children who lost contact with their fathers (as the nonresidential parent) 2 to 3 years after divorce decreased to 18%–26% by the late 1990s (Braver & O'Connell, 1998; Kelly, 2007), and some reports indicated that 35% to 40% of children may have at least weekly contact with their nonresidential parent (e.g., Braver & O'Connell, 1998). However, it is also still typical for the amount of contact between nonresidential parents and their children to decrease to an every-other-weekend schedule following divorce (Kelly, 2007). Although father loss decreased in magnitude, some loss still occurs in most divorcing families.

Research on fathers proliferated as experts and politicians from varying political persuasions began to recognize fathers as an "untapped resource" in the lives of children (C. P. Cowan, Cowan, Pruett, & Pruett, 2007; Tamis-LeMonda & Cabrera, 2002), particularly in families facing numerous risk factors to healthy growth and development, such as those living in father-absent homes (Coley, 2001). As researchers and policymakers increasingly recognized the relevance of each parent's relationship with his or her child to the overall well-being of the child, interest in how the nature and quality of the relationship between those adults impact the child's development likewise grew (see Schulz, Pruett, Kerig, & Parke, 2009). Research has repeatedly shown that interparental conflict is associated with problematic adjustment in children (Braver, Shapiro, & Goodman, 2005; Emery, 1982; Grych & Fincham, 1990; Laumann-Billings & Emery, 2000). Children who are exposed to ongoing and/or high levels of parental conflict are at higher risk of various behavioral and emotional problems (Amato & Afifi, 2006; Grych, 2005; Johnston, Kline, & Tschann, 1989; Johnston & Roseby, 1997) and more problematic parent–child relationships (Amato, 2003; Grych, 2005). Moreover, parents' ability to effectively cooperate as coparents is an important determinant of a child's ultimate level of well-being in divorced families, especially when the children are young (i.e., Adamsons & Pasley, 2005; M. K. Pruett, Arthur, & Ebling, 2007). Recognition in the developmental literature and within divorce and family law that parental conflict is deleterious to children's development—and that cooperation and collaboration are powerful positive forces in child adjustment—led to an intensive and extensive focus on promoting constructive models of shared parenting and interventions to achieve it.

Defining Coparenting: Inside and Outside of Marriage

Shared parenting or *coparenting* refers to the support and solidarity between adults responsible for the joint care of children (see Chapter 1). Such support and solidarity can be related to, but often transcends, the actual division of child-care labor (McHale, 2007). K. Pruett and Pruett (2009) listed six key components of a strong coparenting relationship, four of which pertain to divorced partners as well: (a) acting together as the "kid's team," (b) sharing or dividing up direct child care, (c) managing conflict about the child, and (d) feeling supported in the process of parenting. They further pointed out that successful coparenting in any context requires negotiation, respect, and support. Effective coparents, whether spouses or former spouses, support one another's actions and decisions, make and stick to agreements about how to raise their children, and refrain as best they can from undermining each other by deviating from these agreements unilaterally. Likewise, a successful coparenting relationship, irrespective of the spousal commitment, requires that parents forego "bean counting" or an insistence on "sharing" in which sharing is actually code for a verifiable equal split in tasks or division of time with the child. Instead, effectual coparents recognize and value that each parent brings to the relationship and to the child a different skill set and different life circumstances.

Acknowledging that a coparenting relationship in any context requires certain key components does not, however, imply that coparenting after divorce is identical to coparenting within marriage. One critical difference, which typically wreaks havoc in the family, is the shift in family boundaries and the heightened sense of concern about who is an insider versus an outsider that this change creates for family members.

Divorce: Disrupting Family Boundaries and Instigating Parental Competition

Professionals often use the term *intact* to describe a family with two cohabitating parents in a committed relationship. Intact implies wholeness; nonseparated families are whole, in part, because they are surrounded and protected by a boundary that encompasses the family unit. Boundaries act as the rules that define who may participate in family transactions and how they may participate. When boundaries are operating effectively, the role each family member plays in the family system tends to be clear, as is the relationship between subgroups within the family (e.g., siblings, parent and child) and the functioning of the family system as a whole (Minuchin, 1977). Clear boundaries regulate the content and manner of communication that occurs both within and around the family system. They are indicative of, and support, optimal family functioning. Healthy boundaries as such remain open and flexible enough to allow family members to communicate and collaborate with one another, but sufficiently closed and structured in order to provide family members with autonomy and differentiation to carry out their unique role and position in the family without undue interference from other members.

After divorce, the family boundary splinters—it is no longer intact. Communication and boundaries become ambiguous, especially during the transition from living as one nuclear family in one home. Communication that once flowed predominantly between parents now often passes through children. Communication between parents, and between parents and children, often becomes more difficult and tenuous. Relationships between parents and children shift in ways that may alter secure attachments (Kirkpatrick & Hazan, 1994), potentially leading to increased instability in relationships and a sense of insecurity on the part of one or more family members with respect to the continuity of family relationships. Family members may become uncertain in their perception about who is in and out of the family (Carroll, Olson, & Buchmiller, 2007), and vigilance about inclusion or exclusion can become a preoccupation, galvanized by the threat to a sense of belonging and recognition as a joint parent with authority and legitimacy (Bird, 2009).

The coparental relationship necessarily takes a hit as parents separate physically and emotionally. One partner or both are typically angry, hurt, disappointed, embarrassed, and/or humiliated by the other parent. Without the marriage and the historical "wholeness" of the family to hang onto, there is a powerful desire and tendency to hang on tightly to the children as important vestiges of the relationship that "cannot" legally be torn asunder. When positioned as competitors battling over a scarce resource, coparenting former spouses frequently find their attention inordinately focused on the degree of inclusion—in decisions and in family events—each feels that he or she is afforded and the degree to which the other is entitled. Both parents view themselves as principal stockholders and expect to be treated as such, but one parent—often the father—frequently finds himself feeling like a minority shareholder, lacking authority, respect, autonomy, and sufficient voting power. This struggle for power and inclusiveness typically translates into a contest for equality. Prioritizing equality, however, does not lead to cooperative coparenting. Rather, it is a sense of being viewed as equally valuable, though necessarily not equal, that creates harmonious and effective coparenting. Comparability, not equality, is fundamental. This concept of shared investment and "teamness," however, is difficult to realize when competition, conflict, or hostility finds its way into the coparenting relationship.

Since Ricci (1997) first introduced the idea of divorcing spouses adopting a business relationship, much of the advice on postdivorce coparenting counsels parents to interact with one another in a formal, businesslike approach—for example, to rely on e-mail or a third party to communicate, to communicate rather than discuss major decisions, to negotiate and then adhere to a parenting plan, and to take responsibility for one's own but not the other parent's relationship with the child (e.g., Bird, 2009). This stance is intended to reinforce the notion that despite whatever differences may exist between parents, they continue to have a shared interest and common goal: the well-being of their child. Unfortunately, many former spouses lose sight of the bigger picture in the emotional upheaval of the divorce. Instead of interacting as business partners maintaining a successful joint venture, they act as competitors, frequently creating situations in which one parent's success occurs at the expense of the other, rather than fostering win–win situations in which both parties benefit.

PROMOTING COPARENTING THROUGH
PARENT INTERVENTIONS

To encourage successful coparenting, legal and mental health professionals use various types of interventions aimed at promoting inclusion for both parents while helping them define the boundaries of inclusion and exclusion in ways that support optimal parenting capacities and children's adjustment and well-being. Such interventions are designed to strengthen the coparenting relationship by giving parents the tools and the opportunities to define and discuss with one another the role each will play in the child's life, the scope of authority each will hold, and the amount of time each will have with the child. In addition, interventions attempt to provide parents with the skill and knowledge necessary to converse collaboratively with one another about the children, make joint decisions, and refrain from arguments (M. K. Pruett & R. K. Barker, 2009).

The primary risk for children after divorce is the deterioration of the relationship between the child and either or both parents, with the relationship with the primary caregiving parent more salient for child adjustment and the relationship with the nonresidential parent more vulnerable to damage (Forgatch, Patterson, & Ray, 1995; Hetherington, 1999; Kelly, 2000). When parents remain physically and emotionally engaged with their children, disciplining appropriately, they provide a protective buffer against the multitude of relational and environmental changes that children experience after parental separation (for a summary, see M. K. Pruett & R. K. Barker, 2009). Responding to the relatively greater vulnerability of the nonresidential parent–child relationship to self- or imposed exclusion within the divorced family, an ongoing concern in divorce research is the amount and quality of time children spend with that parent (typically the father) and the institutional, psychological, and parental relationship barriers to continuity that these relationships face after divorce (Kelly, 2007).

Given the gatekeeping role mothers frequently assume after divorce (M. K. Pruett et al., 2007), emphasis is placed on promoting interparental cooperation. There are many strategies to assist parents in establishing a framework for cooperation and defining the boundaries for coparenting. These strategies exist along a continuum of inclusiveness and cooperation. Four approaches that illustrate the range of strategies available are described in the following sections: parent education, group interventions, mediation, and parenting coordination. All of these approaches aim to shore up individual parenting capacity by forestalling conflict, maintaining each parent's sense of inclusion and inclusiveness (i.e., encouraging each parent to support the other's presence in the child's life), and helping parents stay focused individually and together on their children's needs. To accomplish this as a preventive intervention, many U.S. states have put into place universal educational parenting programs. For those families already involved in legal or emotional conflict, secondary prevention and treatment programs, such as parent intervention groups and mediation, are implemented to support the parental alliance. Finally, for families entrenched in high conflict, new and more intensive interventions, such as parenting coordination, have emerged to stave off a complete breakdown of all coparenting behaviors and attitudes.

Parent Education Programs

Parent education programs for divorcing parents began in the United States in the mid-1970s and expanded during the 1980s (Bacon & McKenzie, 2004; Salem, Schepard, & Schlissel, 1996). They have now become widespread, with at least 46 states currently enacting such programs (Pollet & Lombreglia, 2008). These psychoeducational programs are conceptualized broadly as a public health intervention likely to positively impact all families undergoing divorce (Schepard, 2004). Most programs aim to provide parents with information that could help them minimize conflict and understand the benefits children derive from having ongoing relationships with both parents (except in situations of abuse or other family conditions that place children's safety and mental health in jeopardy). Parenting skills and legal options for dispute resolution typically receive less attention than topics involving interparental conflict, such as the negative impact of badmouthing and of encouraging the child to side with one parent (Goodman, Bonds, Sandler, & Braver, 2004). Generally, these programs are short (from 2 to 4 hours) and may be either mandated for all families or made widely available but are not required (Goodman et al., 2004). Although designed as preventive programs, most address topics that affect children's adjustment to parental conflict, making them a potentially worthwhile intervention at most stages of divorce.

Though few rigorous, systematic studies have been conducted on these programs' effectiveness, parents report the acquisition of new information, attitudes, and skills (see Schepard, 2004) and high satisfaction with the programs (Erickson & Ver Steegh, 2001), even when they had initially resisted attending. Testimonials from judges and mediators, and lower relitigation rates by parents who attended such programs, also attest to their short-term positive impact (Arbuthnot & Kramer, 1998; Fischer, 1997; Kramer & Kowal, 1998). Not surprisingly, few short-term programs have reported on positive changes in quality of parenting or child well-being, and there is only sparse evidence of deceased interparental conflict (Goodman et al., 2004).

As educational-type programs cross over from short, universal programs to individual or small group interventions ranging up to 16 hours in length, both reductions in parental conflict (Bacon & McKenzie, 2004) and increases in parental cooperation and coparenting as well as positive parenting have been noted (Goodman et al., 2004). There is also some evidence that greater change occurs in programs of 6 hours or longer (Bacon & McKenzie, 2004), although certain outcomes vary independently of program length (Arbuthnot, Kramer, & Gordon, 1997). Although many programs are described as parenting education models, programs lasting more than 6 to 8 hours could be categorized as intervention and treatment rather than primary prevention models, as described in the following section.

Group Interventions

Group interventions, especially child-focused groups, are the most common forms of divorce interventions (O'Halloran & Carr, 2000; M. K. Pruett & Hoganbruen, 1998). For purposes of this chapter, we focus on adult-oriented interventions targeting the parental relationship. Parent-focused interventions typically use a group-therapy structure to help parents manage stresses of divorce; cope more effectively; and, in more intensive interventions, develop parent management and communication skills. The goal of these interventions is to create a consistent, low-conflict family environment within and between both parents' homes. Parents who have participated in group interventions have reported decreased maternal distress, increased awareness of the negative impact of conflict on children, and more positive feelings toward their former partners (Haine, Sandler, Wolchik, Tein, & Dawson-McClure, 2003; Pedro-Carroll, Nakhnikian, & Montes, 2001). Parenting quality and child outcomes have shown improvement when parenting skills and behaviors are specifically targeted (Sandler, Wolchik, Winslow, & Schenck, 2006). Significant reductions in ex-spousal conflict have also been noted as a result of such interventions (Cookston, Braver, Griffins, De Luse, & Miles, 2007). Innovative therapeutic interventions for high-conflict parents (e.g., see Fieldstone & Coates, 2008) and for parents and children together with the aim of mitigating parental behaviors and family dynamics that contribute to children aligning with one parent and rejecting the other parent, most often the father (Fidler & Bala, 2010), are becoming more prevalent in the clinical and empirical literatures.

These positive results pointing to program effectiveness have undoubtedly supported family reorganization and functioning after divorce. Until recently, however, many of the programs have focused on mothers to the exclusion of nonresidential fathers (O'Halloran & Carr, 2000). Postdivorce parenting interventions might benefit from the knowledge gained in an intervention program for married and unmarried (including some divorcing) couples (P. A. Cowan, Cowan, Pruett, Pruett, & Wong, 2009). Results from this ongoing controlled clinical trial demonstrated that involvement by both parents in a group intervention benefits the couple's communication and relationship, as well as child outcomes, to a greater extent than does a treatment condition that includes only one parent, in this case, the father (P. A. Cowan et al., 2009). It stands to reason that whenever possible, both parents should be involved in interventions together, if the goal is to redefine the postdivorce family as one that includes two parents whose contributions to child adjustment are equally valuable and unique and if the couple's relationship and ability to parent together is viewed as a primary pathway to healthier functioning for all family members.

Mediation

Among the many alternative dispute resolution programs and interventions currently being implemented for divorcing families, mediation remains one of the most widely applied. It functions as both a primary and a secondary prevention strategy, depending on the point at which divorcing parents embark on it and how voluntarily they engage in it. Mediation may occur in a court-based setting, a private practice, an agency, or a community mediation center. Some mediators focus on client interaction and/or integrate therapeutic elements into the process, whereas others emphasize settlement (Folberg, Milne, & Salem, 2004). Regardless, mediation focuses predominantly on the couple's relationship and ability to reach legal and practical agreements concerning how they will coparent their children after divorce. A neutral third party helps the parties consider their varying needs and interests; formulate their own agreement; and ideally, as a consequence, recognize that cooperation is mutually advantageous. Ultimately, the purpose of mediation is to foster cooperative parenting and strong parent–child relationships while reducing parental dependence on the court for arriving at solutions to parental conflict.

The advantages of mediation are touted in empirical studies: Mothers and fathers are quite satisfied with the process, and outcome studies with control groups report reduced parental conflict, increased cooperative decision making and father involvement, and successful development of parenting plans (Emery, Laumann-Billings, Waldron, Sbarra, & Dillon, 2001; M. K. Pruett, Insabella, & Gustafson, 2005). Moreover, compliance with parenting plans and child support agreements remains higher among mediating compared with litigating couples (Dillon & Emery, 1996). Even brief mediation (5 hours) seems to have lasting and impressive effects on parental cooperation, child involvement with the nonresidential parent, and child outcomes as much as 12 years after the mediation (Emery, 2004). Yet empirical research does not support all the assumptions made by mediation proponents; the data are not uniformly positive and mediators, court administrators, and researchers must continue to work closely together to carefully and systematically assess the variables that affect the mediation process and its outcomes (Beck, Sales, & Emery, 2004).

A number of states now mandate mediation before disputing couples come before a judge. Mandatory mediation changes the process from one of private dispute resolution to one that is publicly accessible; visibly accountable; and theoretically, more structured because the process must accommodate non-English speakers, indigent parties, and complex family structures. The imposition of mandated mediation has reduced litigated custody cases in California, and most court-based litigants are satisfied with the service (Ricci, 2004). Yet, there is still much debate in the field about whether mandated mediation serves coparenting and child purposes as well as other forms of conflict resolution. In Connecticut, new court support services have been made available so that families who once had only mediation or a comprehensive evaluation to choose from may now engage in state-funded alternative dispute services of moderate intensity. An evaluation of the new services, and an intake screen that was introduced at the same time as the new services, indicate that the screen and new services have improved families' ability to reach agreements, lowered the return rate of families to court, and resulted in cost savings for the court (M. K. Pruett & Durell, 2009). Mediation, still a highly effective option for separating parents, was made even more effective when other services became available alternatives for higher conflict families.

Mediation is recommended with great caution, if at all, in situations of intimate partner violence (IPV). A traditional mediation process often does not offer adequate protection for parents involved in IPV and the children who are directly involved themselves or as witnesses. A hybrid mediation model that invokes mediation's principles of self-determination but also addresses issues of power, control, and safety is more appropriate in such situations (Milne, 2004). Additionally, cases involving IPV should be facilitated by a mediator who is cross-trained to carry out both assessment and mediation functions (Ricci, 2004).

Parenting Coordination

One of the newest interventions to address high-conflict divorcing families is parenting coordination: a quasi-legal, mental health, child-focused alternative dispute resolution process that combines assessment, education, case management, conflict management, and sometimes decision-making functions (Association of Family and Conciliation Courts, 2005). Parenting coordination is facilitated by the parenting coordinator (PC), a neutral mental health or legal professional ordered by the court or through an agreement of the parties. The role of the PC is to help the parties implement and comply with their parenting plans, reduce conflict, and make timely decisions in a manner consistent with the children's best developmental and psychological interests by providing structured intervention with appropriate boundaries to address impasses in decision making and potential power differences between the parties (Deutsch, 2008). The PC attempts to help the parties come to agreement through mediation and negotiation; if the parties are unable to do so, then depending on the law in that jurisdiction and the agreement of the parties, the PC either makes the decision for the parties or makes recommendations to the parents or the court. The PC role is not subject to the rules of confidentiality that apply to mediation (Deutsch, 2008).

Although recent research on parenting coordination has suggested that it leads to positive outcomes for families (Angaran, Carter, & Fieldstone, 2009; Coates, Deutsch, Starnes, Sullivan, & Sydlik, 2004), the efficacy of this new intervention has not yet been widely evaluated. Results from one recently published study indicated that participation in parenting coordination reduces the number of motions filed in the domestic relations court by relitigating couples and further appears to benefit the parties throughout the duration of the couple's legal process (Henry, Fieldstone, & Bohac, 2009). It is not yet known whether there are subcategories of high-conflict parents who would benefit most from engagement of a PC, although initial indications suggest that parenting coordination is beneficial for couples from diverse populations with varying living situations (Henry et al., 2009). One prominent and challenging issue with this intervention is the cost. For courts that do not provide "in-house" parenting coordination (the majority of jurisdictions), the cost of this approach is borne by the parents, which limits consideration of this option only to parents with adequate financial resources. For courts that do provide such services, adequate court funding may be problematic. Further investigation of this approach is necessary to answer the questions of whether it works and if so, how and for whom.

PATHWAYS OF COPARENTING PROCESSES BETWEEN DIVORCING SPOUSES

In recent research, the senior author of this chapter has attempted to move beyond the question of whether divorce interventions work to understand how they work. She has used path modeling to explicate how relationships between predivorce and divorce processes and child and legal outcomes are mediated by interventions (M. K. Pruett & Barker, 2009; M. K. Pruett, Ebling, & Cowan, in press). The Collaborative Divorce Project (CDP) is a court-affiliated program that combined psychoeducational, mediation, and therapeutic practices under one rubric, creating a randomized clinical trial of promising practices among divorce interventions. The CDP was one of the first programs to make both parents' participation a condition of acceptance into the program. Although the intervention drew parents representing a range of economic, mental health, and conflict levels who were then randomly assigned to the intervention or a control group, the program was still voluntary and likely attracted only those couples with some motivation to succeed at reducing the negative impact of divorce on their family. Parental motivation did vary quite widely among participants, but the study does not inform about couples with little to no motivation, whose children may be in the greatest need for such services.

With this caveat, the CDP (for a complete description, see M. K. Pruett et al., 2005) offered education and intervention that emphasized the need for continuing cooperation and coordination between parents and the necessity of involving both parents in the lives of their children. Results showed that mothers' and fathers' path models were similar in many respects, but also were different in important ways. The primary impact of the intervention for both parents was through reduced parental conflict. Yet one interesting gender difference emerged: Maternal reports indicated that when parents were in conflict, the quality of the mother–child relationship was compromised, as was the child's behavior (averaged across both parents' reports). Paternal reports indicated that it was conflict, cooperation, and the parenting plan— that is, the broader coparental relationship—that shaped the child's behavior (again averaged across both parent reports). Thus, as other divorce researchers have found (e.g., Cohen & Finzi-Dottan, 2005), the coparental relationship after divorce is more salient for nonresidential parents (the fathers in this sample) than for primary care givers (the mothers in this sample). This may be especially true among families with young children, as included here. One implication of these results is that by strengthening the coparental relationship and postdivorce living arrangements through the CDP intervention, the father's role in child adjustment is strengthened as well.

In a second set of path analyses of legal outcomes (M. K. Pruett, 2007), mothers' data show that the intervention led to greater maternal support of fathers during the divorce, which was in turn associated with lower levels of negative legal outcomes from the divorce process. A key finding in the fathers' model was that the intervention led to implementation of parenting plans that supported overnight visits and schedule consistency for children, thereby reducing negative legal outcomes. Here, too, a coparenting intervention that supports maternal inclusiveness of father and paternal inclusiveness in his children's life contributed not only to positive child outcomes but also to lower conflict levels assessed in the legal process of divorce.

COPARENTING IN THE CONTEXT OF VIOLENT CONFLICT

Although recent research has supported the efficacy of joint parenting for child adaptation in particular, and families more generally (see M. K. Pruett & Barker, 2009), there are some situations when spousal exclusion is appropriate. In many high-conflict families involved in IPV, coparenting strategies should be implemented sparingly or not at all. When child abuse allegations are substantiated, there is also cause to protect the child from his or her parent(s). For certain families, IPV is situational and may be intimately connected to the separation or divorce trauma. In these conflict-instigated rather than control-instigated situations of violence (Fuhrmann, McGill, & O'Connell, 1999; Kelly & Johnson, 2008), interventions that mitigate the violence and support the safe separation of spouses strengthen some couples' capacity to cooperate for the benefit of the child. Alternatively, well-founded concerns about the existence of IPV can result in failing to identify families in which coparenting interventions could be beneficial or workable over time (Jaffe, Johnston, Crooks, & Bala, 2008). Efforts aimed at encouraging shared parenting arrangements in families with high levels of conflict should proceed with the utmost caution and careful assessment of the family's conflict history and current situation with regard to the safety of all family members. States and individual service providers vary greatly in the emphasis they place on assessment and monitoring of IPV because of financial constraints, over-large caseloads and crowded court dockets, and lack of specialized knowledge in this area. State-of-the-art knowledge base and intervention design is evolving rapidly, and continuing education in this area for all professionals is urged. For starters, recent advances and controversies in the field are cogently described for mental health and legal professionals by Kelly and Johnson (2008) and Oleson and Drozd (2008).

CONCLUDING REMARKS

The theoretical, clinical, and empirical focus on coparenting after divorce preceded that on married families, in which coparenting was assumed and perhaps taken for granted. The body of empirical evidence supports the usefulness of intervention for reducing parental conflict and promoting cooperation toward the goal of fostering civil parental relationships and paternal inclusion following familial reorganization. But the splintered parental boundary and the resulting opportunities for actual and perceived exclusion of nonresidential parents in particular leave in their wake highly sensitive family dynamics that point to areas of inquiry requiring more attention. Among these is a more differentiated understanding of which kinds of postdivorce interventions (e.g., parenting groups, mediation, parenting coordination, reversal of rigidified child alignments with the primary caretaker and rejection of the other parent) work best for which kinds of families and for children at varying developmental stages. In particular, interventions targeting more vulnerable families with entrenched negative family dynamics are in demand by the courts and legal professionals struggling to secure the child's best interests in these families. How to affect intervention, while amply protecting the children and parents who experience violence in the family, is another area in need of attention. Great strides have been made in this regard in the past decade, but the severity and prevalence of the problem demand more progress. Knowledge generated will be applicable not only to divorcing families but also to those struggling or suffering in intact families, as well.

Leading psychological theories and interventions continue to present the possibilities of, and pathways to, parental cooperation and conflict reduction for separating and divorcing spouses through the promotion of both parents' inclusion in their children's postdivorce life. The recognition of both parents as included and including may promote the responsibility fathers and all nonresidential parents take toward supporting the reorganization of the postdivorce family and enhancing the well-being of all its members, especially the youngest and most vulnerable. The cultivation of a culture of inclusiveness calls on models of professional intervention that creatively help both parents work together and respect one another's place in the life of their child and his or her redefined family unit. Ultimately, the goal is the same for divorced and married families: to share parenting in a way that maximizes the security and well-being of children and to preserve family life in its various structural forms for the generations that count on it to thrive into the future.

REFERENCES

Adamsons, K., & Pasley, K. (2005). Coparenting following divorce and relationship dissolution. In M. A. Fine & J. H. Harvey (Eds.), *Handbook of divorce and relationship dissolution* (pp. 241–262). Mahwah, NJ: Erlbaum.

Amato, P. R. (2003). Reconciling divergent perspectives: Judith Wallerstein, quantitative family research, and children of divorce. *Family Relations, 52,* 332–339. doi:10.1111/j.1741-3729.2003.00332.x

Amato, P., & Afifi, T. (2006). Feeling caught between parents: Adult children's relations with parents and subjective well-being. *Journal of Marriage and the Family, 68,* 222–235. doi:10.1111/j.1741-3737.2006.00243.x

Angaran, R., Carter, D. K., & Fieldstone, L. (2009, November). *Research to practice: Florida's parenting coordination study.* Study presented at the AFCC regional training conference, Reno, NV.

Arbuthnot, J., & Kramer, K. (1998). Effects of divorce education on mediation process and outcome. *Mediation Quarterly, 15*, 199–213. doi:10.1002/crq.3890150305

Arbuthnot, J., Kramer, K., & Gordon, D. A. (1997). Patterns of relitigation following divorce education. *Family Court Review, 35*, 269–279. doi:10.1111/j.174-1617.1997.tb00469.x

Association of Family and Conciliation Courts. (2005). *Guidelines for parenting coordination.* Retrieved from http://www.afccnet.org/pdfs/AFCCGuidelinesfor Parentingcoordinationnew.pdf

Bacon, B. L., & McKenzie, B. (2004). Parent education after separation/divorce: Impact of the level of parental conflict on outcomes. *Family Court Review, 42*, 85–98. doi:10.1177/1531244504421007

Beck, C. J. A., Sales, B. D., & Emery, R. E. (2004). Research on the impact of family mediation. In J. Folberg, A. L. Milne, & P. Salem (Eds.), *Divorce and family mediation* (pp. 447–482). New York, NY: Guilford Press.

Bird, K. (2009, November). *Pro-active strategies for reducing co-parenting conflict.* Paper presented at the AFCC regional training conference, Reno, NV.

Braver, S. L., & O'Connell, E. (1998). *Divorced dads: Shattering the myths.* New York, NY: Putnam.

Braver, S. L., Shapiro, J. R., & Goodman, M. R. (2005). The consequences of divorce for parents. In M. A. Fine & J. H. Harvey (Eds.), *Handbook of divorce and relationship dissolution* (pp. 313–337). Mahwah, NJ: Erlbaum.

Carroll, J. S., Olson, C. D., & Buchmiller, N. (2007). Family boundary ambiguity: A 30-year review of theory, research, and measurement. *Family Relations, 56*, 210–230. doi:10.1111/j.1741-3729.2007.00453.x

Coates, C., Deutsch, R., Starnes, H., Sullivan, M., & Sydlik, B. (2004). Parenting coordination for high-conflict families. *Family Court Review, 42*, 246–262. doi:10.1177/1531244504422006

Cohen, O., & Finzi-Dottan, R. (2005). Parent-child relationships during the divorce process: From attachment theory and intergenerational perspective. *Contemporary Family Therapy, 27*, 81–99. doi:10.1007/s10591-004-1972-3

Coley, R. L. (2001). (In)visible men: Emerging research on low-income, unmarried, and minority fathers. *American Psychologist, 56*, 743–753. doi:10.1037/0003-066X.56.9.743

Cookston, J. T., Braver, S. L., Griffins, W. A., De Luse, S. R., & Miles, J. C. (2007). Effects of the Dads for Life intervention on interparental conflict and coparenting in the two years after divorce. *Family Process, 46*, 123–137. doi:10.1111/j.1545-5300.2006.00196.x

Cowan, C. P., Cowan, P. A., Pruett, M. K., & Pruett, K. (2007). An approach to preventing coparenting conflict and divorce in low-income families: Strengthening couple relationships and fostering fathers' involvement. *Family Process, 46*, 109–121. doi:10.1111/j.1545-5300.2006.00195.x

Cowan, P. A., Cowan, C. P., Cohen, N., Pruett, M. K., & Pruett, K. (2008). Supporting fathers' engagement with their kids. In J. D. Berrick & N. Gilbert (Eds.), *Raising children: Emerging needs, modern risks, and social responses* (pp. 44–80). New York, NY: Oxford University Press.

Cowan, P. A., Cowan, C. P., Pruett, M. K., Pruett, K., & Wong, J. J. (2009). Promoting fathers' engagement with children: Preventive interventions for low-income families. *Journal of Marriage and the Family, 71*, 663–679. doi:10.1111/j.1741-3737.2009.00625.x

Deutsch, R. M. (2008). Divorce in the 21st century: Multidisciplinary family interventions. *The Journal of Psychiatry & Law, 36*, 41–66.

Dillon, P. A., & Emery, R. E. (1996). Divorce mediation and resolution of child custody disputes: Long-term effects. *American Journal of Orthopsychiatry, 66*, 131–140. doi:10.1037/h0080163

Emery, R. E. (1982). Interparental conflict and the children of discord and divorce. *Psychological Bulletin, 92*, 310–330. doi:10.1037/0033-2909.92.2.310

Emery, R. E. (2004). *The truth about children and divorce: Dealing with the emotions so you and your child can thrive.* New York, NY: Penguin.

Emery, R. E., Laumann-Billings, L., Waldron, M., Sbarra, D. A., & Dillon, P. (2001). Child custody mediation and litigation: Custody, contact, and co-parenting 12 years after initial dispute resolution. *Journal of Consulting and Clinical Psychology, 69*, 323–332. doi:10.1037/0022-006X.69.2.323

Erickson, S., & Ver Steegh, N. (2001). Mandatory divorce education classes: What do parents say? *William Mitchell Law Review, 38*, 889–909.

Fabricius, W., & Hall, J. (2000). Young adults' perspectives on divorce: Living arrangements. *Family Court Review, 38*, 446–461. doi:10.1111/j.174-1617.2000.tb00584.x

Fidler, B. J., & Bala, N. (Eds.). (2010). Alienated children in divorce and separation: Emerging approaches for families and courts [Special issue]. *Family Court Review, 48*(1).

Fieldstone, L. B., & Coates, C. A. (2008). *Innovations in interventions with high conflict families.* Madison, WI: Association of Family and Conciliation Courts.

Fischer, R. L. (1997). The impact of an educational seminar for divorcing parents: Results from a national survey of judges. *Journal of Divorce and Remarriage, 28*(1–2), 35–48.

Folberg, J., Milne, A. L., & Salem, P. (2004). The evolution of divorce and family mediation: An overview. In J. Folberg, A. L. Milne, & P. Salem (Eds.), *Divorce and family mediation* (pp. 3–28). New York, NY: Guilford Press.

Forgatch, M., Patterson, G., & Ray, J. (1995). *Divorce and boys' adjustment problems: Two paths with a single model. Stress, coping, and resiliency in children and families* (pp. 67–105). Mahwah, NJ: Erlbaum.

Fuhrmann, G. S. W., McGill, J., & O'Connell, M. (1999). Parent education's second generation: Integrating violence sensitivity. *Family Court Review, 37*, 24–35. doi:10.1111/j.174-1617.1999.tb00526.x

Goodman, M., Bonds, D., Sandler, I., & Braver, S. (2004). Parent psychoeducational programs and reducing the negative effects of interparental conflict following divorce. *Family Court Review, 42*, 263–279. doi:10.1177/1531244504422007

Grych, J. H. (2005). Interparental conflict as a risk factor for child maladjustment: Implications for the development of prevention programs. *Family Court Review, 43*, 97–108. doi:10.1111/j.1744-1617.2005.00010.x

Grych, J. H., & Fincham, F. D. (1990). Marital conflict and children's adjustment: A cognitive-contextual framework. *Psychological Bulletin, 108*, 267–290. doi:10.1037/0033-2909.108.2.267

Haine, R. A., Sandler, I. N., Wolchik, S. A., Tein, J.-Y., & Dawson-McClure, S. R. (2003). Changing the legacy of divorce: Evidence from prevention programs and future directions. *Family Relations, 52*, 397–405. doi:10.1111/j.1741-3729.2003.00397.x

Henry, W., Fieldstone, L., & Bohac, K. (2009). Parenting coordination and court relitigation: A case study. *Family Court Review, 47*, 682–697. doi:10.1111/j.1744-1617.2009.01281.x

Hetherington, E. M. (1999). Should we stay together for the sake of the children? In E. M. Hetherington (Ed.), *Coping with divorce, single parenting and remarriage: A risk and resiliency perspective* (pp. 93–116). Mahwah, NJ: Erlbaum.

Jaffe, P. G., Johnston, J. R., Crooks, C. V., & Bala, N. (2008). Custody disputes involving allegations of domestic violence: The need for differentiated approaches to parenting plans. *Family Court Review, 46*, 500–522.

Johnston, J. R., Kline, M., & Tschann, J. M. (1989). Ongoing postdivorce conflict: Effects on children of joint custody and frequent access. *American Journal of Orthopsychiatry, 59*, 576–592. doi:10.1111/j.1939-0025.1989.tb02748.x

Johnston, J. R., & Roseby, V. (1997). *In the name of the child: A developmental approach to understanding and helping children of conflicted and violent divorce*. New York, NY: Free Press.

Kelly, J. B. (2000). Children's adjustment in conflicted marriage and divorce: A decade review of research. *Journal of the American Academy of Child and Adolescent Psychiatry, 39*, 963–973. doi:10.1097/00004583-200008000-00007

Kelly, J. B. (2007). Children's living arrangements following separation and divorce: Insights from empirical and clinical research. *Family Process, 46*, 35–52. doi:10.1111/j.1545-5300.2006.00190.x

Kelly, J. B., & Emery, R. (2003). Children's adjustment following divorce: Risk and resilience perspectives. *Family Relations, 52*, 352–362. doi:10.1111/j.1741-3729.2003.00352.x

Kelly, J. B., & Johnson, M. P. (2008). Differentiation among types of intimate partner violence: Research update and implications for interventions. *Family Court Review, 46*, 476–499. doi:10.1111/j.1744-1617.2008.00215.x

Kirkpatrick, L. A., & Hazan, C. (1994). Attachment styles and close relationships: A four-year prospective study. *Personal Relationships, 1*, 123–142. doi:10.1111/j.1475-6811.1994.tb00058.x

Kramer, L., & Kowal, A. (1998). Long-term follow-up of a court based intervention for divorcing parents. *Family Court Review, 36,* 452–465. doi:10.1111/j.174-1617.1998.tb01090.x

Lamb, M. E. (2000). The history of research on father involvement: An overview. *Marriage & Family Review, 29*(2–3), 23–42.

Laumann-Billings, L., & Emery, R. (2000). Distress among young adults from divorced families. *Journal of Family Psychology, 14,* 671–687. doi:10.1037/0893-3200.14.4.671

Marquadt, E. (2006). *Between two worlds: The inner lives of children of divorce.* New York, NY: Crown.

McHale, J. (2007). *Charting the bumpy road of coparenthood: Understanding the challenges of family life.* Washington, DC: Zero to Three Press.

Milne, A. L. (2004). Mediation and domestic abuse. In J. Folberg, A. L. Milne, & P. Salem (Eds.), *Divorce and family mediation* (pp. 304–335). New York, NY: Guilford Press.

Minuchin, S. (1977). *Families and family therapy.* New York, NY: Routledge.

Nash, J. (1965). The father in contemporary culture and current psychological thought. *Child Development, 36,* 261–297.

O'Halloran, M., & Carr, A. (2000). Adjustment to parental separation and divorce. In A. C. Carr (Ed.), *What works for children and adolescents: A critical review of interventions with children, adolescents, and their families* (pp. 280–299). New York, NY: Routledge.

Oleson, N. L. J., & Drozd, L. (2008). High conflict, domestic abuse, or alienating behavior: How do you know? In L. B. Fieldstone & C. A. Coates (Eds.), *Innovations in interventions with high conflict families* (pp. 17–40). Madison, WI: Association of Family and Conciliation Courts.

One child, two homes. (1979, January 29). *Time,* p. 61. Retrieved from http://www.time.com/time/magazine/article/0,9171,912328,00.html

Pedro-Carroll, J. L., Nakhnikian, E., & Montes, G. M. (2001). A.C.T. For the Children: Helping parents protect their children from the toxic effects of ongoing conflict in the aftermath of divorce. *Family Court Review, 39,* 377–392.

Pollet, S. L., & Lombreglia, M. (2008). A nationwide survey of mandatory parent education. *Family Court Review, 46,* 375–394. doi:10.1111/j.1744-1617.2008.00207.x

Pruett, K. D. (2000). *Fatherneed: Why father care is as essential as mother care for your child.* New York, NY: Free Press.

Pruett, K., & Pruett, M. K. (2009). *Partnership parenting: How men and women parent differently—why it helps your kids and can strengthen your marriage.* Cambridge, MA: Da Capo Press.

Pruett, M. K. (2007, May). *More on overnights and child outcomes: Pathways demonstrating how an intervention for young children worked.* Presentation at the annual conference of the Association of Family and Conciliation Court Professionals, Washington, DC.

Pruett, M. K., Arthur, L., & Ebling, R. (2007). The hand that rocks the cradle: Maternal gatekeeping after divorce. *Pace Law Review, 27*, 709–739.

Pruett, M. K., & Barker, C. (2009). Joint custody: A judicious choice for families—but how, when, and why? In R. M. Galatzer-Levy & L. Kraus (Eds.), *The scientific basis of custody decisions* (2nd ed., pp. 417–462). New York NY: Wiley.

Pruett, M. K., & Barker, R. K. (2009). Influencing co-parenting effectiveness after divorce: What works and how it works. In M. Schulz, M. K. Pruett, P. Kerig, & R. Parke (Eds.), *Strengthening couple relationships for optimal child development: Lessons from research and intervention* (pp. 181–196). Washington, DC: American Psychological Association.

Pruett, M. K., & Durell, M. (2009, May). *Family Civil Intake Screen and services evaluation: Final outcomes report.* Wethersfield: Connecticut Judicial Branch, Court Support Services Division.

Pruett, M. K., Ebling, R. E., & Cowan, P.A. (in press). Pathways from a U.S. co-parenting intervention to legal outcomes. *International Journal of Law, Policy, and the Family.*

Pruett, M. K., & Hoganbruen, K. (1998). Joint custody and shared parenting: Research and interventions. *Child and Adolescent Psychiatric Clinics of North America, 7*, 273–294.

Pruett, M. K., Insabella, G. M., & Gustafson, K. (2005). The collaborative divorce project: A court-based intervention for separating parents with young children. *Family Court Review, 43*, 38–51. doi:10.1111/j.1744-1617.2005.00006.x

Ricci, I. (1997). *Mom's house/dad's house* (2nd ed.). New York, NY: Simon & Schuster.

Ricci, I. (2004). Court-based mandatory mediation: Special considerations. In J. Folberg, A. L. Milne, & P. Salem (Eds.), *Divorce and family mediation* (pp. 397–419). New York, NY: Guilford Press.

Salem, P., Schepard, A., & Schlissel, S. (1996). Parent education as a distinct filed of practice: The agenda for the future. *Family Court Review, 34*, 9–22. doi:10.1111/j.174-1617.1996.tb00397.x

Sandler, I. N., Wolchik, S. W., Winslow, E. B., & Schenck, C. (2006). Prevention as the promotion of healthy parenting following parental divorce. In S. R. H. Beach, M. Z. Wamboldt, N. J. Kaslow, R. E. Heyman, M. B. First, L. G. Underwood, & D. Reiss (Eds.), *Relational processes and DSM–V: Neuroscience, assessment, prevention and treatment* (pp. 195–210). Washington, DC: American Psychiatric Association.

Sayer, L., Bianchi, S., & Robinson, J. (2004). Are parents investing less in children? Trends in mothers' and fathers' time with children. *American Journal of Sociology, 110*, 1–43. doi:10.1086/386270

Schepard, A. I. (2004). *Children, courts, and custody: Interdisciplinary models for divorcing families.* Cambridge, England: Cambridge University Press.

Schulz, M. S., Pruett, M. K., Kerig, P. K., & Parke, R. D. (2009). *Strengthening couple relationships for optimal child development: Lessons from research and intervention*. Washington, DC: American Psychological Association.

Tamis-LeMonda, C. S., & Cabrera, N. (Eds.). (2002). *Handbook of father involvement: Multidisciplinary perspectives*. Mahwah, NJ: Erlbaum.

Thomas, A. M., & Forehand, R. (1993). The role of paternal variables in divorced and married families: Predictability of adolescent adjustment. *American Journal of Orthopsychiatry, 63*, 126–135. doi:10.1037/h0079390

Wallerstein, J. S., Lewis, J. M., & Blakeslee, S. (2000). *The unexpected legacy of divorce: A 25 year landmark study*. New York, NY: Hyperion.

12

COPARENTING PRACTICES AMONG FAMILIES IN THE FOSTER CARE SYSTEM

DANIELA MONTALTO AND L. ORIANA LINARES

In this chapter, we discuss the coparenting construct as applied to a complex web of adult caregiving arrangements for young children raised in foster homes. We begin by examining the social ecology of the foster care system and the unique rules and regulations for family routines, engagement patterns, and communication channels between caregivers that it imposes, so as to understand how systemic characteristics impact on individual caregiving practices between biological and foster parents. We describe the pioneering work of Patricia and Salvador Minuchin and their colleagues with foster families in New York City in the 1980s, which has had a marked impact on child welfare reform efforts nationwide aimed at promoting more collaborative family relationships in foster care. We discuss Minuchin's structural family systems theory as a foundation for early family-to-family collaborative approaches and describe the Minuchins' influence on our own empirical and intervention work with biological and foster parents sharing a child placed in a foster home.

Afterward, we summarize newer pilot work in which we have been examining the utility of coparenting observations of and self-reports from biological and foster "coparents," joint parenting training for the two sets of caregivers, and the nature of associations between different domains of coparenting and degree of risk for child problems. We conclude by discussing theoretical implications of the extension of the coparenting construct to this unique family constellation and directions for research.

THE SOCIAL ECOLOGY OF FOSTER CARE: A TRIANGULAR SYSTEM

A primary goal of the U.S. public-sponsored foster care system is to provide, expediently, a permanent home for children by either reuniting them with their biological parents or, if this is not possible, finding a suitable adoptive home. The foster care system supports a unique family unit of care fueled by the public threefold mandate to provide child safety and permanency while promoting psychological well-being during placement (Adoption and Safe Families Act of 1997).

A child placed in a foster home enters into a new "reconstituted" family unit, which extends beyond his or her known, immediate kin family. There are three members in this new reconstituted unit: (a) the foster parent, who provides daily caregiving and is often an unknown person to the child at the time of initial placement; (b) the biological parent, who retains custodial rights over the child, is physically absent from the child's home, has family visitation to varying degrees under agency supervision, and serves as a primary attachment figure for the child at the time of placement and subsequently; and (c) an array of caseworkers (from the Department of Social Services and their out-of-home agencies) who are in charge of placement decisions and orchestrate contacts (i.e., family visitation), control communication channels (when, how, and where), and monitor treatments and services for the entire reconstituted family unit.

The stability of the family unit in foster care is often threatened by changes that occur over the course of the child's tenure in care. Biological parents may be "in" and "out" of the picture at various times. Foster parents are replaced, with about half of children changing homes in the first year of placement (Linares, Shrout, et al., 2010). The annual turnover of child welfare caseworkers is between 30% and 40%, with the average duration of employment less than 2 years (http://www.childwelfare.gov/index.cfm). These potential changes in the family unit require reformation and goal realignment, posing additional challenges to building and preserving the collaborative alliance between members of the child's family unit in foster care. The family unit that comprises the biological parent, foster parent, and caseworkers serves as the organizing triangular structure that defines the social ecology of foster care; individual cocaregiving practices that promote and hinder child development are embedded within this structure.

The social ecology in foster care is usually characterized as child focused, adversarial to biological families, hierarchical with the foster parent seen as superior to biological parent, and fragmented in service delivery (Minuchin, Colapinto, & Minuchin, 2007). According to Patricia Minuchin and colleagues (Colapinto, 1995, 1997; Minuchin, Colapinto, & Minuchin, 1998, 2007), the biological parent is at the low point of this triangular social ecology, the foster parent is a step up from the biological parent, and the caseworker is at the pinnacle of the triangle. The caseworker generally perceives foster parents as their competent agents, whereas the biological family is considered inadequate, in need of remediation, and possessing few if any recognized strengths.

Poverty, homelessness, and drug addiction are major facts of life for biological families (Minuchin et al., 2007). Family violence, abusive histories, and mental illness are embedded in the family cycles of this primarily ethnic minority population. These multicrisis families, trapped in a vicious negative cycle, must meet expectations and mandated activities of the larger foster care system if they are to reestablish their family unit. Foster care agencies work hard to offer therapeutic and supportive services to families, but such services are often fragmented (Minuchin et al., 2007). Plans for reunification involve multiple people and various activities and mandates, including parenting classes, substance abuse clearance, housing requirements, and personal counseling. These services create a sharp demarcation between biological and foster families. Further, interventions are implemented with little consideration of positive emotional ties and effective resources from within the original biological family unit, and caseworkers frequently filter through family boundaries and "take over" the family's authority structure, leaving the children vulnerable and adrift (Minuchin et al., 2007).

Paradoxically, professional staff (local protection teams, agency caseworkers, and clinicians) are also vulnerable in this complex social service network; they are generally overworked, governed by hierarchies, and constrained by the way the system works and their place within their agency. These structural characteristics likely impact caseworkers' approach to parenting education as well as their promotion of coparenting behaviors, for agency workers have limited time, energy, or resources to promote bonds and more positive relationships between families. They do not have sufficient support to search for members of the extended biological family who might serve as potential resources, even if they do not live with mother and child. They also rarely make contact with all members of the foster household, even though all will affect the daily life of the child placed in care (Minuchin et al., 2007).

THE FAMILY UNIT: BIOLOGICAL PARENT, FOSTER PARENT, AND CASEWORKER

The biological–foster parent relationship is designed to be temporary, conform to current regulations, and be mediated by agency staff caseworkers who impose unique rules and regulations for family routines, engagement patterns, and communication channels between caregivers. Under these circumstances, the biological–foster parent relationship has been characterized as being initially competitive, hostile, and centered on fear and mistrust (Davies & Bland, 1978).

As described previously, the actions and behavior of biological and foster caregivers (i.e., mothers) who are part of a larger triangle are governed by system regulations. In fact, power does not reside with these women but with the larger system and the professional workers who implement policy and procedures (Minuchin et al., 2007). As is true of divorced parents, biological and foster mothers are not physically coparenting; what's more, they are separated by bureaucratic boundaries and physical limits. But consistent with the imperfect analogy of divorced parents, a goal for these caregivers nonetheless is to achieve a modicum of "collaborative" parenting, acknowledge their caregiving differences, and learn to negotiate interpersonal conflict when it arises.

Biological parents often feel threatened by foster parents' ability to parent effectively (Davies & Bland, 1978) and feel shameful and guilty about the events surrounding the placement (Leathers, 2002a). Deemed as incompetent by the courts, they may view foster parents as better than them, highly invested in their children, and trying to usurp their place. For these biological parents, family visitation is a time to express their dissatisfaction and to "reconquer and capture" the love of their child.

Barriers to a collaborative relationship from the foster parent's vantage may include negative perceptions of the biological parent, a competing agenda, and perceived ingratitude. Foster parents may be reluctant to facilitate prescribed parent–child contacts if they see biological parents as undeserving because of abuse and/or neglect histories. Parents struggling with a chronic addiction or mental illness may be judged weak, ill, and unable to parent effectively. Wishes to become the adopting parent can result in subtle adversarial behavior (e.g., intolerance about lateness for family visitation), designed to sabotage parental efforts at family reunification, and disinterest in any collaborative coparenting efforts. Because no-shows for family visitation are highly disappointing to children of all ages, and foster parents must "pick up the pieces" and contend with disappointed children when they act out in the foster home as a response to their biological parent's "broken promise," visitations may be dreaded by foster parents and are often fraught with tension and hostility (Palmer, 1995).

Not all foster–biological relationships, however, are centered on divergent agendas or ongoing conflict. Foster parents are asked to commit to reunification by encouraging the biological parent and child to stay connected (Sanchirico & Jablonka, 2000). In fact, foster parents are recruited based on a willingness to recognize the temporary nature of the placement and are warned against forming strong child attachments because the courts may order child discharge at any time.

Recent child welfare reforms, such as the Family Conferencing program, hold some promise for reducing barriers that separate the caregivers' roles and promoting more trusting relationships between family systems (Shore, Wirth, Cahn, Yancey, & Gunderson, 2002). Family conferencing allows members of the biological and foster families to agree on a joint permanency service plan on behalf of the child with the goal of reaching family reunification in more expedient ways.

The implementation of a collaborative coparenting approach is also highly contingent on the skills of the professional workers who occupy the top of the triangular unit, and the success of their efforts depends in turn on the support of their agencies—in effect, a circle of mutual dependence (Minuchin et al., 2007). It is not simply agency attitudes that will influence the success of efforts to promote biological–foster parent coparenting; agencies' must also have policies and procedures in place to train workers on how they can support collaborative efforts between foster and biological parents.

The Child in the Family Unit

The ever-changing nature of the family unit, mandated activities rarely oriented to the realities of biological families, and agency procedures undermining the biological family's assertiveness all create barriers to collaboration between parents. Although these barriers are often obvious to caregivers, they may be less apparent from the child's perspective depending on his or her developmental stage. Children can enter care as infants and toddlers, during middle childhood, or in their teens and stay in foster care for an average of 27.2 months (U.S. Department of health and Human Services, 2009). Although removal is not necessarily easier or harder for younger versus older children, emotional understanding and adaptation vary according to age. Every age brings with it a set of developmental strengths and weaknesses that impact children's ability to manage separation, adapt to a new home, and maintain a sense of the original family while accepting new people.

A sound connection between the child and both sets of caregivers stands not only to facilitate the child's return home but also to enhance child well-being while in care by creating a sense of stability, belongingness, and safety that contributes to self-regulatory competence (Brody & Flor, 1996).

Children of all ages, however, may respond to the vicissitudes and uncertainty of the family unit by acting out emotional insecurity when family stability is threatened. Increased child oppositionality, distancing, and/or isolation often follows separations from either or both sets of parents and leaves biological and foster families alike frustrated, upset, and angry. In turn, these sentiments may be redirected toward one another and influence the parent's willingness to form a collaborative relationship.

Early Coparenting Programs in Foster Care

Despite the multiple structural and interpersonal barriers to joint caregiving, the promotion of a harmonious relationship between biological and foster families in the service of enhancing children's emotional and behavioral adaptation has been an aim of child welfare largely because of the seminal efforts of Patricia and Salvador Minuchin and Jorge Colapinto. Their early work with foster care agencies and foster families and their later Foster Care Project conducted under the auspices of the Administration for Children's Services, New York City (Colapinto, 1995, 1997; Minuchin et al., 1998, 2007), exemplify collaborative systems approaches for helping biological and foster families work more closely together. It also inspired a family-to-family movement in child welfare sponsored by the Casey Foundation (Green, 2000) that has had a significant influence in child welfare departments. Here we summarize a few early programs in child welfare developed to promote coparenting practices—loosely defined as family-to-family collaboration. Although most were not rigorously evaluated (using a clinical trial methodology), these programs illustrate the essence of the family-to-family approach.

Landy and Munro (1998), seeking to establish that foster and biological parents working together is key in achieving the goal of reunification, designed a Shared Parenting Project giving foster and biological families support, advice, and guidance in working as a team with family service and foster care workers to develop and plan strategies to best meet child and family needs (p. 307). Program goals were to ensure children's ongoing contact with biological families, with foster parents playing a significant role during the contacts. For example, visits typically began in foster homes but moved into family homes, with both biological and foster parents involved in family visitations at both homes. These interactions not only benefitted children by reducing separation anxiety but also gave foster parents an opportunity to assist biological parents to transfer knowledge and skills to their own environment.

Leathers (2002b) examined whether inclusive practices, reintegrating biological parents into their children's lives while still in placement, are associated with greater family visitation and higher rates of family reunification.

In a study of 230 twelve- and thirteen-year-olds placed in nonkinship (non-relative) homes, she did not find any inclusive practice indicators to be associated with child outcomes (loyalty conflict, emotional disturbance, or behavioral disturbance) but ascribed her failure to detect associations between inclusive practices and child adaptation to a very limited number of children actually experiencing inclusive practices.

Kufeldt (2002) also argued that a biological–foster parent alliance would benefit children's development, advocating a rethinking of the concept of family for children in care so as to include a mix of relatives, professionals, and paraprofessionals. In this model, foster parents—in partnership with social workers—provide a core family milieu, within a system open in its boundaries and inclusive of the children's original extended family to the degree possible (p. 138). Influenced by joint custody research, Kufeldt argued that preservation of family need not depend on cohabitation, existing through shared and collaborative care of the child (p. 137). Most essential for child well-being was a "partnership" between the key players (biological family, foster family, social workers, and other professionals). Practices that integrate birth parents into children's lives while they are in placement are widely seen as an antidote to pervasive negative and hostile sentiments (Landy & Munro, 1998; Leathers, 2002b).

Finally, Barth and Price (1999) proposed adoption of Shared Family Care; their concept involves planned provision of out-of-home care to biological parent(s) and their children together such that they and foster caregivers can simultaneously share the care of the children and work toward independent in-home care by the parent(s).

These early demonstration programs, although not widely implemented and short-lived in the foster care system, all serve as promising models of joint caregiving emphasizing the value of multiple family resources and of explicitly engaging members in inclusive practices to enhance their mutual collaboration and support. The limited impact of these programs, however, underscores Minuchin and colleagues' (2007) central message that genuine organizational understanding and endorsement are critical if there is to be any hope of achieving sustainability of a successful program.

Diversity in Foster Family Arrangements

Nationwide, twice as many children are in nonkinship placements compared with kinship placements (47% vs. 24%; U.S. Department of Health and Human Services, 2009). Although still less common than nonkinship placements, in today's landscape of foster family arrangements, kinship placement has been on the rise (Cuddeback, 2004; see also Chapter 13, this volume). Kinship placement is an arrangement in which a kin relative assumes daily caregiving responsibilities for the child under the formal supervision of the local Department of Social Services. Most, though not all, studies have provided empirical support for benefits of kinship placement on child outcomes. For example, compared with nonkinship, kinship placement tends to be more stable (Price et al., 2008; Rubin et al., 2008); children in kin homes tend to experience fewer behavior problems (Lawrence, Carlson, & Egeland, 2006; Timmer, Sedlar, & Urquiza, 2004). Kinship caregivers are also likely to have a special interest in the well-being of the child in their care, and kinship care placements provide children with a sense of family support (Dubowitz et al., 1994; Iglehart, 1995; Chapter 13, this volume).

These things said, kinship arrangements are seldom simple. Placement with extended family changes the daily roles of family members and their patterns of relating, carrying authority, and resolving conflict (Minuchin et al., 2007). Kinship families often face similar economic challenges, social stressors, and family history to those of the parent in question. For this rearrangement of roles to work, kinship parents must clarify boundaries and move toward a new stage of family equilibrium. Policies that provide these families with the additional support to take on added familial responsibility need to be considered. For more comprehensive coverage of these issues, see Chapter 13.

Understanding the heterogeneity of foster family arrangements is important in identifying demographic and psychosocial characteristics of foster family constellations associated with beneficial coparenting behavior and positive child outcomes. For example, while coparenting conflict and triangulation are higher in kin than nonkin foster arrangements (e.g., grandparents, sisters), so is shared communication, indicating that kin coparenting relationships may be more "intense" (high negative and high positive) than nonkin relationships (Linares, Rhodes, & Montalto, 2010). These data suggest that kin arrangements could benefit from targeted interventions that not only enhance communication but also help parents better manage emotionally intense situations.

Coparenting Studies in Foster Care

From 2001 to 2009, our research team undertook a series of studies designed to better understand the coparenting relationship among families (in kinship and nonkinship arrangements) involved in the foster care system. On the basis of both existing coparenting nomenclature (see Chapter 2) and our clinical understanding of the foster care system, we operationalized collaborative coparenting as parental behaviors (observed or endorsed) that involved support and cooperation of the other parent's parenting efforts, shared communication about child-rearing practices, effectively negotiated conflict, and low child triangulation.

These studies of cocaregiving focused on families with children ages 3 to 10 years living in regular and therapeutic foster homes in New York City with primary histories of substantiated child neglect (with and without presence of physical abuse). Most biological mothers and foster mothers were of ethnic minority background (African American and Latino) and shared common psychosocial maternal risk including low educational achievement, low occupational status, and residence in poor inner city neighborhoods. The focus was on young children, given their prevalence in the foster care system and our overarching interest in developing prevention interventions to reduce risk for early onset of disruptive behavior disorders.

Parent-to-Parent Cooperation

Following the family-to-family perspective in child welfare (Green, 2000) and building on emerging coparenting research (Margolin, Gordis, & John, 2001; McHale & Rasmussen, 1998), we examined whether self-reports of more supportive coparenting (parent-to-parent cooperation) contributed to less harsh discipline practices, even after adjusting for parenting skills and other confounding influences (Linares, Montalto, Rosbruch, & Li, 2006). Controlling for differences in psychosocial profiles (biological mothers tended to be younger, unmarried, and reported higher psychological distress), we determined that biological and foster parents endorsed similar levels of positive, appropriate, and harsh discipline and that the predictors of optimal parental discipline practices were similar for both caregivers. For example, for both sets of caregiver reports, harsh discipline was associated with poorer parent-to-parent cooperation and more child problems. These findings led us to hypothesize that there may be clinical benefits of offering parenting education to both sets of caregivers (biological and foster).

Biological Parent and Foster Parent Interactions

In Chapter 7 in this volume, McHale reviews observational rating systems used to assess coparenting in family systems in which coparents are connected by blood, kinship, or fictive ties. To date, no observational system has been available to assess the unique dynamics of nonkin biological–foster parent interactions. Though the frequency of such interactions likely differs as a function of kinship/nonkinship status, closeness to discharge, and agency policies, there are certainly times during visitations when both families do come together, and the dynamics characteristic of these interactions—along with the underlying themes that these interactions may connote—are poorly understood.

To study the interactions of foster and biological parents with one another, we asked one parent from each family unit to complete a 5-min task in which the aim was to decide together on a family menu (Montalto, 2005). Interactions were videotaped and evaluated using a new Foster Care and Coparenting Rating System. The system, which is based on extant family systems and coparenting theories (Cowan & Cowan, 2000; Cowan & McHale, 1997; McHale, 1995; McHale, Kuersten-Hogan, & Lauretti, 2000; McHale & Rasmussen, 1998; Szapocznik et al., 1985), was designed to assess the dyads on supportive and unsupportive coparenting dimensions (see Table 12.1). Briefly, the main findings were as follows. First, nearly all of the families (92%) showed low coparenting support, and the majority (67%) "rarely" or "never" spoke to one another directly. The coparents made little to no effort to support one another (no working together as a team, sharing of opinions, or asking questions to promote discussion), focusing mainly on the task. None were rated as working together consistently. Most displayed limited affect; they were seen as disconnected (e.g., emotionless, stiff, or robotic; sitting far apart; showing minimal eye contact). However, approximately 30% did show "moderate" to "frequent" competition or rivalry (e.g., challenging or "outdoing" one another), though most "rarely" or "never" competed.

Overall, families showed few disagreements and little triangulation, and almost 80% of interactions were hierarchical (i.e., one parent would take control of and direct or organize the task)—63% directed by the foster parent. The observations revealed largely hierarchical interactions (with foster parents leading the task), with disengagement rather than task collaboration the rule and conflictual interactions rarely, but occasionally, detectable.

The same coparents were also asked to share their personal perceptions of how they coparented. In the solo assessments, inconsistency in house rules and family expectations, triangulation, and limited communication emerged as common themes. Most biological parents reported that foster parents' rules for their children about food, bedtime, and homework differed from theirs and reported that foster parents often tried to get the child to take sides when the adults disagreed. From the other vantage, only one third of the foster parents reported that the biological parents shared the burden of discipline with them—consistent with biological parents' reports that they did not typically discuss with the foster parent how to teach their child right from wrong, how to prepare the child for a visit, or their own fears about the visit. The observational and self-report data confirm a need to bring underinvolved caregivers closer to one another to increase level of engagement on topics concerning child rearing and insight regarding the child, and ideally to also enhance their capacity to rely on one another for support.

A subsequent study (Linares, Rhodes, et al., 2010) linked foster parents' ratings of interadult conflict/triangulation to reported child internalizing and

TABLE 12.1
Dimensions of the Foster Care and Coparenting Rating System

Dimension	Description	Coding type
Positive: Supportive coparenting		
1. Cooperation/ communication I	Parents' active display of facilitating, supporting, and building on one another's suggestions	Dyadic (parent-to-parent)
2. Cooperation/ communication II	Degree of overt, active involvement between parents and their child	Triadic (parents-to-child)
3. Warmth I	Verbal/nonverbal demonstration of affection and positive regard between parents	Dyadic (parent-to-parent)
Negative: Unsupportive coparenting		
4. Competition	Active attempt of one parent to outdo the other parent	Dyadic (parent-to-parent)
5. Disagreement/ anger	Verbal/nonverbal hostility, dislike, disagreement, or disapproval exchanged by the parental dyad	Dyadic (parent-to-parent)
6. Triangulation	Extent to which parents distort parent–child boundaries, drawing children into the parents' conflict through pressure by one parent to side against the other	Triadic (parents-to-child)
7. Hierarchy	Manner in which power and status are distributed in a family	Triadic (parents-to-child)
Descriptive coparenting		
8. Centeredness	Who "drives" the interaction (e.g., who is in charge: one or both parents, the child, or the entire triad)	Triadic (parents-to-child)
9. Task resolution	The level of resolution achieved by the family on each task (conflict)	Triadic (parents-to-child)
Individual parenting		
10. Warmth II	The verbal/nonverbal demonstration of affection and positive regard between parent and child; each parent is rated individually	Dyadic (parent-to-child)
11. Investment	How "tied" a parent is to the child (e.g., the parent's involvement and presence with regard to the child's performance or inclusion; each parent is rated individually	Dyadic (parent-to-child)
Child dimensions		
12. Child discomfort	The child's level of comfort/discomfort during the task	Individual (child only)
13. Child misbehavior	The child's willingness to participate in or otherwise not disrupt the discussion	Individual (child only)

externalizing problems. Such links were found not just in kin but also in nonkin arrangements (see also Chapter 13, this volume). Again, these linkages point to a need for interventions for biological–foster coparents focused perhaps not just on their coparenting relationship in general but also on conflict management in particular. Just as children in divorced families are adversely affected, children in foster situations may also be adversely affected by interadult conflict (undermining) and triangulation (placing the child in the middle of conflict) between parenting adults. These data are also consistent with work on interparental conflict and emotional insecurity (Cummings, Schermerhorn, Davies, Goeke-Morey, & Cummings, 2006). Linkages with child externalizing problems are especially worthy of note, given the high risk for behavioral disorders among youth in foster care (Garland et al., 2001; Linares, Shrout, et al., 2010). Targeted prevention and treatment efforts that consider the potential harmful impact of nonharmonious, conflictual coparenting between adults may help in trying to understand and ameliorate causes of child externalizing problems.

IMPLICATIONS FOR CHILD DEVELOPMENT

By integrating our newer findings with previous coparenting research, we can speculate on how coparenting processes (e.g., low shared communication) may "enter" the child's psyche. McHale and Rasmussen (1998) advanced the notion that when one parent exhibits a significant lack of involvement with both the child and the other parent, this creates a sense of psychological distance and disconnection in the family that can lead to child insecurity, anxiety, sadness, and emptiness—all internalizing spectrum symptoms. As was true of the families described by McHale and Rasmussen (1998), many of the foster and biological parents that we studied showed little connection or engagement as they interacted together, a potential sign of underlying distress. The lack of connection between parents may lead children in foster care to feel discomfort with both sets of parents, triggering child withdrawal, depression, or anxiety. In contrast, open communication between parents may signify to children that they themselves can be free to express a full range of emotions. We speculate that collaborative coparenting can help children identify and keep a meaningful psychological place for each parent, experience less confusion about a placement, and feel comfortable with each of their parents. When they feel safer and more comfortable, children may be more expressive about their likes and dislikes in the foster situation, recognizing emerging attachments to foster parents, dual loyalties, and mixed feelings, and sharing negative feelings such as guilt or embarrassment.

One strategy for promoting a better coparenting connection between biological and foster parents was tested in the New York University family development program (Linares, Montalto, Li, & Oza, 2006), a two-component family intervention designed to improve parenting practices and coparenting collaboration as a means of reducing child externalizing problems. Linked biological and foster parents were randomly assigned in pairs to either a usual care control condition or an intervention condition (Webster-Stratton's [2001] Incredible Years, a 12-week efficacious parenting course with a newly developed coparenting component). Significant gains in both positive parenting and collaborative coparenting were documented for both biological and foster parents postintervention relative to the usual care condition. At follow-up, parents in the intervention group sustained greater gains in positive parenting and clear expectations with a trend for fewer child externalizing problems than did parents in the usual care condition.

These findings are promising. They extend Minuchin and colleagues' earlier work with foster care staff and document how manualized parenting interventions, used by trained foster care staff, can enhance both parenting and coparenting in this difficult-to-reach population. They also support the feasibility of offering parent education jointly to both biological and foster parents and provide preliminary support for the seldom-tested notion that coparenting collaboration can be an outcome that is malleable to change in nontraditional family circumstances, just as it is in traditional two-parent families.

CONCLUSIONS

For almost 2 decades, there has been clinical interest in promoting the best possible partnership between biological and foster parents to benefit young children's psychological development. With more than 500,000 U.S. children placed in out-of-home placement annually (U.S. Department of Health and Human Services, 2009) and the high prevalence of developmental risk for negative child outcomes, there is a pressing clinical urgency to understand family processes in this population so that effective interventions can be developed.

Although the research presented here indicates that collaborative coparenting can be beneficial for children in families consisting of biological and foster parents, there are challenges in any public-sponsored family setting to creating a nurturing, stable family unit promotive of child psychological well-being. Unfortunately, isolated demonstration programs and small clinical trials are insufficient to produce needed systemic changes in the social ecology of foster care, and wider organizational change is needed to achieve sustainability and long-lasting effects from model programs. Greater understanding of aspects of the organizational context (e.g., leadership support, willingness for innovation, supervisory structure) that curtail or promote effective family-to-family practices remains a critical need.

Minuchin et al.'s (1998, 2007) detailed summary of their work in the foster care system in New York City outlines the potential for working with agencies to create these more family-friendly environments; their work and that of others who have conducted promising demonstration programs in the foster care system provide models for effective promotion of collaborations and partnerships between foster and biological parents. Our own work adds to this important literature by documenting the viability of creating collaborative coparenting teams focused on parent education and support, providing preliminary evidence for gains in collaborative coparenting relationships between biological and foster parent dyads and in more effective parenting by each individually, following intervention.

More research is needed to establish the kinds of collaborative relationships between biological and foster parents that can best promote positive parenting (e.g., less harsh discipline). We speculate that an increased sense of togetherness and connectedness resulting from joint trainings has the potential to keep the coparent pair attuned and "in balance," so necessary when raising a child who is overactive, inattentive, or noncompliant. Controlled intervention studies of coparenting behavior among various family constellations in foster care are also sorely needed, as are observational studies with large sample sizes. More attention must be devoted to the range of diversity in family arrangements and constellations (e.g., kinship vs. nonkinship, intergenerational caregiving; culturally matched vs. mismatched families; single vs. sibling groups placements) to begin disentangling critical dimensions of the proximal family environment that contribute to child adjustment to the placement experience. Finally, outcomes involving foster home stability and expedient permanency must be studied to determine whether collaborative parental practices lead to fewer disruptions of foster homes or shorter length in foster care.

Advancements in methodology and instrumentation will be needed to properly capture key characteristics of foster–biological families. We found initial support for the clinical usefulness of adapting existing coparenting scales (observed and self-reported measures) to study the family networks of children in foster care, but more work in this area is needed to further develop and validate measures. Observations of dyadic interactions using large samples are costly. However, unobtrusive observations under natural settings (e.g., the family visit, the family conferencing; see Chapter 13) may provide evidence of the ecological validity of measurement tools in diverse family constellations. Self-report data, although cost-effective, include unknown informant biases owing to the individual perspectives biological and foster parents bring to the coparenting task. Carefully designed multilevel methodological approaches guided by explicit study goals are needed to strike a balance between cost and scientific rigor. Finally, the impact of collaborative coparenting practices at different developmental ages (e.g., infancy, preschool, middle school, adolescents) is yet to be studied. Given the critical yet unique role of the family at every developmental age of the child, the study of coparenting with children at different childhood periods is a highly fruitful area in need of research attention.

In conclusion, the complex mental health needs of children and families involved in the foster care system demand an orchestrated response, which is multilevel and comprehensive to achieve goals of child safety, permanency, and psychological well-being in foster care. The scientific study of coparenting processes in these highly vulnerable families, although relatively new on the scene, promises to contribute to the public mandate in important new ways.

REFERENCES

Adoption and Safe Families Act of 1997, Pub. L. No. 105-89, 111 Stat. 2115 (1997).

Barth, R. P., & Price, A. (1999). Shared family care: Providing services to parents and children placed together in out-of-home care. *Child Welfare, 78,* 88–107.

Brody, G., & Flor, D. (1996). Co-parenting, family interactions, and competence among African American youths. *New Directions for Adolescent and Child Development, 74,* 77–91.

Colapinto, J. A. (1995). Dilution of family process in social services: Implications for treatment of neglectful families. *Family Process, 34,* 59–74. doi:10.1111/j.1545-5300.1995.00059.x

Colapinto, J. A. (1997, November/December). The patterns that disconnect: The foster care system is a classic Catch-22. *Networker,* 43–44.

Cowan, C. P., & Cowan, P. A. (2000). *When partners become parents: The big life change for couples.* Mahwah, NJ: Erlbaum.

Cowan, P. A., & McHale, J. P. (1997). Coparenting in a family context: Emerging achievements, current dilemmas, and future directions. *New Directions for Child and Adolescent Development, 74,* 93–106.

Cuddeback, G. S. (2004). Kinship family foster care: A methodological and substantive synthesis of research. *Children and Youth Services Review, 26,* 623–639. doi:10.1016/j.childyouth.2004.01.014

Cummings, E. M., Schermerhorn, A. C., Davies, P. T., Goeke-Morey, M. C., & Cummings, J. S. (2006). Interparental discord and child adjustment: Prospective investigations of emotional security as an explanatory mechanism. *Child Development, 77,* 132–152. doi:10.1111/j.1467-8624.2006.00861.x

Davies, L., & Bland, D. (1978). The use of foster parents as role models for parents. *Child Welfare, 57,* 380–386.

Dubowitz, H., Feigelman, S., Harrington, D., Starr, R., Zuravin, S., & Sawyer, R. (1994). Children in kinship care: How do they fare? *Children and Youth Services Review*, *16*(1–2), 85–106. doi:10.1016/0190-7409(94)90017-5

Garland, A. F., Hough, R. L., McCabe, K. M., Yeh, M., Wood, P. A., & Aarons, G. A. (2001). Prevalence of psychiatric disorders in youths across five sectors of care. *Journal of the American Academy of Child and Adolescent Psychiatry*, *40*, 409–418. doi:10.1097/00004583-200104000-00009

Green, M. (2000). Family forever: Helping families heal is what family to family is all about. *Children's Voice*, *3*, 4–11.

Iglehart, A. (1995). Readiness for independence: Comparison of foster care, kinship care, and non-foster care adolescents. *Children and Youth Services Review*, *17*, 417–432. doi:10.1016/0190-7409(95)00026-9

Kufeldt, K. (2002). Sharing the care of our children in a changing societal context. *Child & Family Social Work*, *7*, 133–139. doi:10.1046/j.1365-2206.2002.t01-1-00238.x

Landy, S., & Munro, S. (1998). Shared parenting: Assessing the success of a foster parent program aimed at family reunification. *Child Abuse & Neglect*, *22*, 305–318. doi:10.1016/S0145-2134(97)00177-4

Lawrence, C. R., Carlson, E. A., & Egeland, B. (2006). The impact of foster care of development. *Development and Psychopathology*, *18*, 57–76. doi:10.1017/S0954579406060044

Leathers, S. J. (2002a). Foster children's behavioral disturbance and detachment from caregivers and community institutions. *Children and Youth Services Review*, *24*, 239–268. doi:10.1016/S0190-7409(02)00175-5

Leathers, S. J. (2002b). Parental visiting and family reunification: Could inclusive practice make a difference? *Child Welfare*, *81*, 595–616.

Linares, L. O., Li, M., Shrout, P., Ramirez, M., Hope, S., Albert, A., & Castellanos, F. X. (2010). The course of inattention and hyperactivity/impulsivity symptoms following foster placement. *Pediatrics*, *125*, e489–e498. doi:10.1542/peds.2009-1285

Linares, L. O., Montalto, D., Li, M., & Oza, V. (2006). A promising parenting intervention in foster care. *Journal of Consulting and Clinical Psychology*, *74*, 32–41. doi:10.1037/0022-006X.74.1.32

Linares, L. O., Montalto, D., Rosbruch, N., & Li, M. (2006). Discipline practices among biological and foster parents. *Child Maltreatment*, *11*, 157–167. doi:10.1177/1077559505285747

Linares, L. O., Rhodes, J., & Montalto, D. (2010). Coparenting and child problems among families in foster care. *Family Process*, *49*, 530–542.

Margolin, G., Gordis, E. B., & John, R. S. (2001). Co-parenting: A link between marital conflict and parenting in two parent families. *Journal of Family Psychology*, *15*, 3–21. doi:10.1037/0893-3200.15.1.3

McHale, J. P. (1995). Co-parenting and triadic interactions during infancy: The roles of marital distress and child gender. *Developmental Psychology*, *31*, 985–996. doi:10.1037/0012-1649.31.6.985

McHale, J. P., Kuersten-Hogan, R., & Lauretti, A. (2000). Evaluating co-parenting and family-level dynamics during infancy and early childhood: The Co-parenting and Family Rating System. In P. Kerig & K. Lindhal (Eds.), *Family observational coding systems: Resources for systemic research* (pp. 151–170). Mahwah, NJ: Erlbaum.

McHale, J. P., & Rasmussen, J. L. (1998). Coparental and family group-level dynamics during infancy: Early family precursors of child and family functioning during preschool. *Development and Psychopathology, 10,* 39–59. doi:10.1017/S0954579498001527

Minuchin, P., Colapinto, J., & Minuchin, S. (1998). *Working with families of the poor.* New York, NY: Guilford Press.

Minuchin, P., Colapinto, J., & Minuchin, S. (2007). *Working with families of the poor* (2nd ed.). New York, NY: Guilford Press.

Montalto, D. (2005). Co-parenting within foster care: Influences on child development. *Dissertation Abstracts International: Section B. Sciences and Engineering, 65,* 6689.

Palmer, S. E. (1995). *Maintaining family ties: Inclusive practice in foster care.* Washington, DC: Child Welfare League of America.

Price, J. M., Chamberlain, P., Landsverk, J., Reld, J. B., Leve, L. D., & Laurent, H. (2008). Effects of a foster parent training intervention on placement changes of children in foster care. *Child Maltreatment, 13,* 64–75. doi:10.1177/1077559507310612

Rubin, D. M., Downes, K., O'Reilly, A. L., Mekonnen, R., Luan, X., & Localio, R. (2008). Impact of kinship care on behavioral well-being for children in out-of-home care. *Archives of Pediatrics & Adolescent Medicine, 162,* 550–556. doi:10.1001/archpedi.162.6.550

Sanchirico, A., & Jablonka, K. (2000). Keeping foster children connected to their biological parents: The impact of foster parent training and support. *Child & Adolescent Social Work Journal, 17,* 185–203. doi:10.1023/A:1007583813448

Shore, N., Wirth, J., Cahn, K., Yancey, K., & Gunderson, K. (2002, September). *Long-term and immediate outcomes of family group conferencing in Washington state.* EFORUM. International Institute for Restorative Practices. Retrieved from http://www.restorativepractices.org

Szapocznik, J., Hervis, O., Rio, A., Faraci, A. M., Foote, F., & Kurtines, W. (1985). *Manual for the Structural Family Systems Ratings.* Miami, FL: University of Miami School of Medicine.

Timmer, S. G., Sedlar, G., & Urquiza, A. J. (2004). Challenging children in kin versus nonkin foster care: Perceived costs and benefits to caregivers. *Child Maltreatment, 9,* 251–262. doi:10.1177/1077559504266998

U.S. Department of Health and Human Services, Administration for Children and Families. (2009). *Adoption and Foster Care Analysis and Reporting System (AFCARS) FY data (October 1, 2007 through September 30, 2008).* Retrieved from http://www.acf.hhs.gov/programs/cb/stats_research/afcars/tar/report16.htm

Webster-Stratton, C. (2001). *The incredible years: Parents, teachers and children training series. Leader's guide.* Retrieved from http://www.incredibleyears.com

13

COPARENTING IN MULTIGENERATIONAL FAMILY SYSTEMS: CLINICAL AND POLICY IMPLICATIONS

JAMES P. GLEESON, ANNE L. STROZIER, AND KERRY A. LITTLEWOOD

According to the U.S. Census Bureau's (2009) American Community Survey (2006–2008), approximately 6.5% (4,761,786) of children under age 18 in the United States live with a grandparent. Although nearly 41% of the grandparents have primary caregiving responsibility for these children, in only 20% of cases (964,217) neither parent resides in the home. Another 2.6% (1,911,002) of the U.S. child population live in households headed by aunts, uncles, cousins, or other relatives, though the percentage of children for whom relatives are primary caregivers and presence of children's parents in homes are not clear from Census data.

Even when biological parents are not coresident, they nonetheless often share parenting responsibilities, just as divorced, separated, or never-married couples with children do. Contact with a nonresident parent may take place daily or several times a week; the parent may prepare meals for the child, help the child with homework, or otherwise discharge parenting responsibilities (Gleeson et al., 2009; Gleeson & Seryak, 2010). It is also clear that shared parenting responsibilities are not characteristic of all multigenerational households. Some parents who live with their children in the home of a relative assume nearly 100% of the parenting role, whereas others assume virtually none. That is, in some multigenerational households, parents function like siblings with their children, competing for the attention and good will of the children's grandparent, great aunt, or other relative who heads the household. In other multigenerational households, the relatives depend on the children's parent for their own care and well-being and provide little or no parental care for the children in the home. In yet other situations, parents who maintain their own households with their children recruit grandparents, father figures, and other nonresident relatives to serve in coparenting roles (Roy & Burton, 2007). Grandparents may be recruited or volunteer to provide full-time child care to allow the parent to seek and maintain employment and avoid the cost of child care.

In this chapter, we focus on multigenerational families in which at least one child lives in a household headed by a relative other than a parent and in which the parent or parents maintain some parenting involvement, whether coresident with the relative and child or not. We begin by examining the range of multigenerational "kinship care" arrangements and the various ways these arrangements are formed. We then discuss what is currently known about coparenting in these families, followed by clinical issues that affect relative caregivers, parents, and children involved in these arrangements and how they may impact coparenting. Next, we discuss policies that facilitate or impede coparenting among parents and kinship caregivers. We close with a discussion of implications for practice and suggest future directions for coparenting research with families involved in kinship care.

HOW MULTIGENERATIONAL AND CUSTODIAL KINSHIP HOUSEHOLDS FORM

Multigenerational households and custodial kinship care arrangements form for a variety of reasons, and development of these caregiving arrangements is influenced by the motivations of kinship caregivers and parents (Gleeson et al., 2009; Jendrek, 1994). These reasons and motivations influence whether and how some degree of coparenting occurs.

Reasons for Kinship Care

Parents may be unable to care for their children or need assistance from relatives to raise their children for a variety of reasons. Compared with custodial kinship care arrangements, multigenerational families are more likely to form because of financial need, parental divorce, or the parent's work or school responsibilities (Goodman, 2003; Goodman & Silverstein, 2002). It is also common for teen mothers to continue to live with their parents and rely on their parents to help with the care of the child (see Chapter 5, this volume). Other common reasons for the development of multigenerational coparenting include parental substance abuse/addiction, child neglect or abuse, parental incarceration, youth/lack of experience, unstable home life/ homelessness, lack of resources/general inability, mental illness, or physical illness (Burton, 1992; Crewe, 2007; Edelhoch, Liu, & Martin, 2002; Gleeson et al., 2009; Jendrek, 1994; Kelley, Whitley, Sipe, & Yorker, 2000; Waldrop & Weber, 2001). Parents with disabilities or mental illnesses may not have the capacity to raise the child and may rely more heavily on the child's grandparent to be the primary caregiver.

Although kinship care is most often a private agreement between family members, approximately 25% of children living in custodial kinship care arrangements have some level of involvement with the child welfare system; 40% of these children are in the custody of the child welfare system, with the relatives in the role of foster parents and the arrangement referred to as *public kinship care* (Murray, Ehrle Macomber, & Green, 2004). The greater the degree of involvement of the child welfare system in the family's life, the more the child welfare and legal systems shape the ways that families raise children and the degree of involvement parents have in the child's life—and, therefore, the degree and type of coparenting that is possible.

Caregiver and Parent Motivations

The fact that parents need help does not automatically result in a relative stepping forward to care for the child. Some willingness on the part of the relative is required in custodial as well as multigenerational arrangements. Custodial kinship caregivers' motivations to care for the children suggest familial-level protective factors that may also be relevant to creating a coparenting relationship: caregivers' love of the children; their commitment to keep their families together, keep their children safe, and ensure their children's well-being and sense of belonging; a legacy of shared family caregiving and a strong sense of family obligation; and spiritual influences (Gleeson et al., 2009; Jendrek, 1994).

In addition to the motivations of kinship caregivers are the motivations of parents. Parental willingness to participate is required to create a coparenting relationship that includes them. In fact, the custodial or multigenerational living arrangement may result because of the desires and motivations of the child's parent. For example, during periods of incarceration, a mother may desperately want her children to remain with relatives rather than to enter foster care; on release, the mother may expect to join the household, forming a multigenerational living arrangement to facilitate successful transition to the community (Gleeson & Seryak, 2010; O'Brien, 2001; Smith, Krisman,

Strozier, & Marley, 2004). Other parents may rely on a multigenerational coparenting arrangement (shared residence or otherwise) to allow them to complete school or maintain employment (Goodman, 2003). There is also evidence that a caregiver's willingness and motivation to care for children, as well as satisfaction with caregiving, may be influenced by culture, ethnicity, and race (Goodman & Silverstein, 2006; see also Chapter 3, this volume).

CLINICAL ISSUES THAT AFFECT COPARENTING IN MULTIGENERATIONAL AND CUSTODIAL KINSHIP CARE

A small but growing body of literature describes clinical issues affecting coparenting in multigenerational and custodial kinship care, including factors that contribute to willingness to participate in coparenting in these families. Contributing factors include (a) the kinship caregivers' and parents' histories of caring for the child; (b) quality of relationships among parents, kin caregivers, and children; (c) caregiver stress, burden, and depression; (d) needs of children; (e) needs of parents; and (f) complexity of caregiving arrangements.

What Is Known About Coparenting in Multigenerational and Custodial Kinship Care?

Very few studies have specifically examined, described, measured, or otherwise documented the type and degree of shared parenting that occurs in multigenerational or custodial kinship families. Goodman, Potts, Pasztor, and Scorzo (2004) compared the level of shared decision making that occurred between parents and kinship caregivers of school-age children in public (n = 208) and private (n = 373) kinship care. In response to two separate survey items about whether they involved the child's mother and father in decision making about the child (none, some, or most or all of the time), caregivers involved in private kinship care arrangements reported that they were more likely to share decision making regarding the child with the parent, compared with those involved in public kinship care arrangements. It is not clear from this cross-sectional study whether the shared decision making in public kinship care was inhibited by the rules and regulations of the child welfare system or the factors that precipitated kinship care and child welfare system involvement. Public kinship care arrangements were 2.7 times more likely to be precipitated by parental substance abuse and 60% more likely to occur because of child neglect, compared with private kinship care; therefore, it is possible that decreased parental capacity, the caregiver's assessment of the parent's capacity, the child welfare worker's assessment of the parent's capacity and possible structuring of parental involvement, or all three contributed to the lower level of shared decision making. The mother's developmental needs (e.g., teen parent, in school, working) were identified as reasons for kinship care more often for private than for public kinship care arrangements (higher rates of collaboration and shared decision making would be expected when the caregiving arrangement is designed to support the mother's development). It is reasonable to believe that with or without the involvement of the child welfare system, the degree of collaboration, conflict, or animosity involved in formation of the multigenerational or custodial kinship arrangement influences whether and what type of shared parenting might be possible.

In Chapter 5 of this volume, Pittman and Coley describe classifications of adolescent–mother–grandmother coparenting arrangements ranging from the grandparent supporting her daughter's role as mother to replacing the daughter in this role. In Chapter 3, Jones and Lindahl describe what is known about coparenting relationships across four cultural groups. Two studies that are part of a larger research project with mothers detained in a county jail and their children's custodial grandparents have advanced our knowledge of coparenting relationships within families experiencing a number of stressors far beyond those experienced by families in previously studied coparenting samples (Baker, McHale, Strozier, & Cecil, 2010; Strozier, Armstrong, Skuza, Cecil, & McHale, 2011). These included insufficient income, unemployment or underemployment, substance abuse, and involvement with the criminal justice system. In Strozier et al.'s (2011) qualitative study, interviews with 24 mother–grandmother dyads (48 women) from families in which the grandmothers were coparenting young children between the ages of 2 and 6 years, three different types of coparenting arrangements were identified: (a) grandmother with primary power and control, (b) mother with primary power, and (c) parenting shared fairly equally between grandmother and mother. When the grandmother was in control and both accepted this arrangement, mothers often felt that grandmothers were more expert at parenting. One mother stated, "She allows me to have a phone relationship with my son because I know she's older and knows what's best." Less often in this study, the dyads shared the power and control effectively, and least often the mother was in control and the women in both generations agreed that this was best. Dyads demonstrating successful coparenting held similar philosophies regarding child rearing, communicated well with each other, compromised, saw themselves as a team, and had empathy for each other. The women who had less solidarity in their coparenting relationship struggled over power, discipline, and the mother's substance abuse and subsequent disconnection from the family. These coparents often expressed feelings of despondency, guilt, and fear.

Baker et al. (2010) developed and tested the psychometric properties of the Intergenerational Coparenting Incarceration Rating System (ICIRS), which rates coparenting qualities in both grandmothers and mothers using positive constructs (warmth/empathy, listening, validation, and agreement or accommodation) and negative constructs (dismissing, disparagement, competition, defensiveness, and interfering negative affect). The mothers' and grandmothers' ICIRS scores at Time 1 of the study, when the mothers were detained, predicted later coparenting functioning for the 22 dyads that remained in the study at Time 2, when the parents were released; higher coparenting scores were associated with lower levels of externalizing behaviors displayed by the children. Many patterns of coparenting appeared similar to those found in two-parent nuclear families, but two unique dynamics were (a) the tendency of some grandmothers to disallow their daughters' active participation in coparenting and (b) the tendency of some mothers to completely relinquish their parenting role. In addition to providing initial evidence of the integrity and utility of the ICIRS, this study provides some support for the assertion that coparenting solidarity in kinship care benefits children in some of the same ways that it does in other coparenting triads.

A number of studies that examined kinship care more broadly (Gleeson et al., 2009; Gleeson & Seryak, 2010) have confirmed the existence of the three different coparenting arrangements described by Strozier et al. (2011). For some families, this balance of power and authority is stable and long term. For others, it may be temporary and changing. Furthermore, little is known empirically about the ways that coparenting responsibilities and the balance of power, authority, and responsibility are negotiated in custodial or multigenerational kinship caregiving families or how these various arrangements and processes of determining them are associated with the well-being of children, parents, kinship caregivers, or the family system as a whole.

What Factors Contribute to Willingness to Participate in Coparenting?

Although the coparenting relationship is conceptually distinct (see Chapters 1, 2, and 4), it is reasonable to think that the willingness and ability of parents and relatives to participate in any degree of coparenting may be affected by their current relationships outside of their coparenting roles (e.g., mother/father–daughter/son, siblings, cousins), their shared histories, and other stressors and challenges that may impact the kinship caregiver and the parent (see Chapters 3 and 5 as well).

History of Caring for the Child

The parent's and relative's history of caring for the child influence whether coparenting is likely and the form that this coparenting relationship might take. For some parents, their role as primary caregiver has been continuous, and sharing this responsibility with the child's grandparent or other relative may also have continued since the child's birth. For other parents, their role as a primary caregiver has only recently been interrupted by divorce, financial challenges, illness, incarceration, or inpatient mental health or substance abuse treatment, precipitating the need to share this role or relinquish it to a relative. And yet others have had little to no caregiving responsibility for their child from birth and now wish to assume a parental role (e.g., children removed from parents by the child welfare system at birth and placed with relatives). Although some kinship caregivers who have raised the child since birth welcome a parent "getting his or her life together" and gradually assuming a greater parental role, others experience feelings of loss when parents assume greater responsibility and in some ways reduce the relative's time with the child and role in the child's life (Crumbley & Little, 1997).

Quality of Relationships Among Parents, Kin Caregivers, and Children

There is also reason to believe that the type and quality of the birth-parent–caregiver relationship may influence willingness to participate in coparenting and the form that this relationship takes. Their histories as mother and child, aunt and niece/nephew, siblings, cousins, and in-laws, and the degree of closeness, conflict, and collaboration characterizing their relations in the past, are likely to influence the way that the multigenerational or custodial kinship care arrangement is formed and the type of coparenting relationship that may be possible. Positive coparenting in multigenerational families can be compromised by dynamics such as power struggles, relational disputes, disagreements about discipline, and undermining behaviors.

Goodman's (2003, 2007) analyses of relationships in intergenerational triads provide some clarity on associations among relationship closeness, caregiver well-being, and child functioning. Goodman (2003) found that levels of life satisfaction and depression reported by 512 custodial grandmothers and 475 grandmothers raising their school-age grandchildren in multigenerational households were not affected by a weak relationship with the children's parents, so long as the relative reported a close relationship with the child and also between the parent and child. When parents were emotionally isolated and not close to the caregiver or their child, the caregiver's well-being suffered in both custodial kinship and multigenerational households. Life satisfaction was highest and depression lowest for custodial grandmothers, when parent–child, parent–caregiver, and caregiver–child relationships were all close; the reverse was true when the caregiver reported no close relationships between any members of the triad (Goodman, 2007). By contrast, caregivers' ratings of children's behavior have suggested that children function well if they have a close relationship with the relative caregiver, the parent, or both.

Grandchildren who were emotionally isolated from both parent and grandparent, and grandchildren in families with no close bonds between any members of the triad, showed the highest levels of behavioral dysfunction.

Caregiver Stress, Burden, and Depression

Stress experienced by relatives who assume the care of children may influence their willingness and capacity to participate in a coparenting relationship and the quality of that relationship. Many grandparent caregivers experience stress about meeting the demands of parenting a second time in their lives. Grandparent caregivers experience more burdens than grandparents not caring for grandchildren, including limitations of daily activities; increased depression; lower levels of marital satisfaction; poorer health (Jendrek, 1994; Musil, 1998, 2000); and feelings of social isolation, loneliness, exhaustion, anger, grief, despair, and fear about the future (Strozier et al., 2011). Other studies have pointed to stress related to the financial challenges of raising relatives' children, child behavioral functioning, and stressful relationships with the parents of the children living with kin (Hayslip & Kaminski, 2005).

The decision to involve grandparents and other relatives as primary caregivers for children is often sudden and unexpected. In addition to the stresses related to unexpected caregiving, grandparents raising grandchildren assume nonnormative roles. Therefore, they experience dissonance between their expectations to retire and relax and the reality of changing diapers and disciplining teenagers (Young & Smith, 2000). Strozier et al. (2011) quoted a grandmother raising her daughter's children:

> I think that the mother should raise the child and let the grandmother live the role she was designed for: to see that these are the children she would get to spoil. That these are the children that get the gravy of her life and not have to eat so darn many vegetables.

Kin may be reluctant to assume care of a related child or to participate in coparenting the child because of their own developmental needs. Burton (1985, 1990, 1992) noted some of the challenges kinship families face in her seminal work with age-condensed multigenerational Black families. Among the sample of grandmothers in her 1985 study, young grandmothers were far less satisfied with being grandmothers than were grandmothers 12 to 30 years older. Her 1990 study reported that the majority of the young grandmothers sampled refused to act as the primary caregiver to the grandchild. These grandmothers instead chose to involve themselves in such "young-adult" roles as work, romance, friendships, and having their own children. However, Stack and Burton (1993) noted that a refusal to provide "kin work" may have significant costs on the children and mothers who would rely on such help.

Needs of Children

Although most children growing up with relatives function reasonably well, caregivers ratings have indicated that children living with kin are twice as likely to display high levels of emotional and behavioral problems compared with children in the general population, comparable to low-income children living with their parents (Billing, Ehrle, & Kortenkamp, 2002). Children living with kin are more likely than children living with their parents regardless of income to experience behavioral problems in school and one third more likely to experience low engagement in school, both of which are associated with poor academic performance. Children living with kin are twice as likely as children living with their parents to have a limiting condition and poor health. The health status of children living with kin is similar to low-income children living with their parents. The child's behavioral and physical or mental health problems make it challenging for the child's parents and coparenting kin and may contribute to the reluctance of parents previously separated from their children to resume care or participate in a coparenting relationship.

Needs of Parents

For many parents unable to raise their children, the fact that their children are living with relatives is a mixed blessing. Although these parents often express appreciation that their children are in the care of a family member who loves them and provides good care, many also feel a sense of loss of the parental role and awkwardness at reestablishing a relationship with their own children who are being "parented" by their own mother, sister, or even an older child (Gleeson & Seryak, 2010). Parents may be focused on their own needs related to recovery or successful community reentry after release from prison, for example, and need continued assistance with caregiving responsibilities as the parent engages in substance abuse treatment, searches for employment and housing, and participates in other necessary services (e.g., mental health treatment).

Substance abuse is a significant barrier to successful participation in coparenting. One mother stated, "I keep trying and I keep screwing up [with drugs]. And when I'm not with my child, after a while, I don't think about him" (Strozier et al., 2011). A related challenge is parental detachment when parents are absent from the home for extended periods or relinquish parental involvement when home. Sometimes kin caregivers unwittingly encourage this disenfranchisement. As one grandmother said, "I rescue her. . . . If someone would do things for you, you just let them do it, and get into that bad habit" (Strozier et al., 2011). This rescuing can occur because of the caregivers' beliefs that the mothers are not grown-up enough to raise their own children. Guilt and shame for both grandmother and mother may be interwoven with this dynamic.

Complex/Multiple Caregiving Arrangements

This chapter's discussion to this point and the majority of the research on kinship care have focused on one parent or two parents of a child/sibling group and one kinship caregiver or kinship caregiving couple. Many family configurations are far more complex. Both multigenerational and custodial kinship caregiving households may include children from multiple sibships and children within sibships with different fathers. The potential coparenting relationships are extremely complex when considering all of the possible combinations of potential coparents. In addition, parents of some of the children may live in a multigenerational household with the caregiver and children, but parents of other children in the same home may maintain their own residences. Involvement with the child welfare system may also vary, with some of the children in the home in the custody of the child welfare system and kin caregivers considered to be their relative foster parents; other children in the home may not be involved with the child welfare system and therefore considered to be an informal/private kinship care arrangement (Gleeson, O'Donnell, & Bonecutter, 1997). Access to services and financial supports and the degree and type of external regulation of parent involvement and child-rearing practices vary for children in formal and informal kinship care.

POLICIES THAT FACILITATE OR IMPEDE PARENT–KINSHIP CAREGIVER COPARENTING

Many of the reasons for creating multigenerational and custodial kinship care arrangements also contribute to a family's involvement with social services systems that are publicly funded and shaped by public policy. Yet few public policies guiding these systems actually support parent–kinship caregiver coparenting when children live in multigenerational or custodial kinship care. In this section, we examine how financial support policies, policies that guide the child welfare and criminal justice systems, and newer policies that target informal (private) kinship care may also affect coparenting in kinship care.

Financial Support

For many families, poverty contributes to the need for kinship care, and kinship caregiving families have markedly lower incomes and higher rates of poverty compared with families headed by parents (Main, Ehrle Macomber,

& Geen, 2006; Murray, Ehrle Macomber, & Geen, 2004). Three potential sources of public financial support that kinship caregiving families may be eligible to receive are Temporary Assistance to Needy Families (TANF), Supplemental Security Income (SSI), and foster-care maintenance payments. It would be reasonable to expect that receiving financial support would reduce stress and in some ways facilitate parenting and perhaps coparenting. However, in practice, receipt of financial support from each of these sources often serves to hinder rather than enable positive coparenting in the child's best interests. Although all three provide minimal financial support for families headed by relatives under certain conditions, in most cases, if the relative is the primary caregiver, the family is eligible for financial support only if the children's parents do not live in the home.

On the other hand, there are certain situations for which TANF policies do facilitate multigenerational coparenting. Parents with primary caregiving responsibility for their minor children (under the age of 18) may qualify to receive the TANF family grant. Parents and their children can live with a relative in a multigenerational household and receive this grant. For teenage mothers under the age of 18, TANF requirements have the potential to promote cocaregiving relationships. For instance, to be eligible to receive federal cash aid under TANF, a minor parent has to live with a responsible adult (generally her parents) and participate in school or training (Acs & Koball, 2003). This policy promotes coparenting by encouraging the young parent to work with a coresident responsible adult to provide care for the child. However, the TANF family grant promotes coparenting only insofar as the parent and kinship caregiver have a workable relationship already. Coresidence also has the potential to be disempowering for teen parents if the relative caregiver takes control of the baby and excludes the parent from exercising an active parenting role (see Chapter 5). Also, TANF at best provides only temporary financial support because there is a 5-year lifetime limit on receipt of the family grant. Receipt of the family grant requires that parents are looking for employment, participating in employment training, and/or working (some states do exempt parents with mental and physical disabilities).

When a relative is the primary caregiver and neither parent lives in the home, the relative is eligible to receive the TANF child-only grant to help support the related child, unless the relative is receiving SSI or foster-care payments for this child. Although the TANF child-only grant provides only minimal financial support, children who are eligible to receive this grant are also eligible for Medicaid. However, if one of the children's parents moves into the caregiver's home (e.g., after release from prison or discharge from substance abuse treatment), the caregiver is no longer eligible to receive even this minimal support. If the parent is able to assume the primary caregiver role, he or she may be able to receive the TANF family grant or the child-only grant to help support the children. However, bureaucratic procedures required to change recipients of the grant often result in delays and gaps in receipt of financial supports and services. Perhaps as a result, despite the high likelihood of living in poverty, 78% of children living in informal kinship care receive no financial assistance, according to the 2002 National Survey of America's Families (Main, Ehrle Macomber, & Geen, 2006).

Some children qualify to receive SSI, which provides benefits for individuals who are older, blind, or have disabilities and limited income and assets. This program, administered by the U.S. Social Security Administration, provides a cash benefit to the child who is under the age of 18 and meets the SSI disability, income, and asset criteria (Children's Defense Fund, 2004). However, in most cases, children living with relatives qualify for SSI only if the parents are retired, deceased, or seriously disabled (Dayton, Wood, & Belian, 2007). Therefore, this program provides support to a small percentage of kinship caregiving families who may be involved in coparenting.

Custodial kinship families caring for children who are removed from their parent's home because of maltreatment and placed with them by a child welfare agency may be eligible for the Federal Foster Care Program, which is authorized by Title IV-E of the Social Security Act (U.S. Administration for Children and Families, n.d.) if they are willing and able to meet foster home licensing standards. Families who are licensed may receive the same subsidy that is received by nonrelated licensed foster parents, which is generally 3 to 5 times greater than the TANF child-only grant. If the relative is caring for siblings, the subsidy for each child is affected only by the child's age, with higher rates generally paid for the care of older children. Some states, such as Illinois, California, and Florida, also provide a subsidy to relatives who are not licensed as foster parents but are caring for children in the custody of the child welfare system that is higher than the TANF child-only grant but lower than the foster-care payment.

Although public custodial kinship families often receive greater financial support and access to services than do those not involved with the child welfare system, policies governing foster home licensing standards and receipt of foster home subsidies discourage parental coresidence. Parent coresidence in the relative's home violates foster home licensing standards and may result in loss of the foster home license and the foster-care subsidy and possible removal of the child from the relative's home. If children return to the custody of their parents, the child welfare system no longer provides financial support to the kinship caregiver or the parent. These rigid regulations provide little support for the creation or maintenance of multigenerational households that facilitate a parent's recovery from addiction, mental illness, or reentry from prison and the transition of primary parenting responsibility from relative caregiver to parent that may need to occur gradually over time to be successful.

Child Welfare Policies

Other child welfare system policies may facilitate or hinder coparenting. Titles IV-E and IV-B of the Social Security Act, as amended by the Adoption and Safe Families Act of 1997 (ASFA), are the primary federal policies that guide the work with children in the child welfare system's custody and their families. As ASFA's name implies, the primary focus of the child welfare system once children are in its custody is preventing recurrence of the abuse or neglect that led to the child welfare system's involvement in a child's life and ensuring that the child is living in a safe and permanent home as quickly as possible. Once children are in a permanent home, the child welfare system no longer has legal responsibility, and the financial responsibility is generally either eliminated or considerably reduced. ASFA, IV-E, and IV-B do encourage efforts to work with parents to reunify the parent and child, if this can be safely and swiftly accomplished, but provide financial incentives to support adoption that are not available if the child is reunified with a parent. With the enactment of the Fostering Connections to Success and Increasing Adoptions Act of 2008, subsidies are also available to support children who exit the custody of the child welfare system through transfer of guardianship to relatives (Center for Law and Policy, 2009).

Although ASFA requires initiation of termination of parental rights and pursuit of adoption or another permanency plan if the child is in the custody of the child welfare system for 15 of the last 22 months, states are not required to enforce this when children are placed with kin. Nonetheless, when the child welfare system is involved, there is often a sense of urgency to either reunify the parent and child or encourage kinship caregivers to adopt or assume guardianship of the child so that the child welfare system can close the case. This does provide opportunities to build coparenting relationships between parents and relative caregivers, but there is little evidence that this is common practice. The child welfare system's sense of urgency is often inconsistent with the time that parents need to recover from addiction or resume/assume a primary caregiving role after release from prison or jail. Parents involved with the criminal justice system may be left out of case planning because child welfare personnel face so many systemic challenges when visiting the jail or prison, especially if they want to coordinate visitation among the inmate, the child, and the relative caregiver (Center for Advanced Studies in Child Welfare, 2008).

Criminal Justice System Policies

Although the primary focus of child welfare policies is to ensure that children are safe and in permanent homes that enhance their well-being, the purpose of the criminal justice system is to keep society safe and to punish illegal behavior. Building or supporting family relationships is not a central goal. With the dramatic increase in the incarceration of women, the majority of whom are mothers, greater attention is being paid to their parenting role. Although there are growing opportunities for inmates to have contact with family members, prison and jail visiting are both psychologically and physically demanding for children and adults, especially because in most facilities the visiting conditions are poor (Hairston, 1998, 2007). Family ties may be damaged because of the lack of meaningful contact to support an enduring bond between children and parents or between parents and their children's caregivers. Even when incarcerated parents work to maintain a connection to their families while away, they may no longer be kept in the loop of family communications and may not be notified about important events involving their children. Because studies of prisoners consistently show positive outcomes for those inmates who maintain strong family and friendship ties during imprisonment (Laughlin, Arrigo, Blevins, & Coston, 2008; Pimlott & Sarri, 2002), more resources and programs are being developed to eliminate barriers that families face. However, very little attention has been paid to building, maintaining, or strengthening the coparenting relationship between parents in prison or jail and the relatives caring for their children during incarceration or during an extended period of transition back to the community once parents are released.

Policies With Some Potential for Supporting Coparenting in Kinship Care

Two recent policies, the National Family Caregiving Support Act of 2000 (U.S. Administration on Aging, n.d.) and the Fostering Connections to Success and Increasing Adoptions Act of 2008 could be used to provide some support for coparenting, though neither law was designed with kinship caregiver–parent coparenting in mind. States are given the option of using up to 10% of the National Family Caregiver Support Program funding to support grandparents and other relatives raising children. Many states use these funds to establish support groups, respite, or "warmlines" for kinship caregivers. However, there is nothing in this law that would prevent the development of programs to support parent–caregiver coparenting relationships. The Fostering Connections to Success and Increasing Adoptions Act authorizes Family Connection Grants. Two components of these grants have relevance to kinship care. One funds kinship navigator programs designed to connect families to community-based services and supports. The other encourages family group decision-making (FGDM) meetings to engage and promote family and social supports in efforts to make decisions in the best interest of the child. Although these components of the family connections programs were not designed specifically to support coparenting, both could be tailored to assess coparenting capacity and support the development and strengthening of coparenting relationships in kinship caregiving families.

State guardianship and custody laws are also being fashioned in ways that may be supportive to coparenting. Laws in all states allow parents to transfer guardianship to another adult when the child has no other parent to assume responsibility, care, and custody of the child. Designated guardians are better able to prove their eligibility for the TANF child-only grant and can more easily enroll children in school and access medical treatment for the child. Twenty-three states and the District of Columbia (as of July 2008) have standby guardianship laws, developed to address the needs of families living with HIV and other terminal illnesses or disabling conditions who want to plan a legally secure future for their children (Child Welfare Information Gateway, 2008). Although the guardianship may go into effect during the parent's lifetime, the parent retains considerable control over the guardianship and sharing decision-making responsibility with the guardian. The guardian is expected to be in the background during the parent's lifetime, assume responsibility when needed, and relinquish this responsibility to the parent when the parent is healthy. A bill being debated in Florida also appears to be promising. Because kinship caregivers can only levy financial support for a child in their care by legally wresting current support from the child's parents, this state of affairs has the potential to actually create new coparenting conflict in the family. In Florida, Concurrent Custody SB 1519 and HB 1519 were written to amend the Chapter 751 Florida Statute to allow grandparents and other relatives to petition for concurrent custody of kinship children and grant the court the authority to award concurrent custody when parents do not object. This seems to be another family-friendly policy that, if adopted, could actually mitigate the potential for coparenting conflict in families unwittingly caused by current statutes.

PROMISING PRACTICES: EARLY SIGNS AND FUTURE RESEARCH DIRECTIONS

There is a pressing need to develop empirically based assessments and interventions to support coparenting in multigenerational and custodial kinship care. Baker et al. (2010) documented that assessment of the communications of coparents can be reliably measured and that coparenting solidarity between kinship caregivers and parents transitioning from jail is related to child functioning. The work of Baker et al. and Strozier et al. (2011) has indicated that with the cooperation of correctional facilities, it is possible to convene joint meetings with parents and caregivers during the parents' incaceration. Although further replication studies are needed, research developing and testing the feasibility and effectiveness of interventions to strengthen coparenting relationships in families affected by the criminal justice system, the child welfare system, and other families involved in kinship care arrangements is in order. Baker et al. and Cecil et al. (2008) recommended that parenting classes delivered to parents in prison or jail incorporate methods for improved coparenting communication and relationships with the children's caregivers, an apt recommendation for families involved with the child welfare system as well. In many jurisdictions, participation in parenting classes is required of all parents who wish to regain custody of their children. Incorporating knowledge of coparenting and skills for strengthening coparenting relationships makes a great deal of sense. Moreover, bringing parents and kinship caregivers together to negotiate their coparenting roles and to practice positive coparenting behaviors could prove to have benefits long after the child welfare system is out of the family's life. Empirical tests of the effectiveness of these interventions compared with standard practice are urgently needed.

Many questions remain regarding whether and how to engage parents and kinship caregivers reluctant to participate in coparenting. FGDM has been used to reduce family disruption and prevent children's placement in foster care (Crampton & Jackson, 2007) and may be of benefit in determining the feasibility of building coparenting relationships within extended families. The research on FGDM with kinship families has reported mostly positive findings regarding family and child welfare workers' satisfaction, assessments of process and outcomes, and child permanence with family (Merkel-Holguin, Nixon, & Burford, 2003; Sheets et al., 2009). However, although FGDM appears to be a promising intervention for multigenerational kinship families, it has the considerable drawback of requiring a great deal of time to deliver (Merkel-Holguin, Nixon, & Burford, 2003). Moreover, FGDM has never been specifically applied to the assessment of coparenting. With the emphasis on FGDM in recent federal policy, there may be a real opportunity to test its effectiveness in engaging families to identify potential coparents, identify and define coparenting roles, and create a network of support for members of a kinship network who commit to a coparenting relationship on behalf of children in the family. FGDM could also be used for initial engagement, with more intensive coparenting interventions based on communication among coparents following it.

In any attempts to intervene with multigenerational and custodial kinship caregiving families, one is well advised to heed Gibson's (2005) caution that "intergenerational parenting is a very sensitive subject that needs to be handled gently to avoid blame or perceived negative judgment of grandmothers" (p. 293). Potential coparents may feel shame about the parents' failure to raise their children and fear about the "system" intervening to remove the children. In addition, many kinship caregivers have pride in the work they perform as caregivers and feel resistant to accepting help from "professionals." It is essential, therefore, that clinicians approach multigenerational families with special respect, validation, and inclusiveness by collaborating with the family in developing a needs assessment and a treatment plan, recognizing caregivers' expertise and experience, and normalizing the anger and hurt that coparents may feel while also providing hope and training for new ways of collaborating to raise the children (Strozier et al., 2011).

REFERENCES

Acs, G., & Koball, H. (2003). *TANF and the status of teen mothers under age 18* (New Federalism: Issues and Options for States, Series A, No. A-62). Retrieved from http://www.urban.org/UploadedPDF/310796_A-62.pdf

Adoption and Safe Families Act of 1997, Pub. L. No. 105-89, 111 Stat. 2115 (1997).

Baker, J., McHale, J., Strozier, A., & Cecil, D. (2010). The nature of mother-grandmother coparenting alliances in families with incarcerated mothers. *Family Process, 49,* 165–184. doi:10.1111/j.1545-5300.2010.01316.x

Billing, A., Ehrle, J., & Kortenkamp, K. (2002). *Children cared for by relatives: What do we know about their well-being?* (New Federalism: National Survey of America's Families, Series B, No. B-46). Retrieved from http://www.urban.org/url.cfm?ID=310486

Burton, L. M. (1985). *Early and on-time grandmotherhood in multigenerational Black families.* Unpublished doctoral dissertation, University of Southern California, Los Angeles.

Burton, L. (1990). Teenage childbearing as an alternative life-course strategy in multigeneration Black families. *Human Nature, 1,* 123–143. doi:10.1007/BF02692149

Burton, L. M. (1992). Black grandparents rearing children of drug-addicted parents: Stressors, outcomes, and social service needs. *The Gerontologist, 32,* 744–751.

Cecil, D. K., McHale, J., Strozier, A., & Pietsch, J. (2008). Female inmates, family caregivers, and young children's adjustment: A research agenda and implications for corrections programming. *Journal of Criminal Justice, 36,* 513–521. doi:10.1016/j.jcrimjus.2008.09.002

Center for Advanced Studies in Child Welfare. (2008). *CW360: A comprehensive look at a prevalent child welfare issue. Children of incarcerated parents.* Retrieved from http://www.cehd.umn.edu/ssw/cascw/attributes/PDF/publications/CW360.pdf

Center for Law and Policy. (2009). *Fostering Connections to Success and Increasing Adoptions Act (H.R. 6893) Summary.* Retrieved from http://voices.fissiondev.com/wp-content/uploads/2010/03/CDFCLASPSummary1.pdf

Child Welfare Information Gateway. (2008). *Standby guardianship: Summary of state laws*. Washington, DC: U.S. Children's Bureau/ACYF. Retrieved from http://www.childwelfare.gov/systemwide/laws_policies/statutes/guardianship.cfm

Children's Defense Fund. (2004). *Financial assistance for grandparents and other relatives raising children*. Retrieved from http://cdf.childrensdefense.org/site/DocServer/financialassistance0805.pdf?docID=467

Crampton, D., & Jackson, W. L. (2007). Family group decision making and disproportionality in foster care: A case study. *Child Welfare, 86,* 51–69.

Crumbley, J., & Little, R. (1997). *Relatives raising children: An overview of kinship care*. Washington, DC: Child Welfare League of America.

Crewe, S. E. (2007). Different pathways to a common destiny: Grandparent caregivers in the District of Columbia. *Journal of Health & Social Policy, 22*(3–4), 199–214. doi:10.1300/J045v22n03_13

Dayton, A. K., Wood, M. M., & Belian, J. (2007). *Elder law: Readings, cases, and materials*. Danvers, MA: Matthew Bender.

Edelhoch, M., Liu, Q., & Martin, L. S. (2002). Unsung heroes: Relative caretakers in child-only cases. *Policy & Practice of Public Human Services, 60,* 26–30.

Gibson, P. (2005). Intergenerational parenting from the perspective of African American grandmothers. *Family Relations, 54,* 280–297. doi:10.1111/j.0197-6664.2005.00022.x

Gleeson, J. P., O'Donnell, J., & Bonecutter, F. J. (1997). Understanding the complexity of practice in kinship foster care. *Child Welfare, 76,* 801–826.

Gleeson, J. P., & Seryak, C. (2010). "I made some mistakes . . . but I love them dearly." The views of parents of children in informal kinship care. *Child & Family Social Work, 15,* 87–96. doi:10.1111/j.1365-2206.2009.00646.x

Gleeson, J. P., Wesley, J., Ellis, R., Seryak, C., Talley, G. W., & Robinson, J. (2009). Becoming involved in raising a relative's child: Reasons, caregiver motivations and pathways to informal kinship care. *Child & Family Social Work, 14,* 300–310. doi:10.1111/j.1365-2206.2008.00596.x

Goodman, C. (2003). Intergenerational triads in grandparent-headed families. *Journal of Gerontology: Social Sciences, 58B*(5), S281–S289.

Goodman, C. C. (2007). Intergenerational triads in skipped-generation grandfamilies. *International Journal of Aging & Human Development, 65,* 231–258. doi:10.2190/AG.65.3.c

Goodman, C. C., Potts, M., Pasztor, E. M., & Scorzo, D. (2004). Grandmothers as kinship caregivers: Private arrangements compared to public child welfare oversight. *Children and Youth Services Review, 26,* 287–305. doi:10.1016/j.childyouth.2004.01.002

Goodman, C., & Silverstein, M. (2002). Grandmothers raising grandchildren: Family structure and well-being in culturally diverse families. *The Gerontologist, 42,* 676–689.

Goodman, C., & Silverstein, M. (2006). Grandmothers raising grandchildren: Ethnic and racial differences in well-being among custodial and coparenting families. *Journal of Family Issues, 27,* 1605–1626. doi:10.1177/0192513X06291435

Hairston, C. F. (1998). The forgotten parent: Understanding the forces that influence incarcerated fathers' relationships with their children. *Child Welfare, 77,* 617–639.

Hairston, C. F. (2007). *Focus on children with incarcerated parents: An overview of the research literature.* Baltimore, MD: Annie E. Casey Foundation. Retrieved from http://www.aecf.org/KnowledgeCenter/Publications.aspx?pubguid={F48C4DF8-BBD9-4915-85D7-53EAFC941189}

Hayslip, B., & Kaminski, P. (2005). Grandparents raising their grandchildren: A review of the literature and suggestions for practice. *The Gerontologist, 45,* 262–269.

Jendrek, M. P. (1994). Grandparents who parent their grandchildren: Circumstances and decisions. *The Gerontologist, 34,* 206–216.

Kelley, S. J., Whitley, D., Sipe, T. A., & Yorker, B. C. (2000). Psychological distress in grandmother kinship care providers: The role of resources, social support, and physical health. *Child Abuse & Neglect, 24,* 311–321. doi:10.1016/S0145-2134(99)00146-5

Laughlin, J., Arrigo, B. A., Blevins, K. R., & Coston, C. T. M. (2008). Incarcerated mothers and child visitation. *Criminal Justice Policy Review, 19,* 215–238. doi:10.1177/0887403407309039

Main, R., Ehrle Macomber, J., & Geen, R. (2006). *Trends in service receipt: Children in kinship care gaining ground.* (New Federalism: National Survey of America's Families, Series B, No. B-68). Retrieved from http://www.urban.org/UploadedPDF/311310_B-68.pdf

Merkel-Holguin, L., Nixon, P., & Burford, G. (2003). Learning with families: A synopsis of FGDM research and evaluation. *Protecting Children, 18*(1–2), 2–11.

Murray, J., Ehrle Macomber, J., & Green, R. (2004). *Estimating financial support for kinship caregivers.* (New Federalism, National Survey of America's Families, Series B, No. B-63). Retrieved from http://www.urban.org/UploadedPDF/311126_B-63.pdf

Musil, C. M. (1998). Health, stress, coping, and social support in grandmother caregivers. *Health Care for Women International, 19,* 441–455. doi:10.1080/073993398246205

Musil, C. M. (2000). Health of grandmothers as caregivers: A ten-month follow-up. *Journal of Women & Aging, 12*(1–2), 129–145.

O'Brien, P. (2001). *Making it in the "free world"—Women in transition from prison.* Albany: State University of New York Press.

Pimlott, S., & Sarri, R. (2002). The forgotten group: Women in prisons and jails. In R. Sarri & J. Figueira-McDonough (Eds.), *Women at the margins: Neglect, punishment, and resistance* (pp. 55–78). Binghamton, NY: Hayworth Press.

Roy, K., & Burton, L. (2007). Mothering through recruitment: Kinscription of non-residential fathers and father figures in low-income families. *Family Relations, 56*, 24–39. doi:10.1111/j.1741-3729.2007.00437.x

Sheets, J., Wittenstrom, K., Fong, R., James, J., Tecci, M., Baumann, D. J., & Rodriguez, C. (2009). Evidence-based practice in family group decision-making for Anglo, African American and Hispanic families. *Children and Youth Services Review, 31*, 1187–1191. doi:10.1016/j.childyouth.2009.08.003

Smith, A., Krisman, K., Strozier, A. L., & Marley, M. A. (2004). Breaking through the bars: Exploring the experiences of addicted incarcerated parents whose children are cared for by relatives. *Families in Society, 85*, 187–195.

Stack, C. B., & Burton, L. M. (1993). Kinscripts. *Journal of Comparative Family Studies, 24*, 157–170.

Strozier, A., Armstrong, M., Skuza, S., Cecil, D., & McHale, J. (2011). Coparenting in kinship families with an incarcerated mother: A qualitative study. *Families in Society, 92*(1).

U.S. Administration on Aging. (n.d.). *National family caregiver support program (OAA Title IIIE)*. Retrieved from http://www.aoa.gov/aoaroot/aoa_programs/hcltc/caregiver/index.aspx

U.S. Census Bureau. 2009. *American Community Survey 2006–2008, 3-year estimates* (Tables S0901 Children Characteristics, S1001 Grandchildren Characteristics, and Selected Social Characteristics in the United States). Retrieved from http://factfinder.census.gov/servlet/STSelectServlet?_lang=en&_ts=310423107468

U.S. Department of Health and Human Services, Administration for Children and Families. (n.d.). *Title IV-E foster care*. Retrieved from http://www.acf.hhs.gov/programs/cb/programs_fund/state_tribal/fostercare.htm

Waldrop, D. P., & Weber, J. A. (2001). From grandparent to caregiver: The stress and satisfaction of raising grandchildren. *Families in Society, 82*, 461–472.

Young, D., & Smith, C. J. (2000). When moms are incarcerated: The needs of children, mothers, and caregivers. *Families in Society, 81*, 130–141.

AFTERWORD: COPARENTING AS PARADIGM

JAMES P. McHALE

Clinicians, researchers, and policymakers now have a broad, inclusive notion of coparenting that has expanded in much-needed ways the narrow conception of coparenting as visitation between divorced and unmarried couples. This expanded coparenting framework is entering its adolescence—an apropos metaphor, for adolescence is a period of exploration, challenge, contemplation, and self-assessment. Moreover, although the broader coparenting field still lacks a full identity in its adolescence, it is idealistic enough to make some bold initial forays into enduring and decidedly complex issues. Adolescence ushers in a period of more articulated direction and purpose, but it remains uncertain whether coparenting as a coordinated field is moving in this direction. The contemporary notion of coparenting advocated in this volume is certainly greater than the sum of its parts. But if the new coparenting's analytical and prescriptive components are still in search of an overarching, organizing framework, what value can be realized on a practical level?

For more than half a century, family therapists have advocated that educators, social services providers, courts, and mental health practitioners incorporate (or at least acknowledge) a coparenting perspective in their service provision to children and families. Yet at the end of the new century's 1st decade, attention still revolves inordinately around coparenting's analytical and assessment dimensions, with some lingering resistance to even acknowledging and claiming coparenting as a distinctive entity at all. Most all of the contributors to this volume have had to defend, at one time or another, their basic position that coparenting as a paradigm is a fundamentally different way of understanding a child's world than is parenting as a paradigm, or marriage as a paradigm.

Despite the sometimes stoic resistance from advocates of dyadic (mother–infant, fatherhood, and marital) frameworks, limited but encouraging evidence suggests that a few potential seeds of a future nationwide coparenting paradigm—one that embraces all children and their families—have already been sown. Through the fledgling efforts of a few relevant federal departments and agencies, some core coparenting principles have begun making their way from interesting research topics to demonstration projects and even to the "best practice" level, as James Gleeson, Anne Strozier, and Kerry Littlewood expertly detail in Chapter 13 of this volume. Most of the efforts these authors detail are conditioned on delivery of federal financial aid to at-risk families. Yet with some foresight and vision, these fragmented, tenuous efforts could indeed coalesce around a truly comprehensive national approach crafted to support coparenting throughout each phase of every individual's family life cycle.

Such a comprehensive, national approach will require coordination, of course—from the social scientists who carry out relevant studies, pilot programs, and nationwide assessments to the funding agencies that sustain these studies and pilot programs to the policymakers and administrators of courts and human services agencies at state and local levels to the families themselves. In at-risk communities, coparenting interventions may be especially challenging to deliver, but they may also generate great yield. Families raising children in multirisk neighborhoods stand to benefit immeasurably from initiatives that support their own efforts to protect and raise healthy children, for strong coparenting can compensate for the confluence of environmental risk factors that high-risk children—and their parents—must confront on a daily basis. Indeed, as a public health approach carefully conceived, coparenting interventions can significantly lower the prevalence of child and adolescent conduct and externalizing disorders if they succeed in helping children's families create the kinds of coparenting alliances that can serve as buffers against pernicious neighborhood risk factors; at the same time, they can preventively foster important psychological assets such as self-worth, self-esteem, and resilience.

In thinking about how coparenting could be gradually transformed from a sporadic and tenuous best practice among at-risk families to a nationally accepted and supported paradigm for assessing and promoting child development, the U.S. Department of Health and Human Services' Administration for Children and Families Head Start and Early Head Start programs offer some useful clues. Head Start provides grants to local public and private non-profit agencies "to provide comprehensive child development services to economically disadvantaged children and families, with a special focus on helping . . . promote school readiness. . . . They engage parents in their children's learning and help them in making progress toward their educational, literacy, and employment goals" (http://eclkc.ohs.acf.hhs.gov/hslc/About%20 Head%20Start). Head Start's Family Partnerships program was designed to support parents as they identify and meet their own goals, nurture the development of their children in the context of their family and culture, and advocate for communities that support children and families of all cultures. Trusting, collaborative relationships built between parents and staff foster mutual learning and caring. The mutual communication exchange respects family systems and provides a genuine partnership model in which the child is at the center—the core of any functional coparenting alliance.

The federal government has showcased other core coparenting principles—interestingly enough, in the prescriptive sense—through certain programs, centers, institutes, informational pamphlets, and consumer-oriented literature. At present, though, the promulgation of coparenting's core tenets has been selective and sporadic, with a few initiatives scattered across several disparate federal offices (but most of them within the Department of Health and Human Services). However, the fact that such practices appear in federal programming at all provides some early validation that coparenting has gained attention as an advance in raising well-rounded, well-ordered, resilient, and happy children.

A salient (perhaps overarching) assumption here is that the psychological well-being of any child is well served if the child's family can be kept together and intact, whether that integrity is achieved or maintained by biological or adoptive parents, through multigenerational caregivers, or by any other dedicated set of individuals who have stepped forward to assume responsibility for the child's care and upbringing. Longitudinal studies to establish the effectiveness of coordinated and supportive coparenting practices for healthier child adjustment in all family systems could serve as a platform for advocating coparenting policies and practices that can mitigate the "broken-home syndrome." As studies of divorce in middle and upper socioeconomic groups have documented so well, a strong coparenting alliance in the family stands to serve any and every child—across all family systems, up and down the socioeconomic scale.

Although this fundamental premise is clear to the contributors to this volume, there remains the challenge of how to begin to advance this incipient and inclusive new approach as an analytical and prescriptive paradigm for understanding and supporting all family systems. To maximize coparenting's utility, a basic assessment of the myriad general practices that go into raising a child today will be needed. In other words, to elicit interest in coparenting's best practices, we must first inquire into the current state of parenting and what its practitioners find wanting about it. A national conversation about parenting may be the best way to highlight common deficiencies in terms of children's well-being and how the broader, contemporary field of coparenting can address—and go beyond—those seemingly deficient parental practices.

A coordinated national conversation should begin by examining the current state of affairs with respect to coparenting interventions and coparenting supports available from early in the child's life through adolescence. An initiative of the magnitude we envision—State of the Science and Practice in Parenting Interventions Across Childhood—has recently been undertaken by the Office of the Assistant Secretary for Planning and Evaluation and the Administration for Children and Families in the Department of Health and Human Services, albeit with respect to parenting and not coparenting.

If we arrive at some broadly applicable coparenting initiative as the result of such a national conversation, we must also talk about what such an initiative may entail. What best practices do we envision as a result of such a national conversation? A synthesis of research, with the work of this book as one initial starting point, is the evidence-based platform for such a national conversation. The nature of coparenting and its importance for child outcomes, and how coparenting strategies are linked to infant, child, and adolescent development and risk, are the planks of such a platform. The limited number of coparenting interventions and related support services currently available to improve coparenting and child outcomes is an obvious discussion point for this national conversation—along with what currently exists and what is missing from accessible coparenting practices and knowledge chains in support of best coparenting practices.

This set of activities could then contribute to the development of a comprehensive agenda for applied research and practice, clarifying existing needs and gaps in the field and articulating options for future research and program development. A sample of family support programming in a comprehensive approach supporting coparenting at each phase of the family life cycle might include

- coparental education in middle and high school,
- mother–father and mother–coparent models of prenatal care and intervention,
- "coparenting-plus" (job training, education) approaches to help build coparenting alliances in fragile families from the time of paternity establishment,

- true kinship support policies and programming,
- promotion of partnerships and collaboration between parents and both formal and informal (neighbor, family, friend) day care providers,
- preventive postdivorce parenting coordination offered to divorcing parents as alternative dispute resolution,
- coparenting programming for women and men during incarcerations,
- coparenting support services to military families during deployments, and
- coparenting education and support through access and visitation services.

On this basis, more coordinated efforts might then proceed. A comprehensive coparenting framework would span and integrate organizational interests of various governmental—and nongovernmental—administrative and judicial organizations. Its ultimate aim would be to provide coparenting-supportive programming and guidelines that are broadly applicable nationally across diverse regions and administrative jurisdictions. Yet such a framework would be pointless if the programs and services it culminated in did not serve families by asking and providing what they need rather than providing solutions for them. This is an equally important conclusion of this book: Families and support networks attend to the same child concerns (and with the same degree of care) as do professionals, while paying closer attention to child well-being factors. Coparenting efforts that eventuate from the point of this volume must universally ensure that families are supported in their own adaptive efforts to provide their children with happy, well-rounded lives.

Child and family service providers and policymakers can now decide to embrace a deceptively simple coparenting paradigm as an inclusive framework relevant to understanding and supporting all children and their families. There is full consensus among us that children's health, behavior, socioemotional well-being, and academic attainments are fundamentally affected by the supports provided to them via their families. Coparenting relationships stand at the very core of the supportive systems that develop in all manner of family systems.

INDEX

and parental efficacy, 173–174
in preventive interventions,
214–215
as target of intervention, 213
Corboz-Warnery, A., 216
Corcione, C., 164
Coresident families
of adolescent/teen mothers, 107, 279
and foster-care subsidies, 280
fragile families as, 93–95
and grandmothers as coparents,
112, 113
relationship and coparenting quality
in, 83
Cornelison, A. R., 5
Correlates of coparenting, for young
fathers, 108
Couple relationship
coparenting vs., 176–177
in fragile families, 84–86
parallel interventions for
coparenting and, 183
parenthood and strains on, 171
in parenting intervention
programs, 172
of unmarried coparents, 192
Covert coparenting, 40
Cowan, C. P., 140, 177–179, 238
Cowan, P. A., 41, 140, 177–179, 238
CPIC (Children's Perception of
Interparental Conflict) Scale,
163, 164
Criminal justice system
and child welfare policies, 281
and parent–kinship caregiver
coparenting, 281–282
and young fathers, 111
Crnic, K., 43, 47, 48, 50, 54
Crosbie-Burnett, M., 17
Cross-time stability, of coparenting,
45–46
Crouter, A. C., 31, 45
Culture
in assessments of coparenting,
152–153, 161
and relationship stability of fragile
families, 86
Custodial kinship care, 67
clinical issues with, 272–278
formation of households, 270–272
future research directions, 283–285

policies on, 278–283
reasons for, 270–271
Custody laws, 283
Cutrona, C. E., 110

Dads for Life program, 214
Daley, M., 28
Davis, A. A., 118
Davis, E. F., 53
Day care providers, 154–155
Decision making
clear lines of authority for, 18
by coparents, 17, 32
FGDM meetings for, 282–284
by parents and kinship caregivers, 272
Decourcey, W., 51
Dekovic, M., 43
Department of Social Services, 252, 258
Depression and depressive symptoms
and adjustment in two-parent
nuclear families, 50
and conflict, 65, 116
and cooperation in postdivorce
families, 214
and coparenting in fragile families, 95
and coparenting in multi-
generational families, 276
and coparenting quality, 176
and Family Foundations project, 180
in new parents, 171
Detachment, parental, 277
Detouring (coalition), 25, 218
Deutsch, R. M., 241
Developmental needs
of kin, 276
of mothers, 273
Development milestones, attainment
of, 152
Development of child. See Child
development
Dickstein, S., 28
Dillon, P., 82–83
Disagreement, child-rearing, 213
Discipline, 29, 152, 259
Disengagement, 52, 157
Disinhibition, in toddlers, 43
Dissolution of relationship, 109
Dissonance
in assessments of coparenting, 158
in triangular systems, 26

Garfinkel, I., 83
Gatekeeping
    in fragile families, 90
    by grandmothers, 109, 155
    by mothers, 48, 49, 90, 215, 236
    in postdivorce families, 236
    and preventive interventions, 215
    in two-parent nuclear families, 48, 49
Gavin, L. E., 66
Gay couples. *See* Lesbian and gay
        couples
Gee, C. B., 108, 112
Gender (children)
    and adjustment in two-parent
        nuclear families, 52
    and coparenting in fragile families, 95
    and quality of coparenting, 44
Gender (parent)
    and coparenting alliance, 48–49
    and views of parenting/
        coparenting, 203
Gendered specialization, in division of
        labor, 128–129
Genograms, 155
Gibson, P., 284
Goldberg, A. E., 133–134
Gonzalez-Mena, J., 21
Goodman, C. C., 272, 275
Gordis, E. B., 48
Gordon, I., 49
Grandfathers, 16, 118
Grandmothers, 16, 20
    in African American extended kin
        systems, 66, 112–113
    in Asian extended kinship systems,
        68, 69
    as coparents of adolescent mothers,
        112–118
    as coparents of African American
        teen mothers, 64–65
    effect of adolescent pregnancy and
        motherhood on, 117–118
    gatekeeping by, 109, 155
    in Hispanic and Latino families,
        67–68
    in multigenerational families,
        273–274
    and young fathers, 109, 110
Grandparents. *See also* Multigenera-
        tional families

    in Asian extended kinship
        systems, 68
    in assessments of coparenting,
        157–158
    as caregivers, 269, 273
    in coparenting assessments, 154
    in Hispanic and Latino extended
        kinship systems, 67
    in Native American extended
        kinship systems, 70
    stress of, 276
Greenman, J., 21
Group interventions, for divorced
        families, 238–239
Guardianship laws, 283

Hackett, L., 68
Hackett, R., 68
Hamilton-Leaks, J., 118
Hare-Musten, R. T., 6
Harknett, K., 66
Harris, K. M., 112
Hawkins, A., 215
Haxton, C. L., 66
Head Start program, 291
Healthy Marriage Initiative, 98, 183–184
Heterosexual couples
    gay fathers' division of labor vs.,
        134–136
    gendered specialization in division of
        labor, 128–129
    lesbian mothers' division of labor vs.,
        129–134
Hetherington, E. M., 31
"Hidden" forms of work, 139
Hierarchy
    in biological–foster parent
        interactions, 260
    in current coparenting theory, 6
    in structural family theory, 5, 18
High-conflict postdivorce families,
        240–241, 243
High risk families, 19, 214–216
Hispanic families, 67–68
History of caring for child, 274–275
Hochschild, A. R., 138
Holding "envelope" method, 221
Home visiting programs for infants, 28
Horowitz, A., 50, 87, 88
Hossain, Z., 70

Relationship satisfaction
    and Becoming a Family Project,
        178–179
    of gay/lesbian coparents, 135, 137
Relationship stability
    of fragile families, 84, 85
    and young fathers, 109
Relationship status, 184
Remarriage, 92–93
Rescuing, by kin caregivers, 277–278
Resources, connections to, 194
Response rates, for Fragile Families and
        Child Wellbeing Study, 96
Retention, for interventions, 198–199
Reunification
    and ASFA, 281
    and foster care, 252, 253, 255
Rhodes, J. E., 108, 112, 118
Ricci, I., 235
Rights, parental, 281
Risk, in neighborhoods, 65–66, 290
Risk and resiliency approach, for
        interventions, 25, 193–194,
        205–206
Risk factors, for expectant parents'
        outcomes, 176–177
Risky behavior, in adolescents, 31, 45
Robertson, J., 28
Rotman, T., 42, 45, 51, 52

Sadler, L. S., 117, 118
Same-sex couples. See Lesbian and gay
        couples
Satisfaction, relationship
    and Becoming a Family Project,
        178–179
    of gay/lesbian coparents, 135, 137
Sbarra, D. A., 82–83, 214
School-related difficulties, 30
Schoppe, S. J., 43
Schoppe-Sullivan, S. J., 46, 49, 51–52,
        54, 111
Scorzo, D., 272
Scott, M. E., 50
Secondary prevention programs, 212
Secrecy, 30–31
Security
    of children, 42–43
    of parents, 49

Seitz, V., 114, 119
Self-esteem, 49
Self-regulation, infant, 27–28
Self-report surveys
    about interventions for unmarried
        parents, 200–201
    in assessments of coparenting,
        162–165
    for Family Foundations project,
        180–181
SES. See Socioeconomic status
Shared Family Care, 257
Shared method variance, 97
Shared parenting, 233, 272–274
Shared Parenting Project, 256
Shelley-Sireci, L., 133
Sibling relationships, 218, 270
Simoni, H., 42
Sinclair, R., 44
Single-child families, 47
Single-parent families
    adaptive coparenting structures,
        19–20
    African American, 63–66, 71–72
    coresidence of grandmothers, 113
    decision to coparent in, 22
Social competence, 181
Social ecology of foster care, 252–253
Socialization figures, 17
Social Security Act, 280, 281
Social services, 19, 253, 278
Social support
    for adolescent mothers, 108, 109,
        112, 114–118
    for African American fathers, 66
    for African American single
        mothers, 65
    and coparenting quality, 109
    from grandparents, 114–118
    in two-parent nuclear families, 54
    from young fathers, 108, 109
Socioeconomic status (SES)
    in extended kinship systems, 71–72
    of fragile families, 84, 86
    in two-parent nuclear families, 47
Sokolowski, M. S., 49
Solidarity, coparenting.
        See Coparenting solidarity
Sonuga-Barke, E. J., 68, 69
Sperm donor fathers, 16, 154

ABOUT THE EDITORS

James P. McHale, PhD, is chair of the Psychology Department at the University of South Florida, St. Petersburg. He received his doctoral degree in clinical psychology from the University of California, Berkeley, and trained as a family therapist in both Palo Alto, California, and in Philadelphia, Pennsylvania. His research studies of early infant, child, and family adjustment, grant-supported by the National Institutes of Health since 1996, have investigated the nature of children's interpersonal experiences in their families. His theoretical contributions have sought to instigate fresh, inclusive dialogues about how adults in diverse family systems collaborate to support children's care and upbringing. In 2004, Dr. McHale's Decade of Behavior Lecture for the World Association for Infant Mental Health, "When Infants Grow Up in Multiperson Relationship Systems" (published in *Infant Mental Health Journal,* 2007), championed a paradigm shift in the field of infant mental health, and in 2007, his book *Charting the Bumpy Road of Coparenthood* received the Irving B. Harris National Book Award of the Zero-to-Three Press. Professionally, he has provided coparenting trainings for the judiciary, physicians, child care professionals, child welfare advocates and professionals, Healthy Start and Early Head Start care coordinators, foster parents, postdivorce parenting coordinators, statewide fatherhood programs, and other contingents that serve infants and toddlers. Dr. McHale directs the University of South Florida, St. Petersburg's Family Study Center and is a member of the boards of directors for the Florida Association for Infant Mental Health and the Healthy Start Coalition of Pinellas, Inc.

Kristin M. Lindahl, PhD, is an associate professor in the Department of Psychology at the University of Miami, Florida. She received her doctoral degree in clinical psychology, specializing in child clinical psychology, from the University of Denver, Colorado. After completing her internship at Children's Hospital Boston, she accepted a faculty position at the University of Miami, which she has held since 1992. Her research focuses on systemic family functioning and the impact of difficulties in marital and parent–child subsystems, as well as the whole family, on child adaptation. She has been a principal investigator or coprincipal investigator on several National Institute of Mental Health–funded studies examining how family subsystems are interrelated, including how marital conflict is related to family cohesion and parenting strategies, and the role of family functioning on parent and child adaptation to a son or daughter's disclosure of gay or lesbian identity. She has published and presented widely on topics related to coparenting, observational coding of family interactions, and dyadic and triadic family dynamics as they relate to child functioning.